Buddhist Thought

Buddhism has existed for well over two thousand years. It has spread over most of Asia and now it has reached the West. Its philosophy is said to be very difficult. How can we begin to understand it?

Buddhist Thought guides the reader towards an understanding and appreciation of the central concepts of classical Indian Buddhist thought, tracing their development from the time of Buddha, and opening up the latest scholarly perspectives and controversies. Abstract and complex ideas are made accessible by the authors' clear and lucid style. Of particular interest here is by far the most accessible and up-to-date survey of Buddhist Tantra in India. In Tantric Buddhism, under strictly controlled conditions, sexual activity may play a part in the religious path. This apparently shocking and frequently misunderstood topic is absolutely crucial for an understanding of developments in Buddhism that are of wide interest in the West. Detailed bibliographies complete this comprehensive, authoritative and engaging introduction to one of the world's great philosophies.

Paul Williams is Professor of Indian and Tibetan Philosophy and Co-Director of the Centre for Buddhist Studies at the University of Bristol. His numerous publications include *Mahāyāna Buddhism* (Routledge, 1989). **Anthony Tribe** teaches in the Asian Studies Program, University of Montana, and is a specialist on Indian Tantric Buddhism. Both authors have many years' experience of introducing Buddhist thought to non-specialists, and have borne in mind the interests and difficulties of such students when writing this book.

Buddhist Thought

A complete introduction to the Indian tradition

Paul Williams

with Anthony Tribe

Routledge
Taylor & Francis Group
LONDON AND NEW YORK

First published 2000
by Routledge
2 Park Square, Milton Park, Abingdon, Oxon OX14 4RN

Simultaneously published in the USA and Canada
by Routledge
270 Madison Ave, New York, NY 10016

Reprinted 2002, 2003, 2005 (twice), 2006

Routledge is an imprint of the Taylor & Francis Group

Typeset in Times by
Graphicraft Limited, Hong Kong
Printed and bound in Great Britain by
TJ International Ltd, Padstow, Cornwall

British Library Cataloguing in Publication Data
A catalogue record for this book is available
from the British Library

Library of Congress Cataloging in Publication Data
A Catalogue record for this book has been requested

ISBN 0-415-20700-2 (hbk)
ISBN 0-415-20701-0 (pbk)

For Shad

Contents

Preface

The purpose of this book is straightforward. It is to serve as an accessible guide for students wishing to reach as quickly as possible a familiarity with the basic ideas of Buddhist philosophical and religious thought, and the results of some of the latest research in the field. A good understanding of the way Buddhism developed in India is an essential prerequisite for any appreciation of Buddhist ideas elsewhere, in Tibet, China, or Japan and the other countries of East Asia.

The book aims to give a comprehensive first survey of Buddhist thought, devoting adequate balanced space to basic, early, and mainstream Indian Buddhism, the views of some of the philosophical schools, Mahāyāna religious and philosophical developments, and the often neglected and inadequately understood topic of Tantric Buddhism. It will also serve as an introduction to Buddhism as such, providing the reader remembers that the interests of the authors are mainly in religious and philosophical *thought*, that is, essentially in *doctrines*. There is of course much more to a religion as something lived by all its members at all levels in history and society than its ideas on these topics – no matter how central they might be. But it is arguable that without a good grounding in Buddhist doctrine it is very difficult for the student to gain a proper appreciation of what is going on in Buddhism as it occurs in the day to day lives of Buddhists themselves.

The authors of this book have between them many years of experience in teaching Buddhism at school and university level. They have also taught Buddhist thought in the context of centres for Westerners who are interested in practising Buddhism. In writing they have borne in mind the interests and difficulties of such students, particularly students coming from a background in theology, religious studies, and philosophy rather than, say, Asian languages. The authors have tried very hard to make ideas accessible that can sometimes seem abstract and complex. The use of technical terms in Asian languages has been kept to a minimum. Where necessary, both the Sanskrit and the Pāli versions of terms have been carefully indicated. Unless the contrary is stated, however, a technical term is in Sanskrit. Where both terms are given, the Sanskrit is usually given first. The exception is where the context is a discussion of a source in Pāli. In that case the term is in Pāli, or the Pāli version is given first. The reader should have no problem in knowing which language a term is in.

Because this book is intended as a guide for students a central feature is the full Bibliography. This is in order to enable students to know where to find material that might interest them for further study. All the works referred to in the text are carefully listed. In particular all the primary sources – the Indian writings themselves – have been included with reference to reasonably reliable translations where available, and also where to find the Sanskrit, Pāli, Tibetan, and Chinese texts. Thus it is hoped that the book will be of value as well to those who are familiar with these languages, as a study resource.

If there is a common thread running through much of this work it is that of the central distinction for Buddhists between the way things appear to be when seen by ordinary unenlightened people, and the way they actually are. Things are seen the way they actually are by those like Buddhas who are enlightened, that is, awakened to the truth. This distinction has given Buddhism an acute interest in issues of ontology, i.e. what can be said really to exist. Such matters are essentially philosophical. In Buddhism philosophical insight – coming to understand things the way they really are – has transformative moral and spiritual implications. On the other hand there are areas of Buddhist thought that are treated in this book only cursorily or not at all.

For example, there is not a great deal of direct discussion here of Buddhist ethics. Buddhist thinking on the role and potential of women, or ecology, or politics, for example, is scarcely treated at all. For this we offer no apology. Some selection was inevitable. This is an *introduction* to Buddhist thought in India. It naturally reflects the interests of its authors, and their vision of what is central. Paul Williams wrote Chapters 1 to 6, and put the book together. The chapter on Buddhist Tantra (Chapter 7) was written by Anthony Tribe.

It is sometimes said that a book has not really been read unless it has been read three times. Taking either the book as a whole, a chapter, or a section, the first read should be fairly rapid. This reading is in order to survey the topic and get a broad understanding of its nature and scope. It shows you where you are going. The second read should be in detail, making notes as necessary. The final reading is to check any points that are still unclear, pull the topic together, appreciate some of the subtleties, and really *engage* with the material *critically*. The student who reads this book carefully will by the end have a good familiarity with the main Indian Buddhist ideas. He or she will be able to handle with confidence the language and concepts in which those ideas are expressed, and will have met with some of the very latest thinking among scholars working on the topics which have been introduced. After that, with the aid of the Bibliography, the student will have the ability and plenty of help to explore further the astonishingly rich, stimulating, and challenging world that is Buddhism.

Paul Williams
Centre for Buddhist Studies
University of Bristol
October 1999

Acknowledgements

It will be obvious to those who are familiar with the field that this book is heavily indebted to the work of others. In particular I (PW) would like to thank my colleague Rupert Gethin for his generosity with advice and the loan of books related to mainstream and Theravāda Buddhism, on which he is so knowledgeable. Rupert Gethin's own book *The Foundations of Buddhism* (1998) is highly recommended for further reading in areas of Buddhist doctrine and practice which are common to most Buddhist traditions. I would also like to thank my brother Peter Williams for comments and encouragement on an early version of the book's first few chapters, and fun with the computer.

This work is dedicated to my wife Sharon in the confidence that she is unlikely to read it. Her love and complete lack of interest in my religious and philosophical enthusiasms has encouraged in me a degree of critical common sense that has kept me relatively sane through nearly thirty years of wonderfully happy marriage. I am very grateful.

1 The doctrinal position of the Buddha in context

Preliminaries

'Buddhism', and its derivatives like 'Buddhist', are, of course, English words. They have parallels in other European languages, like 'Buddhismus' and 'Bouddhisme'. They refer for speakers of the English (German, French) language to the '-ism' which derives from the (or a) Buddha. The *Buddha* (Sanskrit/Pāli: 'Awakened One') is thought by Buddhists to be one who has awakened fully to the final truth of things, and thus freed, liberated, himself once and for all from all forms of suffering. He is also one who, out of supreme compassion, has taught others the way to attain liberation themselves. Buddhas are not born that way, and they are certainly not thought to be eternal gods (or God). Once (many lifetimes ago) they were just like you and me. They strove through their own efforts, and became Buddhas. A Buddha is superior to the rest of us because he 'knows it how it is'. We, on the other hand, wallow in confusion, in ignorance (Sanskrit: *avidyā*; Pāli: *avijjā*). Thus we are unhappy and suffer.

This use of the English '-ism' termination in 'Buddhism' can be taken to refer to the system of practices, understandings ('beliefs'), experiences, visions, and so on undergone and expressed at any one time and down the ages which derive from, or claim to derive from, a Buddha. The minimum for becoming a Buddhist is spoken of as three times 'taking the triple-refuge' in the proper formulaic way prescribed by the Buddhist traditions. In its broadest sense this 'taking refuge' is firmly taking the *Buddha* as the final spiritual refuge, the final (and only final) place of safety. He has seen in the deepest possible way and taught to its fullest extent how things truly are, and he has thus liberated himself from the suffering and frustrations which spring from living in a state of confusion and misunderstanding of the true nature of things. It is taking refuge also in the *Dharma*. The Dharma is how things truly are and the way to incorporate an understanding of how things truly are into one's being in the deepest possible way, as expressed and taught by a Buddha. One takes refuge also in the *Sangha*, the community of practitioners who are in their different ways and at different levels following and realising the Dharma.

Significant in the above is the notion of practising the Dharma, the Dharma which derives from the (or a) Buddha, and coming to see things the way they really are. While belief is of course a prerequisite for any spiritual path (and this is not denied by Buddhists), Buddhists like to place the primacy not on belief as such but on practising, following a path, and knowing, directly seeing. There is no significant virtue simply in belief. This direct 'seeing things the way they really are' is held to free the person who thus sees from experiences most people would rather be freed from. These are experiences like pain, frustration, anguish, sorrow – experiences which are classed by Buddhists under the broad Sanskrit term *duḥkha* (Pāli: *dukkha*), that is, suffering, unfulfilment, and imperfection. Thus any person who is liberated is finally and irrevocably liberated from all unpleasant experiences. Buddhism is therefore a *soteriology*. In other words it is concerned with bringing about for its practitioners liberation, freedom, from states and experiences held to be negative, unpleasant, not wanted. Being liberated is by contrast a state that is positive, pleasant, and wanted. The primary orientation of Buddhism, therefore, is towards the transformative experience of the individual, for there are no experiences that are not experiences of individuals. Buddhism is thus also concerned first and foremost with the mind, or, to be more precise, with mental transformation, for there are no experiences that are not in some sense reliant on the mind. This mental transformation is almost invariably held to depend upon, and to be brought about finally by, oneself for there can also be no transformation of one's own mind without on some level one's own active involvement or participation. Buddhism is thus a highly individualistic path of liberation. One is bound by one's own mind, and it is by working on one's own mind that one becomes liberated, attaining the highest possible spiritual goal. The transformation is from mental states Buddhists consider as negative to states considered by Buddhists to be positive. That is, it is a transformation from greed, hatred, and delusion, and all their implications and ramifications, to the opposites of these three negative states – non-attachment, loving kindness, and insight or wisdom, and all their implications and ramifications. It is this that liberates. What is meant and entailed by these negative and positive states, what is understood when one 'sees things the way they really are', what sort of 'seeing' is necessary, and how to bring that about, will form the content of Buddhism.[1]

I have referred to 'Buddhism' as what speakers of European languages (or 'the West') think of as the '-ism' that derives from the (or a) Buddha. While one could scarcely be both an orthodox Christian and, say, a Muslim or Hindu at the same time, it is perfectly possible to be a Buddhist and at the same time have recourse to and make offerings to Hindu gods, or other local gods of one's culture. Many, probably most, Buddhists do this. This is because what it is to be a Buddhist, and what it is to be e.g. a Christian, or a Muslim, are different. And if to be a Buddhist and to be a Christian are different, then Buddhism and Christianity *qua* 'religions' are different. Richard Gombrich has succinctly summed up what Buddhism is all about:

> For Buddhists, religion is purely a matter of understanding and practising the Dhamma [Sanskrit: *Dharma*], understanding and practice which constitute progress towards salvation. They conceive salvation – or liberation, to use a more Indian term – as the total eradication of greed, hatred and delusion. To attain it is open to any human being, and it is ultimately

> the only thing worth attaining, for it is the only happiness which is not transient. A person who has attained it will live on so long as his body keeps going, but thereafter not be reborn. Thus he will never have to suffer or die again. For Buddhists, religion is what is relevant to this quest for salvation, and nothing else.
>
> (Gombrich 1988: 24)

Traditionally Buddhists throughout the Buddhist world consider that the universe contains more beings in it than are normally visible to humans. Buddhists have no objection to the existence of the Hindu gods, although they deny completely the existence of God as spoken of in e.g. orthodox Christianity, understood as the omnipotent, omniscient, all-good, and primordially existent creator deity, who can be thought of as in some sense a person. Nevertheless one cannot as a Buddhist take refuge in Hindu gods, for Hindu gods are not Buddhas. That is, they are not enlightened. What this means is that Hindu gods, for all their power, do not see the final way things are, the final truth of things. They do not see it as it is. Power does not necessarily entail insight, and for Buddhists the Hindu gods, unlike Buddhas, do not have that liberating insight. Thus because they are not liberated Hindu gods too ultimately suffer. They have been reborn as gods due to their good deeds in the past (as we have been reborn human for the same reason), and gods too (like us humans) die, and are reborn elsewhere. We may ourselves be gods in our next lives, and, Buddhists would say, we certainly have been infinite times in the past, in our infinite series of previous lives. Gods may be reborn as humans (or worse – the round of rebirth includes e.g. animals, worms, ghosts, and sojourns in horrible hells as well). But none of this entails that Hindu gods do not exist.[2] Therefore none of this entails that Hindu gods cannot exert powerful influence on human lives and activities. There is thus no problem in Buddhists making offerings to Hindu gods, with requests for appropriate favours.

Throughout the Buddhist world there is one very particular way of contacting the gods and asking for their favours. This is through possession. In many Buddhist countries (such as Sri Lanka, Thailand, Burma, or Tibet), and also countries strongly influenced by Buddhism (such as China and Japan) there are people who are both Buddhists and also go into a type of trance. In this trance they are possessed by a god, who may give advice or medical assistance, for example. The only problem with all this would come if a Buddhist took refuge in a god, implying that the god had the key to final liberation. The gods concern only the worldly (Sanskrit: *laukika*). The Buddhas are beyond the world (*lokottara*), both in terms of their own status and also in terms of their final concerns in helping others. Thus whereas one would not expect to see an orthodox Christian making offerings to Hindu gods, prostrating to them, making requests of them, or going into trance and being possessed by them, there is no contradiction to Buddhism in Buddhists doing this. To be a Buddhist for Buddhists is not the same sort of phenomenon as being a Christian is for Christians. Allegiance in different religions does not have the same sort of exclusivity. This is *not* an example of 'Buddhist syncretism', or 'popular Buddhism', or even 'Buddhist tolerance'. Not all religions operate the way we expect them to on the basis of the religion or religions with which we are most familiar. As Lance Cousins puts it:

> It is an error to think of a pure Buddhism, which has become syncretistically mixed with other religions, even corrupted and degenerate in later forms. Such a pure Buddhism has never existed. Buddhism has always coexisted with other religious beliefs and practices. It has not usually sought to involve itself in every sphere of human ritual activity, since many such things are not considered 'conducive to' the path, i.e. not relevant to the spiritual endeavour. Its strength perhaps lies in this very incompleteness. . . . [These other practices, such as contacting local gods] may be practised if desired so long as the main aim is not lost. . . . [As far as the soteriological goal, liberation, is concerned they] are irrelevant.
>
> (Cousins 1998: 372)

As far as we know this has always been the case in Buddhism. There was no period in the past when it was different, or expected to be different. The great Indian Buddhist King Aśoka (third century BCE) made offerings to non-Buddhist teachers and religions. He no doubt also made offerings to non-Buddhist gods.[3] When householders in ancient times met and were impressed by the Buddha and 'took refuge' in him, we need not assume that they thereby ceased entirely to make offerings to other teachers or gods. In their villages they were therefore 'Hindus' as well as 'Buddhists' (if one must use these modern Western classifications). But if they really saw the Buddha as enlightened, and accepted that his teachings differed from those of other teachers, they would no longer take refuge in those other teachers as final sources of truth and liberation. They would be likely to think of the Buddha as their special teacher, the teacher in whom they put their trust for the final concerns of their life, the teacher whom they would most like to see helping them on their deathbed.

The Brahmanical doctrinal background

In the quotation from Richard Gombrich above we saw that from the Buddhist point of view 'religion is what is conducive to salvation'. On the other hand, we might think that making offerings to Hindu gods, whether or not they are worth taking refuge in, is nevertheless indeed 'religious'. But by 'religion', of course, Gombrich (or his Singhalese informants) means here specifically Buddhism. 'Religion' *is* Buddhism, and Buddhism, to a Buddhist, is characterised as what is conducive to salvation, liberation. The term translated by Gombrich above as 'religion' is (in Pāli) *sāsana*, the Teaching, the expression used in e.g. the Theravāda Buddhist tradition of Sri Lanka to refer to 'Buddhism not just as a doctrine but as a phenomenon in history, a whole religion' (Gombrich 1988: 3). Buddhism as a religion in history was founded in ancient India and even the truth as articulated in history, Buddhism itself, it is thought by Buddhists, will eventually cease to exist due to forces of irreligion. As a matter of fact Buddhism in mainland India itself had all but ceased to exist by the thirteenth century CE, although by that time it had spread to Tibet, China, Japan, and Southeast Asia. But eventually all Buddhism will cease in this world. Nevertheless, at some point in the future a *sāsana* will again be established by another Buddha, as indeed its establishment in India this time round was in fact a *re*-establishment. And so on, and so on, apparently throughout all eternity.

Each time a *sāsana* is established it is due to a *re*discovery. But what exactly is rediscovered each time? The answer is the *Dharma*. This is a further term sometimes used by Buddhists for what in the West is called 'Buddhism'. But 'Dharma' cannot of course refer simply to Buddhism as a religion, since we have seen that the Dharma is the second of the three refuges taken by Buddhists, alongside the Buddha and the Sangha. Buddhism as a religion has to include all three refuges. Rather the Dharma is Buddhism as content, that is, what is actually taught by Buddhism as a religion. It consists of the truths, both concerning how things really are, and the way to practise in order to bring about cognition of how things really are. As articulated as part of the *sāsana*, the Dharma consists of the teachings of the Buddha, and thereby of Buddhism. That certain things are really, really, true is central to Buddhism. Buddhists claim that it is really true, for example, that most things form part of a causal flow, and physical matter is not in any sense one's true Self (*ātman*). Buddhists claim too that the state of unenlightenment is ultimately *duḥkha*, unfulfilment, and there is no omnipotent, omniscient, all-good, and primordially existent creator deity, who can be thought of as in some sense a person. That certain practices truly bring about the results they claim to bring about – that, for example, the eightfold path as taught by the Buddha if followed properly with single-minded devotion will eventually lead to liberation (i.e. Sanskrit: *nirvāṇa*; Pāli: *nibbāna*) – is also central to Buddhism. These are objective truths, as truths they are always true, and their truth is quite independent of the existence of Buddhas or indeed any beings existing capable of realising those truths. They form the Dharma, the content of the Buddha's teaching. Buddhism is built on the absolute objectivity of truth, and Buddhists claim that the Dharma (*their* Dharma) is that absolutely objective truth. As Nārada Thera puts it:

> The original Pāli term for Buddhism is *Dhamma*. . . . The Dhamma is that which really is. It is the doctrine of reality. It is a means of deliverance from suffering and deliverance itself. Whether the Buddhas arise or not the Dhamma exists from all eternity. It is a Buddha that realizes this Dhamma, which ever lies hidden from the ignorant eyes of men, till he, an Enlightened One, comes and compassionately reveals it to the world.
>
> (Nārada 1980: 162)

The word 'Dharma' is nevertheless an important word of the Indian cultural context within which Buddhism arose. In using 'Dharma' for his teaching the Buddha intentionally chose a term which was intended to indicate to others that he truly knew and taught how things finally are. Where others disagree, they do not have the Dharma. What they teach is in that respect its negation, *Adharma*. Let us look more closely then at the Indian context that produced the teachings, the Dharma of the Buddha.

First a note on the words 'Brahmanism' and 'Brahmanical' as used here and in the works of other scholars when writing on early Indian religion. We still find it commonly said that the Buddha was a 'Hindu reformer'. This is misleading. The Buddha rejected the final religious authority directly, indirectly, or ideologically, of the social class of brahmins and their primordial scriptures, the Vedas, so important to Hinduism throughout history. And much of what we nowadays call 'Hinduism', such as the centrality of the gods Śiva, or Viṣṇu, the ideas of Śaṃkara's Advaita Vedānta, the themes of the *Bhagavad Gītā*, Tantric practices, and so on developed after the time of the Buddha. In some cases they were influenced positively or negatively by Buddhism. The religious practices and beliefs actually current at the time of the Buddha are associated in early Buddhist texts with two broad groups of practitioners in many fundamental ways radically different from each other. On the one hand we have the *brāḥmaṇas*, that is, (in Anglicised spelling) the brahmins. On the other hand we have the *śramaṇas* (Pāli: *samaṇas*), the renouncers of society, the 'drop-outs'. The religion of the brahmins was pre-eminently a religion of householders, in origins and interests a religion of villagers and very much a set of religious practices geared to the primacy of harmonious ordered social relationships and 'prosperity in this world and the next'. It had evolved out of the religious ideas and practices of the Āryas, migrating speakers of Indo-European languages, who reached India sometime during the second millennium BCE from their home base presumed to be in the grasslands of Southern Russia near the Caspian Sea. The Āryas brought with them horse-drawn chariots, an early form of the Sanskrit language, and perhaps from before arriving in India and anyway soon afterwards the earliest (as yet unwritten and orally transmitted) scriptures of Indian religion, the *Ṛg Veda*. Over many centuries the Vedic scriptures expanded (still not written down), eventually reaching by the time of the Buddha four collections, the *Ṛg*, *Sāma*, *Yajur*, and (originating a little later than the others) the *Atharva Vedas*. Each of these Vedic collections was divided into verses (*saṃhitā*), ritual manuals (*brāhmaṇas* – not to be confused with the same word when used for 'brahmins'), 'forest books' (*āraṇyakas*), and eventually also *upaniṣads*. The Vedic religion was based largely on offerings of sacrifice, and the ritual manuals gave detailed instructions for performance of the sacrifices, which grew more complex as the centuries passed. At first the sacrifices were made as offerings to the various Vedic gods such as Indra – commonly known in Buddhist sources as Śakra (Pāli: Sakka) – Varuṇa, Agni, who was the god of the sacrificial fire, or the sun god Sūrya, in the hope that the gods would reciprocate. Gradually the feeling developed that the gods *must* reciprocate, for a properly performed sacrifice where the appropriate formulae (*mantras*) were correctly uttered needs must bring about the appropriate reward. Just as the very universe itself springs from a primordial sacrifice (see the famous 'Hymn to the Cosmic Man', the *Puruṣasūkta*, *Ṛg Veda* 10: 90), through the sacrifice the universe is kept going. The sacrifice is the action *par excellence*, the 'significant action', the *karman* (i.e. 'karma';

a word which in classical Sanskrit simply means 'action'). From performing one's duty, the correct *karman* appropriate to one's ritual and social status, the fruit (*phala*) of the action necessarily follows, either in this life or in the next. But how is it that the significant action brings about its result? First in the Forest Books, and then very much in the Upaniṣads, we find speculation on the meaning of the sacrifices, and the elaboration of a secret (i.e. esoteric) interpretation which in the Upaniṣads converges on an other-worldly soteriology. The action which takes place here in the space of the sacrifice is seen as a microcosm, which magically corresponds to – is magically identical with – actions, events which the sacrificer desires to bring about in the macrocosm. The esoteric interpretation is a web of magical identifications the knowing of which bestows power over the identified. And it eventually emerges that the most significant identification, the identification whispered in the older prose Upaniṣads, is literally the greatest identification of all. That which is the very core of the universe, that which is unchanging even when all things – 'the seasons and the turning year' – change, is *Brahman* (in origin, the 'priestly power'), the Universal Essence. That which is the true, unchanging, core of oneself, that constant which is always being referred to when one says 'I', that which lies beyond all bodily and mental changes, is the Self, the *ātman*, the Personal Essence. And (clearly the Secret of Secrets in the older prose Upaniṣads) *ātman* is actually identical with *Brahman* – the Personal Essence *is* the Universal Essence. The search for the underlying nature of the universe reached an early apogee in India in the turn inwards. Early cosmology and physics converges with psychology. Magical identification begins its long road in India to spiritual idealism and the overwhelming primacy of personal experience. As the *Bṛhadāraṇyaka Upaniṣad* (1: 4: 10/15) puts it:

> If a man knows 'I am *brahman*' in this way, he becomes the whole world. Not even the gods are able to prevent it, for he becomes their very self (*ātman*). So when a man venerates another deity, thinking, 'He is one, and I am another', he does not understand. . . .

> It is his self (*ātman*) alone that a man should venerate as his world. And if someone venerates his self alone as his world, that rite of his will never fade away, because from his very self he will produce whatever he desires.
>
> (Olivelle 1996: 15/17)

This is the final magical identification. By knowing oneself, by thereby controlling oneself, one knows and controls all.

And after death there will be no more 'coming and going', no more rebirth. The notion of rebirth is not found in the earliest Vedic literature. Rather, the correct performance of the sacrifices, and adherence to one's social duties as laid down by the brahmins, led to 'prosperity in this life and in the next'. The next life here is thought of as some sort of heavenly realm (the 'world of the fathers', the *pitṛloka*), that was expected to go on forever. It is not clear exactly where the notion of rebirth came from, or when. At least, I shall not enter into the speculations here. But inasmuch as *post mortem* existence was linked to 'significant (sacrificial) action' (*karman*) in this life, so the next life as the result of finite actions could not be guaranteed to be infinite. As time passed the idea developed that the ancestors in the 'world of the fathers' needed to be kept alive by further sacrificial offerings on behalf of those who remain behind. And can these further offerings really go on forever? Even in the *post mortem* state one might die again, and be born again. With the notion of rebirth comes redeath, and it seems to have been the idea of continually dying again and again throughout all eternity that gave Vedic thinkers their greatest horror. To be born again is not necessarily a problem. But to die again! For the system was claustrophobic, it seemed to provide no way of getting out. To perform another sacrifice (*karman*) simply perpetuated the problem.

The issue of the broad relationship between these soteriological concerns and the Vedic householder cult of the sacrifice is a complex one. Eventually it begins to crystallise into an opposition between this householder religious world (associated with the *brahmins*), and world renunciation, a complete renunciation of the householder state and a search for some alternative form of practice which would liberate from the abyss of redeath which had opened up. The Buddha was a member of a distinct social group in the Indian religious scene. He was a renouncer, who had 'gone forth from home to homelessness' seeking to know the liberating truth. His life was outside that of the married householder, with his or her social duties within the village or town. He was himself, therefore, a member of the group known as the *śramaṇas*, the drop-outs.

Scholars in the past have debated whether there is any evidence at all that the Buddha was familiar with the ideas of the Upaniṣads, those paradigmatic early Brahmanical treatises on the path to liberation, and whether he was influenced either positively or negatively by them. Louis de la Vallée Poussin expressed a not uncommon view when he denied any knowledge of the Upaniṣads by the Buddha (Gombrich 1996: 14; cf. Norman 1997: 26). Yet if we follow the consensus of opinion that is now emerging on the date of the death of the Buddha the earliest classical Upaniṣads may be a few hundred years earlier than his time. Patrick Olivelle, introducing his valuable recent translation of the Upaniṣads, speaks of the *Bṛhadāraṇyaka* and the *Chāndogya* Upaniṣads, the earliest, as 'in all likelihood, pre-Buddhist; placing them in the seventh to sixth centuries BCE may be reasonable, give or take a century or so' (Olivelle 1996: xxxvi). Thus not only is it possible that the Buddha knew of the earlier prose Upaniṣads, there is a good chance that he had at least some idea of their salient teachings. Others of the classical Upaniṣads may have been composed during or soon after the time of the Buddha, and indeed may have been influenced by Buddhism. Richard Gombrich has recently attempted to show at length references to the Upaniṣads in the earliest Buddhist scriptures (which may or may not go back directly to the Buddha himself), which he holds are directly mocked and criticised by the Buddhists. Gombrich's view is that

> the central teachings of the Buddha came as a response to the central teachings of the old Upaniṣads, notably the *Bṛhadāraṇyaka*. On some points, which he perhaps took for

> granted, he was in agreement with the Upaniṣadic doctrine; on others he criticised it.
>
> (Gombrich 1996: 31; see also Norman 1990–6: paper 99, 1997: 26 ff.)

Scholars refer to the Vedic religion of the sacrificial cult that we have been looking at as 'Brahmanism', because this indicates the centrality of brahmins in both social and religious terms in the world of Vedic civilisation. The brahmins formed the ideologically dominant group in Vedic society. They were and still are a hereditary elite. One is born a brahmin, one cannot become one. Vedic literature was as far as we know composed almost entirely by brahmins, and brahmins were essential to the performance of the sacrifices. What makes a brahmin a brahmin is birth, but what makes that birth significant is the relative ritual purity of a brahmin. Brahmins are ritually pure and, because that purity makes them most suited to approach the gods through sacrifice on behalf of the sacificer (who pays for the sacrifice), that purity must be preserved. Whether or not they actually practise as professional sacrifice-priests, brahmins must therefore not be polluted, and tasks which might involve impurity and thus be polluting (such as the disposal of rubbish, or dead bodies) must be performed by others, specialists in the removal of impurity. These 'others' are held to be by nature, by birth, highly impure, so impure that as time passed they were required to live in separate groups ('outcastes') outside the main hamlet. Other social groups are ranked in accordance with their relative purity and impurity in relationship to these two poles of the system.[4] Thus eventually we have the caste system. But it is not clear how far this system was developed by the time of the Buddha. Scholars tend to think of Brahmanism at the time of the Buddha not in terms of the Indian actuality of caste (*jāti*) as it has developed over many, many centuries, but rather in terms of the Brahmanic ideology of class (*varṇa*). Note this distinction carefully, because confusion between caste and class seems to be almost normal in works on Indian religions. Classical Brahmanic texts dating from Vedic times and beyond refer to society divided into the four classes (*varṇas*) of brahmins (*brāhmaṇas*), warriors/rulers (*kṣatriyas*), generators of wealth (*vaiśyas*), and the rest ('servants', *śūdras*). This division is by birth, it is a division of purity, and it is strictly hierarchical. Each preceding class is purer and therefore superior to the following. Thus the preceding class has a higher social *status* than the following, quite regardless of any wealth one might have. Within this system there is no correlation between wealth or power and social status. Status is determined by relative purity. It is not given by wealth, power or, as such, behaviour or insight. Members of the first three classes are referred to as 'twice-born' (*dvija*), and they are entitled and expected to enter into the world of Vedic religious duties, for most of their lives as married householders. This involves keeping alight the domestic sacrificial fire and engaging particularly in the duty to sacrifice, each in the appropriate and distinctive way determined by relative position (relative purity) in the social hierarchy. Nearly everyone can be fitted somewhere into one or other of these classes. Which class one is a member of determines (according to the Brahmanic lawbooks) a whole range of social behaviour from who one can eat with to which sort of wood is used in making one's staff, or which sacrifices have to be carried out, by whom, and at what age.

Over the years Indian social actuality going back many centuries has seen not just four but hundreds of castes (*jātis*) and subcastes. If we try and relate class to caste, *varṇa* to *jāti*, class is classical Brahmanic *ideology* while caste is historical and modern *actuality*. They are different. The *varṇa* system is what the Brahmanic authors wanted to see, and to the extent that brahmins were the dominant group in society the *varṇa* ideology provided a template for what they sought to realise. The *jātis* represent the actual system of Indian social division within relatively recent historical time. It is important to preserve the terminological separation of the two, and not to confuse them. At the time of the Buddha there was the ideology of *varṇa*, that formed part of the ideology of brahmins, the dominant group in much of North Indian society. No doubt there was within that area also some form of social division influenced to a greater or lesser degree by the ideology of *varṇa*. But the extent to which the *varṇa* ideology influenced the actual social divisions in the region from which the Buddha came, a fringe area in the Himalayan foothills, is still very unclear.[5]

The concept of 'Dharma' is probably the single most important concept for understanding Indian religion, indeed classical Indian civilisation itself. Yet as a concept of the wider Brahmanical culture it is not an easy concept for a modern Westerner to appreciate. This is because it combines in the one concept two facets that we tend to keep distinct. These are the facets of 'is' and 'ought', that is, the dimensions of how things actually *are* and how things *ought* to be (Gombrich 1996: 34). Dharma in the Brahmanic perspective is on the one hand something with the flavour of righteousness and duty. It is the righteousness of those who follow their duty, a duty essentially ordained in the Vedic works and the works of tradition based on the Vedas, as taught and praised by learned Brahmins. On the other hand it is also the objective order of the universe. The universe *is* ordered this way, in accordance with a hierarchy of beings and duties structured in terms of relative purity and the objective workings of the sacrifice. The cosmos in traditional Indian Brahmanism is intrinsically hierarchical, and organisation in terms of ranked hierarchy is absolutely central to most traditional Indian thought. This way of things, including the social and ritual duties that are the way of things, is not created by anyone. At the beginning of each cosmic epoch, when the world is created anew in whatever way it is created, or emanated, or evolved, the sages (*ṛṣis*) directly discern Dharma. Dharma in Brahmanic culture is discovered. It is not created. It is there, objectively existent, waiting to be discovered at the beginning of things. Dharma is not a subject for radical disagreement or debate. Thus when one behaves as one should behave, as laid down in accordance with class (*varṇa*) and stage of life (*āśrama*), whether student (*brahmacārin*), householder (*gṛhastha*), forest-dweller (*vānaprastha*), or wandering ascetic renouncer (*saṃnyāsin*), this behaviour brings conduct into line with the objective order of things. The result is happiness, all one could wish for in this life and the next. And if one seeks to break out of society as ordered by Dharma one can only die. To break the rules of Dharma is a cosmic matter, for to act in a way that is at variance with the objective order of things is to cause a monstrosity. It is to bring about that which cannot *be*, and it is thus the very antithesis of being. This can only lead to the end of the world. No wonder Kṛṣṇa, God himself, in the influential Hindu work the *Bhagavad Gītā* (4: 7–8) declares that he has to incarnate himself to restore Dharma, to prevent God's world coming to nothing. God's salvific action, his intervention in the world, has to be in the interests of the social framework of hierarchy and its duties.

Nevertheless, if significant ritual and social action (*karman*) leads to rebirth and hence redeath, then for some at least it appears that all such actions became suspect. In particular, all sacrificial actions are done with a particular goal in mind. One performs, or has performed on one's behalf, a particular sacrifice in order to have children, more cattle, a long life, or whatever. In general, desire gives rise to action that generates results. There is no significant disagreement with this model, which sees the results as coming from desire through action. But what if one does not wish for the results, since at the best they will involve a heavenly rebirth and therefore redeath, with never an end? Then it was reasoned that one should bring to an end desire, and 'significant action' (*karman*), the actions of sacrifice and duty (or, perhaps, all actions altogether). It is desire, desire for something for oneself or one's group, i.e. egoistic desire, which leads, which projects, generates, rebirth and thence redeath. Thus some might try to discipline their body into less and less action, or less and less dependence upon actions, less and less dependence on even involuntary actions. They might also try to overcome all desires, even so-called 'legitimate' desires. Harsh austerities, it was reasoned, or perhaps suspected, might cut at the very root that leads to redeath. But this could not be done – would not be accepted, has no place – within the social world of reciprocal duties found in the Indian village. The one who would seek to bring to an end all redeath needed to adopt a radically different strategy from that of Brahmanic ritual and obligation. He (perhaps sometimes also she) renounced the world of society, and 'went forth from home to homelessness', seeking the liberating truth which almost by definition could not be found back home. And for some of these renunciates, at least, the means to attaining this knowledge lay not just in finding someone who would whisper it to them. It lay also in bringing about altered states of consciousness through concentration and meditative practices such that access to the liberating knowledge (and perhaps to other extraordinary abilities as well) could be gained in a paranormal or supersensory way.

These renunciates were known collectively (in the early Buddhist sources) as *śramaṇas*. A renunciate was, indeed still is in the modern Indian world, in social terms 'dead', a walking corpse. One who renounces the world performs his death-rites. The presence or even shadow of a renunciate, casteless, homeless, springing up from goodness knows where, pollutes the food of a brahmin about to eat lunch. And having set out on his search Gautama, the Buddha-to-be, both before and after becoming a Buddha, was a *śramaṇa*. In Indian social terms he was a drop-out. His very purpose as a drop-out was to search for that truth the knowing of which will set one free, liberation.

I have stressed that Buddhism is in broad terms to do with transforming the mind in order to bring about the cessation of negative states and experiences, and the attaining of positive states and experiences. It is a soteriology that sees the goal in terms of mental transformation. Buddhism is also in some sense a gnostic soteriology. That is, crucial to bringing about the state of liberation is knowing something, something the not knowing of which by nearly everyone else explains their state of non-liberation, their state of saṃsāra, and hence their *duḥkha*, their pain, misery, and existential *angst*. Contrasting with the centrality of *karman* among Brahmanic householders is the centrality of knowing (*jñāna* = gnosis) among renunciates. Liberation comes not from actions (it is *not* as such a matter of 'good karma'), but from knowing the salvific truth. This centrality of knowing something places Buddhism firmly within other Indian traditions (such as those of the early classical Upaniṣads, or Sāṃkhya, or Yoga) where knowing is thought to bestow soteriological benefits. As we shall see, however, the knowledge of the Buddha was very different from the knowledge of the grand identification associated with the Upaniṣads. In the terminology of the *Bhagavad Gītā*, Buddhism is thus a *jñāna-yoga*.[6] That is, Buddhism is a disciplined course of action based upon, or leading to, knowing something so important and in such a fundamental way that it finally and irrevocably liberates the knower from all unpleasant states and experiences, notably the state and experience of continued rebirth and redeath. We saw above that central to taking refuge in the Buddha is an understanding of the Buddha as one who knows (in the deepest possible way) the way things really are. He is described as 'seeing things the way they really are' (Sanskrit: *yathābhūtadarśana*), and this expression is sometimes found as an epithet of nirvāṇa, liberation itself.

In Brahmanism the ancient sages (*ṛṣis*) discovered an objectively existent Dharma that combines in one concept a description of the objective ordering of things and at the same time a prescription for how one should live to attain the optimum. Similarly the Buddha also taught what he called 'Dharma'. For the Buddha this was *the* Dharma, the actual real Dharma. He had discovered an independent truth, the way things really are that also embraces in the same category the proper code of conduct and set of practices in order to attain the optimum, complete liberation from all suffering and rebirth. In declaring the Dharma, in (as Buddhists put it) 'setting in motion the Wheel of Dharma' after his enlightenment, the Buddha began his teaching (began the *sāsana*) by declaring at the very most the relativity of the Brahmanic Dharma. This Brahmanic Dharma turns out to be not objective truth, but 'mere convention'. The Buddha was a renunciate. For him the Brahmanic Dharma thus does not lead to final liberation, but only to repeated redeath.

It is clear from early Buddhist sources, and from other sources such as those of the Jains, for example, that by the time of the Buddha the institution of wandering renunciates who, by their very nature, lived off alms for which they would give teaching in exchange, was well established. After renouncing the world himself the Buddha-to-be (i.e. the *bodhisattva*, Pāli: *bodhisatta*), then known by his family name of 'Gautama' (Pāli: Gotama), went in search of teachers who could teach him meditation and other associated practices common to his new lifestyle. Buddhist sources speak of six or ten groups of renouncers familiar to young Gautama, with their teachers and teachings, although whether these are very accurate portrayals of the views of their rivals can be doubted. It is not totally clear with some of these how knowing their 'truth' would lead to liberation, at least if liberation is thought of as freedom from rebirth and redeath. Nevertheless, as an indication of views we are told were in circulation among the drop-outs at the time of the Buddha, we have the following:[7]

Pūraṇa Kassapa taught that there is no virtue or sin, no merit or demerit, whatever one does. There is thus no such thing as moral causation.

Makkhali Gosāla taught a sort of fatalism. Rebirth occurs again and again through 'destiny, chance, and nature' (Basham 1951: 14) and nothing we can do will make any difference. We have no control over any of it, and eventually liberation will come when it will come. Makkhali Gosāla was an important founder of the rival religion of the Ājīvikas, which continued for many centuries in India.

Ajita Kesakambalī taught what appears to be a form of materialism, that there is no future life for us let alone repeated rebirth. Mankind is formed of earth, water, fire, and air, which return to their elements after death. There is no merit in good deeds (good *karman*) or demerit in wicked ones.

Pakudha Kaccāyana held the view that earth, water, fire, air, joy, sorrow, and life are stable and unproductive, independent primordial substances. He seems to have drawn the conclusion from this that killing (presumably in terms of moral responsibility) is impossible, since a sword would simply pass between these primordial substances.

The figure of Nigaṇṭha Nātaputta is probably intended to be Vardhamāna Mahāvīra, the twenty-fourth Enlightened Conqueror (*Jīna*) of Jainism. According to the Buddhist source here, which is not very specific, Nigaṇṭha Nātaputta simply held that followers of his tradition surround their mind with a barrier of a fourfold restraint. But what this does show is the emphasis on austere asceticism, moral restraint, and control, characteristic of Jainism, liberating the eternal transmigrating soul from the bonds of matter, transmigration, and suffering.

Sañjaya Belatthīputta was the wonderful agnostic, or perhaps even sceptic, who is reported to have said:

> If you asked me, 'Is there another world?' and if I believed that there was, I should tell you so. But that is not what I say. I do not say that it is so; I do not say that it is otherwise; I do not say that it is not so; nor do I say that it is not not so . . .
>
> (Trans. Basham 1951: 16–17)

And the same for various further questions as well.

We have independent knowledge of Jainism, and Basham (1951) has done an excellent job in retrieving the Ājīvikas from obscurity. The position of Ajita Kesakambalī is sufficiently explicit to suggest his kinship with the materialist wing of a school latter known as Cārvāka or Lokāyata (see Williams, in Grayling 1998: 840–2). But for the others there is not really enough to go on to develop a fair portrayal of a viable position, let alone an appraisal. But what these sources do show is the atmosphere of exciting and excited, vital, debate which was taking place in India at the time of the Buddha. It was a time that was also seeing the breakdown of old tribal federations and measures towards the establishment of powerful monarchies. It saw also the move from an agrarian village-based economy and the growth of cities as mercantile and military bases as well as bases for the exchange of ideas often in an atmosphere of social uprootedness. The Buddha (and other renunciates) stressed existential angst, *duḥkha*, as the starting point for the religious quest. Perhaps this reflects the fact that he also lived in a world of dynamic and upsetting change.

How to read the life-story (hagiography) of the Buddha

When scholars refer to *the* Buddha they invariably mean the Buddha who founded the present *sāsana*. This is the 'historical' Buddha who founded Buddhism in history. That Buddha is called Gautama (Pāli: Gotama). The title 'Buddha' is used for him only after his awakening, his enlightenment. He is also sometimes called in Sanskrit Śākyamuni Buddha, the Buddha who was/is the Sage (*muni*) of the Śākya (Pāli: Sakya) clan. There is a later suggestion that his personal name may have been Siddhārtha (Pāli: Siddhattha), although this is by no means certain. He was born in what is now southern Nepal, in the Himalayan foothills, and he lived for about eighty years. For much of that time he wandered around with no hair, simple robes of a dusty colour, very few possessions, and begged and taught for a living. The Buddha was an outsider – a drop-out and a 'traveller'. As someone considered by his followers to be enlightened, he was a teacher and example rather than a fiery prophet. The Buddha wrote nothing. It is not clear if he was literate, although quite possibly not.

We all like a good story. Books on Buddhism (not to mention regular student essays) often start by recounting, as if it were simple historical fact, the Buddha's life-story. But there is no reason why a book on Buddhism, even an introductory book on Buddhism, should start with the life-story of the Buddha. It is only self-evidently appropriate to start the study of a religion with the life-story of its founder if we hold that the life-story of the founder is in some sense a crucial preliminary to understanding what follows. That is, in the case of Buddhism, if it were true that we could not understand the Dharma without first understanding the life-story of the Buddha.

It is indeed obvious that one begins the study of Christianity as such with the life of Jesus Christ. The role of Jesus as a figure in history is absolutely central for Christians. If Jesus could be shown conclusively not to have lived then necessarily the salvific significance of his life could not have actually, really (i.e. in history), taken place, and this would have radical repercussions for Christian self-understanding. Christianity is a religion founded by a figure in history, embedded in a 'sacred history', and the historicity of that figure is absolutely essential to what the Christian message is all about. Buddhism too is a religion founded by a figure in history, so it seemed obvious when Buddhism was first a subject of study in the Western world to begin its study with the founder. Yet the role of the Buddha for Buddhists is quite unlike the role of Jesus for Christians. The Buddha, as we have seen, attained liberation himself and re-established the *sāsana*, the Teaching. If it could be shown for certain by some clever scholar that the Buddha never existed that need not, as such, have dramatic repercussions for Buddhists. For patently the *sāsana* exists, and the *sāsana* is the *sāsana*, it articulates objective truth 'whether Buddhas occur or do not occur'. The effectiveness of the Dharma does not in itself depend on its discovery by a Buddha. If the Buddha did not exist then someone else existed who rediscovered the Dharma. If it really *is* the Dharma that has been rediscovered, that is sufficient. Of course, if it were shown for certain that no one could become liberated, or ever had become liberated by following this Teaching, that would have radical repercussions for Buddhists. That would be to show the Dharma as not actually the Dharma at all. It would be to show that the central religious event(s) of this religion are and can be nothing for us. This would be the equivalent to showing Christians that Jesus never existed, for it would entail the complete nullity of the claims and practices of the religion.

The role of the Buddha for Buddhists therefore is, as a Buddhist formula has it, simply to show the way, a way which has to be followed by each person themselves in order for its salvific function to be fulfilled. What follows from all this is that the corresponding absolutely central role of Jesus for Christians is performed for Buddhists *not* by the Buddha, but by the *Dharma*. The proper Buddhist place to start the study of Buddhism, therefore, is not the life-story of the Buddha at all but through outlining straight away the Dharma, the practice of which leads to liberation without further ado. The life-story of the Buddha becomes important subsequently as a teaching aid, for showing how it is that the teachings have the validity they do possess – that is, for engendering confidence in the effectiveness of the teachings – and for illustrating themes of the teachings themselves. As one might expect, the Buddha is subordinate to the Dharma, for it is not the Buddha who brings about the enlightenment of his followers, but following the Dharma.

This is a book on Buddhist thought, and not a basic introduction to Buddhism. I do not intend to repeat at any length the traditional life-story of the Buddha here. I am nevertheless interested in drawing your attention to the story as a teaching aid, that is, drawing your attention to what the traditional life-story of the Buddha tells us about Buddhism and the Buddhist orientation. But first some preliminaries.

Our lives would be made much easier if we knew exactly when the Buddha was born, and when he died. In the third century BCE the Indian emperor Aśoka sent various missionary-ambassadors abroad, and it has proved possible more or less to anchor chronologically the lifetime of Aśoka in relationship to various Hellenistic kings apparently visited by these ambassadors. But this still gives rise to problems of how to relate the dates of Aśoka to the time of the Buddha. The view found in the Southern (Singhalese) Buddhist tradition (at least, in its so-called 'corrected' version) is that Aśoka came to the throne 218 years after the death of the Buddha, and suggested correlations with Hellenistic rulers give the date of Aśoka's accession at 268 BCE. Thus this gives 486 BCE for the death of the Buddha. There are other ways of calculating the date of the death of the Buddha however, and in the 'Northern' Buddhist tradition (found in, say, China) Aśoka is said to have come to the throne just 100 years after the death of the Buddha (a suspiciously round figure). Richard Gombrich has recently argued that Aśoka came to the throne about 136 years after the death of the Buddha. Doubt as regards the accuracy of the 486 date is now so widespread among scholars that the one consensus that appears to be emerging is that the 486 BCE date commonly given in books on Buddhism is wrong. The death of the Buddha should be placed much nearer 400 BCE than 500 BCE.[8]

The purpose of mentioning this problem concerning the date of the Buddha here is on the principle that the first stage of learning is to realise that one is ignorant. We do not know even when the Buddha lived. He may well have lived a whole century later than most Western scholars had previously thought. A century is a long time. This uncertainty should also suggest (if not as a direct implication, nevertheless as a methodological strategy) extreme caution as regards the details of the traditional life of the Buddha.

For those unfamiliar with the story let me quote the summary of the Buddha's life from Michael Carrithers, based on traditional Buddhist accounts:

> The Buddha was born the son of a king, and so grew up with wealth, pleasure, and the prospect of power, all goods commonly desired by human beings. As he reached manhood, however, he was confronted with a sick man, an old man and a corpse. He had lived a sheltered life, and these affected him profoundly, for he realised that no wealth or power could prevent him too from experiencing illness, old age and death. He also saw a wandering ascetic, bent on escaping these sufferings. Reflecting on what he had seen, he reached the first great turning-point of his life: against the wishes of his family he renounced home, wife, child and position to become a homeless wanderer, seeking release from this apparently inevitable pain.
>
> For some years he practised the trance-like meditation, and later the strenuous self-mortification, which were then current among such wanderers, but he found these ineffective. So he sat down to reflect quietly, with neither psychic nor physical rigours, on the common human plight. This led to the second great change in his life, for out of this reflection in tranquillity arose at last awakening and release. He had 'done what was to be done', he had solved the enigma

> of suffering. Deriving his philosophy from his experience he then taught for forty-five years, and his teaching touched most problems in the conduct of human life. He founded an order of monks who were to free themselves by following his example, and they spread his teaching abroad in the world. He eventually died of mortal causes, like others, but unlike others he was 'utterly extinguished' (*parinibbuto*), for he would never be reborn to suffer again.
>
> (Carrithers 1983: 2–3)[9]

We simply do not know for certain whether any of the traditional life-story of the Buddha is true, let alone the truth of the details. Comparative work on different versions of the same story preserved in early Buddhist texts in Pāli, and in Chinese and Tibetan translation, by scholars like André Bareau (1963–71) have led to very sceptical conclusions regarding the historicity of the well-known events in this story. The Buddha may not have existed, although there are no serious scholars currently who take this as a significant option. Nowadays scholars would tend to agree with Carrithers when he states that 'There are good reasons to doubt even this very compressed account, but at least the outline of the life must be true: birth, maturity, renunciation, search, awakening and liberation, teaching, death' (1983: 3). The Buddha existed, and he was a renunciate. It is unlikely that what he taught was radically different from broadly what the earliest Indian Buddhist traditions consider he taught. The broad type of his teaching therefore was that of a renunciate, a drop-out teaching of the way to come to know the liberating truth which would free from all negative states including rebirth. But in some cases we now know that certain details of the traditional story of the Buddha are false, at least as they are commonly represented. For example, the Buddha was *not* born a prince, at least if a prince is the son of a king, let alone the son of a powerful king.[10] We know that his clan of the Śākyas had no king. It was one of the North Indian republics soon to be absorbed into the growing empire of the Magadhan monarchy. The Śākya clan was ruled probably by a council of distinguished elders (it was thus perhaps what is known as an 'oligarchy'), with possibly one elder elected for a period of presidency. Perhaps the Buddha's father was one of these presidents, or one of the other elders, or perhaps not. And perhaps also the democratic order of the Buddha's monks and nuns, the Sangha, was based on what he remembered on the political organisation of his home. The view that the Buddha was born the son of a king possibly reflects a retelling of the story by later Buddhists in terms of the political scene that had emerged by their own day. But it also represents a cipher, a code-expression, for the teaching-point significant to understanding the Dharma. This is that the Buddha was born in materialistically the most powerful and richest situation conceivable.

For what we find when we look at the life-story of the Buddha is not a historical narrative but a *hagiography*, and it is as a hagiography that one should read the life-story of the Buddha. A hagiography (nowadays 'spiritual or religious biography' appears often to be the preferred expression) is an account of the life of a saint. The hagiographies of medieval Christian saints provide the classic examples. In the hagiography we meet again the uniting of 'is' and 'ought', in which how it was, how it should have been, and how it must have been if he or she was who he or she indeed was, are united under the overriding concern of exemplary truth. This exemplary truth is the known Truth of the saint's religious system. Within this perspective the interests of veridical historical narrative are sometimes not seen, and are always subordinate. The saint's hagiography is constructed in the light of this exemplary need, and the needs of the construction are the needs of those who undertake it. Thus when the account of the saint's life comes to be written – often, as the Buddha's was, some time, even centuries, after his or her death – the life-story reflects the unification of is and ought in the vision and needs of the subsequent community. Careful intellectual archaeology may revel a core of historical fact (which is what, quite rightly, interests most modern historians, although by no means necessarily the believer), but the 'is' of historical fact was only one dimension, and a subordinate one, in the construction of the original hagiography. Thus the hagiography as a whole is to be read as an ideological document, reflecting the religious interests of the community which put the hagiography together. And the hagiography's survival shows that it indeed fulfilled those interests.[11]

Issues of the historical accuracy of elements in the life-story of the Buddha are therefore tangential to the purposes of one whose primary interest is Buddhist doctrine. André Couture, summarising the sceptical results of the work of Bareau, comments that

> what these studies forcefully bring out is how freely Buddhist writers received accounts deemed edifying. A relatively simple doctrine and a few ancient memories grew little by little into a heap of often contradictory traditions of fictional episodes composed to edify. Anyone claiming to solve unfailingly the enigma of historical likelihood would be shrewd indeed. It can safely be said of Buddhist hagiography in general that the teaching of the Good Doctrine outranks by far what we call attention to history; or as Bareau says, in the minds of hagiographers, the needs of preaching came before concerns over history.
>
> (Couture 1994: 31)

The Buddha's hagiography should be read as an illustration of what is to Buddhists important. It anchors the authenticity of the teachings in a story of wonderful achievement, and illustrates portions of those teachings, parts of the *sāsana* revealing the Dharma. It should be possible to go through each element of the, or a, traditional account of the life of the Buddha and show how that element illustrates this or that aspect of what is to Buddhists important, the Dharma itself.

We are told that even before his birth the Buddha-to-be, unlike us, *chose* to be reborn at the time and place he was reborn, for he was already a supremely advanced Buddha-to-be (Sanskrit: *bodhisattva*; Pāli: *bodhisatta*). Buddhas do not just occur, and to become a Buddha is the result of many lifetimes of devoted practise. The life-story of the Buddha shows a quite superior (albeit still human) being, even before he became a Buddha. Gautama was born into a supremely rich and prosperous family. We are told that had he not chosen to renounce the world and become a Buddha he was sure to become a world-conquering emperor (*cakravartin*; Pāli: *cakkavattin*). He married a beautiful princess and had the supreme joy of an Indian male, a strong and healthy son. No one who follows the householder life could ever hope to be more successful at it than Gautama was and could have been. Thus in successfully renouncing the world Gautama renounced the highest possible attainment within the householder framework. In so doing he announced to all the ultimate frustration, imperfection (*duḥkha*) of the householder's life – the relativity of traditional Vedic Brahmanism – and the spiritual superiority of the life of a religious drop-out.

At this stage in the story we see emerging a key theme, perhaps *the* key theme, illustrated by the life-story of the Buddha. This is the way the story shows so pointedly the central vision of Buddhism, the gap between the way things appear to be and the way things really are. Gautama had been brought up to think that everything was perfect, and it would go on forever. According to the developed life-story, in order to prevent him from having any inkling of suffering and thus becoming a renouncer, Gautama's rich father had resolved to keep his son from ever seeing sickness, old age, and death. It is, for the Buddhist, exposure to this sort of suffering which gives rise to existential doubt, concern, and questioning, and this existential *angst* is what leads one to renounce the world and seek for liberation, freedom. Not ever to see old age, sickness, or death is of course impossible, and the fact that we are told his father kept these facts of life from Gautama until adulthood shows the absurdity of reading this account as narrative history. But it also shows the value of reading it as hagiography. Gautama had been brought up radically to misperceive things. He saw things one way, when they are really another way. His story portrays in acute form the situation that the Buddhist claims all unenlightened people are in, whether they realise it or not. For the Buddhist it is this gap between the way we see things to be and the way things actually are which engenders suffering and frustration. Coming to see things the way they *really* are, actually to see things that way, is to close this gap. That is the final purpose of Buddhist meditation. Closing that gap is how meditation transforms the mind. For Gautama being introduced to old age, sickness, and death and, crucially, abstracting from their occurrence in the case of others to his own case (see *Buddhacarita* Bk 3) was to face reality. It was a revelation, which provoked a crisis. The only resolution was renunciation. That renunciation, it was hoped, would lead to seeing the way things really are in its fullest transformative sense, and thus to attaining liberation. This theme of seeing things one way and their really being another way is the thread running throughout the first part of the life-story of the Buddha. It is not surprising that this thread is the theme of Buddhism, for the whole story of the Buddha exemplifies what Buddhism is all about. The tension set up by this thread is resolved by the enlightenment, after which the gap is closed and the Buddha thereafter is incarnate insight flowing in acts of compassion.

After Gautama had renounced the world he undertook his spiritual practices as a drop-out with supreme seriousness, outdoing all the others in austerity. Gautama entered deep meditation, reducing his food intake dramatically to (we are told) 'as little as three grains of rice a day'. He soon achieved all his teachers could teach him, and went beyond their own attainments. Yet still he felt he had not achieved the goal. Thus Gautama had to discover the *sāsana* anew, discover it for himself, for there was no one left to teach him. Clearly what he discovered went beyond all other teachings, and their teachings therefore could not be the final truth. The result of his extreme austerities was that he too acquired admiring disciples, for such asceticism was surely the way to bring rebirth to an end. But Gautama himself simply became ill. Just as he had shown his superiority over and transcended the householder life, with its extreme of luxury, so he now saw the ultimate pointlessness of much of the contemporary practice of the renunciates, his fellow drop-outs. Buddhism is said to be the Middle Way, and one meaning of this is the middle between sensory indulgence (luxury) and sensory deprivation (extreme asceticism). In eating again, strengthening the body, Gautama showed that true liberation concerns the mind. It is not a matter of ritual action, or of the renunciation of action. It is a matter of knowing. Liberation comes from delving within, beyond fierce asceticism and also any lesser understanding possessed by other renunciates.

Gautama's enlightenment is the enlightenment of a Buddha, completely perfect, relaxed, stillness. He 'had done what was to be done, and there would be no further rebirth for him.' What he had discovered we shall look at subsequently. And yet the Buddha also taught others, founding a monastic order with monks and eventually nuns, wandering, teaching, and living on alms. The Buddhist tradition holds that a Buddha has not just the wisdom of direct insight into the way of things but also complete compassion for others who are suffering as he once was. After forty-five years of teaching the Buddha died, for central to his awakening, his enlightenment, is that all things around us are impermanent. He appointed no human successor, for he affirmed that he has taught all that is necessary to attaining liberation and therefore the only successor needed was the teaching he had rediscovered. What more did they want? His successor, he said – and are we surprised? – should be the Dharma itself.[12] The Buddha at the end directs attention to the Dharma and to its practice. The life-story of the Buddha is not narrative history. It is all about the Dharma. Without the Dharma there is nothing. Without its practice it is useless.

In reading the hagiography of the Buddha in something like the way sketched here we read the life-story as it was intended, we master the Dharma, and (students please note) we stop simply telling stories.

Do we really know anything of what the Buddha taught?

Immediately after the death of the Buddha his teachings, as they were recalled, are said to have been recited. According to tradition they were then assembled into some sort of corpus appropriate for memorisation and oral transmission. They were not written down for some centuries.[13] Over the years, reflecting the growth of different schools of Buddhist transmission and sometimes understanding, a number of different versions of the canonical corpus were assembled. Thus scholars speak of e.g. the Theravāda ('Pāli') Canon, the Mahāsāṃghika Canon, the Sarvāstivāda Canon, and so on.[14] All of these canonical collections reflect what the schools concerned (Theravāda, Mahāsāṃghika, Sarvāstivāda, Dharmaguptaka, etc.) eventually considered to be *the* Canon, the authentic statement of the teaching of the Buddha as remembered, transmitted, and eventually written down. Each school claimed to represent unadulterated the original Buddhism of the Buddha. Not all these canonical collections were in the same language however. The Theravādins (followers of Theravāda) favoured a Middle Indo-Āryan language which has come to be known as Pāli, while the Sarvāstivādins, for example, came to favour the pan-Indian language of high (and Brahmanic) culture, Sanskrit. The Buddha himself may have varied his dialect or language depending on the person to whom he was preaching, but none of these canonical collections is straightforwardly in a language in which the Buddha would have done most of his speaking. To that extent they are all one way or another translations, containing texts that may have been translated sometimes more than once.[15]

The only complete canon of an early Buddhist school surviving in its original Indian language is the Pāli Canon, and the Theravāda school of e.g. Sri Lanka, Burma, Thailand, and Cambodia is the only representative of these early schools of Buddhism to have survived to the modern day. Such a canon consists of three sections. For this reason it is known as the *Tripiṭaka* in Sanskrit, or the *Tipiṭaka* in Pāli, the 'Three Baskets'. In the Theravāda tradition, which uses the Pāli Canon, all the contents of the *Tipiṭaka* are held to stem from the Buddha himself either directly or through his active approval of the teaching of other enlightened monks. The first basket (*piṭaka*) is the *Vinaya Piṭaka*, which broadly speaking treats issues of monastic discipline (*Vinaya*). The *Sutta Piṭaka* is the section of Discourses (*sutta*; Sanskrit: *sūtra*). In its Pāli version it is divided into four sections known as *Nikāyas*: the *Dīgha*, *Majjhima*, *Saṃyutta*, and *Aṅguttara*

Nikāyas. There is also a supplementary collection called the *Khuddaka Nikāya*. The equivalent material to the *Nikāyas* in collections preserved outside the Pāli tradition, particularly in Chinese translation, is called *Āgamas* rather than *Nikāyas*. Finally, and no doubt somewhat later in origin than the other *piṭakas*, is the *Abhidhamma Piṭaka*, the *piṭaka* of 'Higher (or "Supplementary") Teaching'. Here we find seven books treating particularly issues requiring somewhat greater philosophical precision than in the works of monastic discipline or the Buddha's regular discourses. The *Abhidhamma Piṭaka* contains lengthy descriptions of how things really are, and how this relates to the way they appear to be. A great deal of its contents concerns issues of causation, unravelling the dynamic nature of things and explaining how the world nevertheless hangs together. It contains also an attempt to describe the experiential building-blocks which come together to make up our lived world, and how all these relate to issues of moral behaviour and following the path to liberation.

It would be wrong, however, to think unquestioningly that the Theravāda school *is* original Buddhism, and its Canon *is* the original word of the Buddha.[16] There were other early schools of Buddhism, and very substantial sections of their versions of the canons survive either in original fragments or in Tibetan or more importantly here Chinese translations. As we have said, each school considered itself to be simply original Buddhism, and its canon the original word of the Buddha. Scholars have great fun comparing these different versions of the canons, but while there are differences in detail their differences are not normally so great as to suggest very radical divergence in doctrine.

There are differences among scholars however on how far we can use these sources to know exactly what the Buddha himself taught. Lambert Schmithausen has recently referred to three approaches to this issue. The first position he detects, particularly associated by him with British Buddhologists, stresses

> the fundamental *homogeneity* and substantial *authenticity* of at least a considerable part of the Nikāyic [i.e. earliest basic

> canonical, particularly Pāli] materials. . . . On this assumption, the canonical texts are taken to yield a fairly coherent picture of the authentic doctrine of the Buddha himself . . .
> (Ruegg and Schmithausen 1990: 1–2; italics original)

Scholars in the second group (Schmithausen seems to be thinking here in particular of Gregory Schopen and D. Schlingloff) express extreme scepticism about retrieving the doctrines of earliest Buddhism, especially of the Buddha himself. This is because among other things even the earliest texts were not codified until after the first century BCE, and it is difficult without making questionable presuppositions to go much beyond that time as regards the canonical texts, although archaeological sources such as inscriptions may be helpful. Schmithausen himself would side with a third group. This group maintains that notwithstanding these problems it may occasionally be possible to detect in the texts that now exist earlier and later segments and thus sometimes earlier and later doctrines. This approach favours detailed text-critical analysis of canonical versions of particular accounts to detect inconsistencies and contradictions that may suggest earlier textual revisions, stratification of textual content, and therefore different levels of doctrinal development. This may lead to some sort of relative chronology of ideas some of which may (or may not) be capable of being traced back to the Buddha himself. Richard Gombrich (who is considered by Schmithausen very much to fall within the first group of scholars, although he himself rejects being 'painted . . . into a kind of fundamentalist corner') has suggested that jokes in some of the texts may go back to the Buddha himself, for 'are jokes ever composed by committees?'. He also tries to show allusions to Brahmanism in some of the earliest Buddhist texts, which the later tradition appears to have forgotten, thus suggesting the relative antiquity of those allusions. If they refer to doctrines found in e.g. the *Bṛhadāraṇyala Upaniṣad*, and these references have been forgotten by later Buddhists, then it suggests that at least these references *may* go back to the time of the Buddha himself (Gombrich 1996: 11–12). The Buddha himself may well have been self-consciously responding to some of the early prose Upaniṣads like the *Bṛhadāraṇyaka Upaniṣad*.

Of course, we cannot show for certain the falsehood of the claim that none of the teachings attributed to the Buddha goes back to the actual figure of the Buddha himself at all. This logically follows, since it is always possible that the Buddha might not have existed. Nevertheless it seems almost certain that he did exist, and he gave teachings which were considered by his followers to be important and life-transformative. I agree with Gombrich elsewhere, where he considers the possibility held by some scholars that the Buddha may really have taught a Self (*ātman*, Pāli: *attā*) instead of the Not-Self (*anātman*; Pāli: *anattā*) doctrine. He observes, 'I myself find this claim that on so essential a point the Buddha has been misunderstood by all his followers somewhat [to use a Buddhist expression] "against the current"' (Gombrich 1971: 72 n. 18). In other words, if only because it was important to them, barring specific matters of detail the Buddhist tradition as represented in its earliest Indian sources is likely to have preserved the teaching of the Buddha reasonably well. The Dharma is to be practised, for the purposes of liberation. Its preservation, particularly in the hands of the an organised body like the Sangha, created by the Buddha no doubt partly for the purposes of preserving an awareness of the Dharma for as long as possible, is unlikely to have been treated in a cavalier fashion.[17]

The Buddha's attitude to his teaching: the arrow and the raft

The Buddha is said to have used two illustrations in particular to show how to understand what his real concerns were in teaching, and how to take the teaching that he gave. The first is found in the *Cūḷamāluṅkya Sutta* (the 'Shorter Discourse to Māluṅkyā(putta)'), which is the sixty-third sutta ('scripture discourse'; Sanskrit: *sūtra*) in the section of the Pāli Canon known as the *Majjhima Nikāya*, the 'Middle Length Collection'. A monk called Māluṅkyāputta while in retreat became concerned that the Buddha had not answered what were to him certain major philosophical questions. These questions related to whether the world is eternal, or not eternal; whether the world is finite, or infinite; whether the *jīva* (the 'life principle') is the same as the body, or different from it, and whether the *Tathāgata*[18] exists after death, or does not exist after death, or both exists and does not exist after death, or neither exists nor does not exist after death? Upon whether the Buddha can answer these questions or whether he will honestly admit he does not know the answers will depend Māluṅkyāputta's continuing a monk-disciple of the Buddha.

The Buddha's response is simple. These are not questions he has any intention of answering (or, one can be sure, any interest in answering). He had never offered to answer questions like these, so Māluṅkyāputta cannot have decided to become a monk because he thought the Buddha would answer them. If Māluṅkyāputta insisted on answers to these questions before practising the Dharma as a monk then, the Buddha observes, he would surely die before it had been explained to him:

> It is as if there were a man struck by an arrow that was smeared thickly with poison; his friends and companions, his family and relatives would summon a doctor to see the arrow. And the man might say, 'I will not draw out this arrow as long as I do not know whether the man by whom I was struck was a [member of a] brahmin, a kṣatriya, a vaiśya, or a śūdra [class] . . . as long as I do not know his name and his family . . . whether he was tall, short or of medium height . . .' That man would not discover these things, but that man would die.
>
> (Trans. in Gethin 1998: 66)

The one uncontroversial point about this famous image is the comparison of being an unenlightened person in the world, our actual existential situation, with being hit in the eye by a very poisonous arrow. Being in the world as an unenlightened being, being in the world as one who will again be in the world, and again and again throughout endless rebirths and redeaths, is wanted as much as a poke in the eye with a pointed stick. For the Buddha our situation is past discussion, it is lethal (life is a fatal illness), and the very fact we cannot see this is itself a sign of how far we are from seeing things the way they really are. The thick poison is the poison of misconception, of ignorance (*avidyā*; Pāli: *avijjā*).[19] As far as the Buddha is concerned everything else is subordinate to this almost overwhelmingly urgent imperative. The Buddha in this sense is not a philosopher, at least if we understand a philosopher as someone like Socrates, engaged in an activity of reflection and discussion on fundamental issues of metaphysics, ethics, and politics. The image often used in Buddhist texts is not of the Buddha as a philosopher, but the Buddha as a doctor, 'the great physician'. One does not philosophise with one's doctor, at least, not if one's illness is critical but still curable. The teaching of the Buddha is through and through goal-oriented (teleological). It is entirely dependent upon its goal of freedom from suffering and ultimate frustration. And the Buddha's concern is not discussion. It is not pondering or mulling things over. It is action, based on an acceptance not of some abstract philosophising but rather specifically of the Dharma rediscovered by the Buddha. And when the Buddha said that the man would die before he had answered all these questions, what the simile means when applied to the soteriological teaching of the Buddha is not that for one reason or another it would take the Buddha a long time to answer those questions. Rather it must be that before such questions could be answered *all would be lost*. The chance for a cure, i.e. liberation, would have irrevocably passed. So long as one insists on an answer first one will never be liberated. Or, put another way, one will only have a chance of liberation when one abandons the search for answers to such questions.

This image is uncontroversial, and it is this image which shows how to approach the teachings of the Buddha and earliest Buddhism. Not all about the Buddha's response to Māluṅkyāputta, however, is equally uncontroversial. What is it about these questions (and other similar sets of 'unanswered' (Sanskrit: *avyākṛta*; Pāli: *avyākata*) questions found in the Buddhist canon) which meant that the Buddha did not answer them? Here the Buddhist tradition and modern scholars have mooted a number of possibilities (Collins 1982a: 131–8; Gethin 1998: 66–8). One can assume that these questions are being taken as a set. Let us look at the logical options.

Logically, there may be answers to these questions, or there may not. In favour of the view that there is no answer to these questions is that the Buddha seems to think that it would, as it were, 'take forever' to answer them. This seems to indicate that they are actually impossible to answer. Otherwise answers could be given (grudgingly, but if really necessary) and *then* one could follow the path. So on this interpretation, since there is no answer to these questions then not only cannot the Buddha give an answer, but also having an answer to these questions cannot be anything to do with becoming enlightened (because otherwise neither Gautama nor anyone else could have become enlightened).

But if there are answers to these questions, the Buddha may know those answers or he may not. If he does not know the answers then this would certainly be incompatible with later Buddhist tradition that the Buddha was omniscient. It would also suggest that the Buddha was dishonest in not admitting that he did not know the answers, as Māluṅkyāputta wished him to do if that were true. But even if the Buddha did not know the answers it would still show yet again that if the Buddha's Dharma *is* the Dharma, then knowing the answer to these questions could not be relevant to the path to liberation. And the Buddhists are telling this story, so we cannot approach the meaning of the story with an attribution of dishonesty to the Buddha that would be unacceptable to Buddhists.

If the Buddha knows the answers to our questions, then telling the answers may be relevant to his purposes or it may not. But we can assume that if there are answers, and the Buddha knows those answers, it cannot be the case that telling them is relevant to his purposes, or he would have done so. Thus giving answers to these questions simply has nothing to do with attaining liberation. Again and again we return to the same point. The Buddha is by definition an enlightened being, and as such he has understood the true nature of things and all that is necessary to becoming enlightened. That is, he has understood the Dharma. The need to attain liberation is the one overriding imperative. And that liberation simply does not require an answer to these questions, whether or not there is an answer or, if there is an answer, whether or not the Buddha knows it. This interpretation is supported by a subsequent comment made in the text:

> It is not the case that one would live the spiritual life by virtue of holding the view that the world is eternal [etc.]. . . . Whether one holds that the world is eternal, or whether one holds the view that the world is not eternal, there is still birth, ageing, death, grief, despair, pain, and unhappiness – whose destruction here and now I declare.
>
> (Trans. in Gethin 1998: 68)

And that may be about as far as we can go in interpreting the unanswered questions with any reasonable degree of assurance.[20]

The other famous illustration to show the Buddha's attitude to his teaching is that of the Raft. It can be found in another sutta of the Pāli Canon's *Majjhima Nikāya*, this time sutta number 22, the *Alagaddūpama Sutta* (the 'Discourse on the Simile of the Water Snake'). In this discourse a certain rather stupid, or perhaps self-seeking, monk called Ariṭṭha conceives the idea that when the Buddha said that sense pleasures are an obstacle to the spiritual path he was not including in this sexual intercourse.[21] The Buddha is not impressed, calls Ariṭṭha a 'foolish man', and seems astonished that anyone would come up with such a misunderstanding of his teaching. Some people, he observes, learn his teachings but do not apply them. They just chat about them, or use them to accuse others. Thus they simply harm themselves. The teachings here have been 'badly grasped'. It is just like trying to grab a poisonous snake, and catching it not by the head but by the tail. One simply gets bitten. Thus just as the Buddha sees his teachings as intensely practical so, for that very reason, they are also dangerous if misunderstood. And he continues by likening his teachings to a raft. A man comes to an expanse of water, where the near bank (the state of unenlightenment) is ghastly but the far side (i.e. nirvāṇa; Pāli: *nibbāna*) is safe. There is no boat, so he builds himself a raft and crosses over safely. But having got to other side that man does not carry the raft with him. Rather, he leaves it behind. Thus, says the Buddha, the Dhamma (Dharma) is taught for the purpose of crossing over, not for holding onto.

Again we see that the use of the teaching by the Buddha is subordinate to its purpose. The point is the point, but once one has got the point (indeed *if* one has got the point) one certainly should not hold onto the teachings and what they teach with craving and attachment (Gethin 1998: 71 ff.). It follows that there is here no requirement (it seems to me) of rigid literalism. The text adds that by appreciating this simile of the raft one can let go even of the teachings (*dhammā*; following Gombrich 1996: 24 ff.), let alone those things which were not taught by the Buddha (*adhammā*), such as the weird ideas of Ariṭṭha. What the Buddha did not teach is of course not to be adopted, but all that he did teach was for a purpose and having attained that purpose, letting go of craving and attachment, the particular verbal formulations of the teachings are no longer needed.[22]

Note that it simply does not follow from the raft simile that the teachings of the Buddha here are no longer being claimed to be factually *true* but only of relative practical benefit in particular contexts. The Buddha is not saying that any particular teaching is to be abandoned once it has fulfilled its pragmatic purpose because it carries no surplus truth over and above that purpose. The point of the raft simile is much simpler. The teachings may be true, descriptively, factually, cognitively true. But the message of the Buddha concerns liberation through transforming the mind, and the raft simile draws one's attention to a potential incompatibility between the truth of the teachings themselves and the way they are held if they are clung onto with craving and attachment. It is obvious that particular teachings are no longer needed once one has irrevocably understood their point, or their meaning, or what they are referring to. In getting the point one does not need to cling on, and one can let go of the expression. Moreover if necessary one could re-express it, so long as the point eventually turns out to be the same. And whether to utter a particular statement at a particular time may well be completely pragmatic. That is, one utters the statement entirely because in context it will help on the spiritual path. But there is no implication here that the point, i.e. what is being expressed, is not really, objectively true. There is no suggestion that it is only 'pragmatically true' i.e. it is *only* a question of it being beneficial in the context of the spiritual path.

As we have seen, the Buddhist tradition, certainly in India, always considered that the Buddha had discerned a definite 'way things are', and there are teachings which entail practices which do indeed lead to seeing things that way and freedom from all suffering, all *duḥkha*. The teachings of the Buddha are held by the Buddhist tradition to *work* because they are factually *true* (not true because they work). In the Indian context it would have been axiomatic that liberation comes from discerning how things actually are, the true nature of things. That seeing how things are has soteriological benefits would have been expected, and is just another way of articulating the binary 'is' and 'ought' dimension of Indian Dharma. The 'ought' (pragmatic benefit) is never cut adrift from the 'is' (cognitive factual truth). Otherwise it would follow that the Buddha might be able to benefit beings (and thus bring them to enlightenment) even without seeing things the way they really are at all. And that is not Buddhism.

2 Mainstream Buddhism

The basic thought of the Buddha

The four Noble Truths

Books on Buddhism often start with the so-called four Noble Truths, and rightly so since this topic is central to what is traditionally held to have been the first discourse of the Buddha after his enlightenment. That discourse is known in Pāli as the *Dhammacakkappavattana Sutta* ('The Discourse Setting in Motion the Wheel of Dhamma'). Yet, as K. R. Norman has pointed out, there is no particular reason why the Pāli expression *ariyasaccāni* should be translated as 'noble truths'. It could equally be translated as 'the nobles' truths', or 'the truths for nobles', or 'the nobilising truths', or 'the truths of, possessed by, the noble ones' (1990–6, in 1993 volume: 174). In fact the Pāli expression (and its Sanskrit equivalent) can mean all of these, although the Pāli commentators place 'the noble truths' as the *least* important in their understanding (ibid.; see also Norman 1997: 16). Norman's own view is that probably the best single translation is 'the truth[s] of the noble one (the Buddha)'. This would amount to a statement of how things are seen ('truth'; Sanskrit: *satya*; Pāli: *sacca*, derived from '*sat*', being, how it is) by a Buddha, how things really are when seen correctly. Through not seeing things this way, and behaving accordingly, we suffer. Nevertheless, while bearing in mind these alternative ways of reading the expression, let us stick with the (Western) tradition of translating the expression as 'noble truths'.

The formula for the four Noble Truths is probably based on the formula for a medical diagnosis. That is, it states the illness, the source of the illness, then the cure for the illness, and finally the way to bring about that cure. Let me treat each of the four in turn.

Duḥkha/Dukkha

In the Pāli *Dhammacakkappavattana Sutta* the Buddha states:

> Birth is *dukkha*, decay is *dukkha*, disease is *dukkha*, death is *dukkha*, to be united with the unpleasant is *dukkha*, to be separated from the pleasant is *dukkha*, not to get what one desires is *dukkha*. In brief the five aggregates [*khandha*; Sanskrit: *skandha*] of attachment are *dukkha*.[1]

What this amounts to is that absolutely everything pertaining to an unenlightened individual comes under *duḥkha*. A certain amount has been written against the translation of this term by 'suffering'. This is perhaps animated by a feeling that to claim all of our unenlightened life is suffering sounds rather pessimistic, even though it is sometimes added that Buddhism is actually realistic – because it tells it how it is – and optimistic, because it teaches a way to overcome *duḥkha*. It is true that the Buddhist tradition has come to speak of three types of *duḥkha*. The first is literally pain (i.e. in Sanskrit *duḥkhaduḥkha*), the sort of feeling you have when you step in bare feet on a drawing pin. The second type of *duḥkha* is the *duḥkha* of change, a *duḥkha* which things have simply because they are impermanent (Sanskrit: *anitya*; Pāli: *anicca*). They are liable to change, to become otherwise. Thus even happiness is *duḥkha* in this sense, because even happiness is liable to change. This sort of *duḥkha* is considered by Buddhists to be omnipresent in saṃsāra. Perfectly illustrated in the Buddha-to-be's discovery of old age, sickness, and death, radical unremitting impermanence is discovered to be *the* essential ontological dimension of our unenlightened state. And finally there is the *duḥkha* of conditions. This is the *duḥkha* that is part of our very being as conditioned individuals living in a conditioned world. It is the *duḥkha* which is intrinsic to our state of imperfection, unenlightenment. As Rupert Gethin puts it:

> we are part of a world compounded of unstable and unreliable conditions, a world in which pain and pleasure, happiness and suffering are in all sorts of ways bound up together. It is the reality of this state of affairs that the teachings of the Buddha suggest we each must understand if we are ever to be free of suffering.
>
> (Gethin 1998: 62)

It follows from this therefore that as a technical expression of Buddhism *duḥkha* is much wider in meaning than 'suffering'. The Buddhist does not deny that we laugh and are happy, although laughter and happiness still come under *duḥkha*. They come under *duḥkha* not in the sense that they are really miserable but rather in the sense that they are impermanent and anyway they are the laughter and happiness of beings that are not enlightened (as they could be). Nevertheless, while bearing in mind this extended meaning of *duḥkha* in Buddhism, it still is the case that the Buddha chose the everyday word *duḥkha*, pain, suffering, to begin his medical diagnosis of the existential situation of beings. This was true to his position as a world-renouncer who sought complete liberation. Thus 'suffering' is indeed an appropriate translation for *duḥkha*. As a technical term in Buddhist Sanskrit or Pāli it is wider in meaning than simply everyday *duḥkha* (*duḥkhaduḥkha*), and correspondingly therefore we would also have to admit that in Buddhist English 'suffering' is a technical term wider in meaning than it is in everyday English. For the Buddha, from his enlightened vision, all our very being as unenlightened individuals is indeed 'suffering', and that is just how we would expect an Indian renouncer to diagnose the endless cycle of redeath.

Origin (samudaya)

The origin of suffering is said to be craving (literally 'thirst'; Sanskrit: *tṛṣṇā*; Pāli: *taṇhā*). The *Dhammacakkappavattana Sutta*

(Nārada 1980: 51) says of craving: 'It is this craving which produces rebirth, accompanied by passionate clinging, welcoming this and that (life). It is the craving for sensual pleasures, craving for existence, and craving for non-existence.' This passage also indicates the three types into which cravings can be classified. Cravings include not just cravings for sensory pleasures, but also craving for continued existence – eternal life – and craving for complete cessation, non-existence, a complete 'end to it all'. All of these can become objects of craving. Note that 'craving' is a much better translation for *tṛṣṇā* than the common translation 'desire', since in English 'desire' is often synonymous with 'wanting', and it seems to me the Buddha does not wish to say that wanting *per se* is faulty. I take it that if we knowingly engage in rational actions that can be expected to bring about *X* we can be said to want *X* if we are neither acting randomly nor acting under compulsion external to ourselves and counter to our will. The Buddha, when he went on his alms-round, presumably wanted to go on the alms-round. He was not acting randomly, nor being compelled to set off on the alms-round against his will. He acted out of free will. That is, he desired to go on the alms-round. But it does not follow from wanting something that one has craving for it. The Buddha's alms-round was not the result of craving. It did not spring from *tṛṣṇā*. Thus it is not considered faulty, and certainly not contradictory (as people sometimes tell me), for a Buddhist to want enlightenment. A Buddhist wants enlightenment in the sense that wanting something is a condition of freely and intentionally engaging in practices to bring it about. It is indeed faulty to have craving for enlightenment and, since the Buddhist path is precisely designed to bring craving to an end, to want enlightenment is to want the practices which will eliminate among other things craving after enlightenment itself. There is no contradiction in any of this.

No doubt in isolating *tṛṣṇā* as the culprit here the Buddha was following a common move among the *śramaṇas*, the renunciates. This move attributed continued rebirth and redeath to the egoistic concerns, the wish for personal gain, that powered the Vedic sacrificial culture and that led to the results of *karman*, 'good fortune in this life and in the next'. It would have been commonplace among renunciates that the way to bring to an end all rebirth was to cut completely something akin to *tṛṣṇā* which, in order to ensure the results of appropriate actions, projected (as it were) a future rebirth. This craving is in Buddhism, however, a very deep-rooted sort of grasping, since it is considered to be an almost instinctive response in each unenlightened being from birth. He or she does not just want, they *crave*. Craving can lead to attachment (*upādāna*), and the Buddhist tradition speaks of four specific types of attachment (Gethin 1998: 71): attachment to the objects of sense-desire, attachment to views (Sanskrit: *dṛṣṭi*; Pāli: *diṭṭhi*), attachment to precepts and vows, and attachment to the doctrine of the Self. Note the way in which it is not the *object* of craving and attachment that is the determinative factor here. What marked out the Buddha's approach to this topic, in contrast to his fellow *śramaṇas*, was his psychologising. *Tṛṣṇā* is a matter of the mind, and therefore *tṛṣṇā* is eliminated not by fierce asceticism, torturing the body, but by mental transformation through meditation. For the Buddhist it is the mental factor which is crucial. Liberation is all about the mind.

But what exactly is it about *tṛṣṇā*, craving, which has such results, and how exactly does cutting craving lead to liberation? First, what is so insidious about craving, given that one wishes to overcome suffering, is its (psychological) incompatibility with impermanence. Craving *X*, where *X* is sure to cease, is to lead to suffering at the loss of *X* (for frustrated craving is painful), and renewed craving which itself is doomed to eventual loss. And so on, short of liberation, forever, for craving also projects future lives. This craving in the light of impermanence is radically unwise. Essential to seeing things the way they really are, which is liberation, is seeing all these impermanent things as impermanent, and therefore letting go of craving.

Erich Frauwallner (1973: 150 ff.) has suggested that perhaps the Buddha's original idea was that craving resulted simply from contact between the senses and their objects. Craving occurs usually (but clearly not necessarily) from all sensory experience, including mental experiences since Buddhism, in common with all

Indian philosophy, treats the mind (*manas*) as a sixth sense, 'seeing' mental objects like memories and fantasy images. Thus the way to liberation lay in mindfulness, constantly watching sensory experience in order to prevent the arising of cravings which would power future experience into rebirths. Cravings occur subsequent to sensory experience. This is seen in the formula for 'dependent origination' (q.v.; Sanskrit: *pratītyasamutpāda*; Pāli: *paṭiccasamuppāda*) for example, where it is held that conditioned by the six senses is sensory contact, conditioned by sensory contact is feeling, and conditioned by feeling is craving. It becomes possible therefore (it is hoped) through awareness to insert a block between the sensory experience and the resulting craving. Thus the dynamism behind rebirth is also blocked. However, Frauwallner suggests, subsequently the Buddha (or the Buddhist tradition – who can tell?) shifted interest from craving as such as the cause of saṃsāra to the factor behind craving which has such dramatic effects. Fundamentally the factor behind craving and the real cause of suffering is *avidyā* (Pāli: *avijjā*), ignorance or misconception, which produces egotism.

Whether this represents two different phases of the Buddha's understanding remains controversial. Perhaps ignorance and craving can better be seen as two different but inextricably mixed dimensions (the cognitive and the affective) of the saṃsāric experience (Gethin 1997b: 221). Either way, ignorance is not a first cause in Buddhism in the sense of something that chronologically started the whole process off. It is not that once there was nothing and then ignorance occurred and the world came about. The traditional Buddhist view is that the series of lives extends as far as we can tell infinitely into the past. Moreover short of liberation rebirths will as far as we can tell stretch infinitely into the future. Thus there is no chronological (or indeed ontologically necessary) first cause. Rather, ignorance is the conceptual, and, we might say, soteriological first cause. It is that which is taken to act as a conceptually final explanation for suffering and the cycle of rebirth, the root of saṃsāra. It is that from which liberation follows when it is completely overcome. In stating ignorance to be the root cause of suffering Buddhism again displays its credentials as an Indian gnostic system. If ignorance is the cause of saṃsāra, knowing, gnosis (*vidyā* = *jñāna*), becomes the ultimate condition of nirvāṇa.

Ignorance when spoken of as the cause of suffering is explained in the Buddhist tradition as ignorance precisely of the four Noble Truths. 'In other words, it is the not-knowingness of things as they truly are, or of oneself as one really is. It clouds all right understanding' (Nārada 1980: 240). It is thus ignorance of the Dharma, ignorance of what is cognitively and practically seen as the Truth by the Buddha. In particular ignorance is, once more in common with e.g. the Upaniṣads, ignorance of the true nature of the Self. But radically unlike the Upaniṣads (or Jains, for example) which seek to reveal the hidden Self behind all things, the Buddha is going to assert that all the candidates put forward for the Self are 'not Self'. Letting go of all these candidates for Self is the very prerequisite of nirvāṇa. And what makes craving so insidious is precisely the way wanting becomes almost inextricably mixed with a strong assertion of Self, 'I' and 'mine', and thereby becomes craving. Thus the way to liberation lies not just, or perhaps not really, in mindfulness of sensory experience. Rather it lies in cutting forever all false assertion of Self, through knowing (gnosis) that each candidate for Self is really not Self at all. This is a crucial topic to which we shall return.

Cessation **(nirodha)***: on nirvāṇa*

The Buddha has completed his diagnosis. Now he offers the cure. If suffering in all its forms results from craving, then it follows that if craving can be completely eradicated, suffering will come to an end. As we have seen, the way to eradicate completely craving is to eradicate its cause, ignorance, through coming to see things in the deepest possible manner the way they really are. The complete cessation of suffering is nirvāṇa (Pāli: *nibbāna*).

Nirvāṇa is broadly speaking the result of letting-go, letting-go the very forces of craving which power continued experiences of pleasure and inevitably suffering throughout this life, death, rebirth, and redeath. That, in a nutshell, is what nirvāṇa is. It is the complete and permanent cessation of saṃsāra, thence the cessation of all types of suffering, resulting from letting-go the forces which power saṃsāra, due to overcoming ignorance (thence also hatred and delusion, the 'three root poisons') through seeing things the way they really are. Nirvāṇa here is *not* 'the Buddhist name for the Absolute Reality' (let alone, God forbid, 'the Buddhist name for God'). Nirvāṇa is here an occurrence, an event (not a *being*, nor Being). Literally it means 'extinguishing', as in 'the extinguishing of a flame', and it signifies soteriologically the complete extinguishing of greed, hatred, and fundamentally delusion (i.e. ignorance), the forces which power saṃsāra. These forces are thus completely destroyed. This event of extinguishing occurred when the Buddha became the Buddha. He 'attained nirvāṇa' while seated in meditation at the foot of a tree. Having come out of his meditation he knew it had finally been done, once and for all. 'Nirvāṇa' is *not* used by Buddhists to refer to the extinguishing of the person, or the individual. The Buddha did not suddenly go out of existence at the time of his liberation. It does not follow, therefore, from the use of this term alone that liberation in Buddhism is the equivalent (as some people seem to think) of ceasing to exist. Nor does it follow in anything other than the purely grammatical sense that nirvāṇa is entirely negative. After his nirvāṇa the Buddha continued to live and act in the world, living and acting as a person completely free of greed, hatred, and delusion. Note also that to live in this way is thus defined in what we would call moral terms. One who acts free of greed, hatred, and delusion is as such living and acting morally. Nirvāṇa is not understood to be an amoral state.

The tradition refers to the nirvāṇa which the Buddha attained when he completely eradicated greed, hatred, and delusion as 'nirvāṇa with a remainder [of "fuel" or life?]' (Sanskrit: *sopadhiśeṣanirvāṇa*; Pāli: *sa-upādisesanibbāna*). When an enlightened person like the Buddha dies, by definition there is no further rebirth. When that occurs it follows that the psychophysical elements that make him up as the embodied living individual he is (psychophysical elements known collectively as the five aggregates (q.v.)) cease, and are not replaced by further psychophysical elements. This is called 'nirvāṇa without a remainder [of "fuel" or life?]' (Sanskrit: *nirupadhiśeṣanirvāṇa*; Pāli: *anupādisesanibbāna*). As Gethin points out (1998: 76, see also Norman 1990–6, 1996 volume: 12–18), this 'nirvāṇa without a remainder' is sometimes referred to in modern Buddhist usage (probably incorrectly) as *parinirvāṇa*, restricting 'nirvāṇa' to 'nirvāṇa with a remainder'. And what of a Buddha who has attained 'nirvāṇa without a remainder'? What is it like for that person? Is it fun? The question is considered absurd. Without the psychophysical elements (including consciousness, but cf. Harvey 1990: 67 and 1995) there is no sense to the idea of a person (and certainly no sense to 'fun', at least as it is normally understood in saṃsāra). And, as we shall see, the Buddha rejected any additional candidate with the status of a Self that could be the 'real person' undergoing fun. There is nothing left for our minds to fix on ('men and gods will not see him', Norman 1990–6, 1993 volume: 253). Since there is nothing left for the mind to fix on, nothing more can be said. We have seen already that the question whether the Buddha (*Tathāgata*) exists, does not exist, both exists and does not exist, or neither exists nor does not exist after death was one of the useless questions which the Buddha expressed no intention of answering. Any attempt to do so would attempt the impossible, and also contravene Buddhist tradition.[2]

Thus nirvāṇa appears to be expressed in the earliest Buddhist tradition with event-terminology like 'attaining' and 'extinguishing' rather than noun-terms as occur in English metaphysics with 'Absolute', 'Reality', or 'God'. Unfortunately however the issue is rather more complicated than it at first appears. There remains the interesting problem of how to interpret passages like the following, said of nirvāṇa and attributed to the Buddha as an 'inspired utterance' (*udāna*):

> There is monks a domain where there is no earth, no water, no fire, no wind, no sphere of infinite space, no sphere of nothingness, no sphere of infinite consciousness, no sphere of neither awareness nor non-awareness; there is not this world, there is not another world, there is no sun or moon.

> I do not call this coming or going, nor standing nor dying, nor being reborn; it is without support, without occurrence, without object. Just this is the end of suffering.
>
> (Trans. in Gethin 1998: 76–7)

'Domain' would appear to be a noun-term. One way of reading this is that alongside our discussion of nirvāṇa as an event we must also indeed make room for nirvāṇa spoken of here as an Absolute Reality. This would be a Reality rather like the Brahman of the Upaniṣads or perhaps the Hindu school of Advaita Vedānta, or the ineffable 'Godhead' of some religious teachings. Moreover, perhaps, as with the Hindu approaches, this Absolute Reality is also identical with the True Self (*ātman*), really in spite of appearances accepted by the Buddha. Thus his denials were only of what is 'not Self', not of the True Self.[3] I am not convinced by all of this. The Buddhist tradition for its part speaks of nirvāṇa in this context simply as the 'unconditioned' (Sanskrit: *asaṃskṛta*; Pāli: *asaṃkhata*), or the 'unconditioned realm' (*-dhātu*). It is worth noting that the only positive expression in the whole quotation from the *Udāna* cited above (and indeed in expressions like 'unconditioned realm') is 'domain' or 'realm' (*āyatana* = *dhātu*). I do not think that any conclusions sympathetic to the (for want of a better expression) 'Hindu' or 'Absolutist' interpretation can be drawn here from a series of negatives. It simply does not follow that even if I describe identically two things (such as Brahman and nirvāṇa) using negative terminology I am thereby describing the same thing. Think of a banana and an orange both described as 'not apple', 'not cabbage', 'not green', 'not on wheels', 'not powered by diesel', and so on. And one certainly cannot conclude from language like that in the quotation above without considerable further evidence and argument that the Buddhists are speaking of the same *thing* as e.g. the Brahman of Advaita Vedānta. Deference should be given to the mainstream Buddhist traditions that explicitly deny this linkage.

It seems to me that it is from looking more closely at the only positive expressions here, the Buddhist use of 'domain' (*āyatana*) and 'realm' (*dhātu*) that some understanding of what is going on may emerge. Early Buddhist treatment of perception (epistemology) speaks of the twelve *āyatanas* and the eighteen *dhātus*. The twelve *āyatanas* are the six senses (five senses plus the mind) and their six classes of corresponding intentional objects (visual objects, tactile objects, and so on). The eighteen *dhātus* are the same twelve plus the six types of resultant consciousnesses (visual consciousness, which occurs as a result of the 'meeting' of the visual sense with a visual object, and so on). Thus in the context of the theory of perception the term *dhātu* overlaps with that of *āyatana*. It seems clear to me that in referring to nirvāṇa as a 'domain', or a 'realm' the only commitment is to nirvāṇa as an intentional[4] *object of cognition*, where '*X* is an object of cognition' means simply (and nothing more than) 'One can have an *X*-experience'.[5] This is why in another famous passage from the *Udāna* the Buddha states that 'if that unborn, not-become, not-made, not-compounded were not, there would be apparent no escape from this here that is born, become, made, compounded'.[6] All this actually says, in its Buddhist context, is that the attainment of nirvāṇa is not doomed through the mind being unable to cognise in such a way, i.e. there is no such cognitive content. As an intentional object of cognition nirvāṇa is described using almost entirely negatives, for it is described in polarised opposition to that of which it is the complete negation, i.e. saṃsāra (see Norman 1990–6: paper 117, esp. 23–4). Saṃsāra is the conditioned. That is why it is impermanent, and being subject to impermanence it is subject to at least one sort of *duḥkha*. Thus nirvāṇa, being defined deliberately as not-saṃsāra, is specified using precisely negations. It is not conditioned, because it is not part of the formula for 'dependent origination', which pertains to saṃsāra, it is where there are no conditioned things (K. R. Norman), and also it is not impermanent (and thence enmeshed in *duḥkha*) as are conditioned things. And so on. The only commitment in all of this, it seems to me, is that nirvāṇa can be attained. The search for nirvāṇa is not doomed to failure. Cognising nirvāṇa is not impossible, due to there being no such cognitive content or referent. In addition nirvāṇa is the negation of saṃsāra and all that cessation involves. But there is no positive ontological commitment implied at all. Nirvāṇa in this sense is simply – and nothing more than – the perceptual condition for the *event* of nirvāṇa (what happened to the Buddha under the tree of enlightenment) to take place. Thus the only positive expression needed or possible for nirvāṇa is *āyatana* or *dhātu*, translated as 'domain/realm'. All the rest can indicate the negation of the suffering which is saṃsāra, either directly as here through the use of verbal negations, or indirectly through terms like 'supramundane' (Sanskrit: *lokottara*) which unpack as negative expressions (= not of the world). Thus this third sense of nirvāṇa is as the content, or the intentional referent, of enlightening gnosis. That is all.[7]

Way (*Sanskrit:* **mārga**; *Pāli:* **magga**)

The way to nirvāṇa is spoken of in the *Dhammacakkappavattana Sutta* as the 'eightfold path'. In its fullest development this is the eightfold (or eight-dimensioned) way of the Āryas. The Āryas are the noble ones, the saints, those who have attained 'the fruits of the path', 'that middle path the Tathāgata has comprehended which promotes sight and knowledge, and which tends to peace, higher wisdom, enlightenment, and Nibbāna' (Nārada 1980: 50). The path is described as the 'middle path' in this early discourse in the sense that it is the middle path between what renunciates like the Buddha would have seen as the indulgent sensual way of the householder, and the self-mortification, bodily torture, carried out by certain other renunciates. Positive and permissible indulgence in sensual delights (*kāma*) providing it does not contradict Dharma has always been seen as very much the prerogative of the householder in Indian civilisation (*Kāmasūtra*, esp. Ch. 2). For the Buddha this is precisely not suitable for 'one who has renounced', and thus for one seriously engaged in the path aimed at eradicating suffering and rebirth. In talking of the 'middle path' the Buddha directly indicates transcendence of the householder framework. But equally the Buddha understood liberation in psychological terms, as something to do with transforming the mind through correct understanding. Thus asceticism *as such* could not bring about liberation, and indeed certain types of asceticism (such as starving oneself) were no doubt seen as causing serious distraction in working on one's own mind.

The Buddhist path is the overcoming of greed, hatred, and delusion through the cultivation of their opposites, nonattachment, loving kindness, and wisdom or insight. The list of eight elements to the path (perhaps 'dimensions' would be better, as indicating the complementarity rather than successive nature of the set) is early, and is found in the *Dhammacakkappavattana Sutta*. Each element is preceded with 'right' (Sanskrit: *samyak*; Pāli: *sammā*) or 'perfect', 'appropriate', we might almost say 'fitting'. Thus we have:

(i) right view (i.e. *samyagdṛṣṭi*/*sammādiṭṭhi*)
(ii) right intention
(iii) right speech
(iv) right action
(v) right livelihood
(vi) right effort
(vii) right mindfulness
(viii) right concentration.[8]

'Right view' is here glossed as seeing the truth of the four Noble Truths (which in a nice piece of self-reference thus includes of course the eightfold path itself).[9] It means that one speaks, acts, and thinks in conformity with reality, how things actually are. Note that the word 'view' (*dṛṣṭi*/*diṭṭhi*) is used here, and its use in this sense must therefore be distinguished from the sense seen previously in which *all* 'views' are described as finally pernicious. To hold even the right view with craving is to have a *dṛṣṭi* which is ultimately to be abandoned, although it seems clear that to do this must for the Buddhist be preferable to holding a wrong view, necessarily with craving. This is because holding the right view with craving is as such to engage in the path that if followed through eventually erodes all craving and leads to a right view without craving, that is therefore no 'view' at all. 'Right intention' is explained as intentions free from attachments to worldly pleasures, selfishness, and self-possessiveness, and animated by benevolence and compassion (see Nārada 1980: 181–3). In terms of the three major divisions of the Buddhist path – wisdom (*prajñā*; Pāli: *paññā*), morality (or conduct: *śīla*; Pāli: *sīla*), and meditation (Sanskrit/Pāli: *samādhi*) – right view and right intention are classed under 'wisdom'. 'Right speech' is speech that is not false, divisive, hurtful, or merely idle chatter. 'Right action' is refraining from harming living beings, particularly through killing them, refraining from taking what is not given (essentially, stealing), and refraining from sexual misconduct. In the case of monks and nuns this means refraining from all sexual activity.[10] 'Right livelihood' is explained as livelihood not involving the infringement of right speech and right action. Some (Pāli) sources refer to five kinds of trade particularly inappropriate for lay Buddhists (let alone monks and nuns), trade in arms, human beings, flesh, intoxicating drinks (presumably also other 'recreational' drugs), and poison (op cit.: p. 184). In terms of the three major divisions of the Buddhist path, right speech, right action, and right livelihood are classed under 'morality', and the remaining elements of the eightfold path come under 'meditation'. 'Right effort' consists of effort to prevent the arising of unwholesome mental states (e.g. of greed, hatred, and delusion) which have not arisen and effort to abandon unwholesome states that have arisen. It is effort to arouse wholesome states (e.g. of non-attachment, loving kindness, and wisdom) which have not arisen, and effort to develop and promote wholesome states that have arisen.[11] 'Right mindfulness' is constant mindfulness, awareness, with reference to the body, with reference to feelings, with reference to the mind, and with reference to physical and mental processes (following Gethin, based on Theravāda commentaries). In watching these one is aware of their flowing nature, moments arising and falling, aware of their impermanence and aware of letting them go. In watching in this way one perceives them as they are, and abandons any notion that they might be worth craving, as capable of providing lasting happiness, or as an object of attachment as one's true Self. In knowing, seeing the body, feelings, the mind, and physical and mental processes as they are, one begins to erode any basis for craving, and thus the forces that power suffering and rebirth. 'Right concentration' consists of one-pointedness of mind, the mind focusing unwaveringly on a single object, which can be taken to the point where one attains successively the four *dhyānas* (Pāli: *jhānas*), the four 'meditations' or, in this context, perhaps 'absorptions'. These *dhyānas* are said to take the meditator outside, as it were, the desire realm (*kāmadhātu*) in which we humans normally live, and to pertain to the realm of (pure) form, the *rūpadhātu*. The first and lowest of the *dhyānas* is characterised (in the standard scheme) as involving applied thought, examination, joy, happiness, and one-pointedness of mind. The second *dhyāna* has the same features apart from the applied thought and examination, which are no longer experientially present and have dropped away. The third has happiness and one-pointedness, and the fourth possesses just one-pointedness and equanimity.[12] To quote from Peter Harvey:

> The fourth *jhāna* is a state of profound stillness and peace, in which the mind rests with unshakeable one-pointedness and equanimity, and breathing has calmed to the point of stopping. The mind has a radiant purity, due to its 'brightly shining' depths having been uncovered and made manifest at the surface level. It is said to be very 'workable' and 'adaptable' like refined gold, which can be used to make all manner of precious and wonderful things. It is thus an ideal take-off point for various further developments. Indeed it seems to have been the state from which the Buddha went on to attain enlightenment.
>
> (Harvey 1990: 250–2)

The four *dhyānas* are also spoken of as being realms into which one can be reborn as certain types of gods, thus bringing together cosmological realms and mental transformation in an interesting way which shows a blending of 'outer' cosmology and 'inner' psychology on these rarefied levels of Buddhist experience. We shall return to this topic subsequently.

Not-Self (*anātman*; Pāli: *anattā*)

It is often said in books published in English that the Buddha denied the existence of the soul. I do not see this as a very helpful way of speaking. The 'soul' in Western thought is held in its broadest sense to be that which gives life to the body. Some, such as Aristotle, thought of it as the 'form' of the body, that is, what makes the matter of the body alive as the actual living thing it is, rather as the shape is what makes wax *this* wax thing. He apparently did not think of the soul as separable from the body. Others (including Aristotle's Medieval followers such as Aquinas) have seen at least the human soul as something immaterial capable of living apart from the body after the latter's demise, and some others have connected the issues of bodily life, survival of death, and personal identity in a radically dualistic way. As is well known, Descartes identified that which gives life to the body, and survives death, with the mind, and he also identified this mind-soul as the true self, of an intrinsically different stuff from the body. The mind-soul is the factor in which lies the identity of the person over time and change. But these diverse views are diverse views of the thinkers concerned. Christian theology, for example, has no commitment to a particular view of the soul or, as such, personal identity. Its only commitment is that there is *something* that gives life to the body, and death is not the end of the story for the specific person concerned.

It seems to me that very little of this discussion of the soul is relevant to the Buddha.[13] The Buddha stated that a large number of things were *anātman*, not Self, but I see no reason to think that in doing this he was concerned to deny whatever gave life to the body, *whatever that is*. Nor do I think he was concerned to deny that death is not the end of the story. Indeed he was very concerned to assert that the story in some sense goes on after death ('life after death', 'reincarnation'). To say that this is not the case has always been considered to be a cardinal 'wrong view' in Buddhism, the wrong view of *ucchedavāda*, annihilationism. In spite of what is sometimes said nowadays, traditional Buddhism is completely committed to some sense of life after death.[14] But all this has nothing whatsoever to do with the central element in the teaching of the Buddha, the teaching of things as *anātman*, not *Self*.

Strangely, the Buddha makes no mention of Not-Self in the *Dhammacakkappavattana Sutta*. This is particularly strange given that the discourse is supposed to be the Buddha's first sermon. It purports to describe what the Buddha discovered at his enlightenment (apparently the four Noble Truths), and the Not-Self teaching has always been held by Buddhists to be *the* unique discovery of the Buddha, the discovery that ensures his superiority over all other teachers. If what the Buddha discovered was the Truth that sets one free, then in a very real sense Not-Self *is* that liberating Truth. Perhaps in order to reconcile the anomaly here, the tradition holds that the Buddha followed the *Dhammacakkappavattana Sutta* with another discourse, this time on Not-Self, known in its Pāli version as the *Anattalakkhaṇa Sutta* (the 'Discourse on the Definition of Not-Self'). This sutta is probably the single most important source for understanding the mainstream position of Buddhist thought in relationship to its soteriological project. In it we see the Buddha addressing his very earliest disciples:

> Bhikkhus [monks], material form [physical form, *rūpa*] is not self [*rūpaṃ bhikkhave anattā*].[15] If material form were self, this material form would not lead to affliction, and it could be had of material form: 'Let my material form be thus; let my material form be not thus.' And it is because material form is not self that it therefore leads to affliction, and that it cannot be had of material form: 'Let my material form be thus; let my material form be not thus.'
>
> Feeling [sensation; *vedanā*] is not self. . . .
>
> [Determinate] perception [conception; *saññā*; Sanskrit: *saṃjñā*] is not self. . . .
>
> Formations [volitions etc.; *saṃkhārā*; Sanskrit: *saṃskārāḥ*] are not self. . . .
>
> Consciousness (*viññāṇa*; Sanskrit: *vijñāna*) is not self. . . .
>
> (Trans. in Ñāṇamoli 1992: 46)

What the Buddha wants to say, then, is that each of these possible candidates for the status of Self is actually not Self. His grounds for this are that if something were to be the Self it would (i) not lead to affliction, and (ii) it would obey the person of whom it is the Self.[16] In other words, whatever the Self is, it is something over which one has complete control and it is something which is conducive to happiness (or at least, not conducive to suffering). The list of five types of things which might be considered to be the Self but which by simple examination are seen not to fit the description falls into two classes: the physical (material form), and the mental (the other four: feelings, perceptions, formations (e.g. intentions/volitions), and consciousness). These five classes of things are known as the five 'heaps' or 'aggregates' (Pāli (singular): *khandha*; Sanskrit: *skandha*).[17] The Buddha continues with a further characteristic of any putative Self:

> How do you conceive this, bhikkhus, is material form permanent or impermanent? – 'Impermanent, Lord.' – But is what is impermanent unpleasant or pleasant? – 'Unpleasant, Lord.' – But is it fitting to regard what is impermanent, unpleasant and subject to change as: 'This is mine, this is what I am, this is my self?' – 'No, Lord.'
>
> (Ñāṇamoli 1992: 46)

And the Buddha explains that the same can be said as regards the other four aggregates. Thus we can add also that any Self would (iii) have to be permanent. And if it were fitting to regard anything with the consideration 'This is mine, this is what I am, this is my self', that thing ought at least to be permanent, pleasant, and not subject to change. Clearly from all this the Buddha takes it that any part of our psychophysical makeup, anything which can be classed under one or other of the five aggregates, cannot fit the paradigmatic description of what something would have to be in order to be a Self. They are all not Self. And – this is important – they are all impermanent. Seeing things this way is to see correctly:

> Therefore, bhikkhus, any material form whatsoever, whether past, future or present, in oneself or external, coarse or fine, inferior or superior, far or near, should all be regarded as it actually is by right understanding thus: 'This is not mine, this is not what I am, this is not my self.'
>
> (Ñāṇamoli 1992: 46)

And the same applies, of course, to the other aggregates. Elsewhere (in the *Alagaddūpama Sutta*) the Buddha comments that if someone were to burn wood no one would consider that he himself is being burned. Thus not only is our physical body not our Self, but it is patently obvious also that the world cannot be the Self (as some followers of the Upaniṣads might have thought). Of course, on the basis of what we have just seen from the *Anattalakkhaṇa Sutta*, the world also could not be the Self because it too leads to affliction, does not obey the person of whom it would be the Self, and is impermanent. We cannot say 'I am all this, this is my Self'. I cannot gain control over the macrocosm by realising its essence (*Brahman*) is truly identical with my essence (*ātman*), since patently the macrocosm is not my Self. It does not fit the description for a Self.[18]

Now we meet the crucial part of this discourse. Note what the Buddha in the *Anattalakkhaṇa Sutta* considers to be the result of seeing things the way they really are in this way:

> Seeing thus, bhikkhus, a wise noble disciple becomes dispassionate towards material form, becomes dispassionate towards feeling . . . [etc.]. Becoming dispassionate, his lust fades away; with the fading of lust his heart is liberated; when liberated, there comes the knowledge: 'It is liberated.' He understands: 'Birth is exhausted, the holy life has been lived out, what was to be done is done, there is no more of this to come.'
>
> (Ñāṇamoli 1992: 47)

This shows wonderfully well, I think, the connection between seeing things the way they really are, in terms of seeing how the psychophysical world actually is, and liberation. There is built into seeing how things are ('is') a transformation of moral response ('ought'). The Buddha seems to suggest that this transformation is an automatic response to seeing how things really are. In spite of what the eighteenth century Scottish philosopher Hume says, for the Buddha it is very much possible to get an 'ought' from an 'is'. Liberation results from letting-go that which is seen as not being the Self. When one sees things are sources of unhappiness, out of one's control, and impermanent, one sees that they cannot be any kind of Self. With this one lets them go, for having any involvement with them can only lead to misery. In letting all these go there is liberation, for the force of craving which leads to suffering and rebirth is no more. Seeing that all these are not Self is the path to liberation.

The Buddha had characterised the aggregates as being not Self because they lead to affliction, they do not obey the person of whom they are the aggregates, and they are impermanent. It follows from this that if something had the negations of these characteristics (did not lead to affliction, did obey the person, and were permanent) it would be the Self, or at least could be a strong candidate for the Self. On the basis of this there are those who consider that all the Buddha has done here is to show what is not the Self. He has not however said that there is no such thing as a Self at all. I confess I cannot quite understand this. If the Buddha considered that he had shown only what is not the Self, and the Buddha actually accepted a Self beyond his negations, a Self other than and behind the five aggregates, fitting the paradigmatic description for a Self, then he would surely have said so. And we can be quite sure he would have said so very clearly indeed. He does not. It seems that all the other renouncers of his day saw the search for liberation from all suffering as terminating in discovering the Self. Indian systems which do teach the *ātman*, like the *Bṛhadāraṇyaka Upaniṣad*, for example, devote a great deal of attention to the issue, and make it quite clear in what way they assert the Self. No one has ever argued that the Upaniṣads do not teach the Self. Nor could they possibly do so. In early and mainstream Buddhist texts on the other hand all we find are denials, statements that various things are not the Self. If the Buddha had thought there was a Self, and merely wanted to indicate here what is not the Self, it is inconceivable that he would have thought finding the Self really had nothing to do with liberation. Thus in the *Anattalakkhaṇa Sutta* we should expect that he would have continued by explaining how, having seen what is not the Self, one finds the Self and that leads to 'the knowledge: "It is liberated."' But he does not do this. He makes no mention of discovering the True Self in the *Anattalakkhaṇa Sutta.* As we have seen, the Buddha explains how liberation comes from letting-go of all craving and attachment simply through seeing that things are not Self. That is all there is to it. One cuts the force that leads to rebirth and suffering. There is no need to postulate a Self beyond all this. Indeed any postulated Self would lead to attachment, for it seems that for the Buddha a Self fitting the description could legitimately be a suitable subject of attachment. There is absolutely no suggestion that the Buddha thought there is some additional factor called the Self (or with any other name, but fitting the Self-description) beyond the five aggregates.[19]

Just as there are those who think that the Buddha is really teaching a True Self behind all denial (an example of the view of eternalism; Pāli: *sassatavāda*; Sanskrit: *śāśvatavāda*), there are sometimes those who think the Buddha intends to deny that we exist at all. This is a version of the view of annihilationism (Pāli/Sanskrit: *ucchedavāda*). Another sense of 'middle way' when used of Buddhism is the middle between eternalism and annihilationism. This middle is that we do exist in some sort of dependence upon dynamic, causally generated psychophysical bundles. It should be clear from what has been said so far that the individual, in the case of normal human beings the person, is being explained in terms of five classes of physical and psychological continua. Each of these forms a flow with all elements of the flow and the five continua themselves bound together in a dynamic bundle. The principles of this binding, what holds it all together, as we shall see in the next section, are causal. Any idea that there is more to us than is revealed by this reduction is, in terms of how things really are, wrong. An unchanging element, the real 'me', a Self, is simply non-existent. It is a fiction, and as a fiction it is the result of beginningless ignorance (*avidyā/avijjā*) and the cause of endless sorrow. Thus eternalism is false. But note that this explanation of the normal human being, the person, presupposes that there are indeed persons. Thus annihilationism too is false. Although the Buddha himself may have been more interested in his liberating denials, the later Buddhist tradition has been careful to make sure that there is no confusion about what is not being denied here. A practical way of referring to the bundle, giving it one name such as 'Archibald', or as 'Fiona', is generally thought to be acceptable.[20] Persons in the everyday sense exist, and frequently in later Buddhist tradition the person is spoken of as the *pudgala* (Pāli: *puggala*), carefully distinguishing it from the *ātman* which is being denied. The Buddha is denying a particular sort of thing, a Self, which he sees as being at the root of the suffering of those who are unenlightened (whether they know it or not). He is not denying the existence of persons. He is not stating the absurdity that you and me, and he himself simply do not exist, and we would all be better off realising this. Persons exist as practical ways of speaking about bundles.

Dependent origination

In the *Mahātaṇhāsaṅkhaya Sutta* (the 'Greater Discourse on the Destruction of Craving') another stupid monk, Sāti, conceives the idea that consciousness is the unchanging subject of experiences, effectively the Self, and that therefore it is consciousness which transmigrates unchanged from life to life. The Buddha vehemently repudiates this idea. Consciousness comes about in dependence upon some condition or another. 'Consciousness' is just the name we give to e.g. sensory experience, as happens when an unhindered eye meets (as it were) a visual object. Then we speak of 'visual consciousness'. There is a flow of such experiences, and if experiences actually take place no really existing additional subject as consciousness itself, over and above conscious experiences, is needed. Indeed it would be better, the Buddha observes at another point, to take the body as the Self rather than the mind. The mind is patently changing constantly whereas the body at least has a certain perceived stability about it (*Saṃyutta Nikāya* II: 94–5, in Lamotte 1988: 29). Thus the Buddha's response to a claim to have found an unchanging Self is among other things to point to the obviousness that the putative 'Self' (if it occurs at all) occurs as a result of the coming together of causal conditions. It accordingly could not be unchanging, and therefore could not be a *Self*. 'Consciousness' is no more a Self than anything else. It is actually a name we give to the flow of experiences.The Buddha thereby replaces a vision of the world based on Selves underlying change with an appeal to what he sees as being its essentially dynamic nature, a dynamism of experiences based on the centrality of causal conditioning. In other words, the flight from the world into Selves is to be replaced by seeing the world as it truly is and letting it go. The Buddha considered that if we look at the whole of saṃsāra as it is we see that it is pervaded by its three hallmarks (*trilakṣaṇa*; Pāli: *tilakkhaṇa*). It is suffering (*duḥkha*). It is impermanent (*anitya*). And it is not Self (*anātman*). The world truly is a torrent of cause and effect with no stability within it, save the stability we try to make for ourselves as a refuge from change and inevitable death. That stability only exacerbates suffering because it is a fictional stability created by our desperate grasping after security. The only real stability therefore lies in nirvāṇa, just because (as we have seen) nirvāṇa precisely is not the torrent of saṃsāra. This stress on the dynamic nature of saṃsāra throws into relief the still, calm, dimension of nirvāṇa. Causal dependence was important to the Buddha primarily because it indicated the rational coherent structure of the universe. It shows what is to be done in order to bring about liberation, nirvāṇa, through reversing the processes of saṃsāra. The Buddha was interested in the fact that *X* comes into existence due to *Y* particularly because through the cessation of *Y* there will be no more *X*. Causal dependence was also important to the Buddha because it demonstrates how rebirth can occur without recourse to any Self. In addition it shows the mechanism whereby wholesome and unwholesome actions (*karman*) entail appropriate pleasant and unpleasant results. Indicating the way saṃsāra exists as an endless series of causal processes also became important for Buddhists because it rendered any sort of personal divine creator irrelevant. The Buddha intentionally or by implication replaced any talk of God with that of causal dependence. God has no place in a seamless web of natural contingency, where each contingent thing could be explained as a causal result of another contingent thing *ad infinitum*. In the *Mahātaṇhāsaṅkhaya Sutta* the Buddha corrects Sāti by stressing that things originate in dependence upon causal conditioning, and this emphasis on causality describes the central feature of Buddhist ontology. All elements of saṃsāra exist in some sense or another relative to their causes and conditions. That is why they are impermanent, for if the cause is impermanent then so too will be the effect. In particular, our own existence as embodied individuals is the result of the coming together of appropriate causes, and we exist just as long as appropriate causes keep us in existence. Inevitably, therefore, we as the embodied individuals we are shall one day cease to exist. In this particular discourse the Buddha gives a picture of causal dependence (dependent origination) expressed in its most vivid way related to the exhortation to become free. Its very practicality has, it seems, the immediacy of an early source. A child is born, and grows up:

> On seeing a visible form with the eye, hearing a sound with the ear, smelling an odour with the nose, tasting a flavour with the tongue, touching a tangible with the body, cognizing an idea with the mind [this indicates the eighteen *dhātus* of sense, object, and resultant consciousness for each of the six senses], he lusts after it if it is likable, or has ill will towards it if it is dislikable [dependent upon ignorance of its true nature he produces greed and hatred]. He abides without mindfulness of the body established and with mind limited while he does not understand as they actually are the deliverance of mind and the deliverance by understanding wherein those evil unwholesome states cease without remainder. Engaged as he is in favouring and opposing, when

> he feels any feeling, whether pleasant or painful or neither-painful-nor-pleasant [= the three types of feeling], he relishes that feeling, affirms and accepts it. Relishing arises in him when he does that. Now any relishing of those feelings is clinging. With his clinging as a condition, being; with being as a condition, birth; with birth as a condition, ageing and death come to be, and also sorrow and lamentation, pain, grief and despair. That is how there is an origin to this whole aggregate mass of suffering.
>
> (Trans. in Ñāṇamoli 1992: 251 ff.)

This, in a practical sense, is how suffering comes about. It comes about through *causes*. Thus through reversing the causes the suffering can be ended. And the text continues by telling us that perhaps a Buddha may appear in the world. Someone might hear the Dhamma and eventually become a monk. Through following seriously the Buddha's path as a monk he might so develop his ability in mindfulness and meditative absorption that he learns to cut his lust after sensory experiences. Thus each link in the above list ceases through the cessation of the preceding link:

> With the cessation of his relishing, cessation of clinging; with cessation of clinging, cessation of being; with cessation of being, cessation of birth; with cessation of birth, ageing and death cease, and also sorrow and lamentation, pain, grief and despair; that is how there is a cessation to his whole aggregate mass of suffering.
>
> (Op. cit.: 255)

Therefore the Buddha wants to link the emergence of suffering to impersonal lawlike behaviour, and he chooses to anchor this link in the impersonal lawlike behaviour of causation. This impersonal lawlike nature of causation is well demonstrated in its standard formula found in early Buddhist sources: 'This existing, that exists; this arising, that arises; this not existing, that does not exist; this ceasing, that ceases' (Gethin 1998: 141). This is what causation *is* for early Buddhist thought. It is a relationship between events, and is what we call it when if *X* occurs *Y* follows, and when *X* does not occur *Y* does not follow (in Pāli: *imasmiṃ sati, idaṃ hoti; imasmiṃ asati, idaṃ na hoti*). There is nothing more to causation than that. It is because causation is impersonal and lawlike that the Buddha places 'dependent origination' (Sanskrit: *pratītyasamutpāda*; Pāli: *paṭiccasmuppāda*) at the very centre of his Middle Way (cf. 'He who sees dependent origination sees the Dhamma; he who sees the Dhamma sees dependent origination'; *Mahāhatthipadopama Sutta*, Pāli text I: 191). It is this impersonal lawlike causal ordering which is held in the *Saṃyutta Nikāya* (II: 12: 20) of the Pāli Canon to be the case whether Buddhas arise or whether they do not. This is what the Buddha is said to have rediscovered, and it is in this rediscovery and its implications that he is held to be enlightened. Because the emergence of suffering is a direct, impersonal, lawlike response to causes, suffering can be ended automatically through the removal of its causes (without recourse to sacrifices or petitioning divinities). Thus we might argue that (like Not-Self), although the Buddha does not mention dependent origination in the *Dhammacakkappavattana Sutta*, the very significance of the four Noble Truths which formed the content of his enlightenment relies implicitly on the impersonal lawlike behaviour of causation. Perhaps the Buddha's understanding of both Not-Self and dependent origination emerged as he thought more and more (as he meditated) on the implications of what he had discovered. As we have seen, Frauwallner (1973) suggested that the Buddha's tracing all finally to ignorance rather than the immediate cause of craving was a subsequent stage in his understanding and development of the teaching. From this perspective Not-Self and dependent origination together come to form the two pillars of the final gnosis (*vidyā*) which is the antidote to ignorance (*avidyā*).

The account of the *Mahātaṇhāsaṅkhaya Sutta* quite possibly represents an early formulation by the Buddha of the more complex (and much less clear) scheme of dependent origination found for example at length in the *Mahānidāna Sutta* (the 'Greater Discourse on Causes'). The Buddha preached the *Mahānidāna Sutta* to his faithful attendant Ānanda, who had ventured to observe that dependent origination, while profound, seemed to him to be quite straightforward. It is not straightforward, and the Buddha claims here that it is precisely failing to understand dependent origination that has bound people to saṃsāra for so long. Since (as Richard Gombrich 1996: 46 observes) he personally preached it to Ānanda who by tradition remained unenlightened until after the death of the Buddha, Ānanda himself presumably at that time still did not understand it. The full formula for dependent origination (taken for convenience from the Pāli version in *Saṃyutta Nikāya* II: 12: 1; cf. Gethin 1998: 141–2) is as follows:

> Conditioned by (i) ignorance (*avijjā*) are (ii) formations (*saṅkhārā*), conditioned by formations is (iii) consciousness (*viññāṇa*), conditioned by consciousness is (iv) mind-and-body (*nāmarūpa*; *nāma* – name – equals mind here), conditioned by mind-and-body are (v) the six senses (*saḷāyatana*), conditioned by the six senses is (vi) sense-contact (*phassa*), conditioned by sense-contact is (vii) feeling (*vedanā*), conditioned by feeling is (viii) craving (*taṇhā*), conditioned by craving is (ix) attachment (or 'grasping'; *upādāna*), conditioned by attachment is (x) becoming (*bhava*), conditioned by becoming is (xi) birth (*jāti*), conditioned by birth is (xii) old age and death (*jarāmaraṇa*) . . .

And thence come all the sufferings of saṃsāra. Because this is tagged to the impersonal lawlike nature of causation, reversing the process, through overcoming ignorance, can be guaranteed to lead – again, completely impersonally – to liberation.

The reader should stop reading here, and just appreciate the sheer exhilarating wonder the Buddha must have felt at realising the significance of the fact that *effects follow from causes naturally*. We are told that the sharpest of the Buddha's disciples, Śāriputra, immediately left his previous teacher and followed the Buddha when he heard it said that 'of those *dharmas* which arise from a cause, the Tathāgata has stated the cause, and also [their] cessation'.[21] The Buddha had discovered the actual law of things (the *dhammatā* (Pāli); Sanskrit: *dharmatā*), something which clearly others had not realised for they had not taught it to him. Through this law he now had the key to putting a stop to that which all would want to stop if only they knew how. The discovery was absolutely – enlighteningly – liberating. From this sheer wonder of the Buddha at uncovering the inner turnings of the universe, and the overwhelming freedom of stopping their incessant roll, flows the whole history of Buddhist thought.

And yet while it is clear, I think, what is going on here, it is not at all obvious in detail what the twelvefold formula for dependent origination actually *means*. This may reflect its composite origin, for the model we found in the *Mahātaṇhāsaṅkhaya Sutta* was much clearer, and more focused. One theory, widely (but not universally) held in later Buddhist tradition, would have the twelve links spreading over three lifetimes.[22] The twelvefold formula for dependent origination thus becomes crucial among other things in explaining rebirth without recourse to an enduring Self. According to this model, the first link of the twelvefold formula states that as a result of ignorance *karmic* formations – actions of body, speech, or mind, flowing from morally wholesome or unwholesome intentions – take place. The Buddha is reported to have said of *karman* (*kamma*), action: 'I assert that action is volition (*cetanā*), since it is by willing that one performs an action with the body, speech or mind' (*Aṅguttara Nikāya* III: 415, in Lamotte 1988: 34). Thus for the Buddha *karman* as an action issuing in appropriate results (necessitating rebirth) ceases to be the external act itself (as it is within e.g. the Brahmanic sacrificial tradition). What are determinative in terms of 'karmic results' are wholesome or unwholesome volitions, that is, *intentions*.[23] Buddhism is all about the mind. As we shall see in the next section, the Buddha internalised the whole system of 'significant actions' and in so doing moralised it in terms of the impersonal causal law.

The first two links of the process pertain to past lives. It is ignorance in the past, giving rise to morally determinative intentions in the past which brings about the third link, consciousness, in the present life. According to this interpretation, 'consciousness' here is the consciousness that comes about in the mother's womb as the first stage of the rebirth process. And conditioned by this consciousness is the fourth link, mind-and-body. 'Mind' (*nāma*) here refers to the other three aggregates alongside consciousness and held to be mental associates (i.e. not physical matter), that is, feelings, perceptions, and formations. 'Body' (*rūpa*) here is the physical side of the organism, composed of derivatives of the four Great Elements, 'earth', 'water', 'fire', and 'air'. Thus with this link we have an embodied individual, born in dependence upon previous morally determinative acts, traceable to the fact that he or she was not enlightened – was ignorant – in past lives.

The Buddha did not hold that the 'reborn' being is the *same* as the being who died. Thus strictly speaking this is not a case of *re*birth. Likewise the 'reborn' being is not different from the being that died, at least if by 'different' we mean completely different in the way that, say, you and I are different. The reborn being is linked to the being that died by a *causal* process. Let us call the one who dies *A*, and the reborn being *B*. Then *B* is not the same as *A*. For example, *B* is not the same person as *A* (this, at least, seems to me uncontroversial). *B* occurs in causal dependence (of the right sort) on *A*. Among the relevant causal factors here are morally wholesome, or unwholesome, actions (*karman*) performed by *A* (in the sense understood above) in the past (or even by *A*'s previous incarnations as *X*, *Y*, and *Z*, back theoretically to infinity). Thus at death these factors in complex ways enter into the causal process ('karmic causality') which leads to another embodied individual occurring, in direct dependence upon actions performed by *A* in one or more of his or her lives. Therefore the link between the 'reborn being' and the 'being that died' is also explained in terms of causal dependence, where karmic causation is held to be a central factor in holding the whole process together. With causation there is absolutely no need for a Self to link *A* and *B*. This is why one speaks of causal dependence 'of the right sort'. At death the psychophysical bundle reconfigures. One figuration breaks down and another figuration takes place. The bundle is a bundle of the aggregates, but each aggregate taken as a whole is a bundle of momentary impermanent components that form members of that aggregate-class. Thus the person is reducible to the temporary bundle of bundles where all constituents are radically impermanent, temporarily held together through causal relationships of the right sort. All this is in accordance with causal laws (notably of the karmic sort). Because there is this right sort of causal dependence, we cannot say of *B* that he or she is totally different from *A* either.[24]

Thus instead of identity and difference, and instead of eternalism and annihilationism, the Buddha substitutes dependent origination, in the sense of causal dependence. Thereby dependent origination becomes another meaning of the 'Middle Way'. But note that while all this has been said specifically of the rebirth process here (and later Buddhist traditions elaborate that process in great detail), the Buddha would consider that all this also holds throughout life. Throughout life there is constant change in accordance with causal laws and processes of the right sort. Between a person at one stage of their life – whatever stage – and at another stage of their life the relationship between the stages is one of neither identity nor difference, but dependent origination. Death is a particular sort of change, with particular modalities of causal relationships coming into play. But the Buddha does not appear to have thought that there is any fundamental difference in the way things really are between Archibald at age 3 and Archibald at age 73 on the one hand, and Archibald when he died at 81 and his rebirth, baby Fiona, on the other. There is however a difference between Archibald and Fiona on the one hand, and Duncan (who was Archibald's insurance salesman). Between Archibald at 3, Archibald at 73, Archibald at 81, and baby Fiona there is absolutely nothing in common save causal connections of the right sort. With Duncan those connections too are lacking. Thus while we deny that Archibald at 73, Archibald at 81, and baby Fiona, are the same, we also deny they are different. Duncan is different.

Given that we now have an embodied individual, the twelvefold formula interpreted over three lifetimes explains in more detail the process by which in this life we enmesh ourselves yet further in suffering, rebirth, and redeath. As we have seen, suffering arises through craving for sensory experiences (remembering that in India the mind is also treated as a sense). Thus, conditioned by mind-and-body is the fifth link, the six senses. The six senses make contact (the sixth link) with their appropriate objects. Through that contact comes the seventh link, feelings – pleasant, unpleasant, or neutral. This is an important stage in the process, since this link along with all the previous links of the present life (i.e. from the third link, consciousness, on) are the results of former *karman*. They are thus not in themselves morally wholesome or unwholesome. They are therefore morally neutral. But at this stage (no doubt due to previous habits which the wise person should watch carefully and counteract), conditioned by those feelings the eighth link, craving, can so easily arise.[25] From craving comes the ninth link, attachment (see p. 45 for the four types of attachment). And since both craving and attachment are morally negative taints ('passions'; Pāli: *kilesa*; Sanskrit: *kleśa*) from then on it is all downhill. According to the formula, conditioned by attachment the tenth link, 'becoming', arises. It is not immediately obvious what this means. The 'becoming' here is what arises from attachment and explains birth, old age, death, and so on. Since conditioned by becoming is the eleventh link, birth, in order to explain the formula over three lives the 'becoming' here must therefore ultimately equal whatever at the beginning of the formula explained *this* life. Thus 'becoming' is explained to mean the 'becoming' of *karman*, the wholesome and unwholesome intentions arising from attachment (due to craving) which explain future rebirth.[26] And from this occurs birth into a new life, and thence the twelfth link that is old age and death.

This twelvefold formula for dependent origination as it stands is strange. In one way it makes sense spread over three lives, yet this explanation looks like an attempt to make sense of what may well be a compilation from originally different sources.[27] Why, for example, explain the first of the three lives only in terms of the first two links, and explain the tenth link, 'becoming' as essentially the same as the second link, formations? Why introduce explanations in terms of *karman* where none of the links obviously mentions *karman*? Frauwallner (1973) would want to argue that there is certain logic in the eighth to the twelfth link, basing suffering on craving. Perhaps the first to the seventh links were constructed in order to tag craving to ignorance. But it may be impossible at our present stage of scholarship to work out very satisfactorily what the original logic of the full twelvefold formula was intended to be, if there ever was *one* intention at all.

A further note on *karman*

As we have seen, for the Buddha *karman* is essentially volition (intention) which leads to actions of body, speech, or mind.[28] Wholesome and unwholesome karmic intentions entail (in this life or in future lives) pleasant and unpleasant experiences, feelings, as their karmic results, together with the particular psychophysical organism that is capable of undergoing those feelings. Whereas wholesome and unwholesome intentions are by definition morally virtuous or unvirtuous, the results – while pleasant and painful – in themselves are neither wholesome nor unwholesome. A pain in itself has no moral quality. But it is the result of unwholesome karmic intention(s). Thus for a feeling to be unpleasant is not as such for it to be morally wrong. A volition or intention of hatred or greed (produced by ignorance) as a mental response to what is unpleasant, on the other hand, is morally wrong (i.e. unwholesome, not conducive to following the path to liberation). For the Buddha this is all underpinned by the impersonal lawlike behaviour of causality. Thus an unwholesome intention because it is a cause brings about a feeling of pain as a result. A feeling of pain (like all in saṃsāra) *must* be a result, and therefore it must be the result of its cause, an unwholesome intention.[29] And the feeling of pain, as resulting, occurs (by definition) in the same causal continuum as the unwholesome intention occurred as cause. This is why, the Buddhist wants to claim, even with an impermanent psychophysical continuum and without a Self there is no 'causal confusion' or 'confusion of continua'.

Even without a Self, the karmic results occur in the same continuum in which occurred the unwholesome intentions. Feelings of pain are therefore brought about not by others (other persons, God or gods) but by oneself, in the sense that in everyday speech we use 'oneself' to refer to events in the same causal continuum. This is a situation of 'total responsibility' (Gombrich 1971: Ch. 5).

Richard Gombrich has commented that 'just as Being lies at the heart of the Upaniṣadic world view, Action lies at the heart of the Buddha's. "Action", of course, is *kamma*; and primarily it refers to morally relevant action' (Gombrich 1996: 48–9). Gombrich wants to argue that the Buddha did not simply take over a pre-existing Brahmanical doctrine of *karman*, which then sat often uneasily alongside his real interest in gnosis and liberation. The Buddha's attitude to *karman* is different from that of the wider Brahmanic culture, and is of a piece with his vision of what is involved in gaining liberation. That is, the Buddha understood *karman* in quite a different sense from that of his compatriots, and that different sense was soteriologically relevant. In the Brahmanical context *karman* is significant *ritual* action. For Jains (as an example of another renouncer group for whom we have some information) *karman* was seen as quasi-material, like a polluting dirt which weighed down the Self and kept it in saṃsāra. Thus for Jains all *karman* is one way or another bad. Ultimately one should cease acting altogether.[30] The Buddha's position was quite different from either of these groups and (as with his position on the Self) it was different as far as we can tell from all others in India. It was the Buddha who declared that *karman* is intention, a mental event. In so doing, Gombrich comments, the Buddha 'turned the brahmin ideology upside down and ethicised the universe. I do not see how one could exaggerate the importance of the Buddha's ethicisation of the world, which I regard as a turning point in the history of civilisation' (Gombrich 1996: 51). Thus the Buddha turned attention from physical acts cleansing the pollution resulting from 'bad karma' – such as acts of physical asceticism, or the Brahmanic actions of purification, which typically involve washing, or ingesting 'the five products of the cow' – to 'inner purification', mental training. For the

Buddha, as we have seen, craving – a mental state – arises from ignorance – a mental state – and leads to (unwholesome) *karman* – a mental state – and this leads to suffering – a mental state. The Buddha's vision of *karman* as really being intention is of a sort with his stress on overcoming craving through insight into the way things really are. Through understanding how things really are, craving is dissolved. We could relate this to what Gombrich calls 'an ethicised consciousness' (1996: 61). Following the *Tevijja Sutta* (the 'Discourse on the Triple Knowledge [of the Vedas]') Gombrich speaks of the monk engaged in actively pervading the universe with a mind of kindness and compassion. This is a sort of infinite *karman*, the ultimate *karman*, that leads to the overcoming of suffering, liberation.[31]

The universe of the Buddha

I want now to look briefly at how the Buddha (or the early Buddhist tradition) saw the structure of the universe in which he dwelt and which yet he had transcended.[32] The doctrinal framework here is that of the five (or six) types of rebirth, and the 'threefold world'.

First, the Buddha speaks in texts like the *Mahāsīhanāda Sutta* (the 'Greater Discourse which is the Lion's Roar') of five types of rebirth. All rebirth is due to *karman* and is impermanent. Short of attaining enlightenment, in each rebirth one is born and dies, to be reborn elsewhere in accordance with the completely impersonal causal nature of one's own *karman*. The endless cycle of birth, rebirth, and redeath, is saṃsāra. One can be reborn in a hell (sometimes translated as 'purgatory' to stress its impermanent, purifying nature), as an animal (including all creatures other than those of the other types of rebirth), a ghost,[33] a human, or a god. This list of five should be noted, since other Buddhist texts speak of six 'destinies', adding that of the *asuras*, jealous anti-gods who are said to be constantly at war with gods. The list of six types of rebirth, or 'destinies', is rather more familiar in the West, particularly from the Tibetan pictorial representation in the so-called 'Wheel of Life'. It is arguable however that the earliest formula involved only five, and in the *Kathāvatthu* (8: 1) – the fifth book of the *Abhidhamma Piṭaka* of the Pāli Canon – the teaching of six destinies is explicitly contradicted, claiming that the *asuras* can be split between the gods and the ghosts.[34]

Rebirth in a hell, as an animal, or as a ghost is referred to as a bad 'destiny' (*gati*), while rebirth as a human or a god is a good destiny. 'Bad destinies' are so defined due to the preponderance of pain there. Good destinies involve (other things being equal) either a preponderance of pleasure over pain (rebirth as a god), or in general equal pleasure and pain (as a human). There are many hells, and the time spent in them is very, very long indeed. They are, frankly, hellish. The very lowest hell is termed 'without intermission' (*avīci*), although life in a hell does eventually come to an end. Note that what 'destines' one to these destinies is not the action of a God or anyone else, but one's own *karman*. Thus one has a choice over one's destiny. Later tradition is very unsure whether rebirth as an *asura* (given that they are consumed with jealousy) is also a good destiny. The frequent claim that it is a good destiny may reflect more the needs of symmetry (three bad, three good) than doctrinal considerations.

The 'threefold world' divides into (i) the desire realm (*kāmadhātu*); (ii) the form realm (*rūpadhātu*); and (iii) the formless realm (*arūpadhātu*).[35] The desire realm consists of all the realms of rebirth apart from (taken as a whole) that of the gods. Only one group of gods falls under the desire realm, and these gods are appropriately called 'desire gods' (*kāmadeva*). They are the gods who are closest to humans, and into this category the Buddhist tradition has placed the gods it is familiar with from the Vedic Brahmanic and later Hindu traditions. These are the powerful gods it is appropriate to pray to for rewards, or contact through possession, provided one is aware that these gods (and goddesses, of course) are all part of saṃsāra. They are thus subject to greed, hatred, and delusion and their derivatives (such as pride, anger, or lust), and are very definitely unenlightened. The common feature of beings in the desire realm is that they have the five physical senses plus consciousness. In other words, they operate from a base of sensual experience. The desire gods are thought to occupy one or other of six 'heavens', each in certain ways better than the last.[36] If we take all these six heavens together, they can be classed as the 'world of the gods' (*devaloka*), although as we shall see there are many, many gods on higher planes still beyond this sensual 'world of the gods'. Cosmologically these planes where beings have all five senses as well as consciousness form 'world-spheres' (*cakravāḍas*). For a crisp description of a world-sphere I cannot even begin to improve on Gethin, whose recent work has contributed greatly to drawing attention to the interest of Buddhist cosmology and its relationship to meditation and hence Buddhist soteriology:

> At the centre of a *cakra-vāḍa* is the great world mountain, Meru or Sineru. This is surrounded by seven concentric rings of mountains and seas. Beyond these mountains, in the four cardinal directions, are four continents. The southern continent, Jambudvīpa or 'the continent of the rose-apple tree', is the continent inhabited by ordinary human beings; the southern part, below the towering abode of snows (*himālaya*) is effectively India, the land where buddhas arise. In the spaces between world-spheres and below are various hells, while in the shadow of the slopes of Mount Meru dwell the jealous gods called Asuras, expelled from the heaven of the Thirty-Three [Sanskrit: *Trāyastriṃśa*; Pāli: *Tāvatiṃsa*, the second of the desire realm heavens] by its king Śakra [Pāli: Sakka, sometimes, but by no means always, identified with the Vedic god Indra]. On the slopes of Mount Meru itself and rising above its peak are the six realms inhabited by the gods of the sense-sphere [i.e. desire-realm]. A Great Brahmā of the lower realms of pure form may rule over a thousand such world-spheres, while Brahmās of the higher realms of the form-sphere [form realm] are said to rule over a hundred thousand.
>
> (Gethin 1998: 118–19; see also Gethin 1997a)

Note that the description here is of one world-sphere, but there are many, many world-spheres, so many in fact that the number converges on infinity. Thus the Buddhist view is that, taken as a totality, not only is time infinite but space too is effectively infinite. The Buddhist cosmological vision is about as vast as it is possible to conceive. It is clear that in a world-sphere the gods of the desire realm are thought to occupy places in physical space, and while Sakka may rule over the gods most closely related to humans, there are higher gods for whom he too is a subject.[37] There is no final god who rules over either one world-sphere or all the world-spheres, although beings such as some humans may think there is one God who is the supreme ruler and even creator. There may even be a god who mistakenly considers that he is indeed the creator and supreme ruler of the entire system.[38]

Technically the gods of the form and formless realms are known not as 'gods' (*deva*), but as 'Brahmās'. Those of the form realm are ranked in a hierarchy of sixteen levels (in the Theravāda scheme), divided into four classes (in the ratio 3, 3, 3, 7) corresponding to the four *dhyānas* (Pāli: *jhānas*), the four 'meditations' or 'absorptions' that we met earlier. The highest of these levels or planes is the 'Supreme' (Pāli: *akaniṭṭha*; Sanskrit: *akaniṣṭha*). Brahmās within the form realm are said to have only two senses, sight and hearing. The Brahmās of the formless realm are of four types, corresponding to a hierarchy of four formless meditative attainments (*samāpatti*): (i) infinite space; (ii) infinite consciousness (*viññāṇa*); (iii) nothingness, and (iv) neither perception (*saññā*) nor non-perception. This last is also referred to as the 'peak of existence' (Pāli: *bhavagga*; Sanskrit: *bhavāgra*). Brahmās within the formless realm have just consciousness, and so long as they are in that rebirth and have not attained enlightenment they presumably enjoy uninterruptedly the appropriate meditative attainment. In total therefore (including the *asuras*) there are thirty-one different types of beings, or possible states, within saṃsāra. Outside all of this (although not in spatial terms of course) is nirvāṇa. Nirvāṇa is not elsewhere. It is simply not in saṃsāra. It is simply not part of any of this, and can only be specified in terms of its negation.

It is *not* necessary to proceed up all the realms and planes to the very highest before attaining liberation. They are not ranked like a ladder. Many humans have become enlightened, directly from the human plane. As we have seen, liberation is a matter of gnosis and gnosis could in theory be obtained anywhere and at any time. But actually the Buddhist tradition holds that nirvāṇa can be obtained only from the human realm, or a god realm above the human. Indeed the gods of the five very highest planes of the form realm are said to dwell in the 'pure abodes', corresponding to the highest and most perfect development of the fourth *dhyāna*, and as such are all 'never-returners' (*anāgāmin*). We have seen already that the fourth *dhyāna* is held to be a particularly important springboard for enlightenment. Although not yet enlightened they will never again return through the cycle of saṃsāra to the lower realms. They are thus sure of eventually attaining enlightenment, without needing to sojourn in the formless realms.[39]

The Buddhist cosmology, with its realms of rebirth including hells and gods who occupy physical space and undergo sensory experiences as humans do, is reasonably comprehensible. But what is meant by referring 'in the same cosmological breath' to the form and formless realm gods as stages of meditative absorption? Are these places of rebirth, or are they some sort of 'inner state' of a meditator, perhaps encountered during deep meditation? Gethin (1998: 119 ff.) argues that the key to understanding what is going on here is the 'principle of the equivalence of cosmology and psychology. I mean by this that in the traditional understanding the various realms of existence relate rather closely to certain commonly (and not so commonly) experienced states of mind.' Note however that Gethin is *not* saying that the Buddhist cosmology is really all about current or potential states of mind, psychology, or meditation here and now, and is therefore not really a cosmology at all in the sense that these are actually realms or planes of rebirth. These different planes are indeed realms of rebirth. Otherwise either rebirth would always be into the human realm or there would be no rebirth at all. And that is not traditional Buddhism. Moreover if 'cosmos' is defined sufficiently widely there is no reason why this should not be spoken of as 'cosmology'. Thus if someone dies here they may, under appropriate circumstances, be properly thought of as having been reborn (in the sense of 'rebirth' explained above) in, say, a formless realm. Their coarse physical body is perhaps cremated here. Therefore there is no sense of *their* mind left, as the mind of the embodied person they were. But the story has not ended. The tradition does indeed want to speak of an 'elsewhere' here, and 'they' have been reborn elsewhere. Their rebirth in that formless realm is causally dependent on their meditative attainment in a life prior to that rebirth. Thus we cannot be speaking here of states of mind, psychology, or meditation in the sense that these are purely states of mind and so on of a particular embodied individual here and now in this life.

Mental intentions (*karman*) which are wholesome, animated by the three basic virtuous states of mind, non-greed, non-hatred, and non-delusion, give rise to appropriate acts and favourable rebirths. Unwholesome intentions animated by greed, hatred, and delusion produce unfavourable rebirths.[40] The 'favourable rebirths' here are rebirths as a human (possibly as an *asura*) and as a god of the desire realm. Unfavourable rebirths are rebirths in hells, as a ghost, or as an animal (including a fish, worms, bugs, etc.). Thus favourable and unfavourable rebirths spring from states of mind. And there are some specific wholesome states of mind in addition to these that as a matter of fact occur only in meditation. These are states like attaining one of the four meditations (Sanskrit: *dhyānas*; Pāli: *jhānas*). Favourable rebirth as a god of the desire realm, enjoying various sensual pleasures, occurs through acts animated by such states of mind as non-greed, non-hatred, and non-delusion. Similarly the favourable rebirth as a god of e.g. the form realm occurs due to having accustomed oneself to one or more of the four *dhyānas*.[41] A monk who, for example, has cultivated the path to a high level removes various negative factors preventing the attainment of enlightenment and attains the fourth *dhyāna*. After death that monk will be reborn in one of the pure abodes, corresponding to the fourth *dhyāna*, and will there attain enlightenment. Thus given that rebirth accords with mental events, reference to the higher planes as corresponding to meditative states simply describes the sort of mental event which is necessary in order to attain rebirth on those planes. The 'bodies' of those reborn there – defined in terms of experiences of seeing and hearing, plus consciousness for the form realm, and consciousness alone for the formless realm – are the bodies that support and express experience on those planes. Beings reborn on those planes are undergoing the experiences of those *dhyānas*.

It follows from all of this that when in this life the meditator attains to, say, the third *dhyāna*, that meditator is undergoing temporarily the experience of one reborn as a god on that particular plane of the form realm. That is what being reborn there is like. Correspondingly, for one undergoing any of the appropriate mental states in this life, one undergoes temporarily the experience associated with being reborn on the appropriate plane. Thus if one is overwhelmed with greed, hatred, or delusion, one is in the state of one born as a ghost, in hell, or an animal respectively. But one familiar with the third *dhyāna* will, after death, be reborn on the appropriate plane for that *dhyāna*. The appropriate plane of the cosmology is not simply a description of the mental state of a meditator. Similarly, in spite of a common suggestion among some modern Buddhists, the plane of hell is not simply a description of the state of mind of one in this life full of hatred. As one's mind is, so one actually becomes.[42]

Finally there is the destruction of worlds. In Indian thought even for traditions that believe in a creator God there is no such thing as the emergence of the universe from nothing. A common Indian model sees the universe as evolving from a state of what we might call 'implosion' to manifestation. It then remains for a very long time. Eventually the universe implodes again. It remains for a further long period in imploded state before evolving (for theists, due to the action of God) once more. And so on, throughout all eternity. The Buddhists employ a similar model, it being understood that all of this occurs due to an impersonal lawlike causation and not divine whim. Elements of this system are found in works like the *Aggañña Sutta* ('Discourse on Beginnings'), and are elaborated in later Abhidharma works. When the universe implodes it implodes from the lower realms upwards. Thus the hells implode first of all. Sometimes the implosion is through fire, and this implosion stretches as far as the third of the god-planes of the form realm (the *Mahābrahmā* plane), thereby taking in all up to and including the plane corresponding to the first *dhyāna*. The rest remains. Implosion through fire is the most frequent sort of implosion. At other times the implosion is through water, taking in all the above plus the planes corresponding to the second *dhyāna* as well. At other times there is a wind implosion, which includes all that included in the water implosion and also the plane corresponding to the third *dhyāna*. But implosion can stretch no further. Beings reborn in the plane corresponding to the fourth *dhyāna* (and above, for that matter) cannot be affected by any of this. When an implosion occurs, beings that perish are reborn somewhere else that still remains, perfectly in accordance with their *karman*. Let us not worry about them.[43]

Buddhist meditation – the theoretical framework

It is through working with and on the mind that Buddhists consider one can bring about the transformation in seeing required in order to bring to an end the forces generating suffering and rebirth, and thus attain liberation. Earlier I suggested that, for the Buddhist, meditation closes the gap between the way things appear to be and the way they actually are. How does meditation do this? The structure of Buddhist meditation in the oldest texts and throughout much if not all of the Buddhist tradition in India and elsewhere is to calm down and still the mind. One then uses that still, calm, mind to investigate how things really are. This is in order to see things free from the blocks and obscurations that normally hinder our vision. These blocks and obscurations entail our immersion in saṃsāra. Calming the mind is called 'calming (meditation)' (Sanskrit: *śamatha*; Pāli: *samatha*). Discovering with a calm mind how things are really is called 'insight (meditation)' (Sanskrit: *vipaśyanā*; Pāli: *vipassanā*). At least some degree of calming is considered necessary to insight. As we have seen, right concentration is a stage of the eightfold path. Nevertheless depending on the abilities of the meditator it need not be necessary to follow through calming meditation to the actual attainment of the meditative absorptions (*dhyānas/jhānas*) before commencing insight meditation. When calming and insight are linked the mind has the strength and orientation really to break through to a deep transformative understanding of how things truly are.

As one might expect, the Buddhist tradition has elaborated the stages and elements of the path of meditation in great detail. A certain amount of material can be found in early sources such as the suttas of the Pāli Canon, particularly for example the *Sāmaññaphala Sutta* (the 'Discourse on the Benefits of being a Drop-out (*samaṇa*)') and the *Mahāsatipaṭṭhāna Sutta* (the 'Greater Discourse on the Foundations of Mindfulness'). But for the detailed elaboration of the path one must look to the authoritative scholastic compendiums such as the *Visuddhimagga* ('Path of Purification') of the Theravādin Buddhaghosa (fifth century CE), or the *Abhidharmakośa* ('Treasury of Abhidharma') of Vasubandhu. Vasubandhu followed either the Sarvāstivādin (Vaibhāṣika) or the Sautrāntika tradition and wrote in the fourth or fifth century CE. These two sources were constructed independently of one another, and were inheritors of different Buddhist traditions. They are far from agreeing in detail.

Calming meditation aims to still the mind. It presupposes that the meditator has faith in the teachings of the Buddha, has adopted the moral perspective required of a good Buddhist, and is otherwise involved in the religious activities expected of a practitioner who is seriously engaged in the path. In order to bring about the desired state of mental calm the meditator starts by learning to focus the mind, narrowing down its attention so that he or she becomes simply aware. In other words, he or she concentrates. Because concentration requires something to concentrate on, works such as the *Visuddhimagga* list forty different possible objects of concentration. These include concentrating on, for example, a blue disc. This is one of ten objects of concentration known in Pāli as *kasiṇas*, and taking a coloured disc as an object is said (among others) to be particularly suitable for those whose personality is dominated by hatred among the three root poisons. Those who are dominated by greed might take as their object the skeleton. Those by delusion (or whose mind is inclined to instability) might start with mindfulness of breathing. This last has become well known in the modern world through being the very first meditation practice in the *Mahāsatipaṭṭhāna Sutta*, a discourse particularly favoured by more recent Burmese meditation masters and there used, perhaps because everyone's mind is at first inclined to instability, for all meditators. Indeed the text describes itself as 'the sole way':

> Herein, a monk having gone to the forest, to the foot of a tree, or to an empty place, sits down cross-legged, keeps his body erect and his mindfulness alert. Just mindful he breathes in and mindful he breathes out. Breathing in a long breath, he knows 'I breath in a long breath'; breathing out a long breath, he knows 'I breath out a long breath'; breathing in a short breath, he knows 'I breath in a short breath'; breathing out a short breath, he knows 'I breath out a short breath'.
>
> (*Mahāsatipaṭṭhāna Sutta* trans. Nyanaponika Thera: 117–18)

And so on. Or there are the so-called 'divine abidings' (*brahmavihāras*), also known as the 'four immeasurables', again particularly recommended for those of a hate disposition but possibly originally thought of as one sufficient means for attaining enlightenment itself.[44] These entail developing all-pervading loving kindness (Sanskrit: *maitrī*; Pāli: *mettā*). This is the pervasive wish 'may all sentient beings be well and happy'. One develops all-pervading compassion (*karuṇā*), the pervasive wish 'may all sentient beings be free of suffering', all-pervading sympathetic joy (*muditā*) – delight at the happiness of others – and all-pervading equanimity (Sanskrit: *upekṣā*; Pāli: *upekkhā*). In such meditations one practises steadily and repeatedly, gently drawing the mind back to the object when it wanders. The meditator is exhorted to overcome the five hindrances: sensual desire, ill will, tiredness and sleepiness, excitement and depression, and doubt. In abandoning the five hindrances, the *Sāmaññaphala Sutta* observes, the meditator 'looks upon himself as freed from debt, rid of disease, out of jail, a free man, and secure' (*Sāmaññaphala Sutta*, trans. Rhys-Davids 1899: 84). And eventually he or she attains the first *jhāna* (Sanskrit: *dhyāna*). As we saw above, the first *jhāna* is characterised by applied thought, examination, joy, happiness, and one-pointedness of mind. The second *jhāna* has just joy, happiness, and one-pointedness of mind, since ability in meditation has here become so refined that consciously applied thought and examination are no longer needed in order to place the mind on the object. The third *jhāna* lacks even joy, which can become a disturbance, and has only happiness and one-pointedness. The fourth *jhāna* similarly lacks happiness, and possesses just one-pointedness and equanimity. From attaining the fourth *jhāna* it becomes possible (it is said) to develop what might be called supernormal powers (Sanskrit: *ṛddhis*; Pāli: *iddhis*), or 'superknowledges' (Sanskrit: *abhijñā*; Pāli: *abhiññā*). These include the ability to create 'mind-made' bodies, to walk through walls, fly through the air, hear distant sounds, know the minds of others, and to know the past lives of oneself and others.[45]

The general view of the Buddhist tradition is that some considerable ability in calming meditation is necessary in order to develop very effectively insight meditation, although it is not necessary actually to attain the fourth *dhyāna* before commencing insight meditation. Insight meditation involves bringing about a state of meditative absorption where the object of meditation is not one of the objects of calming meditation but rather is how things really are, understood in terms of suffering, impermanence, and not Self and their implications and ramifications. In so doing one attains 'wisdom' (Sanskrit: *prajñā*; Pāli: *paññā*). As can be readily understood from what has gone before, seeing in this manner directly in the deepest way possible is held to cut completely the forces which lead to rebirth and suffering.[46]

The model for the path of insight meditation employed in Buddhaghosa's *Visuddhimagga* (see Chapters 18–22) is that of the 'seven purifications'. The first two purifications concern (i) engagement in proper moral conduct (*sīla*), and (ii) developing calm (*samatha*). The third (iii) is 'purification of view', breaking down the sense of Self through constant direct awareness (mindfulness) of experience in terms of actually being a bundle of e.g. the five aggregates, divided into mind and body in mutual dependence, and nothing more. The fourth (iv) purification is the 'purification by overcoming doubt'. Just as the purification of view involves an awareness of the interdependence of mind and body at any one time, this fourth purification involves examining causal dependence as a continuum in time. Thus one comes to understand *kamma* (*karman*) and to see directly how things are the result of an impersonal lawlike causality and nothing more. In overcoming doubt, Buddhaghosa observes (19: 27), one becomes a 'lesser stream-enterer'. The next purification (v) is that of 'knowing and seeing what is the way [or 'path'; *magga*] and what is not the way'. This involves taking various groups and classes of phenomena and seeing that they are all impermanent, suffering, and not Self. One then sees them as arising and falling in their constant change and impermanence. Thus the meditator comes to deconstruct the apparent stability of things, and to see directly the world as a *process*, a *flow*. Gethin draws attention to the images Buddhaghosa selects (from earlier Buddhist sources) for this stage of the meditator's experience:

> the world is no longer experienced as consisting of things that are lasting and solid but rather as something that vanishes almost as soon as it appears – like dew drops at sunrise, like a bubble on water, like a line drawn on water, like a mustard-seed placed on the point of an awl, like a flash of lightning; things in themselves lack substance and always elude one's grasp – like a mirage, a conjuring trick, a dream, the circle formed by a whirling firebrand, a fairy city, foam, or the trunk of a banana tree.
>
> (Gethin 1998: 190; ref. *Visuddhimagga* 20: 104)[47]

The mind of the meditator at this time is said to be close to absorption (*dhyāna*), and there is a danger that the meditator might become complacent and attached (*Visuddhimagga* 20: sects 105 ff.). Tearing him- or herself away from this, the meditator attains the sixth (vi) purification, 'purification through knowing and seeing the path [or 'way'; *paṭipadā*]'. At this stage the meditator returns to contemplating with renewed vigour and ever deepening awareness the arising and falling of phenomena (*dhammas*), and he or she attains a series of eight knowledges with, it is said 'knowledge in conformity to truth as the ninth' (op. cit.: Ch. 21). Attaining the eight knowledges, in a state of deep equanimity and concentration, the meditator crosses over from worldly meditative absorption to transcendent or supramundane absorption. At this point the meditator 'changes lineage'. He or she ceases to belong to the lineage (family) of ordinary people (Pāli: *puthujjana*; Sanskrit: *pṛthagjana*) and joins the lineage of the Noble Ones (Pāli: *ariya*; Sanskrit: *ārya*). He or she is said now to take as the meditative object nibbāna (nirvāṇa). Nevertheless the complete eradication of defilements may still take time. One is said to become a 'stream-enterer' through abandoning the first three of the ten fetters (*saṃyojana*), the 'view of individuality', doubt, and clinging to precepts and vows. In finally and deeply abandoning these one will be reborn at the most a further seven times before becoming enlightened. In becoming a stream-enterer (or any of the other three 'noble fruits') one is said to attain the seventh (vii) and final purification, the 'purification by knowing and seeing'. On also permanently weakening the next two fetters, sensual desire and aversion, one becomes a 'once-returner', who will be reborn as a human being no more than one further time. On completely abandoning all these five fetters one becomes a 'never-returner' and if one still does not attain full enlightenment, is on death reborn in one of the highest planes of the form realm. On completely and irrevocably eradicating all ten fetters (including in addition the five of desire for form, desire for the formless, pride, agitation, and ignorance) one becomes enlightened, an *arhat* (Sanskrit) or *arahat* (Pāli). In one moment the meditator sees and understands the four Noble Truths, and all the factors leading to enlightenment are fulfilled. In subsequent moments the meditator is said to enjoy the 'resultant' (*phala*) meditative absorption. These four 'noble fruits' may be attained successively, over a long period of time. But there is also a view that their attainment may be in quick succession, or even that one might 'leap' as it were, directly to one or other of the fruits.[48]

Abhidharma (Pāli: Abhidhamma)

As we have seen, the term 'Abhidharma' refers fundamentally to the third section (*piṭaka*) of the Buddhist canon (the *Tripiṭaka*). It also refers derivatively to the teachings, approach, and insight contained in that section of the canon, as well as their explanation, elaboration, and summaries contained in later commentaries, compendiums, and digests, such as the *Abhidharmakośa* of Vasubandhu. Only two complete Abhidharma canonical collections remain: the Theravāda Abhidhamma in the Pāli Canon, and the Sarvāstivāda (Vaibhāṣika) Abhidharma that survives mainly in Chinese translation.[49] Both consist of seven books, but they are quite different books. In the Theravāda Pāli Canon the Abhidhamma section is attributed directly to the Buddha himself, although at least one book (the *Kathāvatthu*) is also said to be the work of a certain Moggaliputtatissa and clearly relates to doctrinal disputes which occurred long after the death of the Buddha. All the books of the Sarvāstivāda Abhidharma are attributed to various elders other than the Buddha, but the claim is that those elders were compilers rather than authors in that they assembled the books from material scattered throughout the canon. Another school, the Sautrāntika, while accepting the approach and many of the tenets of the Abhidharma, appears to have gained its name ('those who follow the sūtras') through a rejection by its adherents of any claim that the Buddha himself actually spoke the Abhidharma.

The controversies concerning the status of the Abhidharma books should indicate that we are dealing here with material that in the form in which we have it now is certainly somewhat later than the Vinaya and Sūtra parts of the canon. The Abhidharma represents a phase of systematisation and clarification of the teachings contained in the Sūtras, and probably grew out of summary lists of the main topics of a teaching prepared for memorisation. With the evolution of the Abhidharma, and Abhidharma style, however, what we find emerging are not just lists of essential points in the discourses. Rather, we find lists which enumerate with the maximum possible exactitude what is *actually* occurring in a particular psychological or physical situation spoken of in the sūtras or occurring in life generally. The lists are lists of what is seen to be the case by one who sees things the way they really are. The Abhidharma lists are exhaustive lists of possible psychophysical *events*. They thus correspond to – and also form a template for – the contents of insight meditation.

The Buddha might say 'Oh monks, on my alms-round I was given a strawberry'. But if he were to speak with maximum possible exactitude there would be no independently real thing referred to by 'I', in the way it is experienced by a person who is unenlightened. Nor would there be that thing referred to by 'strawberry', nor probably a lot of other things that are normally assumed when this simple sentence is uttered in everyday life by unenlightened beings. If we were to speak with maximum possible exactitude here, how would we analyse this situation? The answer would involve listing various psychological and physical factors, each of which is impermanent, and each of which is here relating to the others in a particular sort of causal relationship. Which types of psychological and physical factors are those, and what types of causal relationship are there? How, in this specific situation, do the psychological and physical factors come together in causal relationship? This is what the Abhidharma texts are all about.

As we have seen, implicit in Buddhist philosophy from the very beginning was a distinction between the way things appear to be and the way they actually are. Buddhist thought tends to look beyond apparent stability, apparent unity, to a flow of composite parts which are elaborated by mental processes of construction and reification into the relatively stable entities of our everyday world.[50] There appears to be a Self, but really there is not. Really there is just a flow of material form, sensations, perceptions, formations (i.e. other mental factors like volitions/intentions), and the flow of consciousness. The way things appear to be is one thing, the way they are actually is another. Quite early in the development of Buddhist thought – certainly in the Abhidharma – this distinction issued in a clear distinction between conventional reality (or 'truth'; *saṃvṛtisatya*; Pāli: *sammutisacca*), and the ultimate way of things, how it really is (*paramārthasatya*; Pāli: *paramatthasacca*). The religio-philosophical project of the Buddhist lies in knowing directly the conventional *as conventional*, rather than investing it with an illusory ultimacy. The ultimate truth, how it really is, lies precisely in the fact that what appeared to be ultimate is merely conventional. It appeared that there was a Self, but really there is only a flow of the aggregates and the Self is just an artificial unity, a self, oneself, the person one is, in fact a pragmatic conventional construct. But once we adopt this perspective it is clear that even talk of 'five aggregates' is simply shorthand for a far more complex list of types of psychophysical impermanent factors that might occur.

The common approach of Buddhist philosophy, experienced in insight meditation, is to probe, to investigate. The terminating point of that analysis – what the analysis finds is actually there, what is therefore resistant to the probing, dissolving analysis – is spoken of as 'how it is', i.e. an 'ultimate truth' (or an 'ultimate reality'). In Buddhist thought in the immediate centuries after the death of the Buddha this probing analysis was taken further, and even the five aggregates as simple unities were seen as obscuring a further dissolution, analysis into a plurality of further elements. This analysis rapidly came to embrace not just the psychophysical aggregates of a conscious being but also to include all things in the universe. These elements were known as *dharmas* (Pāli: *dhammas*), 'phenomena', or maybe just 'factors'. The dharmas form the psychophysical building blocks of the world as experienced by us.

For example, take the first aggregate, material form (*rūpa*). If we want to talk about how it really is, material form does not occur. 'Material form' is not a dharma. Rather, this expression is shorthand for the occurrence of particular instances of (in the ancient Indian system) solidity ('earth'), and/or fluidity ('water'), or heat ('fire'), or motion ('air'), and various other possible physical factors derived from these. These are related in some sort of causal connection (perhaps presenting thereby the physical object 'strawberry'). Thus in general under 'material form' comes various classes of things. Is it the same for a specific case of e.g. solidity itself? It seems not. An instance of solidity is irreducible to some further factors. Thus an instance of solidity, transient as it is, is what is really there, seen by one who sees things the way they really are. An instance of solidity is thus a dharma. The Abhidharma texts set out to offer a list of all the types of factors into which experiences can be analysed when we aim to find what is 'really there'. They also explain how these link up causally and relate to each other in order to provide us with the actual world of lived experience. Thus the Abhidharma texts, in contrast to e.g. the Sūtras, are phrased in 'how-it-actually-is language', universally valid, and not in the loose speech of everyday discourse in which the Buddha spoke when he spoke in a manner appropriate to the actual teaching situation he was in. Therefore we also find essential to Buddhist exegesis a distinction between texts or discourses that are definitive and tell it as it is (Sanskrit: *nītārtha*; Pāli: *nītattha*), and those that were phrased the way they are phrased with a particular purpose in view. If we are interested in precision these latter texts or discourses require to be interpreted, to have their meaning 'drawn out' (*neyārtha*; Pāli: *neyyattha*). In general for their advocates Abhidharma texts, and Abhidharma discourses, concern ultimate truth (*paramārthasatya*), and are definitive (*nītārtha*).

The Theravāda Abhidhamma produced a list of eighty-two classes of dhammas.[51] That is, all possible experience can be analysed into events each one of which will be an instance of one or other of the eighty-two classes of dhammas. Eighty-one of these (types of) dhammas are said to be conditioned (Sanskrit: *saṃskṛta*; Pāli: *saṃkhata*: the direct result of causes). One, nibbāna, is unconditioned (*asaṃskṛta/asaṃkhata*). Thus, technically, for the Theravāda Abhidhamma nibbāna is *an* ultimate, a *dhamma*. This means that in the most general sense nibbāna forms the content of an experiential event that cannot be analysed into more fundamental components, and it is in a unique class described as 'unconditioned'. Each *dhamma* has its own specific characteristic, by which it is recognised. Thus the *dhamma* of solidity has physical resistance as its characteristic. Where there is a case of physical resistance that indicates solidity. That is how one knows one has a case of solidity.

The eighty-one conditioned dhammas fall into three classes: consciousness (*citta* = *viññāna* (Sanskrit: *vijñāna*)), mental associates (*cetasikas*; Sanskrit: *caitasikas*), and material or physical form (*rūpa*). Consciousness consists of one *dhamma*. Mental associates consist of fifty-two dhammas. Twenty-five of these are wholesome, including non-greed, non-hatred, and non-delusion, faith, mindfulness, compassion, and so on. Fourteen are unwholesome, including wrong views. Thirteen are morally neutral, and gain their moral colouring from the other dhammas that occur along with them. Seven of these thirteen are common to all mental 'occasions': contact, feeling, perception,[52] volition, mental life, concentration, and attention. Material form consists of twenty-eight dhammas. Other Abhidhamma discussions concern which combinations of dhammas are permissible since, for example, one could not have non-greed and greed occurring in the very same momentary composite mental 'occasion'. Which dhammas occur when one murders Archibald and dances on his grave? Which dhammas occur when one attains the third *jhāna*?

Clearly this is not abstract philosophy, engaging in analysis out of intellectual interest. The purpose is one of direct concern with the path to liberation. The monk engaged in insight meditation will dwell quietly and in concentration, observing the arising and falling of dhammas, seeing how things really are and cutting the sense of Self. He will also know which mental factors conduce to positive, wholesome, mental occasions, and will thus know how to 'cease to do evil and learn to do good'. Lance Cousins (1995) has commented that 'The aim of this *abhidhamma* analysis is not really theoretical; it is related to insight meditation and offers a world-view based upon process in order to facilitate insight into change and no-self so as to undermine mental rigidity'. I would not argue with this, although I would argue with any reading of Abhidharma which would interpret its concern to be solely with practical issues of how to lessen attachment in opposition to the ontology of how things really, truly, are. I have already suggested that there is no such opposition in (Indian) Buddhism. Abhidhamma analysis does indeed involve seeing things as they are, and that is a matter of ontology. The dhammas (excluding, of course, nibbāna) are evanescent events, linked by an impersonal causal law. That is how it truly is.

The Abhidhamma texts are committed to the view that dhammas are how things really are. This does not commit the texts, however, to any particular position on the exact nature of the *dhamma* beyond the contrast between dhammas as what are not further reducible, compared with, say, persons, or tables and chairs which are. What is involved in seeing dhammas as events, in seeing all as based perhaps on an event-ontology, rather than a substance-ontology, seems to be relatively unexplored in the Pāli Abhidhamma or indeed in the Theravāda thought which follows it. To that extent, one could argue, the everyday practicalities of insight meditation remain paramount. An interest in specific questions of the ontological nature of dharmas is found not so much among Theravādins, but among Sarvāstivādins and their rivals.

I do not want to go into many of the details of the Sarvāstivāda Abhidharma here. I shall return in a later chapter to some of their characteristic positions. This system is in many respects very similar to the Abhidhamma of the Pāli Canon and Theravāda tradition. It has seventy-five dharmas, with three dharmas unconditioned.[53] Several of the Sarvāstivāda dharmas are unique to their system, and were the subject of vigorous controversy with other schools (particularly Sautrāntika). I want to mention here briefly, however, the Sarvāstivādin approach to the ontology of the dharma. In India as a whole in classical times the Sarvāstivāda (although it has not survived into the present day as an independent school) appears to have been by far the most important and influential of the Abhidharma traditions. One way or another it is the Sarvāstivāda that appears to have had most influence on the Mahāyāna approaches to both Buddhist philosophy and practice.

It should be clear from what we have seen already that the Abhidharma is characterised by some sort of reduction.

Throughout this reductive process the search is driven by a quest for what factors, what elements, are actually there as the substratum upon which the forces of mental imputation and reification can form the everyday 'life-world'. An 'ultimate truth/reality' is discovered as that which is resistant to attempted dissolution through reductive analysis. This search is animated by the wish to let-go, to bring to an end all selfish craving after things that turn out to be just mental and cultural imputations, constructions for practical purposes. Absurd craving for such things leads to rebirth. It seems to me that all Buddhist thinkers in India agreed in the direction of this analysis. There is no disagreement that you and me, or tables, or chairs, can be analysed into component parts and in reality lack the unities that are imputed upon them simply for practical everyday purposes. Disagreements among Buddhist thinkers in this area centred on claims to have found those elements that are really there behind mere appearance. Major disagreement in Buddhist philosophy concerned claims to the status of ultimate truth or truths. Thus the dissolution of what we might call 'everyday' craving through dissolution of the everyday world is agreed and taken for granted. The real disagreement concerned the craving which one group of Buddhist thinkers would attribute to another in the light of the latter's claim to have found ultimate truths which are not accepted as ultimate by the former. Since this rarefied activity of an elite group of scholars is occurring within the Abhidharma project, all Buddhist philosophy, it seems to me, is Abhidharma philosophy. The great 'Mahāyāna' schools of philosophy (q.v.) Madhyamaka, Yogācāra, possibly also tendencies associated with the Buddha-nature (*tathāgatagarbha*) – involve notably disputes concerning how far this probing, dissolving analysis can go.

In the classical Sarvāstivāda (Vaibhāṣika) system, the plurality of reals discerned through analysis (i.e. dharmas) are of course by their very status as analytic reals ultimate truths. Sarvāstivāda texts also refer to these dharmas, these ultimate truths, as 'primary existents' (*dravyasat*), and those composite entities constructed out of primary existents as 'secondary' or 'conceptual existents' (*prajñaptisat*). Note (and this is important) that to be a conceptual existent (you, me, a chair, table, or a forest) is not thought in Sarvāstivāda to be the same as not existing at all. It is to bear a particular sort of existence, the existence of an entity that is quite correctly treated as a unity for pragmatic purposes but nothing more. It can be analysed into a plurality of constituents which are thus to be taken as ontologically more fundamental. A conceptual existent is genuinely existent, but it is existent (i.e. given as a unity) through a purposeful, pragmatic context and its unity is fixed through conceptual reification. Thus a conceptual existent is the result of a particular sort of causal process, a conceptual reification or unification out of a plurality. A table appears to be a unity in its own right, one thing, and indeed it really can be spoken of and thought of in everyday life as one thing for pragmatic purposes. But it is not really a unity *in its own right* (i.e. a simple). It is not really one thing over and above this pragmatic context. It is actually a name we give for practical purposes to e.g. four legs and a top. And these too can be further analysed, eventually into dharmas. The dharmas into which it can be analysed, however (perhaps here they are actually something more like sense-data), as those factors which must be there irreducibly in order for there to be construction at all, must accordingly be simples. They must be unities in their own right. Otherwise the analysis would not have reached its terminating point.

Thus primary existents must be found as the terminating points of the process of analytical probing. They must be irreducible simples, and they must not be the results of conceptual reification, as are you and me, tables, chairs, and forests. They must thus have, in the terminology of Vaibhāṣika/Sarvāstivāda Abhidharma, an 'own-existence', a *svabhāva*. By way of contrast secondary conceptual existents are the results of conceptual reification and are lacking in 'own-existence', i.e. they are not simples, they are *niḥsvabhāva*.[54] Thus secondary existents are empty (*śūnya*) of own-existence, and to be empty is another expression for lacking own-existence. Note, however, that within this Sarvāstivāda (Vaibhāṣika) framework it is part of the meaning of *niḥsvabhāva* ('lacking own-existence') that some things are *sasvabhāva* ('bear own-existence'), it is part of the meaning of emptiness that not all things are empty. To state that *all* things lack own-existence would be to state that all things are conceptual existents, reified conceptual constructs, without anything left for them to be reified and constructed out of. This would be an absurdity, for it would destroy the very category of secondary, conceptual existence and thus destroy the entire universe – everything – along with the destruction of primary existence. To state that *all* things are lacking own-existence, *niḥsvabhāva*, must entail an absurd nihilism. As we shall see, that is where – in the search for complete letting-go – the Madhyamaka thought of Nāgārjuna will come in. It is heralded by the Mahāyāna Perfection of Wisdom sūtra literature.

But the Buddha, alas, was long dead. With the development of Mahāyāna Buddhism some centuries after the death of the Buddha we encounter a growing awareness among some Buddhist activists of a new dimension to what Buddhism is finally all about, and in the generation of the apocryphal Mahāyāna sūtra literature a radical response.

3 The nature and origins of Mahāyāna Buddhism

I was once asked by an eminent Oxford philosopher 'What sort of "animal" is Indian philosophy?'. If we try and clarify what sort of 'animal' Mahāyāna Buddhism is we find straight away that contemporary scholarship is beginning to indicate – I think convincingly – that there has in the past been considerable misunderstanding concerning the sort of religious phenomenon we are talking about. Talk has all too often been one of schism and sect; the model one of clear-cut doctrinal and behavioural difference, rivalry and antagonism, often one feels, on the model of that between Protestant and Roman Catholic Christianity. This model perhaps has been reinforced by the undoubted antagonism found in some Mahāyāna sūtras towards those who fail to heed the message of the text. These people persistently continue to follow what the Mahāyāna sūtras themselves term – using an intentionally polemical and abusive expression – an 'Inferior Way', a *Hīnayāna*. Thus we have texts, the earliest of which might date in something resembling a form we have now from perhaps the second or first century BCE, that see themselves as genuinely being the word of the Buddha (or *a* Buddha) and thus claim a disputed status as sūtras. These texts advocate a vision, although not necessarily all the same vision, which they term 'Mahāyāna', the Great Way.[1] In some cases, perhaps increasing as time passed, this Great Way is contrasted with an Inferior Way (Hīnayāna), and sometimes this contrast is marked by the use of rather immoderate language. Followers of the Inferior

Way are, as one Mahāyāna sūtra puts it, 'like jackals' (Williams 1989: 21).

Yet notwithstanding the harshness of some Mahāyāna sūtras (all of which were considered apocryphal by non-Mahāyānists), we now know that a picture of schism and sect, with attendant and widespread rivalry and antagonism, would be very misleading. We know from later Chinese sources, for example, that Chinese pilgrims to India found so-called non-Mahāyāna and Mahāyāna monks in the same monasteries. The only obvious and manifest differences between these two groups was that the Mahāyāna monks showed particular reverence towards, 'worshipped', figures of bodhisattvas, compassionate beings on the path to full Buddhahood, while the non-Mahāyāna monks chose not to.[2]

The student should be extremely careful not to extrapolate uncritically from the antagonism of some of the Mahāyāna sūtras to an actual, practical, antagonism 'on the ground'. He or she should also be careful not to extrapolate from the sheer size of the Mahāyāna sūtra literature to the extent or indeed the nature of Mahāyāna identity in Classical India. There is evidence that monks and nuns who did not adopt the Mahāyāna vision viewed it with some scorn, seeing it as an absurd fabrication based simply on the so-called Mahāyāna sūtras claiming a quite unjustified authenticity and consequential authority. Many Mahāyāna scholars such as Nāgārjuna (in e.g. the *Ratnāvalī*) or Śāntideva (in the *Bodhicaryāvatāra*) produced defences of the Mahāyāna, defending the authenticity of the Mahāyāna sūtras. But to the best of my knowledge there is no detailed, systematic refutation of Mahāyāna in *any* non-Mahāyāna Indian Buddhist source yet discovered.[3] Modern scholars are frequently left digging and probing for what are claimed to be occasional and non-systematic references to Mahāyāna in non-Mahāyāna sources such as Vasubandhu's enormous *Abhidharmakośa*. Given the many centuries of Buddhism in India, and the size of the Mahāyāna literature, this is absolutely astonishing if we extrapolate from the size of the Mahāyāna canon to the supposed extent of Mahāyāna in India. But we cannot make such an inference, and one is tempted to suggest that the only explanation for near-silence is that Mahāyāna in Classical India was not a threat, and/or was not taken seriously. This could be because in spite of the size of the literature there were throughout much of the period of Buddhism in India very few monks who actually adopted the Mahāyāna vision, and those monks were just thought by their brethren to be a bit weird – but harmless. Alternatively it could be because in terms of what is to count as a threat among those who have come together to live a simple and cenobitic lifestyle the Mahāyāna was not a rival. I suspect it may be a combination of both of these factors.[4]

Thanks to the work of Heinz Bechert (1982) we now have a clearer idea of what is to count as generating schism in Buddhist monasticism. For Buddhists 'schism' is nothing to do with doctrinal disagreements as such, but is the result of divergence in monastic rule.[5] This makes sense. The whole purpose of Buddhist monasticism is for groups of people to live together a simple life with optimum facilities for inner development. What produces major disagreement in such contexts – and can lead to schism, 'splitting the Sangha' (*saṃghabheda*) – are what for non-monastics would appear to be fairly minor matters of behavioural disagreement. Thus if a monk holds that it is permissible to eat after midday, while all his brethren have to finish their meal before midday, this could cause great problems for the peaceful running of the monastery. Further difficulties could arise for the crucial issue of the harmonious relationship between the monastery and the local lay community. Imagine the response of the lay supporters to their farming day being disrupted by *two* groups of monks from the local monastery on the alms-round at different times. One could see that under such circumstances it might be better for all concerned that the divergent monk (and those who agree) 'split'. Suppose on the other hand that a monk holds the final goal of all should be not nirvāṇa but perfect Buddhahood for the benefit of all sentient beings. Or he believes that in meditation he is receiving personal tuition from a Buddha called Amitāyus unknown to other monks. This might be thought by many of his brethren to be pretty peculiar. But providing it does not lead to intolerable levels of disruptive behaviour – and why should it? – our monk's Mahāyāna views need not lead to a 'schism'.

Buddhism is thus an orthopraxy rather than orthodoxy. What is important is harmony of behaviour, not harmony of doctrines. The role played by doctrinal disagreements in Christian history does not apply in the case of Buddhism. Of course, where there is a genuine schism related to the monastic rule there could also take place subsequently doctrinal variation. But doctrinal difference as such cannot be a matter for schism. Thus since Mahāyāna is, as I shall argue, a matter of vision and motivation which does not (or need not) in itself entail behaviour confrontational to the monastic rule, it could not have resulted from schism. It is not that sort of thing. It is not that sort of 'animal'. Once this is appreciated it can be seen that the opposition between Mahāyāna and non-Mahāyāna could not in any way parallel that of, say, Roman Catholicism polarised against Protestantism, where identity is very, very much a matter of doctrinal allegiance, of rival beliefs. Schism in Christian history is precisely the result of doctrinal disagreement. Identity in Buddhism is supplied by adherence to the monastic code, the Vinaya. Identity is a monastic matter. As time passed, after the death of the Buddha, there were indeed schisms, and there remain a number of Vinayas. The traditional Theravāda account of the Second Council at Vaiśālī in north India (*c.* 40–100 years after the death of the Buddha) describe how it was called to settle issues related to divergent behaviour among certain 'wicked monks'.[6] There is some question about how far we can follow the Theravāda account of this Council, but it is understandable that a Council may have been called over such central issues. The suggestion that the 'wicked monks' were defeated but remained stubborn and broke away is indeed an account of *saṃghabheda*, schism. This account could not be used as it often is, however, in any simple way to explain the origins of the Mahāyāna, since the Mahāyāna as such could not have resulted from schism.

Traditional Theravāda accounts associate the defeated monks with the origin of the Mahāsāṃghikas, a rival Vinaya and doctrinal tradition. In the past there has been a tendency to trace the origins of the Mahāyāna to doctrinal tendencies within the Mahāsāṃghika tradition. On both counts there are however problems. Suffice to say that it is looking very unlikely that the 'wicked monks of Vaiśālī' were the origins of the Mahāsāṃghikas, and few contemporary scholars would identify Mahāyāna in a straightforward way with any particular Vinaya tradition (or non-Mahāyāna 'school'). Inasmuch as we can detect from Mahāyāna sources the Vinaya or perhaps Abhidharma presuppositions of the compilers of those sources, we can see that Mahāyāna tendencies cut across the boundaries of the non-Mahāyāna traditions. For example, there is a clear association between the *Ta-chih-tu Lun* (*Mahāprajñāpāramitā Śāstra*), the enormous compendium of Mahāyāna attributed to Nāgārjuna and translated into Chinese by Kumārajīva in the early fifth century CE, and monks from the Sarvāstivāda/Vaibhāṣika tradition of Kashmir. But the Mahāyāna *Lokānuvartana Sūtra* on the other hand shows a strong tendency towards the idea that the Buddha is in some sense always supramundane, and the teaching of emptiness, which are both associated with the Mahāsāṃghikas (see pp. 128–30).

The Theravāda Vinaya is one particular Vinaya, and indeed a monk can be defined as a Theravādin (a follower of Theravāda) precisely inasmuch as he has been ordained and lives according to the Theravāda Vinaya. In India in classical times, however, it seems likely that one of the most important Vinayas was that of the Mūlasarvāstivāda, the Vinaya which also to the present day guides the monastic vision of Tibetans. In China, and traditions influenced by China, among others the Dharmaguptaka Vinaya was popular. All these Vinayas are Vinayas which evolved over the centuries, but – and this is crucially important – they have absolutely nothing to do with issues of Mahāyāna versus non-Mahāyāna. *There is no such thing as a Mahāyāna Vinaya.*[7] Thus Mahāyāna cannot have originated as such in a schism. Moreover in a very real sense *there cannot have been any Mahāyāna monks in India*, since identity as a monk is a Vinaya matter, although of course there can certainly have been monks who held a Mahāyāna vision and motivation. Once we understand that

Mahāyāna identity is not a matter of the Vinaya and therefore not a matter of publicly significant behaviour in a monastic context, then it becomes perfectly understandable that visitors to India would have seen Mahāyāna and non-Mahāyāna monks in the same monasteries. Why should we expect otherwise? If that still seems strange, then one has still not appreciated the inappropriateness of the schism-model, or that supplied by Christian parallels. Moreover the different Vinayas, although containing what were no doubt significant differences in the context of monastic concerns and precision, are all fairly close to each other. The radical doctrinal differences sometimes found between Mahāyāna and non-Mahāyāna are not matched in what was in public terms what actually counted for Buddhists in Ancient India – monastic behaviour.

I have referred to Mahāyāna as a vision, a vision of what Buddhism is finally all about, rather than a sect, a school, or the result of schism. This picture of Mahāyāna corresponds I suggest with what scholarly research is beginning to indicate both about the nature of Mahāyāna and, more particularly, about what Mahāyāna is not. It also corresponds rather nicely with one of my favourite pictures of what Mahāyāna is really all about, a self-definition admittedly late (but enormously influential in Tibetan Buddhism) found in the *Bodhipathapradīpa* of the eleventh century Indian Buddhist scholar and missionary to Tibet, Atiśa. Based on earlier Buddhist precedents, Atiśa suggests a division of religious practitioners into three hierarchical classes according to their *motivations*. Hierarchical division of persons is a very Indian strategy (cf. caste and class), while division by motivation is quintessentially Buddhist where, as we have seen, from early days it has been the intention behind an act which is the main contributory factor in creating morally significant *karman*. Thus those of the lowest type perform (religious) actions motivated by saṃsāra – unenlightenment – worldly actions with the intention of some material gain either in this life or in another life. Those of the middle type are motivated by the wish for freedom from all suffering and rebirth, in other words the freedom that is nirvāṇa, enlightenment. Note that those who attain such a goal are in fact the group called *arhats*, and within this hierarchical framework they have followed an Inferior Path (a Hīnayāna). But those superior people whose motivation is the very highest take as their goal freedom from suffering for all, that is, perfect Buddhahood, motivated by the wish to attain the greatest possibility to benefit others. These are followers of the Great, the Supreme, Path – the Mahāyāna. In fact those of lowest motivation attain saṃsāra. Those of middle motivation attain nirvāṇa, while those with the highest motivation of all reach what Mahāyāna scholars came to refer to as a 'non-abiding' nirvāṇa (*apratiṣṭhitanirvāṇa*). This nirvāṇa is beyond such dualities. It is not saṃsāra but it is also not a resting in any nirvāṇa that would abandon sentient beings who are still suffering. Thus in the final analysis what makes a follower of Mahāyāna is not robes, rules, or philosophy. It is motivation, intention. The Mahāyāna as a whole is a particular vision of what the final motivation and goal of serious practitioners should be. Atiśa's self-definition of Mahāyāna is particularly useful for us because again it conforms to the picture of Mahāyānists and non-Mahāyānists in the same monastery, and it conforms to the archaeological and early textual evidence that there was no radical break between Mahāyāna and non-Mahāyāna, and no 'Mahāyāna schism'. It reaffirms the centrality of intention in Buddhism, and explains why we find Mahāyāna cutting across the boundaries of non-Mahāyāna traditions. *Mahāyāna is not as such an institutional identity. Rather, it is an inner motivation and vision, and this inner vision can be found in anyone regardless of their institutional position.* Thus, of course, there could in theory be Theravāda Mahāyānists. If that sounds strange it does nothing more than indicate how conditioned we have become to think of the Buddhist world as divided into two schools (or sects) on the model of Roman Catholic and Protestant, resulting from some supposed doctrinal schism.

I suspect it might indeed have been quite possible to visit India in earlier Classical times and as a casual visitor not see Mahāyāna Buddhism as such at all. I am sure that a great Mahāyāna thinker like Nāgārjuna or Śāntideva would not have appeared any different from their non-Mahāyāna brethren. Their public behaviour would not have been different. Perhaps even their public utterances would not have been very different. But if one came to know them well or visited them in their rooms or cells perhaps one could have detected a different vision and intention, a different idea of what, ultimately, it all meant, a different idea of what it was really all about. Nāgārjuna, moreover, was an Indian monk. To meet Nāgārjuna would not have been like meeting a Tibetan yogin, a magic-wielding wonderworker, or a Zen Master. I do not think also that it would have been like meeting the Dalai Lama. In actual fact in appearance and behaviour meeting Nāgārjuna might have been rather more like meeting a Theravāda monk.

So far we have seen that Mahāyāna Buddhism is nothing to do with Vinaya differences, and is not the result of schism. It is a phenomenon that cuts across the boundaries of different Vinaya traditions, and was also capable of cutting across the boundaries of doctrinal (such as Abhidharma) schools without generating an identifiable further school.[8] Mahāyāna is very diverse. It is united perhaps solely by a vision of the ultimate goal of attaining full Buddhahood for the benefit of all sentient beings (the 'bodhisattva ideal') and also (or eventually) a belief that Buddhas are still around and can be contacted (hence the possibility of an ongoing revelation). To this extent the expression 'Mahāyāna' is used simply for practical purposes. It is used as a 'family term' covering a range of not necessarily identical or even compatible practices and teachings. Thus Mahāyāna could not itself form a school of Buddhism. It lacked that sort of unity, it is not that sort of 'animal' either. It is possible to detect in some Mahāyāna sūtras criticism of those who do not accept Mahāyāna, and particularly criticism of those who do not accept the particular sūtra concerned (Schopen 1975). There is also criticism sometimes of or comments on other sūtras and their advocates (Harrison 1978; Pagel 1995: 36 ff.). According to Gregory Schopen (1975), it is quite possible that in origins Mahāyāna was centred on a number of 'sūtra cults', involving the promulgation as well as the worship of particular sūtras which were perhaps in mutual rivalry. These sūtras were held to contain a particular new revelation from the Buddha (or a Buddha).

By far the most important and suggestive work on the nature and origins of the Mahāyāna in India has come from Gregory Schopen, with significant additional contributions by Paul Harrison. Schopen has drawn attention to the importance of archaeological data, such as inscriptional evidence, for the picture it can give us of what was actually happening in India, in opposition to the inferences we might be tempted to draw from written texts.[9] I have argued already that the sheer size of the Mahāyāna literary corpus might suggest that Mahāyāna was a widespread tendency in Ancient India, although this need not follow. After all, one person or one group of teachers could write a very great deal (note the repetitive nature of much of the *Prajñāpāramitā* literature). Schopen's study (1979) of the evidence for Mahāyāna in Indian inscriptions has led to some interesting conclusions which appear to contradict the picture some might be tempted to draw from the literary remains.[10] First, the evidence for Mahāyāna in Indian inscriptions (such as the inscriptions of those donating a statue to a monastery, for example) is actually relatively scarce. What evidence there is shows that with one exception the earliest use of the term 'Mahāyāna' in inscriptions dates from the fifth or sixth centuries CE, although there is the use of certain terms identifiable as having a Mahāyāna reference from the fourth century CE. Therefore we find that inscriptional evidence for Mahāyāna lags many centuries behind the earliest literary evidence (*c.* second/first century BCE), and it is arguable that the use of the term 'Mahāyāna' to give self-identity to a particular group of people took even longer. Thus, Schopen wants to conclude, 'we are able to assume that what we now call the Mahāyāna did not begin to emerge as a separate and independent group until the fourth century' (Schopen 1979: 15). It seems that for perhaps five centuries – the centuries which saw the production of a great deal of the Mahāyāna sūtra literature, and many of the greatest thinkers of the Mahāyāna – Mahāyāna was not seen 'on the ground' as an identifiable 'institution' involving inscriptional allegiance. The one exception is contained in an inscription dating from the second century CE discovered in 1977, which also refers to the Mahāyāna Buddha Amitābha.

But, as Schopen points out (1987b), the amazing point about this inscription and its reference to Amitābha is that it is the only one for many centuries, in spite of the fact that we know Mahāyāna literature and texts treating Amitābha (or Amitāyus) had been in existence for some time. Along with the absence of clear self-identity for the followers of Mahāyāna, we seem to find evidence of their scarcity – or at least, no evidence for their frequency, let alone the prevalence of a 'cult of Amitābha' in North India at that time, as some scholars have claimed. Schopen's conclusions merit quoting at some length:

> even after its initial appearance in the public domain in the 2nd century [Mahāyāna] appears to have remained an extremely limited minority movement – if it remained at all – that attracted absolutely no *documented* public or popular support for at least two more centuries. It is again a demonstrable fact that anything even approaching popular support for the Mahāyāna cannot be documented until the 4th/5th century AD, and even then the support is overwhelmingly by monastic, not lay, donors . . . although there was – as we know from Chinese translations – a large and early Mahāyāna literature, there was no early, organized, independent, publically supported movement that it could have belonged to.
> (Schopen 1987b: 124–5; italics original)

Note also that as far as he is concerned Schopen has failed to find any support for the widespread association of the laity with the origins or growth of Mahāyāna. This is important, for it contradicts a prevalent view that the Mahāyāna represents primarily a move by the laity and those sympathetic to their aspirations, against certain rather remote and elitist monks.[11] It is possible to point to material in the *Pratyutpanna Sūtra*, studied by Paul Harrison (1978, 1990) which gives incidental evidence to support the view that the origins of that particular relatively early sūtra had nothing to do with the laity. It seems to me that the idea that the Mahāyāna in origin was indeed associated with the laity results at least in part from an over-literal and perhaps wishful reading of certain sūtras. These sūtras employ the rhetorical device of lay speakers (such as the rich merchant Vimalakīrti or the young princess Aśokadattā) in order to criticise non-Mahāyāna (in fact definitely Hīnayāna) views associated with rival monks.[12] Mahāyāna was not however the result of a lay movement or lay aspirations, perhaps inspired by the rich mercantile classes, anymore than it was the result of an aristocratic Girl Guide-like movement of precocious juvenile princesses.[13] It seems obvious that in the context of Ancient India enduring religious innovation was made by religiously and institutionally significant groups of people who had the time to do so. This means, among educated laypeople, primarily brahmin teachers working within the caste and class based structures of orthodox householder life. It means as well renunciates, drop-outs, who also taught and survived on alms. It is unlikely that major changes in *Buddhist* ideology occurred inspired and preserved by householder brahmins, but entirely understandable that such changes occurred among Buddhist renunciates, i.e. monks.

Richard Gombrich (1990a) has argued that it seems unlikely that Mahāyāna as we know it could have originated without writing. This seems clear given the association of Mahāyāna in origins with the creation of the Mahāyāna sūtra literature, and also Schopen's (1975) mention of references in early Mahāyāna to worshipping the sūtras themselves in the form of books. This is on the model of the existing cult of *stūpas*, relic-shrines of the Buddha and his eminent disciples. The writing down of the Buddhist canon took place initially in the first century BCE. Thus Mahāyāna as such is unlikely to have occurred – would not have survived – much prior to the use of writing for scriptural texts. Against this, Vetter (1994) has suggested that there is some evidence that early Mahāyāna material was transmitted orally. Even so, Mahāyāna would not have survived without occurring within an enduring respected Buddhist organisation which was prepared to preserve it, and it is difficult to see in the case of Buddhism what that organisation could be if not members of the regular organisation which preserves Buddhist texts, the Sangha. One cannot imagine, on the other hand, the Sangha or indeed any significant Sangha member preserving radical innovative texts that originated in a lay movement against the Sangha itself.

The idea we get from Schopen's work on archaeological sources is also supported by Paul Harrison's concern with some of the earliest extant Mahāyāna literature, the translations into Chinese of Mahāyāna sūtras by Lokakṣema in the late second century CE (1987). Harrison has shown that the picture of early Mahāyāna involvement from these sources is overwhelmingly one of monks, although as well as nuns laity (including lay women) were also addressed in the sūtras. Note that women, however, are far from being treated on a basis of equality with men. We also do not find in these sūtras any antagonism towards monasticism, the Sangha, as such. Central to early Mahāyāna represented by these texts is an aspiration to perfect Buddhahood, that is, taking upon oneself the vow of the bodhisattva, while bodhisattvas as semi-divine beings, the so-called 'celestial bodhisattvas' of later petitionary worship, are at this stage conspicuous by their absence. Early Mahāyāna is also characterised by a fairly antagonistic attitude towards those who follow the 'inferior' path to liberation from merely one's own personal suffering, the state of the arhat, rather than full Buddhahood for the benefit of all living beings.[14] In his recent work Harrison argues that

> some of the impetus for the early development of the Mahāyāna came from forest-dwelling monks. Far from being the products of an urban, lay, devotional movement, many Mahāyāna sūtras give evidence of a hard-core ascetic attempt to return to the original inspiration of Buddhism, the search for Buddhahood or awakened cognition.
>
> (Harrison 1995: 65)

Thus Mahāyāna may in part represent a rather austere, almost ascetic, 'revivalist movement'. This picture is supported in a recent paper by Schopen (1999). He has shown quite convincingly in the case of an obscure Mahāyāna sūtra, the *Maitreyamahāsiṃhanāda Sūtra* (the 'Lion's Roar of Maitreya') that this sūtra can be dated to the Kuṣāṇa period (*c.* first century

CE) and originated in Northwest India. This would make it one of the earliest datable Mahāyāna sūtras. The sūtra advocates a highly *conservative* monastic vision of Buddhism, centred on the inferiority of the laity, austere practice in the forest as the ideal, and condemns less austere monks for their involvement in such inferior practices as stūpa worship. Schopen concludes that

> if there is any 'relationship' of the polemic found in the *Maitreyasiṃhanāda-sūtra* to the 'rise of mahāyāna Buddhism' that relationship remains a mystery. This early 'mahāyāna' polemic does not seem to be connected to the 'rise' of anything, but rather to the continuity and persistence of a narrow set of conservative Buddhist ideas on cult and monastic practice. That is all.
>
> (Schopen 1999: 313)[15]

It is possible that particularly significant in the origins of some of the Mahāyāna literature was a belief that the Buddha (or Buddhas) could still be contacted, and is really still teaching out of his immense compassion. There is some evidence that early Buddhism felt it to be a genuine problem why the compassionate Śākyamuni Buddha had died at the age of 80 when there was a widespread view that at the time of the Buddha the average lifespan was actually 100 years. Lifespan is supposed to be the result of merit, and we have a suggestion in the *Mahāparinibbāna Sutta* that a Buddha can live until the end of an aeon if he so wishes. We also have some grounds for thinking that in the early centuries the inability to see and benefit any more from the actual physical presence of the Buddha was felt by some very acutely. For this reason there was a real doctrinal problem as to why the Buddha actually died when he did die. One strategy was to blame the Buddha's attendant Ānanda for not petitioning the Buddha correctly to remain until the end of the aeon. Such an approach, however, could scarcely harmonise with the image of the Compassionate One, and perhaps one of the few defining dimensions of Mahāyāna Buddhism is a vision and understanding of the Buddha as *not really dead but still around*. When stated and accepted this understanding entailed that Buddhism itself had the potential to change in the light of a continuing revelation.

It is indeed possible that the suggestion that the Buddha is still around may have been (in part) a response to particular visions in meditation, perhaps associated with meditation practices involving visualising the Buddha and known as *buddhānusmṛti* ('recollection of the Buddha'). We know that such practices were popular from a very early period, and that one of the results of these practices is that the meditator feels as if in the presence of the Buddha himself (Williams 1989: 30, 217–20; Harrison 1978). In the *Pratyutpanna Sūtra*, translated into Chinese by Lokakṣema and studied by Paul Harrison, we find details of a visualisation practice in which the meditator visualises Buddha Amitāyus in his 'Pure Land' (Buddha Field; q.v.) in the West, for twenty-four hours a day, for a whole week. After that, the sūtra says, the meditator may have a vision of Amitāyus, and receive new teachings not before heard. Moreover these new teachings the meditator is exhorted to transmit and expound to mankind.

It seems certain that a text like the *Pratyutpanna Sūtra* (and perhaps other early Mahāyāna texts associated with Pure Lands and *buddhānusmṛti*) describes practices which can lead to revelatory visions, and the *Pratyutpanna Sūtra* itself advocates the promulgation of the teachings thus received. But while visions can occur in meditation, the occurrence of visions – messages apparently from a Buddha – does not explain why someone would take those messages seriously. Indeed the Buddhist tradition in general has tended to be very cautious, even dismissive, concerning visions seen in meditation. Of course, if it is correct that for many centuries there were very few followers of Mahāyāna in classical India, then the problem becomes less acute. But certainly some people took these revelations seriously, and those who took them seriously were sometimes great scholars. It is often said that the standard view of early Buddhism is that after the death of a Buddha he is beyond reference or recall, significantly and religiously dead. From such a perspective the idea of seeing a living Buddha in meditation is problematic. One way round this would be to claim that the Buddha visualised is simply a Buddha who has for one reason or another not yet died. That would be to adopt a strategy of doctrinal reconciliation. As we shall see, this is indeed a strategy commonly adopted in Mahāyāna sources. But recent work by Gregory Schopen suggests that the atmosphere in Buddhist circles in Ancient India may have been at least emotionally more receptive to the idea that a dead Buddha is still around than was previously realised. Schopen has argued on archaeological and inscriptional grounds that the Buddha's relics, preserved after his death in stūpas, were felt to be the Buddha himself. The Buddha was thought in some sense to be still present in his relics and even in spots associated with his life (Schopen 1987a, 1990, 1994). Through his relics the Buddha was also treated as if present in the monastery, and was treated legally by the monastery and apparently by the wider community as a person with inalienable property rights.[16] Schopen has shown that in day to day life the Buddha was felt very much to be present among the monks, if invisible.

Perhaps it was little wonder, then, that certain monks, inspired by the common meditation practice of 'recollection of the Buddha', *buddhānusmṛti*, felt the genuineness of their visions of him and what had been revealed to them. Thus they arrived at the possibility of a continuing revelation and of course new sūtras.[17] Little wonder too, then, that eventually we find in some circles forms of religiosity developed centred on the supremacy of Buddhahood above all alternative goals. This religiosity focused too on the great compassion of one who remains present, transcending even death, helping sentient beings. It encouraged the need to attain a palpable immortality through becoming oneself a Buddha. In becoming a Buddha Śākyamuni, after all, is said to have triumphed over the Evil One, the 'Devil', Māra. The etymology of this name shows him to be the personification of death. Little wonder then that we also find in the meantime participation in 'Pure Land' cults, a need to see the Buddha if not in this life in meditation, then after death through rebirth in his presence in the Pure Land where he still dwells.[18]

Thus it seems clear from early Mahāyāna texts that through meditation it was felt to be possible by some Buddhist practitioners to meet with a still-living Buddha and receive new teachings, receive perhaps the Mahāyāna sūtras themselves. That some people actually took this possibility seriously may well have been prompted by a feeling on the one hand of sadness that the age of the living presence of the Buddha as a physical being had passed. But it was also prompted by an awareness of his continuing if rather invisible presence in the monastery, as relics imbued with the qualities of Buddhahood, the *dharmakāya*. These are themes that we shall meet again.

4 Some schools of Mainstream Buddhist thought

Sarvāstivāda / Vaibhāṣika

As with Theravāda, there is a complete Sarvāstivāda Canon with a Sarvāstivāda Vinaya and a Sarvāstivāda ordination lineage to go with it. But the name 'Sarvāstivāda' means 'the doctrine (*vāda*) that all (*sarva*) exist (*asti*)', and holding this 'doctrine that all exist', whatever that involves, is not the same as being ordained into the Sarvāstivāda lineage. To hold and defend this doctrine, and other associated doctrines, is to follow Sarvāstivāda as a doctrinal school. Clearly it is logically possible to be a Sarvāstivādin (one who follows Sarvāstivāda) monk by ordination without being a Sarvāstivādin by doctrine, and vice-versa. The association between a Sarvāstivāda ordination lineage and Sarvāstivāda doctrines is a contingent one, although in practice it may well have turned out to be the case that they were often associated in those monks (no doubt the minority) who were particularly interested in the refinements of doctrinal study. But not all the great doctrinal schools of Buddhism (traditionally there is said to have been eighteen doctrinal schools related to non-Mahāyāna Buddhism) had Vinayas associated with them. As far as we know, for example, 'Sautrāntika' is only a doctrinal school. Thus there could easily have been a Sarvāstivādin monk, i.e. one ordained according to the Sarvāstivāda Vinaya, holding Sautrāntika views. And, as we have seen, Mahāyāna as such is neither a Vinaya tradition nor a doctrinal school. It is rather a vision or aspiration, and an understanding of what the final concern should be for all Buddhists. That final concern should be to obtain perfect Buddhahood for the benefit of all sentient beings, and perfect Buddhahood for all is very much superior simply to becoming an arhat, liberated from one's own suffering. Thus there would be no contradiction in being a Sarvāstivādin monk holding Sautrāntika doctrinal views and also being a Mahāyānist. The universal association of certain doctrinal schools, notably Madhyamaka and Yogācāra, with Mahāyāna is again a contingent matter not one of necessary connection, notwithstanding the fact that the founders and all the great teachers associated with these doctrinal positions do indeed appear to have held the Mahāyāna vision as well.

In this chapter I want to outline briefly some of the more significant positions associated with doctrinal schools *not* historically connected directly with Mahāyāna. The 'doctrine that all exist' was indeed so important to Sarvāstivāda as a doctrinal school that it became a name for the school. But from the time of the composition of the 'Great Commentary' (*Mahāvibhāṣā*) in the second century CE perhaps the expression Vaibhāṣika ('Following the Commentary') was the more formal name for the school.[1] Among the geographical areas associated with Sarvāstivāda, Northwest India (such as Kashmir) was particular important both in doctrinal terms and also for its influence on Afghanistan, Central Asia, and thence China.

The Sarvāstivāda appears to have had a particular interest in ontological issues. This interest should be seen as an understandable response to the basic Buddhist concern with the ontology of the Self, and with seeing things the way they really are. These are essentially ontological issues, and in its concern with ontology Sarvāstivāda is quintessentially Buddhist. We have seen already that Sarvāstivāda drew a systematic distinction between the way dharmas exist, and the way composite entities that are constructions out of dharmas exist. The former are 'primary existents' (*dravyasat*), and those composite entities constructed out of primary existents are 'secondary' or 'conceptual existents' (*prajñaptisat*). Both truly exist, although in different ways. The 'doctrine that all exist' concerns serious and perennial philosophical issues arising out of apparent paradoxes when referring to non-existence, specifically here past and future dharmas.[2] If a dharma is impermanent, and ceases soon after its arising, how can something which has ceased and is thus apparently non-existent *do* anything? How can it serve as the object of cognition (as in the case of memory), and how can it bring about an effect (as in the case of *karman*)? Moreover the same could be said about future dharmas. How can they serve as the objects of cognition or action, as occurs in anticipation and motivated activity? In consideration of all this, the Sarvāstivādin response was that past and future dharmas, while clearly not existing in the same way as the momentary present dharmas, must nevertheless still *exist*. Something simply non-existent could not serve as a cognitive (an 'intentional') referent, nor could it bring about an effect, as in the case of pain now occurring due to wicked deeds done in the past. Thus the 'doctrine that all exist' is specifically the doctrine that if a dharma is a future, a present, or a past dharma it nevertheless still exists.[3]

The idea that dharmas exist when future, present, and past was felt by rival schools (notably Sautrāntika) to sail very close to an entailment that dharmas must actually be permanent.[4] This need not follow, however, providing one distinguishes sufficiently adequately existing as past and future from existing as present. We find a number of attempts to do this even prior to the *Mahāvibhāṣā*, and detailed in that text with priority given to an explanation by a certain Vasumitra. For the Sarvāstivādin it was felt to be clear, as Saṃghabhadra (late fourth or early fifth century CE?) pointed out, that past and future dharmas cannot possibly be absolutely non-existent. They are not non-existent in the way that, for example, the horn of a hare is simply non-existent (i.e. there is no such thing). Anything that can be a cognitive referent exists. But in order to distinguish between existing simply in the way past and future dharmas do, and existing as present (and of course in that respect impermanent) dharmas do, the Sarvāstivādin brought into play the notion of the 'own-existence' (*svabhāva*) of a dharma. The own-existence, as we have seen, is possessed by each dharma inasmuch as it is a dharma and not a conceptual construct. Its own-existence is what makes each dharma an individual unique thing. It was easy to slide from this to the own-existence as the 'what-it-is-ness' of the dharma, and thereby what is referred to every time one speaks of that dharma. Thus the Sarvāstivādin wants to say past and future dharmas exist simply in the mode of their own-existence (*sasvabhāvamātra*). That is, each past and future dharma exists as its 'what-it-is-ness', and it is this that enables one to cognise and to speak about it. This sort of existence is always possessed by a dharma of that type. It is atemporal and is what makes the dharma the dharma it is. In the case of dharmas it enables us to talk in abstract, divorced from particular instances, about dharmas. Thus we can speak of dharmas as 'not further analysable', for example, and we can classify them into a list of dharmas. It is what we might call 'intentional existence'. It is the sort of existence anything has solely inasmuch as it is an object of language and cognition. The Sarvāstivādin wants to suggest that because a past dharma has this sort of existence there is also no longer any paradox in a result occurring of something that is past and otherwise non-existent. But in addition to existing this way, present dharmas also have their characteristic activity (*sakāritra*). That is, a present dharma does what that dharma does, as this is understood in the Abhidharma. The dharma's not yet doing what it does is what makes it a future dharma. Its doing what it does when the appropriate causes and conditions come together makes it a present dharma, and its ceasing to do what it does when the causes and conditions cease is what renders it a past dharma. This 'doing-what-it-does' is instantaneous, momentary. Thus any dharma's being present is momentary. This is fully temporal, and since we live in time and the occurrence (i.e. being present) of a dharma in time is momentary, momentariness is preserved.[5]

A further interesting dimension of Sarvāstivāda thought worth noting in passing is its analysis of causation itself. This is because, in a way that shows remarkable philosophical flexibility and adventurousness, the Sarvāstivādin has no objection to the simultaneity of cause and effect, and is even willing to entertain the possibility that the effect may occur *after* the cause.

Sarvāstivāda speaks of six types of causes (*hetu*) and four types of conditions (*pratyaya*, see Hirakawa 1990: 179–84). The first type of cause is the *kāraṇahetu*, the 'efficient cause'. This consists of every other dharma apart from the dharma that is the effect itself, inasmuch as every dharma either contributes directly towards bringing about a further dharma (the cause as an 'empowered' *kāraṇahetu*) or does not hinder its production (the cause as a 'powerless' *kāraṇahetu*). Thus all things are one way or another linked into the mesh of cause and effect. Here the class of *kāraṇahetu* is specifically said to incorporate causes that can be either prior to or simultaneous with the effect (Saṃghabhadra, in Potter 1999: 704). Simultaneity is even more obvious in the case of the 'simultaneous cause' (*sahabhūhetu*), which occurs where dharmas arise in a simultaneous relationship of mutual cause and effect. Thus, for example, since in a particular composite mental event (like perceiving a strawberry) consciousness and its mental associates arise together, if the consciousness occurs the mental associates must occur, and if the mental associates occur the consciousness must occur. If either consciousness or any of the mental associates is missing here, the others as parts of this composite mental event could not occur.[6] Therefore they are here all mutually and simultaneously cause and effect. The 'homogeneous cause' (*sabhāgahetu*), on the other hand, referring to cases of sequential concordance between causes and effects, must obviously be prior to its effect. Thus, for example, prior good causes give rise to subsequent good effects, prior bad causes to subsequent bad effects.[7] The *Abhidharmakośabhāṣya* (2: 52) considers also the possibility that the cause could occur chronologically after the effect, with support cited both for and against from the central Sarvāstivādin canonical Abhidharma text, the *Jñānaprasthāna*. The *Kośabhāṣya* itself rejects this possibility, but throughout this text its author Vasubandhu frequently rejects even established Sarvāstivādin positions in a way which shows his considerable sympathy with Sautrāntika.[8] From a Sautrāntika perspective it is axiomatic that the cause must precede its effect.

A unique Sarvāstivādin doctrine, and once more a topic of intense debate with others, is that of 'possession' or 'ownership' (*prāpti*). Supposing I have an intense wicked intention. That wicked intention is an unwholesome *karman*, which will eventually produce suffering for me. But the intention itself is impermanent. When it has ceased (in Sarvāstivādin terms, passed from present into past) what entails that its karmic result will occur in the future to a future stage of the same psychophysical continuum in which the original intention occurred? In other words, in imprecise everyday terms, given the Buddhist stress on complete impermanence, what ensures that the karmic result of my wicked intention will occur to *me* (albeit perhaps my reincarnation)? In the future all the factors that make up 'me' will be completely different, even though causally linked, to the factors that make up 'me' now. The answer the Sarvāstivādin wants to say is that when the original intention occurred it was *mine*. That is, in addition to the intention itself there was a further dharma occurring in the series called 'possession', *prāpti*. The intention 'ceased' (i.e. for the Sarvāstivādin, passed into 'past-mode'). As an impermanent dharma, so did the *prāpti*. But the *prāpti* generated another *prāpti*, this time the possession of 'having had that wicked intention'. This *prāpti* too is an impermanent dharma. On its cessation it too generates another similar possession. Thus as a result of the original wicked intention part of my psychophysical continuum consists of an ongoing stream of *prāptis*: 'having had that wicked intention.' Eventually, when the conditions are right, a suffering as the karmic result of that original intention will occur. The original intention still exists in past-mode. And the suffering will occur in the psychophysical continuum which has the *prāpti*-series 'having had that wicked intention', not in another one. In the imprecise everyday terms used above, the karmic result will occur to me because I am the one who has the *prāpti*-series – *I* am the one who possessed the original intention, not someone else.[9] Similarly, an unenlightened being has a possession of the negative taints (passions/defilements). Thus even when these taints are not actually operative in an unenlightened person, he or she is still not equivalent to an enlightened person, since the unenlightened person still has a possession of the negative taints. But in the case of an enlightened person not only has the possession of negative taints been completely disconnected, there is also a different dharma present, called 'non-possession' (*aprāpti*), which keeps the negative taints from ever occurring again.[10] Both *prāpti* and *aprāpti* were simply rejected as unnecessary – indeed a rather absurd reification of abstract qualities into fundamentally existent dharmas – by rival schools like Sautrāntika.

Sautrāntika

The name 'Sautrāntika' refers to 'those who take the sūtras as valid authority (*pramāṇa*), rather than later treatises (*śāstras*)' – where 'later treatises' means the Abhidharma (Yaśomitra, in Cox 1995: 39, 50). It is not clear how early this term came to be used for the group, or how it relates to another expression 'Dārṣṭāntika', 'those who utilise the method of examples'. According to the Japanese scholar Junsho Kato (in Cox 1995: 38–9), Dārṣṭāntika may have been an expression originally used for the followers of Sautrāntika by their opponents, while 'Sautrāntika' was their own name for themselves. As we have seen already, there is no Sautrāntika ordination lineage. Monks who described themselves as 'Sautrāntika' were no doubt frequently ordained according to the Sarvāstivāda rite. Their Sautrāntika affiliation indicated a particular stance in rarefied doctrinal discussion and debate. They were suspicious of the claim of the *Abhidharma Piṭaka* to be the word of the Buddha, and while in fact sharing much in common with their approach they were even more suspicious of the philosophising of certain later Abhidharma scholars. As Collett Cox puts it (drawing on the work of Kato):

> [It] is best not to construe the appellation 'Sautrāntika' as entailing either a distinct ordination lineage or a defined set of doctrinal positions. Instead, it indicates a reliance only upon the Buddha's verified teaching in the *sūtras* that ensures consistency with correct principle in contrast to the faulty reasoning that it is assumed undermines Abhidharma

> treatises. Doctrinally, the Sautrāntika perspective can be characterised only by a rejection of the definitive Sarvāstivādin position that factors exist in the three time periods. Therefore the appellation 'Sautrāntika' could have been used to encompass a broad range of individual opinions that conform to these general guidelines, rather than to a defined and delimited set of doctrinal opinions.
>
> (Cox 1995: 40)

The presence of scholars favouring Sautrāntika shows the vitality and vigour of philosophical debate within the Buddhist tradition. Doctrinal positions were not identical with ordination lineages, and within one monastic group no doubt in the same monastery there could be radical disagreement and discussion concerning doctrinal issues within the context of a common rule of conduct. Followers of Sautrāntika rejected the existence of dharmas in the three times, which they saw as necessarily implying the permanence of dharmas. Actually only the present dharma exists. The past dharma did exist, and the future dharma (assuming the appropriate conditions come together) will exist. But only the present dharma actually exists (see *Abhidharmakośa* 5: 25 ff.). The Sautrāntika took from the Sarvāstivāda, however, the idea that the present stage of a dharma lies in the dharma's exerting its characteristic activity. Thus exerting activity now becomes the mark not of the present stage of the dharma as such, but its very existence. To be in fact *is* to exert activity. But it follows from this that a dharma cannot be something that remains for some time *and then* exerts its activity. If hypothetically it existed for some time before acting then in the moments during which the dharma is not acting it actually could not exist, since to be *is* to act. Likewise if the dharma hypothetically existed for some time *after* exerting its activity then during those moments too it could not actually exist. Thus the dharma must exist only in the moment (*kṣaṇa*) in which it exerts its activity. And that moment cannot itself have any time span, since if the moment had a time span then there would be the first moment of a moment, the second moment of a moment, and so on. If that were the case, then there would be the question of whether the dharma exerted its activity in the first moment of the moment, or in a subsequent moment of the moment. Whatever the answer, it would follow that the dharma actually existed in only one moment of the moment. And this process could be traced to infinity, unless one adopted the position that the temporal moment is not itself divisible into further moments. Thus the moment in which a dharma acts, in which existence occurs, has no time span beyond itself. It is absolutely instantaneous, so short that it can only be said to mark the infinitely short time-difference between the non-existence before its existence, and the non-existence after its existence. To be is to cease. Cessation is the very nature of being, and is said to occur to a dharma through its very nature as existing. We are here stretching the bounds of language. The existence of a dharma is so short in time that we can no longer speak of it in terms of 'being' at all. Life can best be viewed as an ever-flowing process, and all talk of things, of beings, is merely practical convenience that can easily mislead and engender attachment and consequential suffering.

The epistemology of all of this was particularly considered by the philosophers Diṅnāga (fifth or sixth century CE) and Dharmakīrti (seventh century), although it is not clear what the relationship was between their views and the Sautrāntika of, say, Vasubandhu in the *Abhidharmakośabhāṣya*. If what actually exists endures for an infinitely small period of time before ceasing, then it follows that we never really see what we think we see. By the time we have seen something, in any normal sense of 'seeing', that thing has ceased to exist. According to Diṅnāga (*Pramāṇasamuccaya* 1) only the very first moment of a veridical perceptual act apprehends what is actually there, the dharma. This first moment is thus referred to as 'without construction' (*nirvikalpa*). The subsequent moments of what we normally call a 'perception' bring about the construction of a 'thing seen', which as we understand it is of course not a momentary entity at all. These stages are called 'with construction' (*savikalpa*). Since, however, non-momentary entities do not exist these subsequent stages embody a process of falsification through linguistic and conceptual reification, associating the actual momentary real (known as the *svalakṣaṇa*, that which is self-characterising) with a non-momentary recurrently instantiated universal (*sāmānya*) which as something non-momentary cannot really exist at all. Thus what we think we see is actually a constructed image, as such a fiction, and by the time the image (*ākāra*) has been fully constructed the original dharma has long ceased.[11]

Followers of Sautrāntika utterly rejected the Sarvāstivādin theory of *prāpti*, possession, along with the idea that a past dharma is able to cause its effect because the past dharma still exists as past. According to the Sautrāntika theory, what happens in the case of *karman* and its effect is that when e.g. a wicked intention occurs the subsequent psychological continuum or series (*saṃtāna*) of the person who has that intention is no longer what it was. It is directly modified, and each moment of that series now bears the modification (perhaps analogous to a genetic imprint). The last moment of the series *qua* modified series has a special capacity to produce the effect. Thus the effect is the direct result of the preceding moment of the modified series, which is a result of the previous moment, and so on back to the original unwholesome intention. The images used to explain this process are of a 'seed' and 'perfuming'. Thus the unwholesome intention is said to have deposited a seed in the mental continuum, the nature of which is to transform until it issues in a shoot and then a flower, the result. The existence of a flower is the result of a process of transformation from the seed. Lest we are misled by this image to think of the modification of the continuum as itself an additional dharma, it is said that that the influence of the unwholesome intention is like perfuming – there is no additional thing, but the series is now imbued with a different fragrance. It is not obvious however that the 'seeds' and the 'perfuming' could actually be there in the normal everyday level of consciousness (they are not constantly *experienced* as such). Some Sautrāntikas put forward the suggestion that there is a subtle level of consciousness in which this occurs. That subtle consciousness continues through the lifetimes up until its destruction at nirvāṇa. It is held to contain not just the seeds laid down by our intentions but also seeds for the emergence of the whole phenomenal world, implicated as it is in mental construction. Possibly too there are even innate seeds for wholesome activity. These theories contributed to the Yogācāra doctrine of the 'substratum consciousness' (*ālayavijñāna*; q.v.).

Finally, as we have seen, the Sarvāstivāda speaks of three unconditioned dharmas. The most important of these is nirvāṇa itself. As dharmas these bear primary or fundamental existence (they are *dravyas*). Followers of Sautrāntika refused to accept with Sarvāstivāda that any of these unconditioned dharmas are entities, or existents (*bhāva*). They are just ways of talking about negations. Nirvāṇa is not a positive thing, but a simple negation, a non-existent (*abhāva*), the simple cessation and therefore non-existence of greed, hatred and delusion, suffering, and all the factors of saṃsāra.

Theravāda

It is normal in introductory works on Buddhism to equate Theravāda with the Buddhism of its canon, the Pāli Canon. Since for convenience and historical reasons the Pāli Canon is usually the source employed for outlining 'basic' and therefore presumably earliest Buddhism, it is often not properly appreciated that the Theravāda is actually both a Vinaya tradition and a doctrinal school in just the same way as Sarvāstivāda is. Both Theravāda and Sarvāstivāda considered themselves to be simply explicating and defending the original Buddhism of the Buddha. Both could claim great antiquity, and both were nevertheless schools that developed over many centuries. Both schools had a very great deal in common, but also doctrinal differences between themselves and with other schools. As does Sarvāstivāda, the Theravāda as a doctrinal school relies extensively on exegetical works, such as the *Milindapañha* ('Questions of [King] Milinda'), the commentaries to e.g. the *Abhidhamma Piṭaka*, and particularly the great *Visuddhimagga* ('Path of Purity') of Buddhaghosa. The Theravāda also contains among the texts in its *Abhidhamma Piṭaka* one work, the *Kathāvatthu* ('Points of Controversy') which set out to combat other views and thus position Theravāda as a doctrinal school in opposition to its rivals.

According to questionable tradition, doctrinal divisions occurred between Sarvāstivāda and a group known in Sanskrit as 'Sthaviravāda' ('the Doctrine of the Elders') over the issue of the existence of dharmas in the three times. The Sthaviravādins declared themselves to be 'Distinctionists' (Sanskrit: *Vibhajyavādins*; Pāli: *Vibhajjavādins*). They accepted that dharmas exist in the present but denied that they exist in the future. As regards the past, the Distinctionists wished to make a distinction between a wholesome or unwholesome intention that has already issued its karmic fruit, which could no longer be said to exist, and that which has not issued its fruit, which must be held still to exist. The name 'Sthaviravāda' is in Pāli 'Theravāda', and Theravādins are indeed happy also to be called 'Vibhajjavādins'. However the Theravādins clearly cannot actually be identical with the Sthaviravādins of this ancient dispute since the traditional Theravādin position on dharmas in the three times is that only the present dharma exists (see *Kathāvatthu* 1: 6).

A unique Theravādin doctrine is that of the *bhavaṅga*. The *bhavaṅga* is an inactive level of mind that is still present when no mental activity is occurring, as in the case of so-called 'unconsciousness', or deep sleep. When e.g. a visual perception occurs, the mind emerges from the state of *bhavaṅga* and 'adverts' to the visual object, taking its part in a complex process of experiencing, receiving the data, and possibly investigating the object, determining it, grasping, it, and identifying it. But the Theravāda view is that at the end of each process of consciousness the mind returns to the state of *bhavaṅga*, no matter how short that return may be. The *bhavaṅga* is also the level of mind that makes the link between a dying person and the rebirth. When the causal link occurs, and consciousness first arises in the embryo in the womb, that consciousness is the *bhavaṅga*, determined by the karmic forces of previous lives. The link between the consciousness of the dying person and that of the rebirth is direct. The Theravāda denies that there is any intermediate state (*antarābhava*) between death and rebirth, a theory accepted by

Sarvāstivāda and more familiar in the West from its espousal by Tibetans in works like the *Bar do thos grol* (Bardo thödrol; the 'Tibetan Book of the Dead'). The particular *bhavaṅga* is thus the basic level of mind of an individual, linking together all the experiences of a lifetime and making the connection between death and rebirth.

The Theravāda appears to have been much less interested than schools like the Sarvāstivāda in issues concerning the ontology of the *dhamma*. Nevertheless the very nature of the Abhidhamma project necessitated drawing some distinction between entities like cabbages and kings which are constructed out of dhammas, and dhammas themselves which even if the results of causes and conditions are not constructs and thus have their own unshared, unique, existence. This point is reflected in the definition of the *dhamma* which occurs in post-canonical Pāli texts: 'Dhammas are so-called because they hold (*dhārentī*) their own-existence' (Pāli: *sabhāva*; Sanskrit: *svabhāva*). This is of course the same idea that is so central to Sarvāstivāda ontology, even if the Theravāda seems to have had little interest in its implications and development.

Pudgalavāda

The Pudgalavāda, or 'Doctrine of the Person' (*pudgala*) is a notorious doctrine particularly associated with two schools and their offshoots, the Vātsīputrīya and the Sāmmatīya. Unfortunately very little of their texts survives, and most of our knowledge of their unique doctrines comes from attacks by other schools. The Theravādin *Kathāvatthu* begins with this doctrine, there is an important discussion in the Sarvāstivādin Abhidharma work the *Vijñānakāya*, and a lengthy section of the *Abhidharmakośa* is also devoted to its criticism. The best known surviving Pudgalavāda text is only in Chinese translation, but has been given the Sanskrit title of *Sammitīyanikāya Śāstra*. There is also extant in Chinese another Pudgalavādin work given the title of *Tridharmaka Śāstra*.[12]

Scholars often refer to the calculation by the seventh-century

Chinese pilgrim to India Hsüan-tsang, that about a quarter of the Buddhist monks in India at that time were followers of the Sāmmatīya (or Sāmmitīya) school (Lamotte 1988: 542–5, 608). As we shall see, the doctrine of the *pudgala* (Pāli: *puggala*) appears on the surface to be in tension with the Buddhist espousal of Not-Self (*anātman*). It was strongly opposed by other Buddhist schools. Followers of Pudgalavāda were accused of having all but ceased to be Buddhist. I agree very much with Rupert Gethin (1998: 223), however, when he points out that even if Hsüan-tsang is right in his calculation this may well entail only that the Sāmmatīya was the most widespread and popular Vinaya (ordination) lineage. It need not entail that all the monks so ordained held to the actual doctrine of the *pudgala*. Nevertheless, it seems likely that, in spite of the dearth of Pudgalavāda texts, the espousal of its characteristic doctrine was by no means rare among Buddhists in ancient India.

Lance Cousins (1994: 22) has suggested that the earliest source for the Pudgalavāda controversy is the *Kathāvatthu* (third century BCE). This text is quite clear that the Pudgalavādins hold that there exists something called a *pudgala* ('person(hood)') *from an ultimate point of view, as a real thing* (see *Kathāvatthu* 1). That is, the *pudgala* has the status of an additional dharma, an irreducible datum, a primary existent. This contrasts with the position acceptable to other schools, like the Theravāda or Sarvāstivāda, that any personhood, any *pudgala*, is just a conceptual construct (*prajñapti*; secondary existent), a name we give for practical purposes to the patterned flow of dharmas explained in terms of the five aggregates. That the Pudgalavādins wished the *pudgala* to be seen as existing from an ultimate point of view is also confirmed by the later *Vijñānakāya* (*c.* second century BCE – first century CE; Potter *et al.* 1996: 367–70). The issue is complicated, however, by the fact that the *Sāmmitīyanikāya Śāstra* (pre-fourth or fifth centuries CE) asserts that the *pudgala*, while existing and a datum that has to be taken into consideration, is actually a conventional conceptual construct (Potter 1999: 355–7). At perhaps the same time Vasubandhu, in the *Abhidharmakośa*, portrayed the Pudgalavādins as holding that the existence of the *pudgala* is neither by way of a primary existent (a *dravya*) nor by way of a secondary existent (a *prajñapti*; see Cousins 1994: 18). It is possible that under criticism the Pudgalavādins gradually clarified their position.

Adherents of the *pudgala* claim that it is neither the same as nor different from the aggregates. If it were the same as the aggregates then the *pudgala* would be conditioned, and when the aggregates were destroyed the person would be destroyed. This would be annihilationist, and it would also entail that after death the Tathāgata certainly could not be said to exist. In that case why did the Buddha refuse to answer the question concerning whether or not the Tathāgata exists after death? On the other hand if the *pudgala* were different from the aggregates it would be unconditioned, in fact a Self like the *ātman*, and subject to all the Buddhist criticisms of the concept of a Self. This would be to fall into the great mistake of eternalism. Thus the *pudgala* is neither identical to nor different from the aggregates, and neither conditioned nor unconditioned. In fact, it is said to be 'indefinable' (*avaktavya*). The *pudgala* is the subject of experiences, the doer of wholesome and unwholesome deeds, the one that undergoes karmic results, and the *pudgala* is also said to be what transmigrates. It is the *pudgala* that attains nirvāṇa. Unsurprisingly opponents felt that this is in fact the *ātman* in another guise. The so-called *pudgala* necessarily must be reducible to the dharmas which make up the aggregates – in which case the Pudgalavādins would hold the same view as other Buddhists – or must be a separate reality, in which case the Pudgalavādins would hold the *ātman* position of Brahmanic Hindus.

And yet it seems to me that the Pudgalavādins were wrestling with genuine philosophical problems here, and their position is perhaps subtler than it is often portrayed. The Vātsīputrīya-Sāmmitīya tradition may have had a particular interest in Vinaya matters, in which case their concern with personhood could have been significant in terms of an interest in moral responsibility. It is indeed persons who engage in moral acts, and attain enlightenment. For moral responsibility there has to be some sense in which the *same person* receives reward or punishment as the one who did the original deed. It is persons who have experiences of love and hate. All this, as Pudgalavāda sources make clear, has to be taken as given. The question is, what is the status of personhood? It is arguable (as has the modern philosopher P. F. Strawson (1959)) that personhood is an irreducible datum, and cannot be explained away in terms of constructions out of arms, legs, feelings, intentions, and so on, or a series of ever-changing mental and physical moments. Constructions *presuppose* the existence of persons. And it is also arguable that if we cannot say the same person is reborn, or the same person attains nirvāṇa, there would be no point in considering rebirth or the spiritual path. If all this is correct then personhood would not be reducible to the aggregates. And yet it is also clear that it makes no sense to think of personhood as a separate real thing, as if it could float free from the living being of arms, legs, feelings, and so on. Personhood is a different logical category from arms and legs. If we were to take a living human being, or a tree, apart we would not find personhood, or treeness, as an additional component. Thus it seems to me it might make sense to speak of an irreducible datum which is neither the same as nor different from the constituents.[13]

Possibly it was something like this that the Pudgalavādins were thinking of (through a glass darkly) when they started by speaking of the *pudgala* as a reality, existing from the ultimate (i.e. irreducible) point of view, before switching to speaking of the *pudgala* as conceptualised in dependence upon the aggregates. The Pudgalavādins were constrained almost to the point of absurdity by the language of Buddhist scholasticism. The *pudgala* in itself, personhood in itself, cannot be spoken of. One can only speak of personhood in dependence upon living beings, beings with e.g. arms, legs, feelings, and so on, even if personhood is not reducible to arms, legs, feelings, and so on. Thus personhood in itself is indeed indefinable, it is *sui generis*, and personhood can be spoken of, conceptualised in dependence upon the aggregates, without this making personhood a conceptual construction (*prajñapti*) in the way in which this is understood by other Buddhist schools, reducible to the aggregates. Yet personhood is also not a separate reality (*dravya*) capable of being encountered apart from the aggregates. Personhood is not itself a conditioned thing in the way that e.g. the human body is, and for the Pudgalavādin personhood continues from life to life and into enlightenment. Nevertheless personhood also could not be an unconditioned dharma or an *ātman*. For personhood is (possessed by) this person, Archibald or Freda, and it is the person Archibald who marries the person Freda, not some separate eternal reality marrying some separate eternal reality.

The Pudgalavādins found puzzlement and problems where their fellow Buddhists found clarity and simplicity. The problem with unclarity and puzzlement is that they can often seem absurd. But some absurdity, it seems to me, may be profounder than it seems.

Mahāsāṃghikas

The best known Mahāsāṃghika doctrine is that of the 'supramundane nature of the Buddha', and the Mahāsāṃghika 'supramundane doctrine' (*lokottaravāda*) appears to be characteristic of the school. Indeed the Mahāsāṃghikas split into a number of sub-schools, one of which is known specifically as the *Lokottaravādins*. A single text of this school survives in Sanskrit, the *Mahāvastu* (the 'Great Affair'), which describes itself as the Vinaya of the Lokottaravādin sub-school of the Mahāsāṃghikas. The supramundane doctrine itself is found expressed in only a small section of this text, however. Stated briefly, the doctrine asserts that all the actions of the Buddha which appear worldly (*laukika*), to be the same actions as ordinary people engage in, are in reality extraordinary, 'supramundane' (*lokottara*).

All Buddhist traditions agree that once a person has become a Buddha he is radically transformed and no longer the same as an ordinary person. Thus the Buddha has various miraculous powers not possessed by ordinary people, he has the 112 marks of a superior person (*mahāpuruṣa*), his skin is capable of glowing with a golden hue, and he is even said to be able to live for an aeon if he so wishes. A Buddha, as such, is said to be just that – neither a man nor a god, but a Buddha. There is a saying attributed to the Buddha preserved in the Pāli Canon to the effect that though the Buddha was born in the world, he was not tainted by it (see *Kathāvatthu* 18: 1). Perhaps it was sayings such as this which suggested to the Mahāsāṃghikas that although he appeared to need to eat, sleep, bathe, undergo the effects of *karman*, take medicine, get old, and so on, in reality the Buddha was not subject to any of these needs. The Buddha had actually gone beyond all these needs, and did all these things simply in order to conform to the way of things in the world. He appeared to be like the rest of us, but inside he was really quite different. Actually Buddhas do not experience hunger, tiredness, dirt on their bodies, illness, or any of the other taints of ordinary life. Actually, although Buddhas appear to be sleeping or teaching, walking or talking, really they are in constant meditation. That is, a Buddha is not *laukika* (worldly, from Sanskrit *loka*, world). He is *lokottara*. The word *lokottara*, literally 'beyond the world', supramundane, is an expression used throughout Buddhism in the context of enlightenment, the higher reaches of the path to enlightenment, and enlightened beings. To say a Buddha is *lokottara* is to say that he is not *laukika*, that is, he is not unliberated, he really is enlightened. This would be acceptable to all Buddhists. And what a wonderful, almost inconceivable, thing it is to be enlightened. What the Mahāsāṃghikas are doing is giving a specific gloss on what the implications of this supramundane status are. That gloss stretches language and our expectations in admiration and wonder.

Sometimes modern books suggest that the Mahāsāṃghika doctrine is that the Buddha was actually an illusory being, a mere appearance, or a fictitious being, a 'magical emanation' perhaps from some transcendent Buddha who is really on another plane. This is, I think, a misreading of the meaning of *lokottara* here, and is not the doctrine of the Mahāsāṃghikas in the *Mahāvastu*.[14] There is no suggestion in the *Mahāvastu* that the being who was to become the Buddha was not actually born in this world, and did not actually become enlightened here. His birth is indeed accompanied by many marvels, but that is only to be expected in the case of one who had just completed many aeons of progressively more extraordinary spiritual cultivation. What *is* illusory or fictitious about a Buddha, according to the Mahāsāṃghikas, is not his body as such, but his being subject to the normal human needs of food, sleep, washing, and so on. In other words, the illusion of the Buddha is the illusion of an extraordinary being appearing to be ordinary. And, crucially, there is no suggestion in non-Mahāyāna sources like the *Mahāvastu* that the Buddha did not die when he appeared to die. Much about his life may have been mere appearance out of conformity to the world. But his death was not.

There is one other doctrine found among some Mahāsāṃghikas that I also want to mention in passing. There is a text known as the *Lokānuvartana Sūtra* ('The Sūtra of Conformity with the World') which survives in Chinese and Tibetan translation and which also contains strongly expressed the Mahāsāṃghika supramundane teachings. It has been claimed that this sūtra may be one of the sources for the *Mahāvastu* (Harrison 1982: 224). The *Lokānuvartana Sūtra* is quoted and described in a later Indian source as a scripture of the Pūrvaśailas, which is known to be one of the sub-schools of the Mahāsāṃghikas. In that sūtra it is stated that all things, including all dharmas, are lacking in fundamental primary existence, intrinsic existence. This doctrine, of the universal emptiness of all things, even dharmas, is often thought of as characteristic of Mahāyāna sources like the *Perfection of Wisdom* literature and the Madhyamaka. Yet perhaps that is wrong.

5 Mahāyāna philosophy

The Perfection of Wisdom (*Prajñāpāramitā*)

As far as we can tell at the moment, the earliest specifically Mahāyāna literature consists of sūtras of the *Prajñāpāramitā*-type. Since these are Mahāyāna sūtras they thus claim a disputed status as the word of the Buddha. Within India itself the status of Mahāyāna sūtras was always disputed. The circulation of such sūtras was likely to have been much more a matter of individual and small-group activity (carried as treasures by individual wanderers, for example) than the activity of the Sangha of a Vinaya tradition as a whole. Moreover while Indian travellers wandered into Central Asia and thence to China, the wandering was not all one-way. Monks and nuns did indeed leave India for Central and Southeast Asia and China by sea and land routes, no doubt sometimes carrying with them their precious scriptures. These may have included certain scriptures central to the life of the monk or nun concerned but not considered authentic by the wider Sangha community. But of course we know that monks and nuns also came into the Holy Land of India from abroad. Recently Jan Nattier has argued with considerable plausibility that perhaps the most popular Mahāyāna *Prajñāpāramitā* text of all, the short *Heart* (*Hṛdaya*) *Sūtra*, was actually as a sūtra an apocryphal Chinese text abstracted and compiled from a Chinese translation of a much larger *Prajñāpāramitā* text. It may then have subsequently and successfully been introduced into

India itself, probably by the Chinese pilgrim Hsüan-tsang, and translated into Sanskrit (Nattier 1992). The same introduction from outside India has been claimed for the main sūtra of Bhaiṣajyaguru, the Medicine Buddha (Birnbaum 1980: 52 ff.). This sūtra was well known enough in India to be quoted by the great Indian scholar and poet Śāntideva in the early eighth century but could well have been introduced into India at an earlier date.

The *Prajñāpāramitā* literature is large and repetitive. Sūtras are commonly named by the number of verses (the 'Eight-thousand Verse Perfection of Wisdom' (*Aṣṭasāhasrikā Prajñāpāramitā*), for example). There is some agreement among scholars that from an original core the basic text (or idea) was expanded as far as the *Hundred-thousand Verse*, and then contracted into shorter 'summary sūtras'. The earliest version does indeed appear to be the *Aṣṭasāhasrikā*, although what Edward Conze (1960) sees as its verse summary, the *Ratnaguṇasaṃcayagāthā*, may be the very earliest form of the text. The *Pañcaviṃśatisāhasrikā* ('Twenty-five Thousand Verse'), also extremely important, is probably a little later. There is some disagreement as regards the dating of what is one of the most popular *Prajñāpāramitā* texts, the famous *Vajracchedikā Sūtra* (the 'Diamond', or 'Diamond Cutter', otherwise known as the 'Three-hundred Verse'). Edward Conze would take it as an example of a later summary sūtra (see Williams 1989: 40–2).[1]

One has to be very careful in outlining the core message of the *Prajñāpāramitā* literature not to explain it too fully. These are sūtras not systematic philosophical or doctrinal ('Buddhalogical') treatises. They are very clear that they have a message – a message that is repeated again and again – and that message is one of criticism and exhortation. It is a message of inspiration, perhaps the message of a Dharma-preacher (the *dharmabhāṇaka*), rather than the message of a philosopher or doctrinal theorist. The message is a message of exhortation to their fellows in the 'non-Mahāyāna' world. But when we seek to explain more fully, in a more systematically rational manner, the sermon of the Perfection of Wisdom we almost inevitably find ourselves employing the language and perspective of Madhyamaka philosophy or, in explaining the path of the bodhisattva, language of much later path-structures. This systematic explanation we shall come to very soon, but for the moment let us just heed the sermon itself. It has three principal themes, repeated and illustrated again and again as if to seep into the deepest recesses of the Good Buddhist's mind. The first theme is that of the very peak, the perfection (*pāramitā*), of wisdom (*prajñā*). Its content is emptiness (*śūnyatā*). And its context is the path and practices of a bodhisattva, one whose aim is not just enlightenment (obtained by arhats), but Perfect Buddhahood for the benefit of all sentient beings.

The Perfection of Wisdom (prajñā)

Broadly speaking, *prajñā* is the state of mind that comes from properly understanding something. In Buddhism, as a technical term, it is used primarily for that understanding which sees how it really is in contrast to the way things appear to be. Just as that seeing can both be a matter of understanding *that* things are really like this, and also actually being in a state of mind where one *sees* directly how it is, so we can refer to different levels of *prajñā*, from understanding to non-conceptual insight. We have seen already that Buddhist thought was from the beginning marked by a distinction between the way things appear to be and the way they actually are. It should thus come as no surprise to find that within the framework of Abhidharma *prajñā* is used to refer to discernment of the ultimate primary existents. As we have seen, they are to be distinguished from conceptual constructs. Therefore *prajñā* refers to the discrimination of dharmas.[2] The *Prajñāpāramitā* literature refers frequently to *not* discriminating dharmas, but its message is nevertheless encapsulated within the specific Abhidharma project and it is within the Abhidharma framework that we must understand the expression 'perfection' of *prajñā*. The Perfection of Wisdom speaks not of the wrongness of what had previously been considered to be wisdom, but rather of its *perfection*. Previous wisdom is indeed wisdom, but it is imperfect. Mahāyāna texts will treat a series of 'perfections' (*pāramitā*) mastered by the bodhisattva. The common list is six – the perfections of giving, morality, patience, effort, meditative concentration, and finally wisdom – but the perfection of wisdom is primary, said to lead the others as a man with eyes leads those who are blind.

The perfection of *prajñā* is the final *prajñā*, the final proper understanding of the way things truly are. But it seems to me that the perfection of *prajñā* – although it is stated with such missionary zeal in the *Prajñāpāramitā* texts – is in so many ways an affirmation of what has gone before. If, as we shall see, all dharmas are empty, lacking own-existence, then that is merely to confirm their own status as ontologically no more than tables, persons, or forests. There is no question that tables, persons, and forests are conceptual existents, empty, just as the previous Abhidharma thinkers had shown. All are agreed on *that*.

Emptiness (śūnyatā)

What is immediately apparent to anyone who glances at a Perfection of Wisdom text is the endless list of things that are said to be 'empty, like a magical illusion'. This is indeed the principal philosophical teaching of the *Prajñāpāramitā* literature, and it was only possible because of the Abhidharma framework that we have examined previously. Buddhism from the very beginning had used the terms 'empty' (*śūnya*) and 'emptiness' (*śūnyatā*) to apply to the truth discovered by the eye of proper understanding (*prajñā*), the eye of the Buddha. First this was with reference to the five aggregates empty of Self or anything pertaining to a Self. Then it was applied to the whole list of seventy-five, eighty-two or however many classes of fundamental constituents (*dharmas*) discovered by the different Abhidharmas likewise to be empty of Self or anything pertaining to Self. In addition, the term *śūnya* was also used in the Abhidharma (perhaps by an almost imperceptible shift in meaning) to refer to the nature of secondary, conceptual, existents empty of any status other than conceptual existents, empty of own-existence, empty of primary, irreducible, existence. Persons, tables, forests, and so on are empty of Self, but they are also empty of irreducible primary existence. Here these amount to the same thing. But while there is no Self at all, and all things are empty of Self, for the Abhidharma there *must* exist some things which have primary existence, and secondary conceptual existents are themselves empty of that primary existence which is, of course, possessed by primary existents, dharmas. The absence of Self cannot mean there are actually no primary existents at all.

But in the *Prajñāpāramitā* literature the same term *śūnya* is used to refer to absolutely everything, and it entails that absolutely everything is 'like a magical illusion'.[3] We need to be quite clear about the range of this claim, for there are scholars (such as Conze) who would want to limit it and argue for some sort of monistic Absolute – a primary existent, an Ultimate Reality *par excellence* – behind the *Prajñāpāramitā* negations. But the *Aṣṭasāhasrikā* (Eight-thousand Verse) is quite unequivocal:

> Even Nirvana, I say, is like a magical illusion, is like a dream. How much more so anything else! . . . Even if perchance there could be anything more distinguished, of that too I would say that it is like an illusion, like a dream.
>
> (*Aṣṭasāhasrikāprajñāpāramitā*, trans. Conze: 99)

In other words absolutely all things have the same status as persons, tables, and forests.[4] They are all conceptual constructs and therefore cannot be vested with own-existence. Crucially, they therefore cannot be grasped, one cannot substitute grasping after tables and so on with grasping after dharmas as the refuge, the fixed point in a world of disappointment and suffering. Thus the classical earlier *Prajñāpāramitā* literature constantly asks what is referred to by the term *x*, what dharma this is, with the response that nothing can be found, nothing can be grasped, and yet the bodhisattva should heroically resist all fear. To see otherwise is to grasp, and to grasp is to miss enlightenment. Thus enlightenment comes from ceasing to grasp even the most subtle sources of attachment, and this ceasing to grasp requires seeing those things which could serve as sources of attachment as empty, mere conceptual constructs. *All* things are empty. On the level of what is an ultimate, primary existent there is nothing. On such a level therefore there is an endless absence, an endless emptiness. Thus to think that dharmas have primary existence is to grasp. As an exhortation this is an appeal to complete letting-go. For both philosophical reasons and also perhaps existential reasons this teaching of emptiness may for some have been terrifying. It certainly looks like nihilism, and it encourages a deep letting-go in meditation that could indeed be the true spiritual equivalent of the going-forth that the monk underwent in leaving family, friends, and village. At least, that is the impression one gets from the texts. Yet emptiness is also the antidote to fear, a fear which in its frequent mention must have been some problem for Buddhists at this time.[5] For if all is empty, what is there left to fear?

The bodhisattva

The Perfection of Wisdom literature itself does not claim that to see all things without exception as empty is some special teaching for followers of the Mahāyāna. Since any other perspective would involve grasping, it follows that it is necessary to see emptiness in order to attain cessation of grasping and therefore in order to attain *any* state that could be called one of enlightenment. As the *Aṣṭasāhasrikā* puts it, 'whether one wants to train on the level of Disciple, or Pratyekabuddha, or Bodhisattva, – one should listen to this perfection of wisdom, . . . and in this very perfection of wisdom should one be trained and exert oneself' (trans. Conze 1973: 84).[6]

Thus as far as the *Aṣṭasāhasrikā* is concerned it is not possible finally to attain complete cessation of grasping as long as one sees some sort of contrast between the ontological status of dharmas and that of tables, persons, and forests. That is, one cannot cease craving as long as one sees an actual, real, ontological distinction between primary existents and secondary conceptual existents. Under such circumstances it would therefore not be possible to attain *any* degree of enlightenment. Note however that it does not follow from this that there is anything wrong as such with analysis into dharmas. To know that tables are conceptual constructs, as is taught by those who would analyse into dharmas, would I think have been taken as knowing what is correct, and as indeed contributing to letting-go of attachment for tables. The problem however lies in considering that there is some fundamental ontological contrast with dharmas themselves, which might make dharmas suitable objects of attachment.

Although insight into complete emptiness is necessary for any enlightenment, *Prajñāpāramitā* sūtras constantly contrast the aspiration of their hero or heroine, the bodhisattva, with that of one who aims for a lower goal, which is to say one aiming to become an arhat. The idea of a bodhisattva is not new to the Mahāyāna. The bodhisattva is accepted by all Buddhist traditions as one who has seriously taken a vow, properly speaking in the presence of a previous Buddha, to follow the path to Buddhahood. Thus the person who was to become Śākyamuni Buddha also took a vow to become a Perfect Buddha many aeons ago in the presence of a previous Buddha. There is however a problem here. Presumably Śākyamuni actually could have attained enlightenment for himself (the state of an arhat) in the presence of that previous Buddha. Why did he undergo the many, many rebirths necessary in order to follow the path to Buddhahood if the eventual goal of Buddhahood is not qualitatively different to – not in some significant way very much superior to – the state of an arhat? We are told that he undertook the long path to Buddhahood out of compassion, in order to be able to help others more effectively – but why? Clearly it could not have been for some additional quality that would be of benefit to himself, since there is held to be no greater fulfilment *for oneself* than freedom from suffering, nirvāṇa, the state of an arhat. Thus Śākyamuni in his previous life must have taken the vow of a bodhisattva solely out of altruism. This is however absurd if there is nothing about being a Buddha which is qualitatively superior, indeed spiritually superior, to being an ordinary arhat. But if there *is* something qualitatively superior, it can only be described in terms of altruism, since there is nothing left for the Buddha to gain for himself beyond becoming an arhat. And if this Buddhahood is qualitatively superior, then those who do not attain an altruistic Buddhahood must be missing out on the *highest* spiritual goal.

Thus it seems to follow that Śākyamuni Buddha must have taken the vow to become a Perfect Buddha out of altruism, and the state of a Perfect Buddha must be qualitatively superior to that of nirvāṇa, the state of an arhat. That superiority must lie in its altruism. Therefore the bodhisattva vows, in the words of the *Aṣṭasāhasrikā*:

> My own self I will place in Suchness [the true way of things], and, so that all the world might be helped, I will place all beings in Suchness, and I will lead to Nirvana the whole immeasurable world of beings.
>
> (*Aṣṭasāhasrikāprajñāpāramitā*, trans. Conze: 163)

And yet the Perfection of Wisdom literature repeatedly states that the bodhisattva takes such great vows without perceiving that there is any actual being who is saved, for all is really empty. This is truly the Perfection of Wisdom.

Perhaps anyway it was some such reasoning as this that led to the exaltation of the way of the bodhisattva in Mahāyāna literature as a final spiritual career for all who can aspire to it. Whereas in non-Mahāyāna sources accounts of the bodhisattva career are descriptive – this is what great ones have done in the past – in Mahāyāna sources they become prescriptive. All should finally take upon themselves the vow of the bodhisattva, to attain Perfect Buddhahood for the benefit of all. Any other goal is relative to this great goal inferior, i.e. that of a Hīnayāna. Indeed in certain later strata of the Perfection of Wisdom literature we find accounts of the great abilities to help others of those well advanced on this bodhisattva path. Practitioners of this path are encouraged to gain what appear to be miraculous powers in order to benefit those who petition them. Very advanced, perhaps even nearly enlightened, bodhisattvas have immense abilities to help. Thus they become what have been called 'celestial bodhisattvas', such as Avalokiteśvara – particularly associated with compassion – or Mañjuśrī, the bodhisattva of wisdom, who have the ability to help, the wish to help, and great amounts of merit due to their immense good deeds done in the past. This is merit that they are happy to give away to others who are poor in their 'roots of merit' and are thus suffering the many pains of saṃsāra.[7]

Note – and this is important – that in the light of all of this it is far too simplistic to speak merely of 'nirvāṇa' within the context of Mahāyāna Buddhism. There is the nirvāṇa associated with the goal of becoming an arhat; there is the state of a pratyekabuddha; and there is also the full enlightenment associated in Mahāyāna with Perfect Buddhahood. It is common in Mahāyāna texts to refer to nirvāṇa contrasted with saṃsāra and indicate that the bodhisattva, and eventually a Buddha, in attaining freedom from suffering but not abandoning those in saṃsāra, is beyond this duality of nirvāṇa versus saṃsāra. The state of enlightenment attained by a Buddha is thus called a 'non-abiding' or 'not fixed' nirvāṇa (*apratiṣṭhitanirvāṇa*). It therefore becomes very problematic indeed to portray the bodhisattva, as do so many books available in the West, as *postponing* nirvāṇa. What nirvāṇa is he or she supposed to postpone? Clearly not that of an arhat or a pratyekabuddha, since these are said to be inferior nirvāṇas. And it is quite absurd to think (and as far as I know never said in Indian Buddhism) that the bodhisattva, who is portrayed as wishing to attain Buddhahood for the benefit of all sentient beings, literally postpones *Buddhahood*. There is no reason for a bodhisattva to postpone the *apratiṣṭhitanirvāṇa*. If this is what bodhisattvas do of course then any Buddha would have broken his or her vows. The Buddha would have to be taken absurdly as being in some sense deficient in compassion! We saw from the quote above taken from the *Aṣṭasāhasrikā* that the bodhisattva wishes to attain Buddhahood precisely in order better to help others. This is not to say that a text may not exhort the bodhisattva even to abandon Buddhahood as a selfish personal goal, in order to concentrate more fully on helping others. But the result of this is that one attains Buddhahood all the more quickly. This is indeed the true way to Buddhahood. Any alternative would be paradoxical.

Madhyamaka

By 'Buddhist philosophy' here I mean in the broadest sense discussions, speculations, and arguments concerning 'seeing things the way they really are' (*yathābhūtadarśana*). Just as Mahāyāna Buddhism as a whole can best be seen as a vision, an aspiration, within a Buddhism which therefore in itself is non-Mahāyāna, mainstream Buddhism, so I think Mahāyāna philosophy should be understood as a particular expression of and response to Buddhist philosophy as a whole. The name for Buddhist philosophy as a whole, it seems to me, is 'Abhidharma', in the sense that Abhidharma sets the agenda, the presuppositions and the framework for Buddhist philosophical thought, understood in the way in which I have delineated it. Philosophy here developed within Abhidharma discussions among what were probably a minority of elite monks. Mahāyāna philosophy, far from representing a negation of the approach of the Abhidharma, is best seen as a series of strategies within the Abhidharma enterprise.

The name 'Madhyamaka' ('Middling') refers primarily to a school of Buddhist philosophy, and that which pertains to Madhyamaka – a follower or a text, for example – is a Mādhyamika. The use of this name for the school and its characteristic philosophical position appears to be lacking in our earliest Madhyamaka sources. It cannot be found at all in the philosophical works of Nāgārjuna (*c.* second century CE), for example, usually thought of as the founder of Madhyamaka. Nāgārjuna does indicate nevertheless that he considers himself to hold to a distinctive position by employing the expression *śūnyatāvādin*, one who holds to the position of emptiness (*Vigrahavyāvartanī* v. 69). Of course, Buddhism from the beginning had referred to itself as a 'Middle Way'. For a Mādhyamika, however, the principal significance of claiming to be the follower of the Middle Way *par excellence* is an understanding of emptiness (*śūnyatā*) as the middle between eternalism and annihilationism. This understanding undoubtedly can be traced back to universalisation of the idea of dependent origination (*pratītyasamutpāda*) as the middle between those who hold to the eternal existence of an unchanging Self, and those who hold to annihilation at death. Thus it should come as no surprise to find in Madhyamaka sources emptiness equated with dependent origination (*Madhyamakakārikā* (*MMK*) 24: 18). Because even dharmas originate due to causes and conditions they too must be empty of primary, substantial existence.

Therefore the way by which Nāgārjuna and his followers sought rationally to demonstrate the Perfection of Wisdom claim that all things without exception are akin to illusions was through showing that all things are without their own-existence (all things are *niḥsvabhāva*, they are secondary existents, conceptual constructs). They are this way because they are the results of causes and conditions, they are dependently-originated. In general terms a Mādhyamika in Buddhist philosophy is a *śūnyatāvādin*, one who holds to the absolute universality of emptiness, i.e. absence of own-existence. He or she is therefore one who holds and sets out to demonstrate that absolutely everything is nothing more than a conceptual construct.[8] The founder of this approach is always said to be Nāgārjuna, although there is some reason to think that arguments associated with Nāgārjuna may have been extant before his time.

I do not wish to say very much here about the legendary life of Nāgārjuna, or that of his great disciple Āryadeva. Modern scholars do not accept the traditional Tibetan account which would have Nāgārjuna living for some six hundred years and becoming both the great Mādhyamika philosopher as well as a Tantric yogin and wonderworker (*siddha*). They prefer to speak of at least two Nāgārjunas. There is also great debate over which works can be attributed authentically to the philosopher Nāgārjuna.[9] As far as Madhyamaka philosophy is concerned, however, there is some agreement that the following complete works might reasonably be attributed to the Master:

(i) The *Madhyamakakārikā* ('Verses on Madhyamaka', perhaps originally simply called 'Wisdom' (*Prajñā*), commonly abbreviated as *MMK*) – Nāgārjuna's main work, still extant in Sanskrit;

(ii) The *Vigrahavyāvartanī*; verses extant in Sanskrit together with an autocommentary – a reply by Nāgārjuna to his critics.

Save for a few fragments the following works survive only in Tibetan and sometimes Chinese translation:

(iii) *Yuktiṣaṣṭikā* ('Sixty Verses on Reasoning (*yukti*)');
(iv) *Śūnyatāsaptati* ('Seventy Verses on Emptiness');
(v) *Vaidalyaprakaraṇa* – attacking the categories of the Hindu Nyāya epistemologists;
(vi) *Ratnāvalī* ('The Jewel Garland', a long epistle apparently to a king. A shorter royal epistle also attributed to Nāgārjuna is the *Suhṛllekha*);
(vii) The *Catuḥstava* – four hymns also reasonably reliably attributed to Nāgārjuna.

As far as Nāgārjuna's disciple Āryadeva is concerned, by far his most important work is the *Catuḥśatakakārikā* ('Four Hundred Verses'), extant in Tibetan and Chinese translation.

It is not obvious what it means to talk of sub-schools of Madhyamaka in India. Indeed it is not clear how far Madhyamaka thought in India was very influential or taken very seriously. Possible exceptions are the so-called Yogācāra-Svātantrika Madhyamaka from the eighth century onwards, and perhaps Candrakīrti's tradition of Madhyamaka in the eleventh century. This was long after his own death in the seventh century.[10] All Mādhyamikas hold to complete absence of primary, substantial existence, and thus to the universality of conceptual construction. Tibetan scholars, recognising that there were nevertheless differences and debates in India on various issues between Mādhyamikas, subsequently divided Mādhyamikas into Svātantrika and Prāsaṅgika Madhyamaka, dividing again Svātantrika into Sautrāntika-Svātantrika and Yogācāra-Svātantrika. Even so, there was some dispute as to exactly what distinguished thinkers of each sub-school. To take just one influential perspective, if we could follow the view of the

Tibetan Tsong kha pa (fourteenth–fifteenth centuries CE) then a Svātantrika Mādhyamika such as Bhāvaviveka (*c.* 500–70 CE) holds that *ultimately* all things lack own-existence (*svabhāva*). According to Tsong kha pa he appears not to hold this to be the case conventionally, from the pragmatic everyday point of view. For Candrakīrti the Prāsaṅgika, on the other hand, the very notion of own-existence, a *svabhāva*, is contradictory on either ultimate or conventional level. There is sometimes said to be a further difference between Svātantrika and Prāsaṅgika Madhyamaka as regards whether it is necessary to employ the proper logical form or 'syllogistic' structure of reasoning derived from the canons of Indian logic in order to refute the primary existents held by the opponent. The Svātantrikas are said to have argued that one should. For the rival Prāsaṅgikas it is sufficient to employ any reasoning at all which indicates a contradiction in the primary existents of the opponent and which he or she finds convincing, such as the use of favoured *prasaṅga* arguments, a kind of *reductio ad absurdum*. Moreover a Yogācāra-Svātantrika like Śāntarakṣita (seventh–eighth century CE) is held to differ from the Sautrāntika-Svātantrika Bhāvaviveka (not to mention the Prāsaṅgika Candrakīrti) particularly on the issue of the status of objects of experience. While all agree as Mādhyamikas that all things are merely conceptual constructs, Śāntarakṣita seems to have held that those conventional conceptual constructs are all of the nature of mind. In other words subject and object in all experience are of the same fundamental nature, which is in some sense mentalistic. In this respect Śāntarakṣita and his followers are like the Yogācāra (q.v.) school (*cittamātra* – 'mind-only'), although they are held to differ in denying that this mentalistic stuff ('consciousness', 'mind') is itself a primary existent, with its own-existence. Bhāvaviveka does not hold that subject and object are of the same stuff, and in this respect he is said to be similar to the Sautrāntika approach to these issues.[11]

It seems to me that the key to understanding Madhyamaka lies in a proper appreciation of the significance identifying emptiness and dependent origination had within the context of the Abhidharma distinction between substantial primary existence and secondary conceptual existence.[12] Thus I want to argue that Madhyamaka represents a strategy within an Abhidharma debate, an affirmation of the Abhidharma analysis as far as it goes combined with a claim to detect a contradiction in any ontological distinction between primary and secondary existence. Certain followers of Abhidharma had not thought through far enough the full ontological implications of the Abhidharma project. We have seen that to be a conceptual existent is to be capable of being dissolved away under a particular sort of critical analytic investigation. That investigation is an investigation that searches to find if *X* is the sort of thing that has existence in its own right. In other words it searches to find whether *X* can or cannot be dissolved into component parts that, as it were, bestow the existence of *X* upon it when conceptualised in a particular sort of way. Later Tibetan thinkers would refer to this sort of search as an 'ultimate investigation', a search to find out if *X* has ultimate (i.e. primary) existence or not. The existence of a table is a particular way (for particular purposes) of conceptualising the top, legs, and so on. Thus a conceptual existent does not have its existence contained within itself. It does not have own-existence, *svabhāva*. Its existence as such is given to it by conceptual construction. Thus it is *niḥsvabhāva*, lacking own-existence. Therefore in Madhyamaka philosophy a particular sort of analysis is carried out, an analysis which investigates each of the categories held by opponents to contain entities possessing own-existence in order to see whether those entities can be dissolved under this ultimate analysis.

Note also that in previous Abhidharma terms to have a *svabhāva* is to have a particular type of existence, an existence that cannot be dissolved away into component parts. It is therefore to have an existence that is not thought to be the result of the conventional conceptualising process. Not to have a *svabhāva* is still to exist, but that existence is contingent upon a conventional practical conceptualising activity, an existence nevertheless guaranteed by reducibility into primary existents. The contradiction considered within this model and at the heart of Nāgārjuna's demonstration of the truth of the ontology of the *Prajñāpāramitā* sūtras lies in the implication relationship between dependent origination and emptiness. For a previous follower of the Abhidharma, to be a conceptual existent is clearly to be the result of causes and conditions, and notably the conceptualising process. But to be a primary existent is also, in the main, to be the result of the causal process as well.[13] What justifies the primary existent is that it is an irreducible *into which* the secondary existent can be analysed. It is *that which must be.* Thus to be a primary existent is in most cases by no means to be unrelated to causes and conditions. Yet, Nāgārjuna wants to say, a secondary existent cannot be found to have existence in its own right because it can be reduced to primary existents. If that is so then its very being as a secondary conceptual existent is granted to it through existence being bestowed upon it by its causes and conditions. The concept of the *svabhāva* must therefore reduce (slide?) from that of own-existence when contrasted with constructed existence to that of *inherent*, or *intrinsic*, existence, i.e. self-contained existence, existence that is not bestowed upon it at all from outside. Inherent or intrinsic existence is an equivalent of existing from its own side, quite independent of the causal and conceptualising process. But anything that is the result of causes and conditions must lack its own inherent existence.

Thus while there may still be a relative distinction between 'primary' and 'secondary' existents (a table can still be analysed into parts), anything which is the result of causes and conditions must be *niḥsvabhāva*, that is, empty. If *X*, whatever it is, cannot be found when searched for under the sort of analysis that is investigating the (ultimate) existence of *X*, then *X* is empty. If *X* is the result of causes and conditions – particularly if it can be shown to be the result of conceptualisation – then *X* is empty. Hence Nāgārjuna applies analytic investigation to some of the principal categories of Buddhist thought as well as those of non-Buddhists, such as causation itself, movement, time, the Buddha, nirvāṇa, as well as the Self. He declares emptiness whenever anything is found to be the result of some sort of causal process. In this way the assertions of complete emptiness 'like an illusion' in the *Prajñāpāramitā* sūtras can be demonstrated through analytic investigation. It is shown through using dependent origination in the most impeccable Buddhist, even Abhidharma, manner.[14] As Nāgārjuna puts it:

> Whatever comes about conditioned by something else is quiescent from the point of view of inherent existence. Therefore both the process of origination and the act of production itself are quiescent. . . . Like an illusion, a dream or a castle in the air are production, duration and cessation declared to be.
>
> (*MMK* 7: 16/34)

Nāgārjuna's approach, therefore, is to take a category held to be capable of withstanding analysis – such as causation itself (in the famous *MMK* 1) – and analyse it. This is the sole concern of the Mādhyamika, to analyse the positions of the opponent, not to put forward counter-positions which might entail something of their own capable of resisting analysis. Hence Nāgārjuna's famous statement on *Vigrahavyāvartanī* 23 that he has no thesis (*pratijñā*) to prove. How can there be causation, since it cannot be rationally explained between a cause and effect that are the same. This is because such causation would be pointless, and lead to an infinite regress. Causation also cannot be demonstrated where cause and effect are different, since then there would be no actual connection between the two. Cause and effect could not be both same and different, for such a position would be subject to both sets of problems. Nor could there be an effect coming from no cause at all, because then production would be random, and without a proper causal connection intentional action would become pointless.[15] The Self cannot be the same as the five aggregates, taken separately or together, nor could it be different from them. And so on.

Note that in Abhidharma terms to find that *X* does not resist ultimate analysis (i.e. it is empty of own-existence, *niḥsvabhāva*) should not be taken as entailing that it does not exist at all. No follower of the Abhidharma maintains that tables and chairs do not exist. They can still be used for everyday purposes, and that usage is quite correct. Thus Nāgārjuna can argue in his *Vigrahavyāvartanī* that the fact that his own words lack inherent existence does not entail that they cannot carry out their function of refutation. His position is not contradictory in that sense. Once it is appreciated that emptiness is an implication of dependent origination and is by no means identical with non-existence it can be seen that for something to be empty implies that such a thing must in some sense *exist*, since it must have originated through some sort of dependence.

Emptiness here is not some kind of Absolute Reality approached perhaps through a 'way of negation' (*via negativa*). It is the very absence (a pure non-existence) of inherent existence in the case of *X*, whatever that *X* may be, which is the result of *X*'s arising due to causes and conditions. If a table is empty it is because it has come into existence in the dependent way that tables come into existence. The table is *empty of* inherent existence, and that quality, that complete absence of inherent existence, possessed by the table is its emptiness. In a famous discussion in *MMK* 24 an opponent accuses Nāgārjuna with having destroyed the whole of Buddhism with his teaching of emptiness. Nāgārjuna replies that his opponent has misunderstood emptiness and its purpose, and his commentator Candrakīrti reiterates the relationship between emptiness and dependent origination. It is necessary to understand the two truths taught by the Buddha. Without relying on everyday practice (*vyavahāra*) the ultimate is not taught, while without resorting to the ultimate there is no nirvāṇa. The ultimate truth here is emptiness, in that it is what is ultimately true about things. Things themselves as empty of inherent existence are the conventional. Without reference to things there could be no teaching of emptiness. Moreover, Nāgārjuna continues, where emptiness is seen to be rational and acceptable all things are seen to be rational and acceptable. This is because since emptiness is an implication of dependent origination, the alternative to emptiness would be inherent existence and therefore an unchanging block-universe (or of course literally nothing at all). If *X* exists but is not empty, *X* would be inherently existent and thus would never go out of existence. And in a wonderful reversal, Nāgārjuna accuses his opponent who denies emptiness with destroying the teaching of the Buddha. Who could become enlightened if their state of unenlightenment were inherently existent, and thus not the result of causes and conditions?[16]

Note also that there is a very real sense in which emptiness is dependent on things. Emptiness is the absence of inherent existence in the case of *X*. If there were no *X* then there could not be an emptiness of *X*. In a hypothetical case in which absolutely nothing existed, there could also be no emptiness. Thus emptiness exists in dependence upon that which is empty. As dependently originated, emptiness is itself therefore empty. While emptiness is the ultimate truth in that it is what is ultimately true about *X*, it is not an ultimate truth in the sense that it is itself a primary existent. The ultimate truth is that all things, including any emptiness itself, lack ultimate truth. Therefore Madhyamaka uses 'ultimate truth' in two senses:

(i) The first is the ultimate truth as *an* ultimate truth, i.e. something resistant to analysis, a primary existent. In this sense, Madhyamaka is saying that there is no such thing as an ultimate truth.
(ii) The second is the ultimate truth as the ultimate way of things (the *dharmatā*), how it ultimately is, what is found to be the case as a result of ultimate analysis, searching for primary existence. This is the lack, the absence, of that primary existence, i.e. emptiness.

Thus it is the ultimate truth in sense (ii) that there is absolutely no ultimate truth in sense (i).

It is important in studying the Madhyamaka approach to ultimate and conventional not to separate the two and think that Madhyamaka is advocating the ultimate truth as the final *goal* beyond the conventional. Buddhism is not a move away from conventional to ultimate, but rather is a move of gnosis, an understanding of the conventional as merely conventional rather than bestowing it with a false sense of inherent, and therefore graspable, existence. The whole point is to see things the way they really are, to understand the ultimate way of things. Then the follower of Mahāyāna engages in the world for the benefit of others. The point is not to move (as it were) from this world to another realm of the ultimate, a pure emptiness.[17] Perhaps it was partly to prevent this move away from the world to a supposed ultimate that Nāgārjuna made his famous and much misunderstood statement about there being nothing whatsoever which differentiates nirvāṇa from saṃsāra (*MMK* 25: 19–20). This statement cannot be taken in context as meaning that this world is itself the realm of enlightenment. Nor can it be taken as indicating that enlightenment (or emptiness itself) lies just in a way of looking at the world, let alone that the life of monastic renunciation has somehow missed the point. Emptiness is not a way of looking at something. It is the quality of that thing which is its very absence of inherent existence. Moreover in context Nāgārjuna equates saṃsāra and nirvāṇa only and simply as regards that quality of emptiness. Nāgārjuna appears to have been a monk who fully expected the normal monastic lifestyle (as were all the great Mādhyamikas in India), and there is no suggestion that he would have compromised on the supremacy and superiority (in realistic practical terms the necessity) of that monastic lifestyle. It is not the case, Nāgārjuna wants to say, that saṃsāra is empty but nirvāṇa is not. Nirvāṇa (or indeed emptiness itself) both lack inherent existence and the one cannot be taken as an ultimate refuge from the other. According to universal Buddhist tradition Nāgārjuna was a follower of Mahāyāna, and he did not want his teaching of emptiness to entail a flight from the welfare of sentient beings.

In spite of its popularity outside India and among modern scholars the Madhyamaka system actually seems to have been rather neglected in the history of Indian thought. Hayes (1994) has suggested that this may well be because many of Nāgārjuna's arguments are simply fallacious. But I do not believe that fallacies in Nāgārjuna's arguments, even if true, really gets to the core of what was felt to be wrong with Madhyamaka. We have seen already that Nāgārjuna appears to slide from own-existence in the sense of the type of existence that is not the result of conceptual construction to inherent existence, existence uncaused in any way. This enables Nāgārjuna to maintain that all things are lacking inherent existence and are *prajñaptimātra*, merely conceptual constructs. This *prajñaptimātra* status of all things is a particular feature of Madhyamaka. Yet for the followers of Madhyamaka it is always held that such a position does not reduce to one of nihilism – nothing exists at all – since emptiness is said to be the same as dependent origination, not non-existence. I suggest that most Buddhists in India, familiar with the Abhidharma, still felt that the Madhyamaka position was tantamount to nihilism for the simple reason that it is incoherent to maintain that *all* are merely conceptual constructs. It is, we might say, part of the meaning of 'secondary, conceptual existence' that there is primary, substantial existence. It makes no sense to talk of all things being secondary existents. If all things were secondary existents then *all things would be constructs with nothing for them to be constructed out of*. This must mean that nothing exists at all. It is not sufficient to reply with Nāgārjuna that this ignores the two truths, since if all is merely a conceptual construct then there could be no foundation for the two truths. Everything is foam which dissolves into nothing.[18]

Thus through focusing on the Abhidharma background to the Madhyamaka project we can see that those who accused Madhyamaka of nihilism did not misunderstand Madhyamaka. They did not fail to understand the implication between emptiness and dependent origination. Rather they simply failed to be convinced that all as merely conceptual constructs could avoid nihilism.[19] It is not surprising, therefore, that in opposing as nihilism a position of *prajñaptimātra* clearly that of Madhyamaka, Yogācāra scholars precisely had to put forward the primary existence of something, something which could serve as an alternative to the primary existents (*dharmas*) of the other Abhidharma approaches.

But there may be one way of reading Nāgārjuna that his critics would have appreciated and which might have provided some suggestion of a response to their doubts. This would be to see a work like the *Madhyamakakārikā* as providing a rare series of (perhaps mnemonic) notes originally intended to guide Nāgārjuna's students in insight meditation. Let us return to our discussion of insight meditation in Chapter 2 above. Although we cannot assume that Nāgārjuna's model for practice was exactly that repeated in Buddhaghosa's *Visuddhimagga*, it was probably something like that model. We saw that in the third purification the practice involved breaking down the sense of Self through constant direct awareness of experience in terms of actually being a bundle of e.g. the five aggregates, divided into mind and body in mutual dependence, and nothing more. This corresponds exactly with the direction of the Sarvāstivāda analysis in terms of primary and secondary existence. As we saw, the fourth purification involves examining causal dependence as a continuum in time, coming to see directly how things are the result of an impersonal lawlike causality and nothing more. The fifth purification involves taking various groups and classes of phenomena and seeing that they are all impermanent, suffering, and not Self. One then sees them as arising and falling in their constant change and impermanence. Thus the meditator comes to deconstruct the apparent stability of things, and to see directly everything as a process, a flow. And we saw also that the images used by Buddhaghosa for this stage are to see all things as 'like a mirage, a conjuring trick, a dream' and so on – precisely the images used by the Perfection of Wisdom literature and Madhyamaka for the ontological status of everything.

It may be possible to read Nāgārjuna's work as a guide to something like the stages of meditation corresponding to Buddhaghosa's fourth and fifth purifications. Just as the dharma-lists, and an understanding of causal linkage, provide one framework for analysis by a monk undertaking insight meditation, so the *Madhyamakakārikā* gives a structure for the analyses a monk practising at this level is expected to undertake.[20] In other words, Nāgārjuna is prescribing taking the sort of analysis found in e.g. Sarvāstivāda dharma ontology and extending it through *time*. Rather as with Diṅnāga and Dharmakīrti's version of Sautrāntika, everything is then seen as a fluctuating flow, with no actual *things* at all. Hence the stress for Nāgārjuna on what follows from dependent origination. The centrality of dependent origination for Nāgārjuna is the centrality of things as processes in time. The stability of things is appearance only. They collapse into processes. Thus Nāgārjuna is not concerned to question the reduction to dharmas, but rather to probe what happens when it is realised that all things, including dharmas, are actually dependently originated.[21] Nāgārjuna accepts that everyday things are constructs out of, or conceptual imputations upon, dharmas. But if we turn our attention round and 'project', as it were, both the everyday thing and the dharmas into which they are analysed into time we find that things become processes. When things are processes the constituents of things must be processes too. There can thus finally be no ontological difference at all between the things and the dharmas themselves.[22]

Yogācāra

The *Saṃdhinirmocana Sūtra*

Not all Mahāyāna sūtras advocated universal emptiness, absence of inherent existence, as did the Perfection of Wisdom literature. Particularly interesting in this context is a text known as the *Saṃdhinirmocana Sūtra*. Among those Buddhists who knew of the teaching of emptiness many (I suggest most) felt it to be a quite absurd nihilism. Yet for some who claimed to follow the Mahāyāna this gave rise to a dilemma since it seems clear that in the *Prajñāpāramitā* literature the Buddha did indeed teach emptiness as the very *perfection* of wisdom. If emptiness as complete lack of primary existence cannot be taken literally, how is it to be understood? In Chapter 7 of the *Saṃdhinirmocana Sūtra* the Buddha is asked directly what was his intention behind declaring that 'all dharmas [and therefore all things] lack their own essential nature' (*Saṃdhinirmocana Sūtra*, trans. Powers: 96/7)? In other words, why say such a thing since it could scarcely be taken seriously without entailing that literally everything is a conceptual construct with nothing for it to be constructed out of? In the sūtra the Buddha replies that the correct way of understanding his teaching of emptiness is in terms of the 'three aspects' (*trisvabhāva*; q.v.) which, when properly appreciated, will be seen not to entail nihilism at all. It is a misunderstanding of emptiness to take it as meaning that literally *all* things are conceptual constructs. As we shall see, it must follow therefore that at least one thing is not a conceptual construct (*prajñaptisat*), at least one thing must have primary existence (*dravyasat*), must exist with its own-existence (i.e. in *this* sense – as a substratum to construction – have a *svabhāva*). In the *Saṃdhinirmocana Sūtra* the Buddha gives a vision of the history of Buddhism which pinpoints both how he has been misunderstood and also the position of his present teaching as its final explanatory clarification.

The sūtra recollects that at the very beginning of Buddhism, at the discourse in the Deer Park at Sarnath called 'setting in motion the Wheel of Dharma', the Buddha taught such topics as the four Noble Truths and so on. Nevertheless, this teaching was not intended to be a philosophically definitive teaching reflecting exactly the ultimate way of things. It is interpretable, *neyārtha*. For example really there are no persons as ultimate realities, they are, of course, conceptual constructs. Eventually this first teaching became a topic of controversy and dispute. Likewise he taught what was in fact a second 'setting in motion the Wheel of Dharma', a more advanced teaching, in the *Prajñāpāramitā* literature. This was a teaching of dharmas (therefore all things) lacking their own essential nature. This teaching too, however – and this is important – was taught for a practical spiritual purpose and was not intended to be philosophically definitive. In time this teaching too was in fact misunderstood and became a basis for controversy and dispute. Note, therefore, that the teaching of universal emptiness as understood by Madhyamaka is itself declared to be not a philosophically definitive teaching reflecting exactly the ultimate way of things. Thus it is *not* the final ultimate truth. Once again we see that the logic of denying that all things lack *svabhāva* (i.e. are empty) must be to claim that at least one thing has a *svabhāva*. The final, definitive (*nītārtha*) teaching, which can be no basis at all for controversy and dispute, is contained within this *Saṃdhinirmocana Sūtra* itself. It is the third and final 'setting in motion the Wheel of Dharma'.[23] Those who unfortunately took the teachings of the second turning as definitive, on the other hand, either over-negated as a consequence and completely destroyed everything, or they decided that this nihilism could not really be the teaching of the Buddha. Thus they unfortunately committed the great mistake of denying the Dharma of the Buddha (*Saṃdhinirmocana Sūtra*, trans. Powers: 118/19 ff.).[24]

Yogācāra teachers and texts

The *Saṃdhinirmocana Sūtra* maintains that a literal understanding of the universality of conceptual construction (i.e. emptiness) must be wrong. Therefore we can see that at least one thing must have the status of being a primary existent. A Mahāyāna school of thought that holds such a position must obviously differ in at least this respect from Madhyamaka.[25] This school of thought is called *Yogācāra* – an expression that may indicate originally a particular interest in the data of meditation experience (*yoga*) – or sometimes *Vijñānavāda*, *Vijñaptimātra* or *Cittamātra*. The terms *vijñāna* ('consciousness'), *vijñapti* ('cognitive representation'), and *citta* ('mind'), all indicate the orientation of this school towards what we might call the mentalistic side of our being. The addition of the term *mātra* – 'only', or 'merely' – also suggests that this school not only accepts at least one thing as a primary existent, but indeed it accepts *only* one thing. That thing is variously termed, but clearly in some sense it must be mentalistic. Thus this is the school of 'Mind-only'.

It seems to me that Yogācāra was probably one way or another the most popular and influential of philosophical schools in India associated with Mahāyāna. Within the Yogācāra tradition we find extensive discussions of Mahāyāna religious ideas and ideals – the status of the Buddha or the bodhisattva path, and meditation practice, for example – as well as issues relating to philosophical ontology. There is also – I would argue not surprisingly – a whole Yogācāra Abhidharma system. However at this point it is the Yogācāra approach to issues of ontology and the mind that interests us. The suggestion that 'all that belongs to the triple world is mind only' is found in a number of sūtras that are quite early such as the *Pratyutpanna Sūtra* and *Daśabhūmika Sūtra*, as well as the *Saṃdhinirmocana Sūtra*. Other sūtras that contain important Yogācāra material include the *Avataṃsaka Sūtra* and the *Laṅkāvatāra Sūtra*. Note that commonly in the sūtras the introduction of this *cittamātra* point occurs within the context of a discussion of visions seen in meditation experience. If certain Mahāyāna Buddhist thinkers, disturbed by Madhyamaka, wanted to find a primary existent to serve as a substratum for all things, saṃsāra and nirvāṇa alike, the fact that they chose something that was mentalistic might well reflect the general mentalistic orientation of Buddhism through meditation practice. In particular it shows an interest in the implications of alternative and yet seemingly real worlds of meditation visions.

It is possible that the earliest named Yogācāra teacher was the shadowy Maitreyanātha. Tibetan tradition however holds that works attributed to him were in fact delivered to his pupil Asaṅga (*c.* fourth century CE) by none other than the great 'celestial' bodhisattva – to be the very next Buddha here on earth – Maitreya himself. Five works are sometimes attributed to Maitreya, whoever he was:

(i) *Abhisamayālaṃkāra* ('Ornament for the Realisations') – a text on the *Prajñāpāramitā* path;
(ii) *Madhyāntavibhāga* ('The Discrimination of the Middle from the Extremes');
(iii) *Dharmadharmatāvibhāga* ('The Discrimination of dharmas and their True Nature (*dharmatā*)');
(iv) *Mahāyānasūtrālaṃkāra* ('Ornament for the Mahāyāna Sūtras'); and the
(v) *Ratnagotravibhāga*, otherwise known as the *Uttaratantra*, on the *tathāgatagarbha* or Buddha-nature teachings (q.v.).

It is quite likely that not all these five texts stem from the same hand. Actually it is the middle three with their commentaries that form some of our most important sources for classical Yogācāra. Asaṅga himself wrote some commentaries, as well as an important compendium of Yogācāra Mahāyāna, the *Mahāyānasaṃgraha* ('Compendium on Mahāyāna') and a work specifically establishing Yogācāra Abhidharma, the *Abhidharmasamuccaya* ('Collection on Abhidharma'). One of the very earliest Yogācāra texts, however, is a large work probably of multiple authorship but sometimes attributed to Asaṅga, the *Yogācārabhūmi* ('Stages of Yogācāra'). There is also a story – rather doubted by some modern scholars – that Asaṅga converted his brother Vasubandhu to Mahāyāna. There may have been two (or more) Vasubandhus. Attributed to a Mahāyāna Vasubandhu are the *Triṃśikā* ('Thirty Verses'), the *Viṃśatikā* ('Twenty Verses'), the *Trisvabhāvanirdeśa* ('Teaching on the Three Aspects') and other texts including commentaries on some of the above works of 'Maitreya'.[26]

Mind and the 'three aspects' (trisvabhāva)

We have seen that in Yogācāra a mentalistic factor – let us call it Mind – is the one primary existent that serves as the substratum for everything else, both enlightenment and unenlightenment.[27] In the *Saṃdhinirmocana Sūtra* the antidote to nihilism is said to be the 'three aspects', and this teaching of the three aspects explains what Mind is, and the relationship of Mind to phenomenal illusion. How are these explained in the classical Indian Yogācāra texts?

The first of the three aspects is the 'constructed aspect' (*parikalpitasvabhāva*). What this amounts to is the aspect of our life which is a polarisation into separate subjects (called the 'grasper'; *grāhaka*) confronting objects (the 'grasped'; *grāhya*). This is the realm of subject–object duality, the world as seen by the unenlightened and also the realm of linguistic operation. Since as we know Yogācāra thinks in terms of just one primary existent, substratum for delusion as well as enlightenment, clearly duality cannot actually be correct. Duality is a wrenching apart of what is actually a unity, one basic 'substance' (*ekadravya*). This polarisation is erroneous.

The second aspect is the 'dependent aspect' (*paratantrasvabhāva*). It is the flow, a dependently originated continuum, of cognitive experiences (*vijñapti*), the substratum, that *which* is erroneously polarised into subjects and objects. If we settle down and examine carefully we will see that all the world of objects, and ourselves who confront those objects, are nothing more than a series of experiences. Actually there is *vijñaptimātra*, merely cognitive experiences, or merely representations. As a flow of experiences this flow must, of course, be mentalistic in nature. Note this. It could not be physical, and in Abhidharma terms there is realistically nothing else for it to be other than something mentalistic. Also it could not be the case that this flow does not exist at all – there is really no substratum – or there would be no experiences at all and therefore there would be nothing. Thus in Madhyamaka terms a flow of experiences must be found under ultimate analysis.[28] But note also that since the constructed aspect is the realm of language, the other two aspects including this flow of experiences as it actually is are strictly beyond language and can only be indicated obliquely through linguistic usage.

The 'perfected aspect' (*pariniṣpannasvabhāva*) is the true way of things, which has to be seen in meditation. It is also said to be emptiness. But in Yogācāra texts emptiness is redefined to mean that the substratum which must exist in order for there to be anything at all is *empty of* subject–object duality. Thus emptiness must indeed be known for liberation, but this emptiness which is the perfected aspect – the highest aspect inasmuch as it is that which is to be known by those avid for liberation – is defined as *the very absence of the constructed aspect in the dependent aspect*. Students often get very confused about this, but it is not as difficult as it might appear. What we have to know in order to let go of the grasping which is unenlightenment is that the flow of experiences which we erroneously understand in terms of subjects and objects is actually, finally, all there is. It is therefore empty of those subjects and objects as separate polarised realities. That emptiness, the quality of 'being empty of' is the perfected aspect. As in Madhyamaka, emptiness is an *absence*, a pure negation. This time, however, it is not absence of own- or inherent existence but rather absence of subject–object duality. For Yogācāra it is very much not the case that there is universal absence of own-existence (*svabhāva*). In order for there to be absence of subject–object duality there has actually to exist *something* which is erroneously divided into subjects and objects.

It is crucial in understanding Yogācāra philosophy to understand properly the three aspects. Note that while the perfected aspect is the highest aspect in the sense that it is the highest thing to be known, it is *not* in Classical early Indian Yogācāra the highest aspect in the sense that it is itself the one reality. One should be very careful not to confuse the one reality in Classical Indian Yogācāra with the perfected aspect. Being the ultimate reality in an ontological sense, and being the highest thing to be known, the ultimate way of things, are in Yogācāra different. If Yogācāra teaches one mentalistic primary existent as substratum, in terms of the three aspects that is the *dependent* aspect. But what has to be known for liberation, the supreme in *that* sense, is that the flow of experiences which makes up our life is empty of polarised subjects and objects (empty of the constructed aspect). That emptiness, that very absence itself, is the *perfected* aspect, and it has to be known directly on the deepest possible level, in meditation.

Thus for Yogācāra the teaching of the three aspects is the final teaching, the antidote to Madhyamaka 'nihilism', inasmuch as it denies what is to be denied – the constructed aspect – but does not deny what should not be denied – the dependent aspect. This dependent aspect which once served as the substratum for saṃsāra is thus potentially still there to serve as the substratum for enlightenment. Texts therefore talk about the tainted dependent aspect, and the purified dependent aspect. This teaching is held to be the true Middle Way between over- and under-negation.

Certain Yogācāra texts, notably Vasubandhu's *Viṃśatikā*, also give arguments to counter any objections to the idea that all is simply experience, that there are no (subjects and) objects external to consciousness, all is one primary existent (*ekadravya*). For example, the existence of spatial and temporal distinctions is no problem since that can be explained on the model of dream experiences where we experience spatio-temporal difference. The fact that unlike in the case of an hallucination many experience the same thing can be explained on the model of the Buddhist hells, where it is accepted that many undergo a common collective hallucination. Also it is difficult for opponents to explain the actual existence of 'external' objects, since things cannot be wholes in their own right because they are not experienced that way. They are experienced as having parts, and the division into parts threatens to extend to infinity. Objects also cannot be constructs out of fundamental minute 'atoms'. This is because an atom, that is not further indivisible and therefore without spatial extension, capable of aggregation into spatially extended gross objects, is simply incoherent. Thus there can be no explanation of the world of matter. Yet clearly there is *something*. Since there is no matter (*rūpa*), but nevertheless there must be something, that something must itself be mentalistic (*citta*).[29]

The dependent aspect as a flow of experiences is the base, the substratum, 'ultimate reality' in Yogācāra. But note that this is not some immutable Absolute, and Yogācāra thinkers seem to differ over whether it is ever in itself really tainted. Inasmuch as we can look at consciousness from the point of view of the working-out of the phenomenal illusion of everyday saṃsāric experience, however, the Yogācāra tradition speaks of eight types of consciousness. There are the normal five sensory consciousnesses, the mental consciousness (*manovijñāna*) that, among other things, experiences mental events and also synthesises the data from the senses, the 'tainted mind' (*kliṣṭamanas*) and the 'substratum consciousness' (*ālayavijñāna*). The substratum consciousness is the flow, texts say the torrent, of underlying consciousness. While changing from moment to moment it serves to provide a necessary substratum for individual experience and also individual identity not just throughout one life but over the infinite series of lifetimes.[30] The 'tainted mind' observes the substratum consciousness and mistakenly conceives it to be a Self. Clearly such a changing flow could never be an actual Self in the sense in which Buddhists deny the Self. One of the main functions of the substratum consciousness is to serve as the 'seedbed', the repository for seeds (*bīja*) which result from karmicly determinative deeds and which therefore issue in future experiences, including from particular sorts of seeds the very experiences of the 'intersubjective' world itself. The seeds, which are momentary, form a series within the substratum until their fruition, and the substratum consciousness is 'perfumed' by their presence. Yogācāra thinkers disagreed over whether all seeds were the results of karmicly determinative acts, or whether perhaps some were primevally latent in the substratum, and differed also over whether the substratum consciousness continued even at enlightenment. In China the Indian missionary Paramārtha (490–569 CE) seemed to think that the substratum consciousness would cease, to be replaced by an ninth 'immaculate consciousness' (*amalavijñāna*). But notwithstanding this, the general view in Indian Yogācāra appears to be that at enlightenment the consciousness that was the substratum consciousness would continue to exist forever in a completely radiant and purified form.[31]

The Buddha-nature (tathāgatagarbha) in India

Broadly speaking, the teaching of the *tathāgatagarbha* in Indian Mahāyāna is concerned with that factor possessed by each sentient being which enables him or her to become a fully enlightened Buddha. It is, as the leading contemporary scholar of the *tathāgatagarbha* David Seyfort Ruegg has put it, 'the "buddhamorphic" Base or Support for practice of the Path, and hence the motivating "cause" (*hetu: dhātu*) for attainment of the Fruit (*phala*) of buddhahood' (1989a: 18–19). The earliest sources strongly advocating the possession of the *tathāgatagarbha* appear to be sūtras such as the short and appropriately named *Tathāgatagarbha Sūtra*. According to its recent translator this sūtra may well have been composed in the mid-third century CE. This century corresponds with one estimate of the date of another crucial *tathāgatagarbha* sūtra, the *Śrīmālādevīsiṃhanāda Sūtra* ('Discourse that is the Lion's Roar of Queen Śrīmālā', trans. Wayman and Wayman: 1–4). This latter sūtra, however, seems to show a much more elaborate doctrinal understanding of what the *tathāgatagarbha* might be, and how exactly it relates to Buddhahood. Also vitally important for understanding the *tathāgatagarbha* doctrine in the Indic cultural world – and important in the transmission of these ideas to East Asia where they have become an integral part of the Buddhist vision – is the (Mahāyāna) *Mahāparinirvāṇa Sūtra*. There are also some other significant *tathāgatagarbha* sūtras such as the *Aṅgulimālīya Sūtra* as well as interesting and important references to the *tathāgatagarbha* and related ideas in such sūtras as the *Laṅkāvatāra* and *Avataṃsaka Sūtras* (see Gomez 1995). Given the importance of these teachings particularly in Far Eastern Buddhism, it is striking that the only developed attempt in India to understand them within the systematic context of a philosophical treatise (*śāstra*) is in the *Ratnagotravibhāga* (*Uttaratantra*) and its commentary (*Vyākhyā*), both works of disputed authorship.[32]

So far we have followed through in particular one crucial strand in the development of Buddhist philosophical thought – the ontological issue of construction and substratum, *prajñaptisat* and *dravyasat*. Such an issue is indeed soteriological, related to a letting-go, and the range of that letting-go and the possibilities of its occurrence. Issues of ontology in Buddhist thought take place, it seems to me, within the context of debates which are first and foremost broadly those of Abhidharma. I strongly suspect, however, that notwithstanding issues of the ontology of the *tathāgatagarbha* that developed later, particularly outside India, the topic of the *tathāgatagarbha* did *not* originate in India within this broadly Abhidharma ontological context. In other words the very context within which the issue of the *tathāgatagarbha* emerged was conceptually not one which was concerned with relating it to questions of ontology.

We can willingly understand, starting with the distinction between conceptual construct and primary existent, how some might argue that complete letting-go and philosophical consistency required that literally all things are conceptual constructs (Madhyamaka). We can also understand how some others (Yogācāra) might feel that this in fact collapses into nihilism and there must actually be a primary existent that is the non-dual flow of experience itself (which after all, cannot be denied even if we can deny certain things about it). While not exclusively so, nevertheless these are very much ontological issues. It is clear from our earliest sources such as the *Tathāgatagarbha Sūtra*, on the other hand, that the topic of the *tathāgatagarbha* is more to do with specifically religious issues of realising one's spiritual potential, exhortation, and encouragement, not ontology. We are not as such in an Abhidharma world. Our context, our immediate conceptual world, is quite different. It is perhaps rather the world of advocating the supremacy of the Mahāyāna against rival 'lower' paths, for if the *tathāgatagarbha* – the Buddha-nature – is in all sentient beings, all sentient beings should, and presumably in the end will, follow the path to a supreme Buddhahood. This path will leave the arhats and pratyekabuddhas far behind. Issues of the ontological status of the *tathāgatagarbha* developed later. In China Fa-tsang in the seventh century claimed that the *tathāgatagarbha* tradition represents a fourth turning of the Dharma-wheel. In other words the tathāgatagarbha tradition represents a different philosophical and ontological position from Madhyamaka and Yogācāra. In spite of this, however, I do not believe that in its Indian origin this was the intention of the teaching of the *tathāgatagarbha*.

The *Tathāgatagarbha Sūtra* consists mainly of a series of examples showing that even though one is in the midst of defilements there dwells within all sentient beings a *tathāgatagarbha*. This *tathāgatagarbha* is a tathāgata-womb, or a tathāgata-embryo, or a tathāgata-calyx, or a tathāgata-inner sanctum, or a tathāgata-husk, or a tathāgata-seed, or a tathāgata-interior (trans. Grosnick 1995: 92–3). In other words something supremely valuable is contained within all this dross. The sūtra even goes so far as to have the Buddha state that hidden within the defilements is 'the tathāgata's wisdom, the tathāgata's vision, and the tathāgata's body . . . eternally unsullied, and . . . replete with virtues no different from my own. . . . the tathāgatagarbhas of all beings are eternal and unchanging' (op. cit.: 96). The Buddha exhorts people, 'do not consider yourself inferior or base. You all personally possess the buddha nature' (op. cit.: 101). This short sūtra is a cry of encouragement, not a philosophical treatise.

Some examples used suggest the *tathāgatagarbha* as a potentiality, some – perhaps wishing greater encouragement – use examples that speak of an actuality already achieved. Either way (and this ambiguity gave rise to endless doctrinal debates later), the message of the sūtra is that we *all* have a tremendous and probably unrealised spiritual potential.[33]

Problems might start to arise, however, with the actual choice of terms used to refer to this *tathāgatagarbha* in some other sūtras, notably perhaps the *Mahāparinirvāṇa Sūtra*, a sūtra which is boldly prepared to use the term *ātman*, Self, for the *tathāgatagarbha*. Perhaps it was this that began the attempt to clarify or explain the nature and ontological status of the *tathāgatagarbha* given the difficulties that would inevitably arise through using such a problematic term in a Buddhist context. The *Mahāparinirvāṇa Sūtra* is a long sūtra with a complex textual history. It does not always appear to be very consistent. But it is obvious that the *Mahāparinirvāṇa Sūtra* does not consider it impossible for a Buddhist to affirm an *ātman* provided it is clear what the correct understanding of this concept is, and indeed the sūtra clearly sees certain advantages in doing so. For example, since non-Buddhists are portrayed as considering the Buddha a nihilist due to his teaching of Not-Self, provided there is no compromise of Buddhist tenets – and there does not *have* to be such a compromise – portraying the *tathāgatagarbha* as *ātman* might help convert non-Buddhists to Buddhism. It might thus help them to realise that Buddhism is not a form of spiritual nihilism. After all, if there is a *tathāgatagarbha* that serves as the very foundation for attaining Buddhahood then Buddhism could not be nihilism. No questions have to be begged on what actually corresponds to the term *tathāgatagarbha*. Moreover adherents of the *tathāgatagarbha* argued that by structural opposition, if saṃsāra is, as Buddhists say, impermanent, not-Self, suffering and impure then Buddhahood (i.e. the *tathāgatagarbha*) as the negation of saṃsāra can indeed be portrayed without further commitment as permanent, Self, bliss, and purity. Furthermore the *tathāgatagarbha* is by definition that very thing within sentient beings which enables them to become Buddhas, which means that the spiritual path is not impossible, and which shines forth in Buddhahood. Thus it does indeed fit some of the characteristics associated with a Self. Nevertheless the sūtra as it stands is quite clear that while for these reasons we can speak of it as Self, actually it is not at all a *Self*, and those who have such Self-notions cannot perceive the *tathāgatagarbha* and thus become enlightened (see Ruegg 1989a: 21–6).

Problems in the teaching of the *tathāgatagarbha* can thus be neutralised by claiming among other things that it was just a skilful strategy to bring Buddhism to non-Buddhists who might otherwise be frightened by the truth. Alongside this approach, provided we are clear what the *tathāgatagarbha* is, calling it a Self need not be seen as in any way compromising Buddhism. But what, therefore, *is* the *tathāgatagarbha*? There is some suggestion in the sūtra that it could be taken as actually the very absence of Self itself. After all, all Buddhist traditions agree that this is what one has to know directly in order to become enlightened ('the Tathāgata has spoken of not-self (*bdag med pa*) as self, in reality there is no self'; trans. Ruegg 1989a: 23). Or, as the *Laṅkāvatāra Sūtra* (trans. Suzuki: 68 ff., 190 ff.) suggests, the *tathāgatagarbha* could actually be another name for the substratum consciousness. It is the answer to the question what it is about sentient beings *qua* sentient beings that enables them to become Buddhas. It must therefore be something permanent in sentient beings. It is thus also possible to link the *tathāgatagarbha* with an old Buddhist concept of the 'natural luminosity of the mind' (*prakṛtiprabhāsvaracitta*), the idea that the mind is in its own nature never defiled. Defilements are simply adventitious to it. Therefore it is the primeval innate purity of the mind – taints are not essential to it – which enables Buddhahood to occur. We accordingly find the *Avataṃsaka Sūtra* referring to the wisdom, the mind, the gnosis of a Buddha which is present although unrealised in each sentient being (Gomez 1995: 109–11). Or the *tathāgatagarbha* could be, in Yogācāra terms, as the *Mahāyānasūtrālaṃkāra* suggests, the pure dependent aspect (Griffiths 1990: 62–3). Or, again, if one is a Mādhyamika then that which enables sentient beings to become Buddhas must be the very factor that enables the minds of sentient beings to change into the minds of Buddhas. That which enables things to change is their simple absence of inherent existence, their emptiness. Thus the *tathāgatagarbha* becomes emptiness itself, but specifically emptiness when applied to the mental continuum. None of this, even the fact that the *tathāgatagarbha* is permanent, need entail any compromise with the Buddhist teaching of Not-Self, since while speaking of an *ātman* none of these things *need* be thought of as an unchanging, inherently existing, ontologically real and independent, eternally enlightened True Self.

Perhaps it was the *Śrīmālādevīsiṃhanāda Sūtra* that first introduced the explicit association of the *tathāgatagarbha* with the *dharmakāya* (q.v.), the Buddha's highest 'body', what a Buddha finally is in him- or herself. The term *tathāgatagarbha* is said to be actually the name we give in the case of unenlightened beings to what in the case of Buddhas is called the *dharmakāya*. The *dharmakāya* is said to be 'beginningless, uncreate, unborn, undying, free from death; permanent, steadfast, calm, eternal; intrinsically pure. . . . This Dharmakāya of the Tathāgata when not free from the store of defilement is referred to as the Tathāgatagarbha' (*Śrīmālādevīsiṃhanāda Sūtra*, trans. Wayman and Wayman: 98; see also Williams 1989: 101). The *tathāgatagarbha/dharmakāya* is also explicitly said to be empty (*śūnya*). But as we have seen with Yogācāra, the mere presence of an attribution of *śūnya/śūnyatā* to something in Buddhism does not in itself entail that these expressions are being used with the Madhyamaka sense of 'absence of inherent existence', or 'merely having conceptual existence'. If the question of the actual ontological status of the *tathāgatagarbha* arises, it has not yet been settled simply by the use of *śūnya/śūnyatā*. In *tathāgatagarbha* texts, as with the *Śrīmālā Sūtra*, the *tathāgatagarbha* is said to be empty inasmuch as it is intrinsically free of defilements, but also not empty inasmuch as it truly and intrinsically possesses all the qualities of the Buddha (op. cit.: 99). The *tathāgatagarbha* is moreover explicitly said here not to be a Self (op. cit.: 106), although the *dharmakāya* for its part is nevertheless said to have the 'perfection of self' (op. cit.: 102).

The *Ratnagotravibhāga* (*Uttaratantra*) appears to be the only systematic treatise on the *tathāgatagarbha* tradition composed in India. It is not clear just how influential it was, although its influence might have been relatively slight.[34] Anyway, for this text the true way of things ('Suchness', 'Thusness'; *tathatā*) as tainted is called the *tathāgatagarbha*. As immaculate, on the other hand, that same *tathatā* is called the *dharmakāya* (Ratnagotravibhāga (Uttaratantra), trans. Takasaki: 186–7). In itself, this *tathatā* is said to be 'unchangeable by nature, sublime and perfectly pure' (op. cit.: 287). Crucial to understanding the *Ratnagotravibhāga* is the idea of the intrinsic purity of consciousness. Buddhahood precisely is permanent and unconditioned because it does not involve bringing anything about – adding or removing anything – but rather realising what has always been the case.[35] The impurities that taint the mind and entail the state of unenlightenment (saṃsāra) are completely adventitious. From the point of view of the mind itself, in terms of its essential nature, they are simply not present. That is how they are able to be (as it were) 'removed', never to return. On the other hand from the point of view of the mind's pure radiant intrinsic nature, because it *is* like this it is possessed of all the many qualities of a Buddha's mind. These do not need actually to be brought about but merely need to be allowed to shine forth. Because they are intrinsic to the very nature of consciousness itself they, and the very state of Buddhahood, will never cease. How it is possible for consciousness to be intrinsically pure and yet defiled is one of a number of mysteries said by the *Ratnagotravibhāga* to be understandable by Buddhas alone (op. cit.: 188 ff.), for issues concerning the *tathāgatagarbha* are precisely the deepest issues accessible only to Tathāgatas themselves. For the rest of us and for the time being there can be only faith (op. cit.: 296).

6 The Buddha in Mahāyāna Buddhism

Some further sūtras: 'Garland' (*Avataṃsaka*), 'Lotus' (*Saddharmapuṇḍarīka*) and 'Skill in Means' (*Upāyakausalya*)

Let me now introduce briefly some of the main ideas of two large Indian Mahāyāna sūtras that have become particularly important in East Asian Buddhism. These are the enormous and heterogeneous *Avataṃsaka* ('Garland') *Sūtra* (Chinese: *Hua-yen*) and the famous *Saddharmapuṇḍarīka* ('Lotus') *Sūtra*. The *Upāyakauśalya* ('Skill in Means') *Sūtra* will serve as an additional sūtra source devoted entirely to one of the principal doctrines of the *Lotus*, the teaching of skill in means (*upāya/upāyakauśalya*).

The *Avataṃsaka Sūtra* is a composite sūtra some portions of which may well have been composed in Central Asia where perhaps the whole was also put together. Parts of this composite sūtra certainly circulated in India as independent sūtras in their own right. The most important of these are the sūtra on the ten stages of the bodhisattva path to Buddhahood, the *Daśabhūmika Sūtra*, and the climax of the *Avataṃsaka*, known as the *Gaṇḍavyūha Sūtra*. This is an extraordinary sūtra that takes up the *Avataṃsaka* theme of stretching language to try and portray what it must be like to see the world as a Buddha does. That vision is said to be 'inconceivable; No sentient being can fathom it . . .' (*Avatamsaka sūtra*, trans. Cleary; quoted in Williams 1989: 122). Inasmuch as it can be spoken of it is one of the presence of Buddhas and the realms of the Buddhas in each realm of the cosmos, and in each atom of existence. It is also one of infinite interpenetration: 'They . . . perceive that the fields full of assemblies, the beings and aeons which are as many as all the dust particles, are all present in every particle of dust' (trans. Gomez, in Williams 1989: 124). Yet in spite of infinite interpenetration things are not confused, each slightest thing keeps to its own place. Buddhas and also advanced bodhisattvas are forever engaging in innumerable deeds to help others, emanating innumerable further Buddhas and bodhisattvas whose only being is to help. Using a wonderful image, the word as seen by a Buddha is said to lack hard edges, it is a world of radiance without any shadows. On another level the universe itself is said to be the very body of the Buddha, or the Buddha is himself the ultimate truth – emptiness, or radiant nondual consciousness, as the case may be. The sūtra is not particularly concerned with the rigid distinctions of separate philosophical systems. The Buddha here is no longer spoken of as Śākyamuni but rather as Mahāvairocana, the Buddha of Great Radiance, Great Splendour of the Sun. In the world as seen by the great splendour of the sun how can there be any shadows? Nothing is unseen, and nothing is hidden. Things lack inherent existence, or they are all the play of pure, radiant consciousness. A world like this is, to use an expression Stephan Beyer applied to the *Prajñāpāramitā*, a world of 'the vision and the dream: a universe of glittering and quicksilver change' (Beyer 1977: 340). It is a universe of what are for us miracles precisely because we superimpose upon the real way of things a rigid and exclusive fixity. The *Avataṃsaka Sūtra*, particularly its *Gaṇḍavyūha* portion, delights in describing the supranormal – even hallucinogenic – experience of advanced mental transformation wherein 'body and mind completely melt away', 'all thoughts depart away from consciousness', and 'there are no impediments, all intoxications vanish'. It also contains the 'pilgrim's progress' story of Sudhana and his path to this astonishing Buddhahood, meeting along the way many great bodhisattvas including gods, goddesses, and laypeople such as Vasumitrā the courtesan, who is said to teach the Doctrine through the use of embraces and kisses!

While the *Lotus Sūtra* is of crucial importance in East Asian Buddhism (in Japan many consider it to be the final and all-sufficient word of the Buddha) it is not totally clear how important this sūtra was in Indian Mahāyāna Buddhism. Commentaries on it and references to it in other Indian writings are not that common. Like so many others the sūtra appears to have grown over a number of centuries, and since it was translated into Chinese in the late third century CE its earliest version may perhaps date from sometime between the first century BCE and the first century CE. The sūtra is primarily concerned with issues relating to the Buddha and Buddhahood. In it the Buddha is portrayed as employing a device known as *upāya* ('means') or *upāyakauśalya* ('skill in means', or 'skilful means'). According to this perspective the Buddha adapts his teaching to the level of his hearers. Out of his compassion he gives the teaching which is appropriate to their needs. Thus he may give one teaching at one time, and completely the opposite teaching at another.[1] This is why given the vast and disparate nature of the textual corpus claiming to be the word of the Buddha there is so much diversity in it. The Buddha taught the non-Mahāyāna goals of arhat and pratyekabuddha to those to whom it was appropriate. Subsequently he taught the path of the bodhisattva that leads to perfect Buddhahood, a goal which, the sūtra itself reveals, is infinitely beyond the goal of an arhat or pratyekabuddha. Indeed these inferior attainments are shown to be no real goals at all, but simply fabrications generated by the Buddha out of his skill in means for those who would otherwise be discouraged when told of the long, long career to Buddhahood. Thus in reality there is not at all three vehicles to liberation – the arhat-vehicle, the pratyekabuddha-vehicle, and the bodhisattva-vehicle to Buddhahood. Really there is only one vehicle, the Solitary Vehicle (*ekayāna*), the Supreme Buddha Vehicle. Those who think they have attained a goal called that of an 'arhat' are far from having really finished their spiritual careers. All (or perhaps most), including even great arhats like Śāriputra, will eventually become Perfect Buddhas. One of the most attractive features of the *Saddharmapuṇḍarīka Sūtra* is its use of several striking and famous parables to illustrate the skill in means of the Buddha. Thus we have the parable of the burning house, a metaphor for saṃsāra from which the Buddha as a loving father entices his children with the toys of arhatship and pratyekabuddhahood, before giving them the real treasure of Buddhahood. The sūtra illustrates the travelling of all in the One Buddha Vehicle by the parable of a poor man with a forgotten jewel (the future attainment of Buddhahood) sewn into his clothing.[2]

Skill in means is the educational and ethical equivalence of emptiness. Teachings are actually delivered relative to context. In time this was taken also to mean that the behaviour of enlightened beings too is relative to context. It will be underpinned certainly by the great compassion of the Buddha and bodhisattvas but it will not be necessarily predictable in advance or indeed even understandable by those whose vision does not encompass that of enlightenment.[3] The actions of such spiritually advanced beings are all appropriate to context, solely for the benefit of the recipient. Just as contexts differ and in a sense are never exactly the same so those actions are quite unpredictable, or rather are predictable only in their truly compassionate motivation and the wisdom of their application.

Not in the *Lotus Sūtra* itself, but in the *Upāyakauśalya Sūtra*, we find all the key actions of the traditional life of Śākyamuni explained with reference to their compassionate purpose in helping and teaching others. A spiritually advanced practitioner may not behave in what would normally be considered to be an appropriate manner. This is illustrated through recounting a tale in which the Buddha (as a bodhisattva in a previous life before he became a Buddha) was in a situation where the only way of saving the lives of five hundred other bodhisattvas was to kill a man who was plotting their deaths. He did indeed do so, recognising that to kill leads to a hellish rebirth. He was nevertheless willing to undergo such a rebirth in order to save not only the five hundred but also the potential murderer from the karmic results of carrying out his evil designs (trans. Chang 1983: 456–7). In another story we are told that the Buddha in a previous life as a bodhisattva was a celibate religious student who saved through sexual intercourse the life of a poor girl who had threatened to die out of love for him (op. cit.: 433).[4]

The other great teaching of the *Lotus Sūtra* concerns the revelation of the lifespan of the Buddha. The Buddha was actually enlightened aeons ago, and what is more although he now manifests the appearance of death he has not really died. He is really still around helping in myriads of compassionate ways. The Buddha's demonstration during his life of seeking enlightenment, becoming enlightened and dying was also an example of skill in means in order to give various lessons that would help others (*Saddharmapuṇḍarīka Sūtra*, trans. Hurvitz: 239). Conviction that the Buddha is still around is of course religiously transformative. It opens out the possibility of reciprocal relationships with the Buddha – petitionary prayer, visions, devotion, and continuing revelation for example – as well as the possibility that all the infinite previous Buddhas throughout the universe also are still around helping sentient beings. In East Asian Buddhism (influenced by the work in China of Chih-i (538–97 CE)) it is commonly held that the Buddha of the *Lotus Sūtra* is actually eternal, but I do not find this clearly stated in the sūtra itself. If a Buddha is eternal then it is difficult to see how anyone else could become a Buddha, short of combining the teaching of the *Saddharmapuṇḍarīka* with that of the *tathāgatagarbha* (Buddha-nature) and claiming that we are actually already fully-enlightened Buddhas if we but knew it. This is exactly what Chih-i himself did. It seems to me however there is no evidence that the *Lotus Sūtra* itself accepts a teaching of the *tathāgatagarbha*, and without it a literal acceptance of the Buddha as eternal would destroy the very possibility of attaining Buddhahood and with it the Mahāyāna path.[5]

Among other themes found in the *Saddharmapuṇḍarīka Sūtra* which were to become one way or another so important in the development of Mahāyāna Buddhism are those of the immense significance of even small acts of devotion to the Buddhas and indeed devotion to the sūtra itself. There is the possibility that faith in the sūtra and the efficacy of its practices might save even great sinners from hell-fires. The sūtra speaks of the immense salvific abilities also of bodhisattvas like Avalokiteśvara, who are so full of compassion and advanced on the path to Buddhahood that they are willing and able to employ miraculous powers in order to save those who call upon them. It recounts how even an 8-year-old princess from among the *nāgas*, snake-deities, could be an advanced bodhisattva and capable (with, it seems, change of gender) of enlightenment. Finally, perhaps most strange in a sūtra no stranger to things strange, the *Lotus Sūtra* explains at length the great virtues of burning oneself to death in honour of the Buddhas.

The Buddha's multiple 'bodies' (*kāya*)

The English term 'body' bears much of the ambiguity of the Sanskrit *kāya*. This expression can refer to an actual physical body possessed by living beings, or a body similar but perhaps rather less obviously 'physical' (such as, perhaps, an 'astral body'). It can also refer to any collection of things classed together by some principle of classification, as in the case of a body of texts or a body of people. If this ambiguity of 'body'/*kāya* is borne in mind then much of the initial mystification when looking at the case of the Buddha's multiple bodies will disappear.

According to what Paul Griffiths (1994) has called the Mahāyāna 'classical doctrine' a Buddha is said to have three types of 'body'.[6] These bodies consist of the *dharmakāya* (or *svabhāvakāya*) – the 'real body' – the *saṃbhogakāya* – the 'body of communal enjoyment' – and the *nirmāṇakāya* – the 'body of magical transformation'.[7] Although variations on it have become standard in later Indian Buddhism and Buddhism outside India, it took some time for this classical doctrine to develop. In an important paper Paul Harrison (1992) has argued, that in early and even relatively late Mahāyāna sūtra literature in India, such as the *Prajñāpāramitā* and the *Laṅkāvatāra Sūtra*, the idea of the *dharmakāya* was not one of any kind of metaphysical or cosmic ultimate. It was not a 'unitary cosmic principle'. It rather preserved a notion well known in non-Mahāyāna sources of this body – according to texts the highest and most important body of the Buddha – as either the 'body of the doctrine' (*Dharma*) or the 'body of dharmas'. In the latter sense, found also in Sarvāstivāda, the *dharmakāya* refers to those factors (*dharmas*) the possession of which serves to distinguish a Buddha from one who is not a Buddha.[8] Commonly in these sources, Harrison argues, the expression *dharmakāya* should be taken rather as an adjective – truly, really, the Buddha is possessed of a body of *Dharma*, his teachings, or perhaps a body of dharmas, his Buddha-qualities. Thus it is possible to contrast the actual physical body of the Buddha – which has now passed away and anyway always was just a physical body with all its physical frailties – with the Buddha's true body. This true body is either his teachings (*Dharma*, his Doctrine), that remain and lead to enlightenment, or the qualities the possession of which to their fullest degree made him a Buddha and that can still be attained by his followers. These are the *true* body of the Buddha. The Buddha's true body has not passed away but remains.[9]

Reference to the *dharmakāya* in works reasonably attributed to Nāgārjuna is rare.[10] However there is some interesting material in a collection of four hymns which have been attributed to the Master (Tola and Dragonetti 1995: Ch. 4; cf. Lindtner 1982). Particularly important in this context is the *Niraupamyastava* (the 'Hymn to the Incomparable One'). Here (v. 16) Nāgārjuna speaks of the Buddha's splendid physical body, a body which manifests in many apparently miraculous ways for the benefit of others and which accords with the behaviour of the world, although having no need to do so (cf. the Mahāsāṃghika *lokottaravāda*). But he also notes that the Buddha is seen actually not through a physical form that can be seen (with the eyes). It is when the *Dharma* is seen that he is properly seen. But the true nature of things itself (*dharmatā*) cannot be seen at all. Thus through understanding his teachings one sees the true body of the Buddha, yet the very point of those teachings is that emptiness is not something that can be seen at all in the normal way of seeing. And Nāgārjuna continues (v. 22) by singing of the Buddha's body as eternal, unalterable, auspicious, made of *Dharma*. He thus remains even after his death (*nirvṛti*), although he demonstrates a death through his skill in means to help others. The Buddha's true body is his teaching, and yet we also find a move here – admittedly still perhaps partly unconscious – towards the Buddha's final true body as that which is demonstrated by the teaching, emptiness itself. For, as Nāgārjuna puts it in his *Paramārthstava* ('Hymn to the Ultimate'), the Buddha himself has not been born, remains nowhere, neither existing nor non-existing. This is actually the way of things (*dharmatā*), emptiness itself.[11] Other later Madhyamaka sources also speak of the *dharmakāya* – the body which is the collection of ultimates (i.e. for Abhidharma, dharmas) – as emptiness. But of course while emptiness applies to everything, one specifically refers to the *dharmakāya* in the context of Buddhology. That is, the *dharmakāya* is spoken of in the context of uncovering the true nature of the Buddha, or what it really is to be a Buddha.

Let us turn now to the basic structure of the 'classical doctrine' associated with Yogācāra. The *dharmakāya* is said in the *Mahāyānasaṃgraha* (Ch. 10) to be equivalent to the actual true way of things (*tathatā*), the purified dependent aspect.[12] In other words, the *dharmakāya* is the intrinsically radiant consciousness of a Buddha. It is a gnosis completely empty of subject–object duality, beyond all conceivability or speculation, free of all cognitive and moral obscurations. It is the wisdom-body (*jñānakāya*) of the Buddha possessed of all the superior qualities intrinsic to the nature of a Buddha, eternal and in itself unchanging. It is said to serve as the support for the other bodies of the Buddha, which manifest out of infinite compassion in a form suited to help others. This *dharmakāya* is in fact what a Buddha is in himself, as it were from his (or her) own side.[13] It is, to use Griffiths' (1994) expression, 'Buddha in eternity'. The *dharmakāyas* of the Buddhas are in many respects the same (in their aspirations and their types of actions, for example), and *in themselves* they do not have qualities which could differentiate them. Nevertheless they are not literally the same, since many other beings become Buddhas and not just one being. The 'revolution of the basis' from unenlightened egotism to enlightened altruism is not in history a once and for all occurrence.

The *saṃbhogakāya*, the 'body of communal enjoyment', and the *nirmāṇakāya*, the 'body of magical transformation', are both wonderful 'form-bodies' (*rūpakāya*). That is, they appear as if physical bodies, based upon the *dharmakāya* and manifested by Buddhas spontaneously for the benefit of others. They manifest as automatic ways of fulfilling the Buddhas' great aspirations to help others made throughout their long career as bodhisattvas. The body of communal enjoyment is Griffiths' 'Buddha in heaven'. Strictly speaking, however, the body of communal enjoyment is paradigmatically the classic appearance of a Buddha according to the needs of sentient beings in a glorified body ornamented with the 112 marks of a Buddha (often seen on statues, such as long ears, cranial bump, etc.). He appears seated on a lotus throne not in a heaven (*svarga*) but in a Pure Land. The Pure Land where a *saṃbhogakāya* form of a Buddha appears is on another plane, a 'Buddha-field' said to include 'ponds of nectar, wish-granting trees and the like' (trans. in Griffiths 1994: 145). There he teaches the Doctrine to an assembly made up mainly or entirely of advanced bodhisattvas. There is of course an infinite number of bodies of communal enjoyment, since in infinite time infinite beings have become Buddha. As a *saṃbhogakāya* teaches only the Mahāyāna it is possible for Mahāyāna to claim that its own teachings are truly those of the Buddha manifesting in a superior *saṃbhogakāya* form. This contrasts with the lower *nirmāṇakāya* manifestation that includes Śākyamuni Buddha appearing in India in history, teaching as a preliminary to the higher doctrine the non-Mahāyāna teachings. To have direct access to the body of communal enjoyment it is necessary to have spiritual attainments that will allow one, either in this life or in another, to reach the relevant Pure Land.

A Buddha, however, wishes to help everyone. To benefit even those of lowly attainments, or the wicked, Buddhas emanate *nirmāṇakāyas*. The 'body of magical transformation' – 'Buddha in the world' (Griffiths) – is frequently described on the model of Śākyamuni Buddha and the great deeds of his life. Later sources make it clear, however, that a body of magical transformation can appear in any form that will benefit others and is not limited to appearing in accordance with the classic model of the life of the Buddha. Thus the historical figure of Śākyamuni Buddha and the events of his life, as a body of magical transformation, were simply emanations. In effect they were a magical show teaching out of compassion, manifested by a *saṃbhogakāya* Buddha but ultimately, as it were, the spontaneous compassionate 'overflow' of the *dharmakāya*.[14]

How to become a Buddha

Mahāyāna sources are quite clear that the path to full Buddhahood takes a long time. It is often said to take three incalculable aeons. The reason for following it is compassion. As we saw above when considering the three motivations for religious practice outlined by Atiśa, having the motivation of wishing to attain freedom of suffering for all, and from that motivation embracing the long path to Buddhahood, is definitive of the Mahāyāna practitioner. The 'vehicle' which makes that possible is definitively the Mahāyāna.

Details of the path of the bodhisattva to Buddhahood differ between Indian Buddhist sources, not to mention sources from outside India. I shall base my outline of the path mainly on the great *Bodhicaryāvatāra* ('Introduction to the Conduct which leads to Enlightenment') of Śāntideva, together with the *Bhāvanākramas* ('Stages of Cultivation') of Kamalaśīla (both from the eighth century), and Atiśa's *Bodhipathapradīpa* ('Lamp for the Path to Enlightenment'). The latter has a commentary attributed to Atiśa himself.[15]

The proper commencement of the path of the bodhisattva is not thought to be just some vague sense of care, but an actual revolutionary event which occurs in the trainee bodhisattva's mind, an event which is a fundamental switch in orientation from self-concern to concern for others, to compassion. This event is called the 'arising of the Awakening Mind (*bodhicitta*)'. The incredible implications of such a thing occurring – in effect the *real* deep wish and intention to be kind in every way to all without discrimination – and the importance of preserving it, are hymned by Śāntideva in the opening chapters of his poem:

> It satisfies with every happiness those starved of happiness, and cuts away oppressions from those oppressed in many ways.
>
> It also drives off delusion. How could there be a holy man its equal, how such a friend, or how such merit?
> (*Bodhicaryāvatāra* 1: 29–30, trans. Crosby and Skilton)

But just as there is a distinction between really wishing to travel somewhere and actually undertaking the journey, Śāntideva notes, so too we can distinguish two types of Awakening Mind, the 'Mind resolved on Awakening' and the 'Mind proceeding towards Awakening' (1: 15–16).

Later Tibetan traditions have isolated two analytic meditation patterns from the Indian sources which it is thought will facilitate the occurrence – give compelling reasons for the generation – of this revolutionary mind. The first meditation pattern, called 'equalising self and others and exchanging self and others', can be traced to the eighth chapter of Śāntideva's *Bodhicaryāvatāra*. It is taken for granted by Śāntideva that if we are talking about morality then we require no special pleading. We must be completely objective. Now, all are equal in wanting happiness and the avoidance of suffering (8: 95–6). As regards the need therefore to treat everyone equally that is all there is to it. Viewed objectively there is nothing special about me such that I strive for just *my own* happiness and the avoidance of *my own* suffering: 'I should dispel the suffering of others because it is suffering like my own suffering. I should help others too because of their nature as beings, which is like my own being' (op. cit.: 8: 94).

First one sees all as of equal weight. Then one actually 'exchanges self and others' by seeing all the problems that arise from cherishing oneself and the benefits that accrue from cherishing others. One meditates that:

> All those who suffer in the world do so because of the desire for their own happiness. All those happy in the world are so because of their desire for the happiness of others.
>
> Why say more? Observe this distinction: between the fool who longs for his own advantage and the sage who acts for the advantage of others.
>
> (Op. cit.: 8: 129–30)

The result is an imperative to always put others first.

The other meditation pattern can be traced in the second *Bhāvanākrama* of Kamalaśīla and in the commentary to Atiśa's *Bodhipathapradīpa*. As with Śāntideva's reasoning above it is based upon a sense of equality, since all are equal in wishing for happiness and the avoidance of suffering. Moreover if we take cognisance of previous lives then throughout the infinite series of previous lives all sentient beings have been one's friends many times. Indeed, as Atiśa notes, all sentient beings have been one's mother in previous lives and from this reflection arises the wish to repay their kindness. That is called 'love' (*maitrī*) and from that in turn arises compassion (*karuṇā*) for one's 'mother sentient beings' that are suffering so much. For his part Kamalaśīla meditates systematically on these sufferings. From all this, Atiśa hopes, comes the Awakening Mind, a wish and a path to help them in all possible ways but ultimately through attaining full Buddhahood for their welfare (see Sherburne (trans.) 1983: 42–3).

In actually following the journey which has been vowed, to perfect Buddhahood for the benefit of all sentient beings without distinction, the bodhisattva practises in particular the six (or ten) perfections (*pāramitā*) and traverses the five paths (*mārga*) and the ten stages (*bhūmi*). According to this model when the Awakening Mind has arisen one has nevertheless not yet technically entered the first of the bodhisattva stages. It is necessary to cultivate 'means' (*upāya*) – that is, the first five perfections of giving (*dāna*), morality (*śīla*), patience (*kṣānti*), effort (*vīrya*), and meditative concentration (*dhyāna*) – as well as the sixth perfection of wisdom (*prajñā*), without neglecting either.[16] At the true arising of the Awakening Mind the new bodhisattva begins the first of the five paths, the path of accumulation (*saṃbhāramārga*), accumulating the 'twin accumulations' of merit (through the 'means') and wisdom. The bodhisattva then attains the path of preparation (*prayogamārga*), which develops in four stages a deepening direct realisation of emptiness.[17] When direct non-conceptual awareness of emptiness first occurs in meditation, the bodhisattva attains the path of seeing (*darśanamārga*). He or she is no longer an ordinary person, but becomes a fully-fledged *ārya* bodhisattva. With this, Kamalaśīla says, the bodhisattva attains the *first* of the ten bodhisattva stages, the stage called that of 'Joyous'. This stage is associated with the particular (although by no means exclusive) cultivation of the perfection of giving. It follows that actually to attain to the full degree the perfections of giving and so on it is necessary to have had direct non-conceptual awareness of emptiness. They are not truly *perfections* unless they are underpinned with a direct realisation that e.g. the giver, recipient, and gift all lack inherent existence. Giving is explained as being of three types: (i) material goods; (ii) fearlessness; and (iii) the Doctrine (*Dharma*).[18]

The other nine bodhisattva stages all occur on the fourth of the five paths, the path of cultivation (*bhāvanāmārga*). It should be noted, incidentally, that at each of these stages the bodhisattva is said to employ twelve particular abilities such as the ability to see Buddhas, visit Pure Lands, live for aeons, shake and illuminate worlds, and emanate or otherwise manifest versions of his or her body. At the first bodhisattva stage this applies to sets of one hundred and can be attained in one instant (see in one instant one hundred Buddhas, visit one hundred Pure Lands, and so on). The number is multiplied by ten at the next stage (i.e. in one instant see one thousand etc.), one hundred at the stage after that (i.e. in one instant see one hundred thousand etc.), and so on. By the time the bodhisattva reaches the tenth stage the figure is said to be inexpressible (see *Madhyamakāvatāra* Ch. 11, cf. Lopez 1988b: 203).

The second bodhisattva stage is called the 'Pure' ('Stainless'; *vimalā*). At this the bodhisattva attains the very perfection of morality. Morality remains perfectly pure even in his or her dreams. At the third stage, the 'Luminous', the bodhisattva perfects the virtue of patience. Patience does not quarrel with others, and also it is capable of putting up with any misery. Then the bodhisattva attains the fourth stage, that called the 'Radiant', on which the bodhisattva acquires the perfection of effort that counteracts on heroic scale all laziness and faintheartedness. The fifth stage is 'Difficult to Conquer', and the bodhisattva attains the perfection of meditative concentration. Then comes the crucial sixth stage, that of 'Approaching', in which the bodhisattva finally achieves the perfection of wisdom, understanding dependent origination (*pratītyasamutpāda*) in all its implications.[19] We have now reached the end of the six perfections. But the bodhisattva continues for a very long time yet, attaining the seventh to tenth stages and according to sources like the *Daśabhūmika Sūtra* a further series of four additional perfections. Thus at the seventh stage, the 'Gone Afar', the bodhisattva attains the perfection of skill in means and completes the eradication forever of the obscuration of moral taints (*kleśāvaraṇa*). The bodhisattva is thus free from rebirth (*Madhyamakāvatāra*). Were he or she not a bodhisattva with the bodhisattva vows to attain perfect Buddhahood for the benefit of others, it would have been possible to attain the final peace of the arhat.[20] The remaining three stages are thus called the pure stages, and bring about the final eradication of the other fundamental obscuration often spoken of in Buddhist doctrinal texts, that of the knowable (*jñeyāvaraṇa*). The process of dissolving the obscuration of the knowable is the process of attaining the unique omniscience of a Buddha. At the eighth stage, the 'Immovable', the bodhisattva begins to see the world in a completely different way, even when not meditating, 'like a person awaking from a dream'.[21] From this stage all the activities of a bodhisattva have become instinctive ('spontaneous'), the natural overflow of his or her great vows of compassion. There is no more striving. The perfection is called that of the 'vow'. The ninth stage is 'Good Intelligence', the perfection 'power' or 'strength' (*bala*). The tenth and last stage is the 'Cloud of Doctrine', the perfection that of gnosis (*jñāna*). The bodhisattva appears on a special jewelled lotus seat, surrounded by other bodhisattvas. Light rays pervade the universe, many sufferings are eradicated, and all the Buddhas appear and consecrate the hero to full Buddhahood. As the *Daśabhūmika Sūtra* makes clear, the powers of the bodhisattva already are such that he or she can even put an entire world region into an atom of dust, or infinite sentient beings into a pore of his or her skin, without any harm occurring. The tenth stage bodhisattva can emanate innumerable and any forms in order to help others, even the forms of Hindu gods like Śiva. Yet this is nothing, a minuscule droplet compared with the powers of a fully enlightened Buddha. Buddhahood is attained with the final complete eradication of the obscuration of the knowable, that is, with the attainment of omniscience. With this the bodhisattva transcends the ten bodhisattva stages and, of course, ceases to be a bodhisattva. In attaining Buddhahood he or she also attains the fifth of the five paths, that of 'no more learning' (*aśaikṣamārga*). It is a path to nowhere, for now the bodhisattva is a Buddha – and the Buddha is everywhere.

Buddha and bodhisattva cults in Indian Mahāyāna

We know from the work of Paul Harrison (1987) that the earliest Mahāyāna appears not to have thought of the bodhisattvas as people to prostrate and pray to (the 'celestial' bodhisattvas) but rather as a group to join. The bodhisattva is a model for one's own spiritual career. One should oneself out of compassion become, or aspire to become, a bodhisattva and eventually a Buddha. But as we have also seen, early Mahāyāna may well have embraced a number of separate cults centred on particular sūtras and their teachings. Some sūtras which were relatively early were concerned almost entirely with a description of the nature and delights of the Pure Land (or Buddha Field; *buddhakṣetra*) of the particular favoured Buddha and how to be reborn in that Pure Land. Examples might be the *Akṣobhyavyūha Sūtra* or the *Sukhāvatīvyūha Sūtra*. With time particular advanced bodhisattvas also became associated with Pure Lands and the focus of cults which seek to involve their beneficial activities.

Indian Mahāyāna Buddha and bodhisattva cults appear to be concerned first and foremost with techniques of access. That is, they concern techniques for reaching a Pure Land and its attendant Buddha and bodhisattvas, through meditation and rebirth, and bringing into play in this very life the beneficial qualities of those Buddhas and bodhisattvas. The concept of the Buddha Field perhaps represents a result of a consideration of Śākyamuni's range of influence and authority, his field of awareness, and the actual geographical context of his activities (Rowell 1935). This was combined with the development of the idea – found also in non-Mahāyāna sources – of a multiplicity of world-systems throughout the infinity of space, in some of which at least there must surely be other Buddhas. Thus a Buddha's range of awareness (and compassion) is infinite, but the actual range of his direct spiritual influence is finite although vast, and in the case of Śākyamuni he was actually born and had immediate influence in a very limited historical and geographical context. Throughout infinite space there are however infinite Buddhas, each located in a particular place, each with infinite awareness and compassion, and each with a vast but finite direct spiritual influence. Their location, and the range of their direct influence, is their Buddha Field. The Buddha Field exists in order to help sentient beings that can be helped by that Buddha Field.

A bodhisattva on his or her path to Buddhahood is said to 'purify' his or her Buddha Field, which is the result of their great acts of compassion. Thus the Buddha Field of a Buddha is thought in some sense to be brought into existence by his or her great deeds on the bodhisattva path. Not all Buddha Fields are fully-fledged Pure Lands however. Since Śākyamuni Buddha was born in ancient India his Buddha Field would appear to have been extremely impure. Some Mahāyāna texts refer to three types of Buddha Fields: pure, impure, and mixed. One response to the apparent impurity of Śākyamuni's Buddha Field was that of the *Karuṇāpuṇḍarīka Sūtra* ('the "Lotus of Compassion" Discourse'), which claimed that Śākyamuni was a superior type of Buddha precisely *because* his compassion was so great that he appeared in such an impure place. Another response was to suggest, with the *Vimalakīrtinirdeśa Sūtra* (the 'Discourse concerning the Teaching of Vimalakīrti'), that purity and impurity are matters of the mind. For a person who sees correctly, the 'impure' sphere of Śākyamuni is indeed itself a full Pure Land.

A bodhisattva can be born in the Buddha Field of a Buddha, or it may be possible to visit a Buddha Field in meditation. It is quite possible that the very idea of the Pure Land – and indeed the 'continuing revelation' which is represented by the Mahāyāna sūtras – had some connection with the experiences of visions seen in meditation. Central here is the practice of 'recollection of the Buddha' (*buddhānusmṛti*). Indeed it may even be possible to associate geographically some of the developments in *buddhānusmṛti* practice which contributed to the rise of Pure Land cults with the region of Kashmir and associated areas of Central Asia during the first few centuries CE (Demiéville 1954).[22] Kashmir at this time was renowned for its meditation masters, and for meditation practices in which elements often thought of separately as Mahāyāna and non-Mahāyāna were mixed. It was renowned particularly for *buddhānusmṛti* practices. Especially important to the Kashmiri meditators of the period was the bodhisattva Maitreya, the only current bodhisattva completely acceptable in both Mahāyāna and non-Mahāyāna contexts.

Broadly speaking recollection of the Buddha involves recollecting systematically and with a concentrated mind the great qualities of the (or 'a') Buddha. We know from quite early Pāli sources that among the results of such a practice is that 'it is possible . . . to see him with [the] mind as clearly as with [the] eyes, in night as well as day' (*Sutta Nipāta*, trans. Saddhatissa: v. 1142). Through recollection of the Buddha, the Theravāda scholar Buddhaghosa observes, one can conquer fear and come to feel as if one were actually living in the Master's presence, and '[one's] mind tends towards the plane of the Buddhas' (*Visuddhimagga*, trans. Ñāṇamoli: 230). It seems very likely that one spur to the cultivation of such practices was regret at living in an age after the life of the Buddha has passed.[23] But there is clearly a paradox in the popularity of practices that lead to feeling as if one is in the presence of a Buddha when the Buddha is held to be dead and gone, and quite inaccessible. This is particularly the case when certain texts not specifically Mahāyāna speak of the possibility of nirvāṇa through *buddhānusmṛti* (Harrison 1978: 38). For their part relatively early Mahāyāna sūtras like the *Pratyutpanna Sūtra*[24] describe austere and rigorous visualisation practices which lead to a vision (or a dream) of a Buddha, in this case the Buddha Amitāyus in his Pure Land of Sukhāvatī in the West. Amitāyus is seen not with the (psychic) 'divine eye' but with one's present fleshly eyes. The meditator receives teachings directly from Buddha Amitāyus, and transmits those teachings to humankind. Thus in this Mahāyāna context through practice of recollection of the Buddha it is held to be possible to reach a Buddha who is still present albeit elsewhere, and to receive teachings – including new teachings – from that Buddha. If compassionate Buddhas are present throughout space 'in the ten directions' (up, down, the four cardinal points, and the four intermediate points) then it must be possible to come into contact with them and draw on their compassion. All that needs to be added is that it must be possible also, through use of the correct techniques, to bring about rebirth in their presence – not through any selfish reason but in order, of course, to further one's spiritual path under the best possible circumstances. It ought to be possible to become enlightened if taught directly by a Buddha, as we know so many became enlightened at the time of Śākyamuni Buddha. Thus while it may take a very long time to become enlightened under present circumstances, if one can bring about rebirth in the Pure Land of a Buddha then the path will be very much shortened.

Buddhas

As we have seen, Gregory Schopen suggested (1975) that early Mahāyāna may have involved a series of largely independent (though presumably in some as yet unclear sense linked) 'book cults' centred on particular sūtras and their teachings. If so, then some of these book cults involved sūtras which set out to teach how in meditation and rebirth the Pure Land of a chosen Buddha can be reached.[25] It is possible that the earliest Pure Land

Buddha cult was centred on the Buddha Akṣobhya and his Buddha Field in the East. This cult is reflected in the *Akṣobhyavyūha Sūtra*, a sūtra which was translated into Chinese as early as the second century CE and which may well have been written originally in Gāndhārī, the language of Northwest India (including Kashmir) at that time. The Pure Land of Akṣobhya is modelled rather on a heavenly realm. It is the ideal realm, the world as it ought to be, a world in which Māra (the 'Devil') does not interfere, a world without mountains, a world of flowers, gentle breezes, and music. There is no ugliness, no menstruation, no gross physical sexuality, and gestation and birth is gentle and pleasant. All is clean, and all are interested in practising the Doctrine. This Pure Land is so wonderful as a direct result of the merit deriving from great vows of morality made by Akṣobhya when engaged in the bodhisattva path. Rebirth in this wonderful Pure Land comes from following oneself the bodhisattva path and vowing to be reborn in Akṣobhya's Pure Land (Abhirati). One should also dedicate all merit to being reborn there in order to become fully enlightened in the presence of Akṣobhya, and visualise the Pure Land with Akṣobhya within it teaching the Doctrine, while wishing to be like him (Chang 1983: 315 ff.).[26]

A further Buddha Field cult seems to have been associated with the Buddha Bhaiṣajyaguru, the Medicine Buddha, and indeed it is possible that this cult originated outside the country and was subsequently introduced into India (Birnbaum 1980). But by far the most well known of the Pure Land cults is that of Buddha Amitābha – sometimes known as Amitāyus and sometimes perhaps as Amita – and his Pure Land of Sukhāvatī in the West.[27] The significance of the Pure Land cult of Amitābha is largely due to its considerable importance in China and particularly Japan. There is surprisingly little evidence for its widespread importance in Indian Buddhism.[28] The specific cult of Amitābha, assuming there was such an identifiable cult in India and abstracting from the key sūtras in the East Asian Amitābha tradition, is centred on two, or possibly three, sūtras. Principal among them is the longer *Sukhāvatīvyūha Sūtra*, first translated into Chinese during the second century CE and like the *Akṣobhyavyūha* perhaps written originally in Gāndhārī. Again, rather as with the *Akṣobhyavyūha*, the *Sukhāvatīvyūha Sūtra* tells of a previous time many years ago when the bodhisattva Dharmākara, having visualised the most perfect Buddha Field possible, made (in the Sanskrit version) forty-six vows. These vows are expressed in a series of conditions through the formula 'If this is not fulfilled, may I not become a fully enlightened Buddha'.

This Dharmākara is now the Buddha Amitābha. All therefore is as he vowed. Thus in accordance with the vows all those who are born in this Pure Land of his will never return to the lower realms, and they will be firmly established in a state set on enlightenment. Those who having heard his name meditate on Amitābha will be taken by him to Sukhāvatī at the time of death. Those who have directed their 'roots of merit' to be reborn in Sukhāvatī will do so. This will occur even if they have generated the thought of Amitābha only ten times, always providing they have not committed one of the five great crimes of murdering father or mother, or an arhat, harming a Buddha, or causing schism in the Sangha.[29] Thus all those who wish to be reborn in the Pure Land of Amitābha should generate the Awakening Mind, hear the name of Amitābha, think of him and meditate on him. They should make vows to be reborn in Sukhāvatī and turn over their stock of merit in order that this should come about.

A further description of Sukhāvatī is given in the shorter *Sukhāvatīvyūha Sūtra*. There is some uncertainty among scholars as to the chronological priority between the two *Sukhāvatīvyūha Sūtras*. The shorter sūtra particularly stresses that Sukhāvatī is a Pure Land and not a heavenly realm or a sensual paradise. Even the birds of Sukhāvatī sing the Doctrine. The proper way to be reborn there is undistracted holding of the name of Amitāyus for up to seven days. The *Pratyutpanna Sūtra* is also another important Amitāyus text, describing by way of contrast how it is possible to have a vision of Amitāyus in this very life itself. But the East Asian tradition always classes along with the two *Sukhāvatīvyūha* sūtras not the *Pratyutpanna Sūtra* but another sūtra available only in Chinese and known by its Chinese title as the *Kuan-wu-liang-shou-fo Ching*. It has become normal to translate this title into Sanskrit as the *Amitāyurdhyāna Sūtra*, but if appropriate to translate it into Sanskrit at all perhaps a better translation would be the significant *Amitāyurbuddhānusmṛti Sūtra*. There has been some doubt however as to whether in fact this sūtra was originally written in India. Some scholars consider it a Chinese 'forgery', although it could have been composed in the Indian cultural areas of Central Asia. Julian Pas (1977) sees the sūtra as one of a number of visualisation sūtras composed in the area around Kashmir or associated areas of Central Asia, with a series of significant Chinese interpolations. Also included among these visualisation sūtras is one that involves rebirth in the Tuṣita heaven if one calls on the name of its most famous resident, Maitreya, and practises *buddhānusmṛti* (op. cit.: 201). Seeking rebirth in Tuṣita in the presence of Maitreya was and is a practice perfectly acceptable within the non-Mahāyāna tradition. The only significantly different factor with Amitābha, therefore, is that Amitābha is a *Buddha* who exists presently in a *Pure Land*. Here, perhaps, we see the results of visionary encounter plus the possibility that if there are past and future Buddhas so there surely must also be other contemporary Buddhas somewhere in the cosmos.

Although it is not homogeneous, let us take the '*Amitāyurbuddhānusmṛti Sūtra*' as an Indic text. The sūtra teaches a series of thirteen visualisations in which one builds up an elaborate scene of Sukhāvatī with Amitāyus seated on his lotus throne, flanked by his two bodhisattvas Avalokiteśvara and Mahāsthāmaprāpta.[30] The meditator prays for rebirth in Sukhāvatī and visualises him- or herself indeed reborn there within a lotus. There are different levels of rebirth in the Pure Land (reflecting perhaps Chinese social categories). Nevertheless, as it stands the sūtra suggests that even someone who *has* committed the five worst crimes may be reborn in Sukhāvatī as a result of calling on the name of Amitāyus before death even as few as ten times. They are born inside a closed lotus in Sukhāvatī. After twelve aeons the lotus opens and they behold the two bodhisattvas preaching the Doctrine. Thus they generate the Awakening Mind and eventually they too become enlightened.[31]

Bodhisattvas

Mahāyāna bodhisattva cults can perhaps be contrasted with those devoted to Buddhas. The contrast, such as there is, is that while Buddha cults appear primarily (perhaps with the exception of Bhaiṣajyaguru) to be concerned with visions, teachings, and rebirth, bodhisattva cults have a certain tendency to want to bring into play the bodhisattva's compassion and power for direct tangible 'this worldly' benefits. We have noted already the importance of Maitreya, who is Śākyamuni's successor, and is held by both Mahāyāna and non-Mahāyāna traditions to be the next Buddha in this world. The idea that Śākyamuni Buddha was not the only Buddha but was the latest of a long line of Buddhas – and therefore there will also be Buddhas in the future – developed fairly early in the history of Buddhism. It was thought reasonable to assume, therefore, that the next Buddha can be named and is already in the final stages of his bodhisattva path. The *Maitreyavyākaraṇa* ('Prediction of Maitreya') is a text that describes the tempting wonders of the 'millennium', the world many years hence when Maitreya finally arrives and in becoming a Buddha completes his bodhisattva path. Maitreya appears to have been almost a 'patron saint' of the Kashmiri meditation schools and his cult was carried to Central Asia (also as the subject of a number of enormous statues) where it was extremely important, and thence to China.[32]

One of the earliest sources for the cult of Avalokiteśvara is the *Lotus Sūtra*. In the twenty-fourth chapter of that sūtra (Sanskrit version), which appears to have circulated sometimes as a separate text, the salvific activity and benefits of Avalokiteśvara are described in tempting detail. He is a truly useful bodhisattva, saving from fire, rivers and oceans, murder, execution, demons, ghosts, prison, bandits, and moral negativities like greed, hatred, and delusion. He grants excellent offspring – sons or daughters – to those who wish for them.[33] Avalokiteśvara is a bodhisattva who appears in whatever form is necessary to help others, be it as a follower of Mahāyāna, non-Mahāyāna, householder, monk, animal, or god. Avalokiteśvara also acts as an assistant to Amitābha, and is thus associated with Amitābha and is sometimes portrayed in art with a small figure of Amitābha in his turban or hair.[34] Particularly important in terms of the Avalokiteśvara cult is the *Kāraṇḍavyūha Sūtra*. This sūtra describes Avalokiteśvara's activities for the benefit of others. It includes his descent into the hells in order to help the hell-dwellers, and his appearance in the form of a bee in order to hum the Doctrine to save thousands of worms. Avalokiteśvara even apparently placed the Hindu gods like Śiva in their appropriate ranks, ruling by Avalokiteśvara's permission. It seems to be the *Kāraṇḍavyūha Sūtra* that is the source for the great mantra associated with Avalokiteśvara, *oṃ maṇipadme hūṃ*, perhaps modelled on the use of the Śaivite mantra *oṃ namaḥ śivāya* (Studholme 1999). In Indian art there is also some marked iconographic association of Avalokiteśvara with Śiva.[35]

A female bodhisattva that has become important in Tibetan Buddhism, frequently associated with Avalokiteśvara and taking over from him some of his salvific functions, is Tārā. It is not clear how important she was in Indian Buddhism, although praises of her date from just possibly as early as the third century CE and the great missionary to Tibet Atiśa is said, at least by Tibetans, to have been a particular devotee of Tārā (Willson 1986). The fact that Tārā is held to be perpetually 16 years old, and yet the 'Mother of all the Buddhas' suggests some possible connection between her and the figure of *Prajñāpāramitā* – a female personification for ritual and meditation purposes of Wisdom itself – who is also described this way.

Another figure who is regularly described as 16 years old, and is often said to be the very incarnation of the Perfection of Wisdom, is Mañjuśrī, 'the birthplace of all the Buddhas'. He is described – as wisdom should be – as both the progenitor of all the Buddhas and also their most excellent son (Williams 1989: 240). Indeed, in Tibetan art Mañjuśrī is commonly portrayed holding aloft the sword of gnosis which cuts aside the bonds of ignorance.[36] In Indian Buddhism Mañjuśrī gains his significance mainly as the supremely wise interlocutor in a number of Mahāyāna sūtras, such as the *Vimalakīrtinirdeśa Sūtra*. The importance of this sūtra in Chinese Buddhism may go some way towards explaining the possibility that a particular concern with Mañjuśrī could have originated in Chinese or perhaps Central Asian Buddhism. Anyway, in India Mañjuśrī appears in Indian art fairly late, and his association with the sacred mountain Wu-t'ai Shan in China seems to have been known in ancient India itself. Mañjuśrī is sometimes spoken of in the sūtras as actually already a fully enlightened Buddha, and in these sūtras – such as the *Mañjuśrībuddhakṣetraguṇavyūha* and the *Mañjuśrīparinirvāṇa* (in Lamotte 1960) – the categories of tenth-stage bodhisattva and Buddha begin to break down or merge. Mañjuśrī has in the past appeared as a Buddha, manifested all the deeds of a Buddha, and apparently entered final nirvāṇa, although he remains acting tirelessly for the benefit of sentient beings. In fact he has done this many times, even leaving holy relics behind. In the *Ajātaśatrukaukṛtyavinodana Sūtra* Śākyamuni Buddha describes how in the past he was a disciple of Mañjuśrī and has indeed become a Buddha through Mañjuśrī (quoted in Lamotte 1960: 93–4). Such observations, whether for the believer true or not, may well indicate also the way in which sūtras establish the identity and prestige of their teachings in rivalry with traditions associated with other Buddhas and bodhisattvas, and perhaps also any associated cults.

In the final analysis are all these Buddhas and bodhisattvas considered by Mahāyāna Buddhists to be real or not? This question often becomes a question about whether 'sophisticated', 'educated', 'brainy' Mahāyāna Buddhists believe there really are such beings, or whether these are mere concessions to the masses, 'popular Buddhism', or perhaps ways of speaking symbolically of positive qualities like compassion and wisdom. The answer, at least from the point of view of traditional Mahāyāna as it has existed down the centuries, is that of course Buddhas and bodhisattvas – as actual beings with arms and legs – do not really, really exist. This is because from an ultimate point of view all is either empty of inherent existence, or merely non-dual consciousness, or the Buddha-nature, or some other ultimate truth. But to think that this entails that they therefore do not exist,

exist that is in the non-inherent etc. way that we all do – and are thus really symbols for, say, positive qualities – would be precisely to confuse ultimate negation with conventional negation. From a Madhyamaka point of view, for example, Mañjuśrī has as much reality as we do and is genuinely working for the benefit of all of us. We can indeed *see* Mañjuśrī, and enter into a reciprocal relationship with him. The fact that he is in other contexts also spoken of as being actually wisdom itself personified is irrelevant. To say that Mañjuśrī, or Buddha Amitābha, are merely symbolic and do not really (in the everyday sense of 'really') exist would be to say that there are no advanced bodhisattvas with the qualities spoken of in the sūtras, or no Buddhas as understood by Mahāyāna. They do not exist, not in the ultimate sense in which all things do not exist (i.e. in Madhyamaka in the sense of having inherent existence), but they do not exist at all. This is certainly not entailed by the teachings of emptiness and so on. And it would probably be to destroy Mahāyāna Buddhism, and the great Mahāyāna aim of striving through pure altruism as a bodhisattva throughout innumerable existences in order to attain perfect Buddhahood for the benefit of all sentient beings.

All conditioned things are impermanent, Mahāyāna Buddhism as well. But to hasten its end would seem to me to be a pity.

7 Mantranaya/Vajrayāna – tantric Buddhism in India

Introduction

As this book has demonstrated, scholarly understandings of, and attitudes towards, the history of Buddhist institutions and thought in India have changed considerably in recent years. Tantric Buddhism, with its focus on particular sorts of meditation and ritual, is no exception. The present chapter takes on the task of depicting the 'sort of animal' that tantric Buddhism is. It is a task that in a number of respects should deter the wise. One problem is the lack of availability of materials. A large number of primary texts – tantric scriptures, commentaries, and related works – survive in Sanskrit, and in Chinese and Tibetan translation, yet only a very few have either been edited (to give a reliable text from surviving manuscripts) or translated into European or other modern languages.[1] This has inevitably limited attempts to understand the nature and development of tantric Buddhism in India. The tantric tradition is also complex and multiform, containing what may appear to the beginner as a baroque and dizzying array of deities, practices, and symbols that challenge his or her previous understanding of Buddhism. As a result most introductory works make little more than passing reference to tantric Buddhism.[2]

A further problem concerns attitudes, both scholarly and popular. Until comparatively recently scholarly investigation of tantric Buddhism has been unfashionable. One reason for this has to do with a series of presuppositions held by some scholars who were involved, particularly in the early period of Buddhist scholarship in the West, in what Donald Lopez (1996: 99) has termed the 'European construction of an original Buddhism'.[3] In this perspective tantric Buddhism was seen as degenerate – typified by disgusting practices and a welter of gods – and far removed from the conception of (early and 'true') Buddhism as a rational, humanistic, and morally uplifting philosophy, free from the taints of magic and idolatry otherwise found in Indian religion. Buddhism was clearly not a tantric 'sort of animal'. To take just one example of this type of thinking, Louis de La Vallée Poussin (1922: 193), one of the great Buddhist scholars of the twentieth century, concluded that tantric Buddhism was 'practically Buddhist Hinduism, Hinduism . . . in Buddhist garb'. Not surprisingly, evaluations such as these contributed both to the neglect of the field and the paucity of available materials.

Today, the academic study of tantric Buddhism is more acceptable. The project of reconstructing an 'original Buddhism' is seen to be misguided, as is the attempt to identify narrowly religion with soteriology. There is a growing interest in the ritual dimension of religion – a dominant feature of tantric Buddhism – allied with a recognition that understanding a religious tradition requires a balance of textual and anthropological perspectives. In consequence, a number of more recent (generally non-introductory) publications dealing with Buddhism and the religions of India give tantric Buddhism, and tantric traditions in general, a weighting that is more appropriate to their historical and religious importance.[4]

Non-scholarly attitudes, especially in the contemporary West, are also often problematic. Words like 'tantra', 'tantric', 'tantrism', have an array of popular, but on the whole misleading, connotations derived from a range of representations of Indian tantric traditions. The negative associations these words carried for scholars in the past are now largely absent. On the contrary, more often they carry a sense of allure and excitement. Contemporary connotations are generally sexual – i.e. 'Tantra' is about (particularly exciting and unusual) sex, or sexual ritual. Perhaps it is the very antinomian and sexual elements in Indian (Buddhist and otherwise) tantric religion that have laid hold of both scholarly and popular imaginations and received contrary evaluations. The difficulty with such popular representations is not that there is no sex, or sexual ritual, in Indian tantric religion. There is – though it may not be the sort of thing constructed by (for differing reasons) past scholars or present popular imaginings. The problem is that any attempt to identify tantric religion with forms of sexuality (or transgressive behaviour) is to understand it too narrowly. In tantric Buddhism – and this is not the place to address the issue within Indian religion as a whole – sexual elements come to play a role comparatively late in the development of the tradition.

How significant is tantric Buddhism, then, to the understanding of Buddhism in India? If we provisionally define tantric Buddhism as the set of religious ideas and practices promulgated in or related to texts classed as tantras by the Buddhist tradition itself, then tantric texts appear by the third century CE.[5] They continue to appear until Buddhism's effective disappearance from India during the twelfth century. From approximately the beginning of the eighth century, tantric techniques and approaches increasingly dominated Buddhist practice in India. One reason for this is that tantric meditation and ritual start to be seen as powerful and effective tools in the quest for Buddhahood, as well as a means for attaining worldly powers and goals. In other words, tantric Buddhism develops a soteriological function. Historically tantric Buddhism also took root in China, as one of a number of schools, and from there spread to Japan where, as the Shingon school, it still flourishes. Tibet, inheriting Indian Buddhism between the eighth and twelfth centuries, developed a tradition that was thoroughly tantric in complexion, with the result that all schools of Tibetan Buddhism regard tantric Buddhism as its highest and most effective form.

Some idea of the importance of tantric Buddhism in India can be gained by the very large number of Indian Buddhist tantric texts that have survived in their original language or in Tibetan translation. More than one thousand five hundred Sanskrit texts are known to survive and the actual total – the work of identifying and listing extant manuscripts continues – remains to be ascertained: Isaacson (1998: 26) suggests it may be over two thousand. The Tibetan Kanjur (*bKa' 'gyur*) collection of scriptures – works regarded as the word of the Buddha – contains more than four hundred and fifty texts classified as tantras, and the Tenjur (*bsTan 'gyur*) collection of commentaries and other authored works has, in its tantric section, more than two thousand four hundred texts.[6]

Tantric Buddhism in India did not evolve in isolation from the rest of Indian religious culture. The development of tantric forms of religion was a pan-Indian phenomenon, which had a profound and pervasive effect on the group of traditions that have come to be known as 'Hinduism'. Much of contemporary Hinduism shows the influence of tantric ideas and practices. The Jains also developed a tantric tradition in western India, which has as yet been little studied. A sense of the broader Indian tantric tradition can give a deeper understanding of tantric Buddhism, and an encouraging feature of more recent scholarship is the recognition, and increasingly nuanced discussion, of the relationship of tantric Buddhism to this broader Indic context (see, for example, Nihom 1994; Sanderson 1994).

Returning to the question of what 'sort of animal' we are dealing with, it has been noted that tantric Buddhism is in general concerned with particular types of meditation and ritual that are seen as especially powerful and efficacious. The goals of these practices may be both worldly – alleviation of illness, protection from danger, control over weather – and (more latterly) soteriological. Tantric techniques are generally centred on the ritual evocation and worship of deities who are usually conceived of as awakened, enlightened. Key to this process is the use of mantras – utterances of various kinds understood to have especial power – and methods of visualisation. Successful evocation of a deity would give the practitioner power to achieve his or her desired goal. Access to tantric practice is not open to all, but restricted to those who have received initiation, a ritual that empowers the practitioner to evoke a particular deity. Monastic vows are neither necessary nor sufficient qualification for tantric practice. Leaving aside for the time being the question of tantric Buddhism's origins, it is clear that these techniques were located within the context of Mahāyānist soteriological and ontological thinking.[7] Over time, however, tantric Buddhist ritual and Mahāyānist doctrinal categories can be seen modifying one another. None the less, insofar as tantric Buddhism is concerned largely with technique, it can be viewed – from within the perspective of Mahāyāna doctrine – as being primarily within the sphere of compassionate method or 'means' (*upāya*) rather than that of wisdom (*prajñā*).

A significant point in the history of tantric Buddhism occurs, probably sometime during the late seventh century, with the appearance of the term *Vajrayāna*, 'The Diamond Way'. This expression, which was to become one of the standard self-descriptions of tantric Buddhism, emerged at a time when the word *vajra*, meaning equally 'diamond' and 'thunderbolt', had assumed a major symbolic role in certain texts, standing for the indestructibility and power of the awakened, enlightened, state (*bodhi*). It is worth stressing that the term 'Vajrayāna' was not employed before this period, and that, therefore, the expressions 'Vajrayāna Buddhism' and 'tantric Buddhism' are not synonymous. What is true of Vajrayāna Buddhism is not necessarily true of tantric Buddhism as a whole. Thus, while Vajrayāna Buddhism has the speedy attainment of Buddhahood as a goal, this is not the case for tantric Buddhism overall, which had no such goal for perhaps its first four hundred years.

An earlier term used to distinguish tantric from other forms of practice was *mantranaya*, 'the path (*naya*) of mantras'. This expression was paired with *pāramitānaya*, 'the path of perfections' (i.e. the path elaborated in the Mahāyāna Perfection of Wisdom literature).[8] Together, the two paths were considered to constitute the Mahāyāna. The value of the Mantranaya was understood to be its particular efficacy in aiding the bodhisattva's compassionate activity in the world for the benefit of suffering sentient beings. Two points should be noted here. First, the label 'Mantranaya' indicates that the use of mantras was perceived to be the distinctive and distinguishing feature of tantric practice. Second, Indian tantric Buddhism, in its pre-Vajrayāna phase at least, saw itself as part of the Mahāyāna, a fact that can be obscured by suggestions that Buddhism is comprised of three paths – the Hīnayāna, Mahāyāna, and Vajrayāna.

Significant features of tantric Buddhism

Attempts to specify the nature of tantric Buddhism in any detail quickly run into difficulties since it proves hard to formulate a definition without excluding or including too much. Donald Lopez, who deals with the problem of defining tantric Buddhism at some length (1996: 83 ff.), tables the possibility that a search for one common defining characteristic is misplaced. If this is the case then what makes something an example of tantric Buddhism is not the possession of a single feature but, according to this argument, the possession of a significant proportion of a set of features. This way of defining, rooted in Wittgenstein's notion of 'family resemblances', and which can be termed 'polythetic' as opposed to 'monothetic', leaves the problem of how to decide on the base set of features on which individual instances of 'tantric Buddhism' draw.

Despite the limitations of this approach, it is worth enumerating some of tantric Buddhism's more important features, if only for the purpose of gaining a better overview of tantric Buddhist terrain, before turning to examine the nature of specific texts and historical phases.[9] None the less, it is important to remember that, in accordance with the notion of polythetic definition, individual features may or may not be present at any given historical or functional level of the tradition. The central concern of tantric Buddhism with technique has been noted, as has the importance of the evocation and worship of deities, the use of mantras and visualisation, and the necessity for initiation before undertaking tantric practice. Other features, some of which (ritual use of maṇḍalas, foul offerings and antinomian acts, and revaluation of the status and role of women) will be revisited at greater length later, include the following.[10]

Esotericism

Tantric Buddhism is often termed esoteric (see Wayman 1987), a notion that is related to the requirement of initiation. Some tantras threaten dire consequences to those who reveal their contents to the uninitiated. The *Vajrabhairava Tantra*, for example, after describing a number of rites, warns that 'these deeds must not be spoken of to others. Should the foolish devotee do this he will certainly fall into hell' (*Vajrabhairava Tantra*, trans. Siklós: 35). The same text (op. cit.: 43) also states that a painting of the deity Vajrabhairava should not be displayed openly. Another way in which secrecy was maintained was to use varying degrees of allusive, indirect, symbolic and metaphorical forms of language (*saṃdhyābhāṣā*).[11] This tradition can give rise to acute problems of interpretation. Not only is there the issue of whether statements are to be understood literally or not, there is also the question of how to understand them once it is agreed they are intended metaphorically. Indian tantric commentators themselves, aware of these problems, often failed to agree on an interpretation, as well as admitting that a passage could have multiple meanings.

Importance of the teacher

The role of the teacher (*guru*) or Vajra-master (*vajrācārya*) in tantric Buddhism is especially important. It is the teacher who gives access to tantric practice and who transmits the teachings of the various tantric scriptures. The *Guhyasamāja Tantra* (see Snellgrove 1987a: 177–8) identifies the tantric teacher as both the *bodhicitta* ('awakening mind'; q.v.) and as the father and mother of the Buddhas (in that the existence of Buddhas depends on their having teachers). That this text portrays the bodhisattva Maitreya being frightened on hearing this teaching suggests that the accordance of such high status to Vajra-masters was a new development.

Deriving from this status is the view that one should never speak ill of one's teacher. Again, the *Guhyasamāja Tantra*, while apparently recommending the contravention of all major ethical precepts, adds the qualification that 'those who speak ill of their teacher never succeed despite their practice' (quoted in Snellgrove 1987a: 170). In the later phases of tantric Buddhism the teacher's instruction is essential to the successful practice of what became quite complex psychophysical meditation techniques. Also the teacher is identified, in meditation, with the deity at the centre of the *maṇḍala*.

Ritual use of maṇḍalas

The employment of maṇḍalas – two, occasionally three, dimensional representations (or creations) of a sacred space or enclosure, often understood as the particular domain of a deity – are a ubiquitous feature of tantric Buddhism, used both in initiation rituals and in post-initiatory practice.

Foul offerings and antinomian acts – the transgressive dimension of tantric Buddhism

It is apparent that not everyone accepted tantric Buddhism, more especially in its latter phases, as genuinely Buddhist. There is evidence that a number of monks at Bodhgayā found the tradition sufficiently offensive to warrant the destruction of tantric texts and images (Sanderson 1994: 97). Controversial features included the use of impure and forbidden substances as offerings, the (seeming) advocacy of unethical behaviour, the employment of ritual sexual intercourse, and the worship of terrifying, wrathful, blood-drinking deities.

Revaluation of the body

It is not hard to find negative evaluations of the body in both Mainstream and Mahāyāna Buddhism (e.g. Chapter 8 of Śāntideva's *Bodhicaryāvatāra*) that often emphasise its impurity and disgustingness with a view to lessening the practitioner's attachment to it, and its cravings. Tantric valuations, on the other hand, are often highly positive.

> Without bodily form how should there be bliss? Of bliss one could not speak. The world is pervaded by bliss, which pervades and is itself pervaded. Just as the perfume of a flower depends on the flower, and without the flower becomes impossible, likewise without form and so on, bliss would not be perceived.
>
> (*Hevajra Tantra* II: ii, 36–7, trans. Snellgrove)

Two related factors are at play in the creation of such revaluations. First, the use of the expression 'great bliss' (*mahāsukha*) to describe the goal, and second, the employment of a yogic model of the body as the basis for generating blissful experience that is seen as functioning as the stepping-stone to the great bliss of awakening. The model of the body is essentially one shared by the Indian tantric tradition as a whole, and sees the body as possessing a subtle anatomy comprised of energy channels (*nāḍi*) and centres (*cakra*; literally 'wheel'). Through this system the vital energy (*prāṇa*) of the body flows, and under certain circumstances it can be yogically manipulated to generate a transformation in the awareness of the practitioner.[12] A range of meditation methods employing this model were developed, and came to form part of what was known as the 'perfection stage' (*niṣpannakrama*) of tantric Buddhist meditation. In the later tradition practices of this type were seen by some as an indispensable part of the path to Buddhahood.

Revaluation of the status and role of women

In the later phases of tantric Buddhism female deities become increasingly prominent, either at the centre of the maṇḍala as sole principal deity, or as the (wild and dancing) attendants of the central figure or figures. In scriptures women are given high status, and regarded as the embodiment and source of wisdom. In the milieu of tantric practice there is evidence that women functioned both as practitioners and teachers.

Analogical thinking

Employment of sets of correspondences and correlations is characteristic of much of tantric Buddhism. This approach involves the systematic elaboration of connections between the features of key aspects of tantric practice – such as deities, maṇḍalas, mantras, practitioners' bodies – and other elements or factors that they are seen to symbolise or embody. As Wayman has noted (1973: 30), this sort of thinking can be observed in India from as early as the (pre-Buddhist) *Ṛg Veda*.[13]

One of the more developed and better known sets of correspondences is based on a group of five cosmic Buddhas. These become associated with a whole range of other sets of five: directions, colours, hand-gestures, elements, aspects of awakened cognition or gnosis (*jñāna*), aggregates (*skandha*), negative mental states ('taints'; *kleśa*), to name but a few (see Table 1, p. 211). Significantly, some of these correlations link saṃsāra, or that which is unawakened – for example, the aggregates and negative mental states – to what is awakened, i.e. the five Buddhas. This is a connection that can be seen as reflecting a view that it is possible to use negative mental states to help traverse the path.

More generally, iconographical features of deities are encoded in terms of doctrinal categories. For example when the deity Cakrasaṃvara is portrayed trampling on Hindu deities, it might be explained as symbolising the destruction of craving and ignorance, or as the avoidance of attachment to either saṃsāra or nirvāṇa. Correspondences can also be established between microcosmic and macrocosmic levels. Thus, a maṇḍala and its deities may be identified as the body of the practitioner and as symbolising the cosmos as a whole. Identifications may also be multi-layered. The yogin's staff can symbolise his female partner, who in turn symbolises awakened wisdom (*prajñā*). Analysed into its components, the staff may then be the subject of further identifications.

Revaluation of negative mental states

The notion that mental states ordinarily conceived of as negative could be employed as a means of effectively traversing the path to Buddhahood becomes an significant feature of the Vajrayāna phase of tantric Buddhism. The *Hevajra Tantra* (II: ii, 51) declares that 'the world is bound by passion, also by passion it is released'. It gives a homoeopathic argument by way of justification: 'One knowing the nature of poison may dispel poison with poison, by means of the very poison that a little of which would kill other beings' (op. cit.: II: ii, 46).

Of the passions, it is sexual craving and pleasure that tend to be placed in the foreground, sexual bliss being homologised with the great bliss of awakening. In a general discussion of tantric religion, André Padoux (1987: 273) cites the French Indologist Madeleine Biardeau's summary of tantric doctrine as 'an attempt to place *kāma*, desire, in every meaning of the word, in the service of liberation'. Although this will not do for tantric Buddhism as a whole, it satisfactorily epitomises much of later Vajrayāna ideology.

Tantric texts: classification and characteristics

The very large number of Indian Buddhist tantric texts that survive in their original language, as well as in Chinese, Tibetan, and Mongolian translation, has been noted. These texts are of diverse kinds. There are the scriptures, many of which have one or more commentaries devoted to them, some of considerable length. There are ritual manuals and compendia that contain detailed prescriptions for a range of rituals associated with the consecration of monasteries, temples, and statues, the preparation and construction of maṇḍalas, initiation and empowerment (*abhiṣeka*), and the evocation of tantric dieties (*sādhana*).[14] There are also collections of tantric songs, hymns to individual deities, as well as texts on doctrine.

The classification of scriptures by the Indian commentarial tradition is not a straightforward matter. There are a number of classifications and no wholly consistent terminology. To complicate matters, the classification used in most secondary sources (i.e. books on Buddhism) appears not to be one used in the Indian context. Some categorisation of tantric scriptures into classes had occurred at least by the late eighth century, when a tripartite division of texts as either *Kriyā* ('Action'), *Caryā* ('Practice'), or *Yoga* ('Union') tantras is found.[15] This division is broadly chronological. Kriyā tantras are generally earlier than the Caryā, with the Caryā generally preceding the Yoga tantras. Scriptures appearing from the time of the Yoga tantras – approximately, from the early to mid-eighth century onwards – are often conscious of the classification tradition. What one sees is a development and expansion of categories, particularly of the Yoga tantra class. Scriptures begin to use these categories to describe themselves as tantras of particular kinds.

A classification that appears to have been fairly widely adopted by the end of the development of tantric Buddhism in India, at least as suggested by its usage in commentaries, is a fivefold division of scriptures into Kriyā, Caryā, Yoga, *Yogottara*, and *Yoganiruttara* tantras. This classification may be seen as an expansion of the earlier tripartite division, accomplished by a sub-division of the Yoga tantra class into three by the addition of two 'superior' categories, Yogottara ('Higher Yoga') and Yoganiruttara ('Highest Yoga'). Alternative terminology is found for these two categories. Yogottara tantras are also known as *Mahāyoga* ('Great Yoga'), and the term 'Yoganiruttara' may have sometimes been replaced by its synonym *Yogānuttara*. The Yoganiruttara tantras were also known as *Yoginī* tantras, a name that is descriptive of the focus these scriptures have on female figures (*yoginī* is the feminine of *yogin*, 'a practitioner of yoga').

This fivefold classification continues broadly to reflect historical developments in Indian tantric Buddhism. Thus scriptures called Yogottara or Mahāyoga generally appear before those called Yoganiruttara or Yoginī, and both types generally appear after the Yoga tantras. In what follows, I shall use this division to structure discussion of the different sorts of tantric texts, and in particular tantric scriptures. I shall also generally use the terms

Mahāyoga and Yoginī rather than Yogottara and Yoganiruttara for the fourth and fifth classes. This is largely for the reason that for one who does not read Sanskrit the former terms are probably more distinctive. It should be remembered, however, that some commentators used other categorisations of tantric scriptures, though these can generally be related to the fivefold division. For example, the great teacher Atiśa, writing in the mid-eleventh century, distinguishes seven categories, adding *Upāya* ('Means') and *Ubhaya* ('Dual') tantras between the Yoga and Mahāyoga tantras of the fivefold system. The different classes, moreover, are not discrete. A number of texts are clearly transitional, and there was not always agreement as to how to assign individual cases, or what were the defining features of the different categories. The project of classification is essentially scholastic in nature, and reflects the attempts of exegetes to give some order to the extensive and growing array of tantric texts they were faced with. None the less, bearing these factors in mind, the fivefold division can help clarify some of the key features and historical development of tantric Buddhism in India. It also has the advantage of being a significant self-representation developed by the Indian tantric tradition itself.

It should perhaps be noted that this fivefold division into Kriyā, Caryā, Yoga, Mahāyoga, and Yoginī tantras is not generally found in books on Buddhism. The most common classification is fourfold, into Kriyā, Caryā, Yoga, and Anuttarayoga ('Highest Yoga') tantras. The Anuttarayoga class is further divided into Father tantras and Mother tantras, sub-divisions that broadly correspond to the Mahāyoga and Yoginī categories of the fivefold classification. Despite its ubiquity there are disadvantages in using this fourfold categorisation to understand the nature and development of tantric Buddhism in India. First, the amalgamation of the Mahāyoga and Yoginī classes into one Anuttarayoga class tends, despite their recognition as Father and Mother subdivisions, to obscure similarities between Yoga and Mahāyoga texts as well as differences between Mahāyoga and Yoginī texts. Second, the fourfold classification appears to be Tibetan rather than Indian in origin, and one that represents a particular Tibetan conceptualisation of the Indian tradition. Moreover, the term *anuttarayoga* has not been found in any of the surviving Sanskrit manuscripts (Isaacson 1998: 28).[16]

Kriyā tantras

The Kriyā class is by far the largest. Over four hundred and fifty works are assigned to this category in the tantra section of the Tibetan Kanjur.[17] The earliest Kriyā texts probably date from the second century CE.[18] They continue to appear until at least the sixth century. They form a miscellaneous collection of largely magical texts that contain an array of rituals designed to achieve a variety of worldly (*laukika*) goals. No suggestion appears that they can be used to attain awakening. The range of pragmatic ends is wide. Among other things, the user of these texts and their rituals aims to alleviate illness, control the weather, generate health and prosperity, oppose enemies, placate deities, and protect himself and others from an array of dangers. Kriyā rituals employ mantras and early forms of maṇḍalas. However, the word 'tantra' – the common term for tantric texts in the later period, and literally meaning little more than 'text' – rarely occurs in the title of Kriyā texts. A variety of other names are more common: *dhāraṇī*, *kalpa*, *rājñī*, or *sūtra*. Thus the *Mahāmegha Sūtra*, 'Great Cloud Sūtra', a work concerned with the control of weather, is classified as a Kriyā tantra despite it being called a sūtra. One reason for such anomaly is that the exegetical classification of these texts as 'tantras' was most likely retrospective. The rationale for the designation of a text as a tantra was also as much to do with content – prominence of rituals employing mantras etc. – as with its particular title. Indeed, it is not until the period of Yoga and Mahāyoga texts that the title 'tantra' comes into general use.

An important type of Kriyā text is the *dhāraṇī*, and many works classified in the Kriyā class are either dhāraṇīs or texts that locate dhāraṇīs within a ritual context in texts called *kalpas*. A dhāraṇī is seen as having a particular power when read or recited, a power either in the world or on the mind of the reciter.

They may be shorter or longer strings of words, and are understood to bear in condensed form a particular meaning or intention, often of a teaching of the Buddha. Yukei Matsunaga (see de Jong 1984: 95–6) has distinguished two principal meanings of *dhāraṇī*: 'memorisation' (of texts) and 'magical spell'. A number of non-tantric Mahāyāna sūtras contain dhāraṇīs – for example the *Lotus Sūtra*, and the Perfection of Wisdom text, the *Heart Sūtra* – and these generally use the term in its sense of memorisation.[19] The link between this and the second meaning is found in the idea that the memorised dhāraṇī contains the power of the word of the Buddha, which is able to protect one from harm and overcome enemies. The word *dhāraṇī*, found only in Buddhist contexts, derives from the verbal root *dhṛ*, meaning 'to support' or 'to hold' (the word *dharma* derives from the same root). Strings of words, taken as summarising or holding the teaching of the Buddha, can therefore function as utterances of magical power, much in the same way as do the *paritta* ('pirit') verses of early Buddhism and contemporary Theravāda. As utterances of power dhāraṇīs resemble mantras and the terms are indeed sometimes used synonymously.

One of the few Kriyā texts that has been even partially translated into a European language is the large and heterogeneous *Mañjuśrīmūlakalpa*, 'The Root Ritual Instruction of Mañjuśrī', in which the bodhisattvas Mañjuśrī and Avalokiteśvara play important roles. The bodhisattva Tārā is also mentioned, in possibly the earliest textual reference to this important female figure (see Willson 1986: 39–43). The *Mañjuśrīmūlakalpa* is significant in representing an early stage of development of the notion that deities can be grouped into 'families'. Depicted within a somewhat sprawling non-symmetrical maṇḍala are three groups of figures comprising the Buddha, Lotus (*padma*) and Thunderbolt (*vajra*) families, with peaceful and fierce deities assigned to the Lotus and Thunderbolt families respectively (for a translation of the relevant passage see Snellgrove 1987a: 192–4).

The history of translations of Kriyā texts (especially into Chinese; see Matsunaga 1977: 169–71) suggests that they were not superseded in importance by later Indian tantric developments, in the way that the rituals of the Caryā and Yoga texts were, by the supposedly more advanced methods of the Mahāyoga and Yoginī tantras. On the contrary, individual Kriyā texts can be seen expanding and developing over a number of centuries. Such sustained interest may be the result of the worldly focus of these texts – the very reason why they have been little studied by western scholarship. Kriyā rituals addressed needs that continued to be important, especially perhaps for non-monastics. In locating these Kriyā texts in broader context, Snellgrove (1987a: 232–4) has argued against taking them as anything more than an aspect of Mahāyāna practice. They should not, he believes, be seen as constituting a separate Way (*yāna*). On the contrary they should be placed within the normal Mahāyāna Buddhist world and the bodhisattva's practice of altruism. If this is the case, and the issue of tantric Buddhism as a separate *yāna* will be taken up later, then the performance of Kriyā type tantric rituals by monks for the benefit of householders can be seen as a way in which the monastic community could act altruistically. Such activity involves a shift in the traditional role of monks functioning as a passive source of merit for householders (see Lewis 1995). A more active function, however, could be effective in attracting needed patronage, especially if Kriyā rituals were seen as powerful and efficacious.

Caryā tantras

In contrast to the Kriyā, very few texts are standardly assigned to the Caryā Tantra class. In the Tibetan Kanjur classification there are just eight, making it the smallest of the five categories. The most important Caryā text is the *Mahāvairocana Sūtra*, known more fully as the *Mahāvairocanābhisaṃbodhi Sūtra*, which was probably composed during the early to middle seventh century (see Hodge 1994: 65). Also in this group, and probably earlier than the *Mahāvairocana Sūtra*, is the *Vajrapāṇyabhiṣeka Tantra*. Apart from occasional quotations in commentaries, neither of these works survives in its original language of composition. An important commentary on the *Mahāvairocana Sūtra* was written by the mid-eighth century figure Buddhaguhya, who also composed commentaries on Kriyā texts.

A significant feature of Caryā tantras is the role played by the Buddha Vairocana, 'The Luminous One'. In the *Mahāvairocana Sūtra* he is depicted at the centre of a symmetrical maṇḍala, with four other Buddhas placed in the cardinal directions. It has been observed (Orzech 1987) that Vairocana's centrality is founded on his role as a symbol of ultimate reality developed in two non-tantric Mahāyāna scriptures, the *Gaṇḍavyūha* and *Daśabhūmika Sūtras*. These are both part of the large composite work the *Avataṃsaka Sūtra* (q.v.). For the *Gaṇḍavyūha* Vairocana is *the* Buddha, residing in a transcendent world of luminosity, fluidity, and magical transformation, while simultaneously being present at all levels and in all things. From this perspective Śākyamuni, the historical Buddha, is a magical transformation produced for the benefit of suffering sentient beings. In the *Mahāvairocana Sūtra* Vairocana is presented as the cosmic Buddha. Moreover, he appears as all deities and as revealing all religions, suggesting the omnipresence of Buddhism.

The world of the *Gaṇḍavyūha Sūtra* can be transformed at will by the mental acts of Buddhas and advanced bodhisattvas. It provides an eminently suitable perspective for the tantric practitioner, who from this point onwards is increasingly concerned to transform, within the context of visualisation meditation, the appearance (and hence the reality) of him- or herself and of the external world. The idea of the tantric practitioner developing intense meditative identification with the deity being evoked appears to develop during the period of the Caryā texts. Practitioners identify themselves, visualise themselves, as the awakened deity occupying a luminous universe that can be magically transformed, precisely in the way that it can be transformed in the *Gaṇḍavyūha Sūtra*. It appears that soteriological goals continue to be absent from the Caryā Tantras. The powers (*siddhi*) and purposes pursued remain worldly. Yet, conceptually at least, it is a small step from identifying oneself as a Buddha in order to gain worldly ends to using that identification to accelerate the process of actually becoming such a Buddha.

Yoga tantras

The number of texts usually designated as Yoga tantras makes it a slightly larger class than the Caryā (some fifteen works in the Tibetan Kanjur). The key text in this class is the *Tattvasaṃgraha Sūtra*, also known as the *Sarvatathāgatatattvasaṃgraha Sūtra*. Other works in this category include the *Sarvadurgatipariśodhana*, *Sarvarahasya*, and *Vajraśekhara Tantras*, and the short but influential *Nāmasaṃgīti*, 'The Litany of Names'. This last text enumerates the dimensions or 'Names' of wisdom as embodied in the figure of Mañjuśrī, who is conceived of as the non-dual wisdom underlying all phenomena.[20] Yoga tantra commentators of the eighth century include Buddhaguhya, Mañjuśrīmitra, and Vilāsavajra. Buddhaguhya wrote a *Tattvasaṃgraha* commentary, the *Tantrāvatāra*, which has a sub-commentary by Padmavajra. Mañjuśrīmitra and Vilāsavajra wrote commentarial and other works focused on the *Nāmasaṃgīti*.[21]

Historically, it appears that the Yoga tantras closely followed the Caryā. Matsunaga (1977: 177–8) dates the *Tattvasaṃgraha* in its earliest form to the beginning of the eighth century. More recently Yoritomi (1990) has argued that it was virtually complete by the latter half of the seventh century, and that in its original form it is older than the *Mahāvairocana Sūtra*. The centrality of Vairocana continues in the Yoga tantras, as does the use of maṇḍalas with a symmetrical arrangement of five principal Buddhas. The names and directions assigned to Buddhas vary somewhat from text to text in the Yoga tantras. Over time, the arrangement of the *Vajradhātu* maṇḍala in the *Tattvasaṃgraha* became standard, with Vairocana in the centre surrounded by Buddhas Akṣobhya (east), Ratnasaṃbhava (south), Amitābha (west), and Amoghasiddhi (north).[22]

The most significant development in the Yoga tantras is their concern with soteriology. Awakening is included as a legitimate goal of tantric practice and from this period tantric Buddhism begins to promote itself not only as an effective way to gain worldly ends and powers. It is also an especially powerful way to gain Buddhahood.[23] Other developments include an increase in the number of Buddha-families. Initially, it appears this was from three (as found in the Kriyā texts) to four in the *Tattvasaṃgraha*, by the addition of a Gem (*ratna*) family. Yoritomi (1990) suggests that a fifth, Action (*karman*) family, first appears in the *Vajraśekhara Tantra*. At this point each of the five principal ('cosmic') Buddhas of the maṇḍala was thus considered to have its own retinue or 'family', comprised of bodhisattvas, offering goddesses, and so on. The system of five families developed, therefore, after the system of five Buddhas onto which it was mapped. The *Vajraśekhara Tantra* also contains a reference to a sixth family, that of Vajradhara, a Buddha (or principle) seen as the source, in some sense, of the five Buddhas. From this perspective Vajradhara takes on the foundational role played by Vairocana. This is a function also given in some contexts to the figure of Vajrasattva. A further shift that occurs with the expansion of the number of Buddha-families is that all five (or six) families can be conceived of as Buddha-families in that they each have a presiding Buddha surrounded by awakened or near-awakened figures. In the three-family system of the *Mañjuśrīmūlakalpa* only members of the central Buddha family were recognised as awakened. Members of the Lotus and Thunderbolt families were unawakened peaceful and fierce deities that had none the less allied themselves with the Buddhist tradition.

The combination of the five-Buddha and five-family system encouraged the establishment of sets of correspondences between the Buddhas, their families, and other sets of five. Table 1 gives some of these, though not all shown were established by the Yoga tantras. The correlations with the aggregates (*skandha*) and poisons ('taints'; *kleśa*) were made by the *Guhyasamāja Tantra* (a Mahāyoga tantra) and the *Hevajra Tantra* (a Yoginī tantra) respectively (Yoritomi 1990).

Mahāyoga tantras

Historically, Mahāyoga tantras, appearing by the end of the eighth century, have clear connections with Yoga tantras. Indeed, there is evidence that these texts were not initially seen as distinct from

Table 1 Correspondences established between the Five Buddhas of the Yoga tantras and other sets of five

	Vairocana	*Akṣobhya*	*Ratnasambhava*	*Amitābha*	*Amoghasiddhi*
Family (*kula*)	Buddha	Vajra	Gem (*ratna*)	Lotus (*padma*)	Action (*karma*)
Direction	Centre	East	South	West	North
Colour	White	Blue	Yellow	Red	Green
Hand Gesture (*mudrā*)	Teaching	Earth-touching	Giving	Meditation	Fearlessness
Throne	Lion	Elephant	Horse	Peacock	Garuḍa
Seed-Mantra	*oṃ*	*hūṃ*	*traṃ*	*hrīḥ*	*āḥ*
Offering Goddess/ Consort	Vajradhāteśvarī	Locanā	Māmakī	Pāṇḍaravāsinī	Tārā
Element	Consciousness	Water	Earth	Fire	Air
Cognition ('consciousness'; *vijñāna*)		Store	Defiled Mind	Mental	Five Senses
Wisdom ('awakened cognition'; *jñāna*)	Perfectly Pure Dharma-sphere	Mirror-like	Sameness	Discrimination	Practice
Aggregate (*skandha*)	Consciousness	Form	Sensation	Perception	Volition
Poison ('taint'; *kleśa*)	Ignorance	Hatred	Envy	Craving	Pride

the Yoga tantras.[24] As has been noted, and as their name suggests, Mahāyoga tantras can be seen as an additional division of the Yoga tantra class. The most influential work classified as Mahāyoga is the *Guhyasamāja Tantra.*[25] Also included in this class are the *Vajrabhairava*[26] and *Māyājāla Tantras*, the latter of which is seen by Yoritomi as the exemplar for the *Guhyasamāja*. The Father tantra section of the Tibetan Kanjur – the equivalent class of the Mahāyoga tantras – contains thirty-seven texts.

The Mahāyoga tantras maintain the five-Buddha and five-family system of the Yoga tantras. However, the *Guhyasamāja Tantra* has Akṣobhya as its central deity. This reflects a general shift in the Mahāyoga tantras away from the Caryā and Yoga tantra emphasis on Vairocana. Akṣobhya and his Thunderbolt family move to the foreground, paving the way for the ascendance of semi-fierce and fierce deities that dominate the last period of development of tantric Buddhism in India as represented by the Yoginī tantras. Two other features of the Mahāyoga tantras should be noted: the use of sexuality and the (ritual) consumption of forbidden and impure substances. The sexual elements are immediately apparent in the iconography of the five cosmic Buddhas, who are depicted sitting (peacefully and multi-armed) in sexual union with female partners. Also, according to the ritual manuals, the person to be initiated was required to engage in ritualised sexual intercourse as part of initiation into the observances and practices of this class. Although ritualised sexual activity is not completely new – it has a marginal presence in some Yoga tantras – it is in the Mahāyoga tantras that it is first given prominence. The male and female figures in sexual union – whether in iconographical or ritual contexts – are given symbolic value, as are all elements of a maṇḍala, a process known as 'purification'. The female figure is equated with wisdom (*prajñā*) and the male with compassionate method ('means'; *upāya*). Their union represents the union of wisdom and method, the twin aspects of awakened cognition.

Use of impure or otherwise forbidden substances appears in descriptions of post-initiatory practice, where the consumption of alcohol, meat, and bodily substances such as urine and faeces are recommended. The issue of transgressive activity is discussed later. For the present, it can be noted that one reason for such behaviour lies in the idea of non-dual (*advaya*) practice, that is, practice that transcends dualistic categories such as permitted and forbidden, pure and impure. This idea is in turn rooted in the view that the true nature of cognition is in some sense non-dual, and that this non-dual and awakened state can appropriately be approached through non-dual practice.

Within the Mahāyoga commentarial literature, two traditions of *Guhyasamāja Tantra* exegesis evolved, known as the *Ārya* and *Jñānapāda* schools. The Ārya school, which emphasised the importance of the oral tradition in its interpretations (Wayman 1995: 148), was founded by (the tantric) Nāgārjuna. His work on the stages of tantric meditation, the *Pañcakrama*, is available in Sanskrit, as is a *Guhyasamāja* commentary, the *Pradīpoddyotana*, by (the tantric) Candrakīrti. The Jñānapāda school stressed the importance of interpreting the *Guhyasamāja Tantra* within the doctrinal context of the Mahāyāna. According to tradition its founder, Buddhajñānapāda, had studied with the famous Perfection of Wisdom exegete Haribhadra (mid-ninth century CE).[27]

Yoginī tantras

Texts designated as Yoginī tantras are generally thought to have appeared during the ninth and tenth centuries, and may be taken as representing the final phase of tantric Buddhism in India. The Mother tantra division of the Tibetan Kanjur, the equivalent of the Yoginī class, contains some eighty-two works, making it the second largest category of tantric scriptures. Yoginī tantras take a variety of figures as the principal deity of the maṇḍala, some of whom have more than one tantra associated with them. As a result, it is possible to speak of the Yoginī tantras as comprising a number of different tantric 'cycles' (i.e. comprised of a number of tantras that centre on particular figures).[28] Thus the *Hevajra Tantra*, the first major tantra to be translated into English, is centred on Hevajra ('Oh Vajra!'). The *Caṇḍamahāroṣaṇa Tantra*, on the other hand, also named after its principal deity, places

Caṇḍamahāroṣaṇa at the centre of the maṇḍala. The tradition associated with Caṇḍamahāroṣaṇa became established in Nepal where there are still shrines dedicated to him (see Gellner 1992: 256). A major Yoginī tantric cycle, centring on the important figure of Cakrasaṃvara, includes the *Laghusaṃvara* (also known as the *Herukābhidhāna*), *Abhidhānottara*, *Saṃvarodaya*, *Yoginīsaṃcāra*, *Vajraḍāka* and *Ḍākārṇava Tantras*. Although mostly surviving in Sanskrit, of these texts only parts of the *Saṃvarodaya Tantra* have been edited and published in English translation.

The Yoginī tantras continue to place most importance on Akṣobhya's Thunderbolt family, and all the deities mentioned above are fierce or semi-fierce in appearance. Employment of sexual and transgressive elements also continues. What is distinctive about the Yoginī class is its incorporation of symbolism, deities, and practices associated with cremation grounds. These are traditions that were strongly influenced, if not dominated, by tantric Śaivism (i.e. traditions focusing on the 'Hindu' god Śiva as the ultimate deity). It is this context that determines the appearance of Yoginī tantra deities. Mahāyoga figures such as Guhyasamāja, though multi-headed and multi-armed, wear the ornaments and attire of royalty, typical of non-tantric Mahāyāna Buddhas and bodhisattvas, and are generally peaceful in appearance. The multi-limbed Yoginī tantra deities, on the other hand, have human bones for ornaments, flayed human and animal skins for clothes, are garlanded with strings of skulls or severed heads (fresh or decaying), and drink blood from cups made of human skulls. They are generally portrayed standing, often in a dancing posture, in sexual union with a female partner of similar appearance. Grimacing expressions, protruding and bloody fangs, flaming hair and eyebrows, and a third eye in the centre of the forehead, indicates their 'Hindu' ferocious nature.

The title given to the Yoginī tantras derives from the importance and distinctive roles accorded to female figures in them. The central maṇḍala deities, whether alone or in sexual union, are generally surrounded by dancing female figures called *yoginīs* or *ḍākinīs*, whose appearance mirrors that of the central figure or figures. Thus, Hevajra and his consort Nairātmyā ('Selfless') are standardly encircled by eight yoginīs. Yoginī tantra maṇḍalas can also have female figures as their central deity. For example, Cakrasaṃvara's consort, Vajravārāhī, is important in her own right as a deity who appears without a male consort at the centre of the maṇḍala.[29] Vajrayoginī, Vajraḍākinī, and Kurukullā, often seen as a form of Tārā, are among a number of other female figures that also function in this way.

Two further Yoginī tantras should be mentioned. These are the *Kālacakra Tantra* and one sometimes alluded to, somewhat confusingly, as the *Saṃvara Tantra*,[30] a short form for the rather daunting *Sarvabuddhasamāyogaḍākinījālasaṃvara Tantra*. The *Kālacakra Tantra*, which refers to the threat of Muslim incursions and is generally therefore dated to the early eleventh century, is probably the most recent major tantra of Indian tantric Buddhism. This tantra is familiar to some in the West as a result of the large initiations given into its practice by the present Dalai Lama. It contains a myth of a Buddhist world saviour hidden in the land of Shambhala (prototype for the Shangri La of James Hilton's 1936 novel *Lost Horizon*) and a prophesy of future world peace and harmony. As well as having a highly elaborate maṇḍala the *Kālacakra Tantra* differs from other Yoginī works in being composed in a fairly sophisticated Classical Sanskrit verse-form. This contrasts with the Sanskritised Middle Indo-Āryan dialects and irregular Sanskrit typical of most Yoginī tantras. It is also a religiously syncretistic text and may therefore represent an attempt to form an alliance with Hinduism against the threat of Islam.[31]

The *Saṃvara Tantra*, in contrast, may well be one of the earliest Yoginī works and also the exemplar for the *Hevajra Tantra* (Yoritomi 1990). The second part of its full title, *ḍākinījālasaṃvara*, 'the assembly of the host of ḍākinīs', is a key expression for the Yoginī tantras. It denotes both the assembly of practitioners, who come together for ritual celebrations (*gaṇacakra*), and also the maṇḍala, or assembly, of Buddhas and their emanations that the assembly of practitioners mirrors and recreates.[32] The full title of the *Saṃvara Tantra* – 'the assembly of the host of ḍākinīs, which is the fusion of all the Buddhas' – denotes the (ritual) identity of these two assemblies. Moreover, the unified gathering of all the Buddhas, equated with that of the ḍākinīs, can also be seen as identical with, or emanating from, a single Buddha. This is an idea articulated in the *Hevajra Tantra*'s full title, *Śrīhevajraḍākinījālasaṃvara Tantra*, 'The Assembly of the Host of Ḍākinīs, [namely] the Glorious Hevajra'.

Also, implicit in the understanding of these titles is a play between the meanings of *saṃvara* ('assembly') and *śaṃvara* ('bliss'). These are words that were not always distinguished in the script. The assembly of ḍākinīs, or of practitioners, was also one that gave rise to bliss, which could be homologised with the great bliss (*mahāsukha*) that was seen as characterising the experience of awakened cognition. Another expression found in these texts to describe this non-dual and blissful state is the rather opaque term *mahāmudrā* ('The Great Seal'). The sense of this is derived from the use of the word *mudrā* (seal) to denote the yogin's tantric consort who, as the symbol of wisdom, is also known as the *prajñā* (wisdom). The experience of *mahāmudrā* is thus the awakened blissful experience engendered by one's consort (*mudrā*), which is identical with wisdom (*prajñā*).

Practitioners of the Yoginī tantras were generally known as *siddhas* ('accomplished ones') or 'great siddhas' (*mahāsiddha*). A late account of their legendary and often unconventional lives is found in Abhayadatta's *Caturaśītisiddhapravṛtti* ('Lives of the Eighty-four Siddhas'). An important term, or principle, employed by the siddhas is *sahaja*, literally meaning 'born-together'. This was taken to denote the innate and spontaneous nature of the awakened mind. This idea underlies much of the unconventional behaviour of the siddhas. From the perspective of conventional society, they appeared to be crazy. From their point of view, however, they were delighting in the spontaneity of non-dual cognition.[33]

A number of works composed by siddhas survive. These include the song cycles of Saraha, the *Dohākośa*, a collection of variously attributed songs, the *Caryāgīti*, which were used in ritual contexts,[34] as well as commentaries on tantras such as

Kāṇha's *Yogaratnamālā* (on the *Hevajra Tantra*) and Nāropa's *Sekoddeśaṭīkā* (on a section of the *Kālacakra Tantra*). Altogether, there are a very large number of commentarial and other secondary works on the Yoginī tantras, mostly preserved in Tibetan. Important authors include the towering and prolific figure of Abhayākaragupta,[35] whose work includes invaluable summaries of maṇḍalas and maṇḍala rituals (*Niṣpannayogāvalī* and *Vajrāvalī*), Advayavajra (*Advayavajrasaṃgraha*), and Ratnākaraśānti, also known as Śānti pa, the Yogācāra exegete. The large anonymous *Kālacakra Tantra* commentary, the *Vimalaprabhā*, quickly became an influential work and in Tibet was given canonical status.

Vajrayāna – how distinct a way?

We have seen that tantric Buddhism from the time of the Yoga Tantras conceived of itself as the Vajrayāna, 'The Diamond Way'. The Sanskrit word *vajra* has two primary meanings, 'thunderbolt', the weapon of the Vedic god Indra, and also 'diamond'. Both are significant in the context of its emerging importance within tantric Buddhism. The power of the thunderbolt was seen as symbolic of the power of tantric methods to achieve both worldly and trans-worldy goals. In the Pāli suttas the vajra appears as the weapon of Śākymuni's *yakṣa* (demigod) guardian Vajrapāṇi, a name meaning 'Vajra-in-hand'. Vajrapāṇi, after undergoing a transformation of status into an advanced bodhisattva, becomes a prominent figure in Vajrayāna texts, often functioning as the Buddha's principal interlocutor. The meaning 'diamond' for *vajra* also has important connotations. Diamonds are the hardest of gems. They are also precious, beautiful, and translucent. In the symbolic language of the Yoga Tantras the ultimate nature of things was also diamond-like, pure and radiant, but also strong and indivisible. The *Tattvasaṃgraha*, in a reworking of the story of Śākyamuni's awakening, has him visualise an upright vajra in his heart. The visualised vajra is portrayed as stabilising – giving indestructible strength to – the *bodhicitta* ('awakening mind') in Śākyamuni's heart, and also as symbolising his inner nature. As a result Śākyamuni is given the name *Vajradhātu*, 'Vajra-Sphere', on his attainment of the state of Buddhahood.

In the Kriyā Tantras the word *vajra* in a deity's name indicated a wrathful nature. Moreover, there was no assumption that such figures were awakened. By the time of the Yoga Tantras, however, the word tended to indicate a deity's awakened, or vajra-, nature. Their appearance may or may not be wrathful. From this point on one sees a proliferation of vajra names. For example, the maṇḍalas of the *Tattvasaṃgraha* have Vajrapuṣpā ('Vajra-flower') and Vajranṛtyā ('Vajra-dance') as offering goddesses, bodhisattvas such as Vajraratna ('Vajra-gem'), Vajrarāja ('Vajra-king'), and Vajrarāga ('Vajra-passion'), and gate-keepers named Vajrapāśa ('Vajra-noose') and Vajrāṅkuśa ('Vajra-hook'). The importance of the ex-yakṣa Vajrapāṇi has been noted. Two other figures with vajra names should be mentioned: Vajradhara ('He who holds a vajra') and Vajrasattva ('Vajra-being'). Both of these have central and complex roles as Tathāgatas in a range of Vajrayāna texts. Vajrapāṇi's rise to prominence has been traced by Snellgrove (1987a: 134 ff.), who suggests that Vajrapāṇi is essentially the same figure as Vajradhara.

In its adoption of the vajra as a symbol for the nature of reality the Vajrayāna sets about what may be called a vajra-isation of Buddhism. Thus the name *Vajradhātu*, given to Śākyamuni in the *Tattvasaṃgraha*, vajra-ises the Mahāyāna concept of the *Dharmadhātu*, the 'dharma-realm' or 'dharma-sphere', the totality seen as it truly is by the awakened, enlightened, mind. The vajra-ised *bodhicitta* of the *Tattvasaṃgraha* is embodied as the Tathāgata Bodhicittavajra, an important (albeit transitional) figure of Yoga and Mahāyoga Tantras. The role of the vajra as a core symbol in tantric Buddhism continues for the remainder of its history in India, vajra names being characteristic of both Mahāyoga and Yoginī Tantra deities. For example, the principal figures of the Mahāyoga Guhyasamāja cycle are Akṣobhyavajra and Mañjuvajra (based, respectively, on Akṣobhya and Mañjuśrī). Hevajra (from the *Hevajra Tantra*), Vajrayoginī, and Vajravārāhī are all major figures of the Yoginī tantras.

The vajra also became a key ritual object for the Vajrayāna. Generally made of metal, it is comprised of a central sphere from which two prongs emerge at one hundred and eighty degrees to each other. These prongs may each be surrounded by a number of other prongs – usually four, though occasionally two or eight – which also emerge from the central sphere, curving away from and then back towards the central prongs. Held alone, usually in the right hand, the vajra stands in general for the non-dual and indestructible nature of awakened awareness. In particular, the unity of the two sets of prongs in the central sphere is seen as representing the unity of wisdom (*prajñā*) and compassion (*karuṇā*). Held along with a bell, the latter usually in the left hand, the vajra now symbolises compassion and the bell wisdom. Together they stand for the non-dual unity of the awakened mind. As has been noted, this unity can also be symbolised by the sexual union of male and female tantric deities. This sexual unity can itself be symbolised by holding the vajra and bell in a particular way, known as the embrace gesture (*mudrā*). The vajra thus comes to be associated with the male figure in sexual union. In some contexts the vajra stands more specifically for the penis, a process of association probably aided by the phallic shape of the ritual object. The bell, on the other hand, did not come to stand for the vagina. This is a role often taken by the lotus flower, anatomical comparisons again probably being influential in the choice.

It is not until this period, then, that the vajra appears to have been accorded any symbolic status in Buddhism. Its rise to prominence within tantric Buddhism probably led to the use of the term *Vajrayāna* for the path followed by its proponents. The new nomenclature raises the question of the relationship between the Vajrayāna and the Mahāyāna. How distinct a 'way' (*yāna*) is the Vajrayāna? Is it a special path that is none the less part of the Mahāyāna, or is it a path that is distinct from and supersedes the Mahāyāna? The classical hierarchy of three *yānas* – Hīnayāna, Mahāyāna, and Vajrayāna, (where 'Hīnayāna' is, of course, the pejorative Mahāyānist term for mainstream non-Mahāyāna Indian Buddhism) – seems to suggest that Vajrayānists saw themselves as following a path distinct from the Mahāyāna. But, as we have seen, pre-Vajrayāna tantric Buddhism – the Mantranaya – took itself to be a branch of the Mahāyāna. On the whole, Vajrayānist commentators maintained this position, locating the Vajrayāna as a special path within the Mahāyāna. Nevertheless, the inclusion of Buddhahood as a legitimate tantric goal made the Vajrayāna an especially significant, for some even necessary, aspect of the Mahāyāna.

Just as the Mantranaya was an especially efficacious way of attaining this-worldly goals, so the Vajrayāna saw itself as also especially efficacious in the task of attaining the goal of awakening. In particular, it was seen as enabling the practitioner to traverse the path at a much faster rate than before. The *Nāmasaṃgīti* describes itself as 'the quick success of those bodhisattvas implementing their practice by means of mantras, and the realisation in contemplation for those intent on the perfection of insight'.[36] Instead of taking three incalculable aeons to attain Buddhahood – the time generally required according to non-tantric Mahāyāna texts – one could collapse the process into a single lifetime by following the Vajrayāna.

What, then, made the Vajrayāna so effective? One answer, developed in the later Vajrayāna, was to depict its efficacy as owing to its being a 'Result-Path'. In contrast, the non-Vajrayāna is typified as a 'Cause-Path'. A non-Vajrayānist, in this light, pursues the goal of Buddhahood through the careful maturation of the causes (*hetu*) that lead to it, for example through the practice of the six or ten Perfections (*pāramitā*). That is, he or she attains Buddhahood through following the classical bodhisattva path. Vajrayānists, on the other hand, following the result-path, assume that they have achieved the 'result' (*phala*) – the goal of Buddhahood – already. They perceive themselves, through visualisation and other techniques, as fully awakened, and as inhabiting a pure and radiant world (i.e. the world 'as it really is'), the external reflex of their awakened cognition. In other words, Vajrayānists, through the process of tantric ritual and meditation, are said to make the result (Buddhahood) part of the path. That is what, according to this view, is unique to the

Vajrayāna and what makes it so particularly effective. It should perhaps be reiterated that this conception of the Vajrayāna still locates it as part of the Mahāyāna.

Is there, none the less, a case for saying Vajrayāna goals (and therefore paths) differ from those of the Mahāyāna? Although new conceptions of the goal are found in the Vajrayāna, it is hard to say whether these amount to the goal changing. The use of the expression 'great bliss' (*mahāsukha*) as descriptive of the goal has been noted, as has the fact that it signposts a Vajrayāna revaluation of the significance of pleasure. Also, Vajradharahood is sometimes used in lieu of Buddhahood, though, again, it is not clear that becoming a Vajradhara is essentially different from becoming a Buddha. Snellgrove, who argues that the Vajrayāna is 'as distinguishable from the Mahāyāna as this is distinguishable from the so-called Hīnayāna' (1987a: 129), takes the view that the word *Vajrasattva* ('diamond being') denotes the Vajrayānist conception of the highest state. It is formed on analogy with its Mahāyāna equivalent *bodhisattva* ('awakening being') (op. cit.: 131). However, this equation seems problematic, in that, practically speaking, the term 'bodhisattva' stands not for the goal but for one who is aiming at the goal. Technically at least, the bodhisattva is precisely one who had not attained the goal. Approaching the issue of *yānas* from a different direction, Gellner (1992: 261) has suggested that separate soteriological ideals – arhat, bodhisattva, and siddha – can be assigned to the Śrāvakayāna (Mainstream Buddhism), Mahāyāna, and Vajrayāna respectively. The siddha is perhaps a better Vajrayānist equivalent of the bodhisattva, and the typology serves to give a sense of the differing emphases of the traditions (though the siddha is not present as a type during the early Vajrayāna). Strictly speaking, however, the three ideals are not equivalent. This is because the siddha and arhat have attained the highest goals of their *yānas*, whereas even the most advanced bodhisattva has not (though some Mahāyāna sūtras point out the futility of trying to distinguish a tenth stage (*bhūmi*) bodhisattva from a Buddha).[37]

Although the Vajrayāna is more often than not seen as part of the Mahāyāna, it may, none the less, be seen as a necessary part, in which case tantric initiation and post-initiatory practice become mandatory. But if this view is to be consistently maintained, the historical Buddha cannot be an exception. He too should have been initiated into tantric practice. Yet none of the traditional Mahāyānist or Mainstream accounts of the life of Śākyamuni refers to such an event. This omission is remedied by reworking the life-story of the Buddha. The first and paradigmatic tantric version of the Buddha's awakening may well be the one found in the *Tattvasaṃgraha*.[38] Here, the future Buddha, known by the variant name 'Sarvārthasiddhi' (rather than Siddhārtha), seated on the seat of awakening under the bodhi-tree, is visited by a host of Tathāgatas who tell him that he will not gain awakening by acting like that. Sarvārthasiddhi asks for instruction and the Tathāgatas give him a number of mantras to recite. These generate a series of visual images in his heart, which produce and then stabilise the *bodhicitta*, the 'awakening mind'. Next, all the Tathāgatas enter Sarvārthasiddhi's heart and he is empowered with their combined wisdom. At this point he too becomes a Tathāgata, and is given the name *Vajradhātu* ('Vajra-Sphere'). The newly awakened Buddha, accompanied by all the Tathāgatas, is then taken to a palace on the summit of mount Meru where he is installed on a lion-throne. Around him four other Tathāgatas each takes a place in one of the cardinal directions to form a maṇḍala of five Buddhas. Later in the text, the Buddha returns to the bodhi tree on the banks of the river Nairañjanā and the traditional awakening story is resumed.

This retelling of the Buddha's awakening is remarkable in a number of ways. Not only does it legitimise the place of tantric practice as a key part of the Buddhist path, it also provides the exemplar for tantric initiation and practice. Thus, the tantric practitioner can be seen as rehearsing the actions and experience of the Buddha. The centrality of vajra symbolism is repeatedly underscored: Sarvārthasiddhi sees a vajra in his heart, understands his vajra-nature, is consecrated as a Tathāgata by all the Tathāgatas entering the vajra in his heart, and given a vajra name.

Elements of practice

Mantras

Despite the vajra's symbolic centrality, the use of mantras was at the heart of actual Vajrayāna practice. This is just as it was for pre-Vajrayāna tantric Buddhism which, as we have seen, identified itself precisely as the Mantranaya, the 'Way of Mantras'. But what exactly are mantras? In the introduction they were provisionally described as utterances understood to have especial power. They may consist of a syllable or a word, or a series of syllables, or a series of words, and they may or may not make sense. What is important about a mantra is that it has some effect (or power) beyond that of just uttering the sounds of which it is composed. Mantras may be understood as a form of what the philosopher J. L. Austin called 'performative utterance'. This is an utterance that does something, that is action as well as speech.[39] In the right context the action of a mantra is guaranteed. The mantras given to Sarvārthasiddhi in the *Tattvasaṃgraha* retelling of his awakening are described as 'successful by nature'. Accordingly, he has only to utter the mantra *oṃ bodhicittam utpādayāmi* , '*Oṃ* I generate the *bodhicitta*', and the *bodhicitta* arises in his heart.

The 'right context' for the use of mantras – outside narrative contexts found in scriptures – is that of ritual, and mantras have a range of functions in the effecting of a variety of ritual ends within tantric Buddhism. One common enumeration of (worldly) rituals lists four: pacifying, prospering, subjugating, or destroying. The narrative of the *Tattvasaṃgraha* provides an example of a mantra's use to subjugate, in this case to subjugate Hindu gods.

> Then Vajrapāṇi pronounced his own vajra-syllable: HŪṂ! As soon as he pronounced this, all the great gods who belong to the threefold world, fell down on their faces, emitting miserable cries, and they went to Vajrapāṇi for protection.
>
> (Trans. Snellgrove 1987a: 137)

Perhaps the most important use of mantras in tantric Buddhism is in the ritual evocation and visualisation of deities and the universes they inhabit. Mantras – appropriately called 'seed-mantras' – generate both the maṇḍala and its deities. Following the primacy of sound over image in Indian religion, the utterance of the mantra almost invariably precedes the visual form. Thus the mantra *bhrūṃ* creates a floor made of vajras for the maṇḍala, and Tārā and Mañjuśrī emerge from – are transformations of – their respective seeds, *tāṃ* and *dhīḥ*.

Once a deity has been fully visualised different mantras – often called 'heart-mantras' – are employed for its contemplation or for performing functions as the deity. These mantras are generally flanked by mantra particles, which may function independently in other contexts. Thus, a heart-mantra often opens with *oṃ* and may close with *svāhā*, *hūṃ*, or *phaṭ*. The heart mantras of Tārā and Mañjuśrī are *oṃ tāre tuttāre ture svāhā* and *oṃ a ra pa ca na dhīḥ*, respectively. The former is usually understood to be a set of variations on her name. The central five syllables of Mañjuśrī's are regarded as the opening of an esoteric syllabary. Uses of mantra particles include the empowering of objects and deities (with *oṃ*, *āḥ*, and *hūṃ*, that represent the triad of body, speech, and mind) and the introduction of deities into a maṇḍala. Thus we have *jaḥ* to summon them, *hūṃ* to draw them in, *vaṃ* to bind them, and *hoḥ* to ensure they pervade the maṇḍala. *Phaṭ* can be put to use as a weapon mantra. Also, mantras are frequently accompanied by ritualised hand gestures (*mudrā*), as in making visualised offerings to a deity (for diagrams of some of these see Beyer 1973: 147 ff.).

Historically, the use of mantras is not restricted to tantric forms of religion, and they certainly predate their development. Their origin can be traced at least as far back as the Vedic period where, within the context of brahmanical ritual, they were employed for inviting the various gods to the sacrifice. It would be a mistake, however, to think that the existence of mantras in tantric Buddhism simply represents a borrowing from Hinduism. There are significant continuities between the non-tantric and tantric Buddhist traditions. In Pāli and Theravāda Buddhism *paritta* verses function similarly to mantras, being used as protective formulae and as talismanic or auspicious words.[40] In the non-tantric Mahāyāna context, the use of dhāraṇīs in sūtras has been noted. Also, the 'recollection the Buddha' (*buddhānusmṛti*) practices of sūtras such as the *Pratyutpanna* and the *Saptaśatikā Prajñāpāramitā* recommend single-minded mantra-like repetition of a Buddha's name in order to evoke a vision of that Buddha.

Visualisation and self-identification with the deity

Visualisation plays a central role in tantric practice. Whether the goal is awakening or the protection of a locality's crops, the relevant ritual usually requires the visualisation of a deity or set of deities, often located within the sacred space of a maṇḍala. Underlying this process is the notion that visualisation transforms the world of appearances to accord more closely with its actual nature, thereby allowing greater opportunity for the practitioner to enact change. This idea becomes prominent from the period of the Caryā tantras, which took the luminous, translucent, magical world of the *Gaṇḍavyūha Sūtra* as the measure for how awakened cognition would perceive the world.

The employment of visualisation as such in tantric practice is nothing new. Visualisation plays an important role in Mainstream and Mahāyāna 'recollection of the Buddha' practices (see Beyer 1977 for a broader contextualisation). Arguably, what is new is the self-visualisation of the practitioner as the deity. Doctrinally, this transformation is underpinned by the Mahāyāna doctrine of emptiness (*śūnyatā*). This is the view that the individual is not a fixed entity but a changing process that is empty of – depending on ones allegiance – either own-existence (Madhyamaka) or subject-object duality (Yogācāra). In this perspective, the practitioner is not adopting the identity and powers of an external deity when visualising him or herself as a deity. On the contrary, the practitioner when seen with the eyes of awakened perception *is* the deity. Moreover, if the universe is characterised by emptiness then the fluid world of appearances created by tantric visualisation is more real than the hard-edged world of ordinary perception.

As Beyer (1973: 69) comments, 'In a universe where all events dissolve ontologically into Emptiness, the touching of Emptiness in the ritual is the re-creation of the world in actuality'. Without the metaphysical context, however, such self-identifications, and the ritual processes by which they are achieved, look very similar to the local traditions of possession found throughout South and Southeast Asia (Gombrich 1996: 155). Also, the doctrine of emptiness can cut both ways. While the deity is no more real than the practitioner, it is also no less real. It is not inconsistent with the Mahāyāna perspective, therefore, to consider tantric dieties as actual external entities.

The process of tantric visualisation can be strikingly dynamic. Visual elements transform into one another, or are transformed out of mantras, also visualised. Light rays emanate from and return into deities, acting for the benefit of and transforming the world. The central figure or figures generally dominate a tantric visualisation, and their appearance may be prescribed in minute detail. The *Saṃvarodaya Tantra* instructs the practitioner to visual the deity Cakrasaṃvara as follows (for a description of Tārā, see Gomez 1995: 320):

> He should imagine the auspicious *Heruka* situated in the midst of the solar disc. He is the hero, three-faced, six-armed and standing in the posture of *āliḍha*. His central face is deep black; his right face is like a *kunda*-flower; and his left face is red and very terrible, and is adorned with a crest of twisted hair. Treading on *Bhairava* and *Kālarātrī*, he abides in the great pleasure (*mahāsukha*), embracing *Vajravairocanī* in great rejoicing of desire of compassion.
>
> (*Saṃvarodaya Tantra*, trans. Tsuda: 283)

Maṇḍalas

The use of maṇḍalas is one of the distinctive features of tantric Buddhism, and they play an important role in initiation rituals as well as in post-initiatory observance throughout the tradition. The word *maṇḍala* is the common Sanskrit term for a circle, a disc, or a halo. Within a religious context it came to denote the generally circular diagram representing, or delineating, a sacred and auspicious space or enclosure. For tantric Buddhism the maṇḍala is primarily understood as the domain of the deity located at its centre. Yet, to the extent that such deities are fully awakened, the maṇḍala also represents the universe as perceived by awakened cognition. Within this base meaning there are some variants. As well as being the abode of deities – their 'residence' – a maṇḍala can be the deities who occupy the abode – its 'residents'. Often the term is taken to cover both residence and residents.

Commentarial discussions of maṇḍalas reinforce and elaborate on the notion of a maṇḍala as a sacred space. Employing the tradition of hermeneutical etymology (*nirukti*), one account explains that the word maṇḍala means 'that which receives (*-la*) an adornment (*maṇḍa-*)', deriving the word from the Sanskrit root *maṇḍ*, to adorn. For this explanation to make sense one needs to understand that the Indian Sanskrit (especially poetical) tradition did not view an adornment as something arbitrary. On the contrary, an adornment is seen as an elaboration, or organic expression, of that which is being adorned. In this interpretation then, a maṇḍala is an expression of the nature of the central deity. An alternative, though not incompatible, explanation is that *maṇḍala* means 'that which contains (*la-*) the essence (*maṇḍa*)', *maṇḍa* being taken in its sense of 'essence' or 'best part'.[41] A maṇḍala, in this reading, is that which envelopes the central deity as its essence.

Some features of any given maṇḍala depend on the nature of its central deity, the 'lord of the circle'. Others are common to most Buddhist maṇḍalas, especially those from the period of the Yoga tantras onwards. Thus, the maṇḍala as a residence is conceived of as a temple-palace, comprised of a square courtyard, with a gateway in the centre of each side. The central courtyard will occasionally have one or more other courtyards surrounding it concentrically, each with four gates. For instance, the maṇḍala of the *Kālacakra Tantra* has three major courtyards (see Brauen 1998). The gateways are surmounted by more or less elaborate archways, which like the courtyard walls are adorned and ornamented. In addition there may be an inner circular pillared space within the main courtyard. The whole complex rests on a floor composed of interlinked vajras, and is enclosed within a protective circle, which is frequently composed of three sub-circles of lotus-flower petals, vajras and, on the outside, flames. Once the residence has been constructed, the maṇḍala deities can take their place, with the main deity, or deity and consort, enthroned at the centre, surrounded by the remaining figures of the 'retinue', such as yoginīs, Buddhas, bodhisattvas, offering goddesses, and gate-keepers.[42]

Maṇḍalas were created (and still are, in Tibetan Buddhism) for use within ritual contexts in which a deity was evoked. They could be created either physically or mentally through visualisation (or both). Their design might be simple or highly elaborate, with a few or hundreds of maṇḍala deities. Occasionally three-dimensional maṇḍalas were built, but two-dimensional representations were more common. More permanent maṇḍalas would be painted on cloth, or onto temple walls as murals. Less permanent were maṇḍalas constructed from coloured powder or sand and used for the duration of a particular ritual. It can take a little practice to 'read' two-dimensional maṇḍalas since they represent the three-dimensional temple-palace (minus the roof but with the door archways) viewed simultaneously in plan and section view. Descriptions of maṇḍalas are found in both tantric scriptures and commentarial material. Important sources for the study of maṇḍalas and their associated rituals are Abhayākaragupta's *Niṣpannayogāvalī* and *Vajrāvalī*, composed during the late eleventh and early twelfth centuries. The first contains detailed descriptions of twenty-seven maṇḍalas from across the range of tantric texts. The second deals with rituals that precede initiation into a deity's maṇḍala.

A range of factors appears to have contributed to the evolution of the standardised and stylised symmetrical maṇḍalas depicted by Abhayākaragupta. Part of the process of development may have involved the symbolism and circular architectural form of the stūpa – an important type of Buddhist monument, in origins a burial mound – combining with Mahāyānist conceptions of Pure Lands and cosmic Buddhas (Leidy 1997: 17 ff.). The oldest surviving Buddhist maṇḍala is arguably the remarkable monument at Borobudur, in central Java, which dates to around the late eighth or early ninth century. Although Borobudur clearly shows the influence of the Yoga tantras (Wayman 1981), it is none the less a composite work that can equally be seen as a complex form of stūpa. Temple murals of Yoga and Mahāyoga type maṇḍalas, dating from the late eleventh to early twelfth century, have survived at Alchi in Ladakh, and Tabo in the Indian state of Himachal Pradesh.[43]

Sādhana – the framework of practice

Mantras, visualisation, and maṇḍalas are brought together in texts called *sādhanas* (literally, 'means of accomplishment'), works specifically designed to guide the tantric practitioner through a sequence of practice focused on a particular deity.[44] Most sādhanas came to have a basically similar structure. The components of the sādhana may be more or less elaborated, depending on factors such as the tantra class of the principal deity, the sādhana's purpose, and the interpretive perspective (and enthusiasm) of the author. Three main phases can be distinguished: (i) preliminaries; (ii) main visualisation; (iii) conclusion. The preliminaries often have as their main function the situation of the main ritual within a Mahāyānist ethical and doctrinal context. This involves what Beyer (1973: 29, 33) has appropriately called the 'ritualization of moral attitudes', and 'the ritualization of metaphysics'. The ethical setting is characteristically established by a liturgy that develops the positive emotional and altruistic attitudes embodied by the 'divine abodes' (or 'abidings') (*brahmavihāra*), and that generates the 'awakening mind', the *bodhicitta*. Also, a more or less elaborate worship (*pūjā*) may be offered, using mantras and ritual hand-gestures (*mudrā*) to a visualised assembly of Buddhas and bodhisattvas.[45] To set the doctrinal context, an experience of the ultimate nature of things – its emptiness or natural purity – is ritually evoked. This is achieved by the recitation of one or more mantras. For example, the pure nature of things is evoked with the mantra *oṃ svabhāvaśuddhāḥ sarvadharmāḥ svabhāvaśuddho 'haṃ* ('*Oṃ* all things are pure by nature, I am pure by nature').

The visual evocation of the main deity – either identified with or as distinct from the *sādhaka* ('one who practices a sādhana') – follows these preliminaries. It may be more, or less, complex. When the deity is fully evoked the ritual purpose of the sādhana, worldly or otherwise, may then be effected. The conclusions bring the sādhaka out of the ritual space, back to the ordinary world of 'public non-reality' as Beyer nicely puts it (ibid.: 130). Two ways of structuring the main visualisation phase of a sādhana should be mentioned. One employs a distinction between what is called the 'conventional being' (*samayasattva*) and the 'knowledge being' (*jñānasattva*). The former expression is used to refer to the main deity as initially visualised. This figure is understood to be the deity in appearance only, i.e. the deity 'by convention'. This 'conventional being' is seen as preparing the way for the actual deity (or the actuality, the *jñāna*, of the deity), the *jñānasattva*. Often sādhanas have a phase where the *jñānasattva* ritually descends into the *samayasattva*, merging with it. At that point the sādhaka becomes the deity, or the deity 'really' appears.

The other structuring method divides the main visualisation into two phases, a 'generation stage' (*utpattikrama*) and a 'perfection (or 'completion') stage' (*niṣpannakrama*). From the perspective of this distinction, the merging of the *samayasattva* and *jñānasattva* is seen as preparatory. It becomes part of the generation stage. The business of 'really' becoming the deity now falls to the perfection stage. This stage in turn can be sub-divided into a phase 'with signs' and a (subsequent) 'without signs' phase.[46] In the former can be found a whole range of yogic practices that involve manipulation of the energies (*prāṇa*) of the subtle body, thought to 'underlie' the gross physical body, with a view to generating a subtle awareness often characterised as radiant and blissful. These yogas – a well known set is the 'six yogas of Nāropa' – are termed 'with signs' since the sādhaka continues to visualise him or herself as the deity. In the 'without signs' phase the visualisation of the deity is dissolved and the sādhaka remains in a blissfully radiant and awakened but formless state. This is not the end, however, for now the sādhaka emerges from this formless state, arising instantaneously as the deity, 'like a fish leaping from water', in order to relieve the suffering of sentient beings. Now the sādhaka really is the deity.[47]

Access to tantric practice: initiation and empowerment

As has been emphasised earlier tantric practice is not available to anyone simply by virtue of their being a Buddhist who has taken either lay or monastic vows. In addition to any such vows, it is necessary to receive consecration or empowerment (*abhiṣeka*)[48] through a ritual of initiation. In any given initiation ritual the pupil, who has previously requested initiation from a tantric teacher or – within the context of the Vajrayāna – Vajra-master, will receive a number of empowerments. These have the function of introducing the pupil to the deity, and legitimising and requiring post-initiatory practice. The empowerments take place within a ritual space that contains the maṇḍala of the appropriate deity. The precise number of empowerments bestowed depends on the nature of the tantric cycle involved. Generally speaking, initiations into Mahāyoga and Yoginī tantras require more empowerments than those into Yoga, Caryā, and Kriyā tantras.

In detail empowerment rituals are often complex. The history of their development is as yet only partially understood. Despite considerable overlap, the number of empowerments, as well as their interpretation, varies somewhat from text to text in each phase of the tradition. Nevertheless, by the time of exegetes such as Abhayākaragupta some standardisation is apparent. His *Vajrāvalī* describes a set of six or seven empowerments regarded as preliminary for initiation into Mahāyoga and Yoginī tantras. These may be taken as typifying those required for Yoga tantra initiation.[49] The set of seven is composed of the garland, water, crown, vajra, bell, vajra-name, and Vajra-master empowerments. Omitting the Vajra-master empowerment, which is required only for those intending to conduct tantric rituals themselves, gives the set of six.

The first empowerment, the garland, which determines the initiand's Buddha-family and follows a number of preliminary rites, broadly proceeds as follows. The pupil is led blindfold before the maṇḍala and given a flower. He (or, more occasionally, she) imagines himself to be the flower, visualises the central maṇḍala deity in front of him, and casts the flower to the deity. The place where it lands on the maṇḍala – east, south, west, or north of the centre, or on the centre – reveals the identity of his Buddha-family. The flower is then fastened in the initiand's hair as part of the garland from which the empowerment takes its name. Next, the blindfold is removed and the rest of the empowerments continue. As they do so, the Vajra-master is engaged in what may be quite complicated visualisations that accompany the external ritual actions. Thus, an empowerment ritual into the Hevajra maṇḍala contains the following instructions to the Vajra-master for the water empowerment:

> Then from the three places (forehead, throat and heart) of Hevajra he [the Vajra-master] envisages manifestations coming from lightrays and filling the sky, and the (eight) goddesses thus manifest hold a jewelled jar and they consecrate the pupil on the top of the head with a stream of *bodhicitta*. Thus he envisages it, as he takes the water in the scoop and bestows the Water Consecration, reciting the mantra: OṂ Vajra-Jar consecrate HŪṂ!
>
> (Prajñāśrī, *Abhiṣekavidhi*, quoted in Snellgrove 1987a: 254)

The water empowerment is clearly linked with ideas of purification, and in Prajñāśrī's text water is homologised with *bodhicitta*, the latter understood as being what is truly purifying. Prajñāśrī also links the water empowerment and the four that follow with the five Buddhas (Akṣobhya etc.), giving the ritual an extra layer of symbolism. Thus, in the fourth and fifth empowerments the person being initiated is given the vajra and bell. As the two major Vajrayānist ritual implements, these already carry a heavy load of symbolic meaning. Onto this Prajñāśrī adds all that

Amitābha and Amoghasiddhi stand for. The mandatory part of the ritual culminates with the Vajra-name empowerment. Here, the pupil is given a new name, which is determined in part by his or her Buddha family as identified during the first empowerment.

If one desires initiation into the maṇḍala of a Mahāyoga or Yoginī deity, for example Guhyasamāja or Cakrasaṃvara, further empowerments are required. The earlier set of six or seven is taken now together and counted as a single empowerment, sometimes known as that of the jar. To this two or three further, or 'higher', empowerments are added. These additional empowerments are generally known as 'the secret', 'the knowledge-of-wisdom' – or just 'wisdom' (*prajñā*) – and, when it occurs, 'the fourth' (*caturtha*). This nomenclature of the final empowerment does no more than describe its place in the new fourfold series that starts with the (multiple) jar empowerment.

The secret and wisdom empowerments were controversial in India for the sexual elements in them. They may still seem shocking today. The secret empowerment, which follows the completion of the jar empowerments, requires the person being initiated, who in the texts is generally presumed to be male, to lead the woman who will be his tantric partner to the Vajra-master. The Vajra-master sexually unites with her. After ejaculating, the Vajra-master collects some of the combined sexual fluids, which is symbolically equated with *bodhicitta*, from the woman's vagina. This he places on the tongue of the person being initiated who must swallow it without hesitation, exclaiming 'O Bliss!' (*Caṇḍamahāroṣaṇa Tantra* iii). For the wisdom empowerment the Vajra-master returns the woman to the person being initiated who in turn unites with her. As he does so, he (in theory) should experience a series of four states of bliss (*ānanda*). These are understood to arise progressively as a result of this union of wisdom (i.e. the female partner) with compassionate method (i.e. the male partner). The fourth empowerment, when it occurs, consists of an explanation by the Vajra-master of the nature of the four blisses that the person being initiated has just experienced. During this the Vajra-master may quote from tantras and songs composed by the siddhas.[50]

This highly abbreviated description of Mahāyoga and Yoginī tantra empowerments broadly follows the more extended summary of Abhayākaragupta's *Vajrāvalī* given by Sanderson (1994: 90). It should be sufficient to indicate the reason for their controversial nature. One reaction to such practices and the texts that justified them was to argue that they could not be Buddhist. This was the response of at least some Indian Buddhists, as it was of Chinese Buddhists, including those who followed the Vajrayāna of the (somewhat expurgated) Yoga tantras (Sanderson 1994: 97). If, however, they are accepted as Buddhist practices, then for a monk to receive the secret and wisdom empowerments as described would be to infringe monastic vows of celibacy. Moreover, if it is accepted that this form of tantric Buddhism is necessary for the attainment of the highest goal an especially awkward consequence follows. It appears that the goal is now only available to non-monastics or laypersons. Even if these practices are regarded as no more than highly efficacious means of realising the goal, they still appear to be closed to the monastic Sangha.

Aside from the rejection of the controversial empowerments and their associated practices as non-Buddhist, it is possible to distinguish three sorts of strategy that evolved in India in response to these problems. The first takes the position that sexual elements are a mandatory part of the secret and wisdom empowerments. Monks therefore should not receive them. Atiśa takes this stance in his *Bodhipathapradīpa*, but qualifies it by adding that as long as the Vajra-master empowerment has been taken a monk may listen to and explain all tantras, and may practice and officiate in appropriate tantric ritual. He further states that the omission of these empowerments does not impair a monk's wisdom in any way (see Sherburne 1983: 176–8).[51] This tactic, while admitting the necessity of sexual activity in the secret and wisdom empowerments, downplays their value.

A second strategy was to argue that monks could take the secret and wisdom empowerments, but only by using an imagined (*jñānamudrā*) rather than an actual (*karmamudrā*) partner. This approach rests on reading textual descriptions of outer physical actions (i.e. of sexual acts) as symbolising, or as ideally symbolising, internal actions and experiences. Thus, texts can be interpreted either as intending visualised partners, or as intending physical partners only for those of poor spiritual capacities.[52] Downplaying the importance of actual sexual activity becomes increasingly typical of the later, and largely monastic, exegetical literature. (The tantric) Nāgārjuna exemplifies this perspective: 'He who does not indulge in the union of Vajra and Lotus according to common practice gains success due to mastery of *yoga*, even if he has experienced it only once' (*Pañcakrama*, quoted by Kvaerne 1975: 103).

Abhayākaragupta (*Vajrāvalī*) and Darpaṇācārya (*Kriyāsamuccaya*) adopt a third approach. They argue that monastics (as well as non-monastics) can take all the 'higher' empowerments, understood literally, i.e. as requiring ritualised sexual intercourse. They can do so, moreover, without contravening the monastic code. This is provided they have attained insight into the empty nature of things. The purpose of this qualification is to ensure that candidates' motives are pure and that they will be capable of benefiting from the empowerments. The relativist ethics of the Mahāyāna permits that 'even the forbidden is allowed in the case of the man who is compassionate and intent on the welfare of others' (*Kriyāsamuccaya*, quoted by Sanderson 1994: 101). Thus, according to these authors at least, there is no contradiction between an individual's vows as a monk and as a Vajra-master.

Impure substances and antinomian acts: the transgressive dimension of tantric Buddhism

The sexual elements in initiation rituals and post-initiatory practice were not the only aspects of the Vajrayāna that had the potential to shock. The existence of a transgressive dimension as a feature of tantric Buddhism has been noted, as has the use of impure or forbidden substances as a characteristic of Mahāyoga tantras. Mahāyoga tantras are also striking for their seeming recommendation that the practitioner should contravene fundamental Buddhist ethical precepts. Passages referring to both of these types of activity are also prominent in Yoginī tantras.

Post-initiatory gatherings (*gaṇamaṇḍala*) – often referred to as 'tantric feasts' – of tantric practitioners can be seen to particularly focus on the impure and forbidden. The *Hevajra Tantra* (II: vii) recommends corpses or corpse-shrouds for the participants' seats, both highly impure because of their association with death. For the feast itself the text specifies that there should be alcohol to drink (forbidden to monks), and to eat there should be 'spiced food' – a mixture, according to Kāṇha's *Yogaratnamālā* commentary, of cow, dog, elephant, horse, and human meat – as well as 'kingly rice'. This 'kingly rice' is the flesh of particular sorts of humans. Consumption of impure substances is also emphasised in descriptions of individual post-initiatory observance. As a part of yogic practice with his female partner, the practitioner is enjoined (among other things) to 'drink her mouth-wash and wash-water of her Lotus', and to 'wash his mouth with the wash-water of her anus' (*Caṇḍamahāroṣaṇa Tantra* vii: 9–10, trans. George).

In the earlier discussion of the Mahāyoga tantras, it was suggested that an important notion underlying the use and consumption of what was considered impure or forbidden was that of non-dual (*advaya*) practice. This is the idea that since awakened cognition (*jñāna*) is in some sense non-dual, the tantric practitioner can approach that non-dual state by transcending attachment to dual categories such as pure and impure, permitted and forbidden. Thus the *Caṇḍamahāroṣaṇa Tantra* (op. cit.: vii: 18–19) states that 'never should the practitioner think in terms of "edible" or "inedible", "to be done" or "not to be done" '; on the contrary, he 'should remain with a composed mind, the embodiment of Innate Bliss alone'. The *Guhyasamāja Tantra* concurs, declaring that 'it is thus that the wise man who does not discriminate achieves buddhahood' (quoted by Snellgrove 1987a: 171). From this perspective, since contact with what was considered impure would be repulsive to most Indians at this time, it was precisely such contact that needed to be practised.

Another factor possibly at play here is related to a view that tantric forms of religion are at heart concerned with the quest for power or, more precisely, powers (*siddhi*), whether worldly or soteriological. One sphere where power is to be found is in those things or activities that are seen as impure. As Gombrich (1996: 155) notes, Indian (largely Brahmanical) ideas and rules of purity presume 'that the world is full of dangerous forces' that have to be controlled and contained. One way of doing this is by designating them as impure. From this perspective, contact with the impure is a means to harness its inherent power. Within a ritual context it can be drawn upon, but in a controlled way. The power and benefit of using the impure is acknowledged in the *Caṇḍamahāroṣaṇa Tantra* (vii: 14–5) when it explains that eating unclean things is like applying manure to a tree so that it will become fruitful.

The apparent endorsement of unethical behaviour found in Mahāyoga and Yoginī tantras can be illustrated by Vajradhara's declaration in the *Guhyasamāja Tantra* that 'those who take life, who take pleasure in lying, who always covet the wealth of others, who enjoy making love, who purposely consume faeces and urine, these are the worthy ones for the practice' (quoted by Snellgrove 1987a: 171). Almost identical recommendations are found in the *Hevajra Tantra* (II: iii 29): 'You should kill living beings, speak lying words, take what is not given, consort with the women of others'.[53] How should these passages be understood? Should they be taken literally, as further instance of non-dual practice, or of the drawing of power from the forbidden? The passages quoted invert the universal Buddhist precepts concerning killing, stealing, lying, and sexual activity. The intention seems, in part at least, to be to shock. In the *Guhyasamāja Tantra* the assembled bodhisattvas all faint and fall to the ground on hearing Vajradhara's words.

Whether these recommendations were ever taken literally or not, non-literal interpretations are often found in adjacent passages of the same texts. Thus, the *Hevajra Tantra* follows its statement with explanations. For example, to kill is to develop one-pointed cognition by destroying the life-breath of discursive thoughts. To lie is to vow to save all living beings. The whole device – of saying something that appears shocking and then explaining what is really meant – is reminiscent of passages from the Perfection of Wisdom sūtras. An alternative interpretive strategy is to see such passages in the light of the expanded and relativistic perspective of Mahāyānist ethics. Under certain circumstances precepts may be broken if compassion is the motive. Both of these approaches are found in the commentarial literature. For instance, by using the Mahāyāna device of explicit (or definitive, *nītārtha*) and implicit (*neyārtha*) meanings, the *Vimalaprabhā* commentary to the *Kālacakra Tantra* gives two explanations for each exhortation to unethical activity. Hence, at the explicit level, killing denotes a Buddha's ability to kill in some specific situations. At the implicit level, killing refers to the (yogic practice of) retaining of semen (Broido 1988). In conclusion, the recommendations to transgress Buddhist ethical norms seem not intended to be taken in their most literal sense. In contrast, those advocating association with what is impure do seem, for the most part, so intended.

Tantric practitioners

If we ask who were the practitioners of tantric Buddhism, the answer will depend, as so often, on the phase of tantric Buddhism being considered. The evidence suggests that the practitioners of the Kriyā and Caryā tantras were probably monks. We have seen how these texts tend to speak of their rituals as valuable tools for the bodhisattva following the Mantranaya, the 'Way of Mantras', conceived of as part of the Mahāyāna. Despite the existence of late Indian texts describing the practices of householder bodhisattvas, these forms of tantric Buddhism probably had their primary location in the monastic arena. It is not clear whether this changes at all with the appearance of the Vajrayāna as a self-conscious tradition in the Yoga tantras. The issue of the origins of tantric Buddhism, to be discussed in the next section, should not be confused with the question of who its practitioners were. Although it may well be the case that a number of the rituals found in these three classes of tantras had their origins outside the Buddhist monastic context it is still likely that they were in the large practised by monastics. Significantly the major figures in the transmission of the Caryā and Yoga tantras to China in the eighth century – Śubhakarasiṃha, Vajrabodhi, and Amoghavajra – were all monks.

With the Mahāyoga and the Yoginī tantras the characteristics of the practitioner change. The ideal of the Yoginī tantras is the siddha, portrayed in Abhayadatta's *Caturaśītisiddhapravṛtti* ('Lives of the Eighty-four Mahāsiddhas'), as typically a non-monastic, non-celibate yogin or yoginī, living on the margins of society, frequenting cremation grounds, and generally behaving in an unconventional manner. Abhayadatta's text, however, is written perhaps some two hundred years after many of the figures it portrays were living, and has a somewhat stylised and stereotyped presentation. In consequence, as historical evidence, its descriptions have to be treated with caution.[54]

Nevertheless, it is clear that the Yoginī tantras were also practised in a monastic setting – witness the debate over whether monks should or should not take the secret and wisdom empowerments. That both householder and monastic Vajra-masters coexisted during this period is also clear from a passage in the *Vimalaprabhā* that – revealing its monastic bias – criticises monks who take a householder Vajra-master as their teacher in preference to a monk Vajra-master when one was available (Sanderson 1994: 92). The same text also denounces the use of married Vajra-masters to perform rituals of consecration for monasteries. Scholars disagree on the issue of whether the Yoginī tantras were initially practised by monastic or non-monastic Buddhists. The tendency of some Yoginī tantra commentaries to give internal or symbolic readings of the more controversial material in the primary texts can be taken as evidence of monastic Buddhism incorporating forms of practice that were initially non-monastic. Alternatively, some practices may have been incorporated directly into a monastic context from outside the Buddhist tradition.

Women in tantric Buddhism

The introduction to this chapter suggested that the high status and crucial roles given to women and to female deities could be counted as one of tantric Buddhism's distinctive features. This characterisation seems applicable, essentially, to just the phase of the Mahāyoga and (more especially) the Yoginī tantras. The earlier discussion of the Yoginī tantras observed that they were so named as a result of the central role played in them by female figures. As yoginīs and ḍākinīs, they comprise the maṇḍala deities surrounding the central figure. As (among others) Tārā and Vajrayoginī they may function as the central deity.[55] There is no question as to the high status accorded to female figures in the Yoginī texts:

> Women are heaven, women are the teaching (*dharma*)
> Women indeed are the highest austerity (*tapas*)
> Women are the Buddha, women are the Sangha
> Women are the Perfection of Wisdom.
> (*Caṇḍamahāroṣaṇa Tantra* viii: 29–30)

This same text warns (in Chapter 6) that those who slander women will be tortured in hell for three aeons. Rather, women should be honoured and respected as embodiments of female deities. Non-tantric Mahāyāna texts often take a perspective that appears – in spite of the rhetorical intent – to contrast vividly:

> You have plenty of filth of your own. Satisfy yourself
> with that!
> Glutton for crap! Forget her, that other pouch of filth!
> (Śāntideva, *Bodhicaryāvatāra*,
> trans. Crosby and Skilton 8: 53)

The shift in attitude towards women exemplified in the *Caṇḍamahāroṣaṇa Tantra* can be seen as part of the broader revaluation of (sexual) pleasure and the body found in these texts. Moreover, if what is impure is not to be seen as disgusting but is equally to be embraced with the pure, then Śāntideva's emphasis on the impurity of women becomes counterproductive.

Despite the status given to women in the Yoginī tantras there is controversy as to whether this status was mirrored 'on the ground' in the world of tantric practitioners. Freedom from social subordination does not necessarily follow from high ideological status.[56] One perspective is that tantric Buddhism, whatever its rhetoric, was generally for men. This is the view of Snellgrove (1987a: 287), who argues that 'despite the eulogies of woman in these tantras and her high symbolic status, the whole theory and practice is given for the benefit of males'. It has further been suggested that not only were the practices of these tantras essentially for men but that, in the process, women – particularly low-caste women used as tantric consorts – were often exploited. A very different view of the role of women in late tantric Buddhism has been advanced by Miranda Shaw (1994).[57] Shaw argues that not only did women have a key role in tantric theory but that they were prominent as adepts in tantric circles, and that they figured as founders and pioneers in tantric Buddhism's history. She suggests, moreover, that their position in relation to male tantric practitioners was not one of being exploited but, on the contrary, one of intimacy and equality, if not of superiority (as their teacher).

The paucity of historical evidence makes the assessment of the social realities of eighth to twelfth century tantric Buddhism especially problematic, and the issue of the actual role of women in this phase of the tradition is likely to remain controversial. In support of Shaw's case, there is evidence of women functioning as tantric teachers as well as practitioners, and a number of tantric texts are attributed to women. Many of the siddhas in Abhayadatta's *Caturaśītisiddhapravṛtti* receive decisive teachings from their female tantric partners, who are often also portrayed as their long-term companions.[58] That there was no restriction on the full involvement of women in tantric practice is suggested by later Tibetan histories of tantric Buddhism in India. For example, Kāṇha's foremost disciple is said to have been a woman, and among the disciples of Nāropa who gained awakening it is stated that one thousand were women whereas just two hundred were men.

On the other hand, the Mahāyoga and Yoginī tantras generally (the *Caṇḍamahāroṣaṇa Tantra* is a partial exception) fail to provide for women taking the secret and wisdom empowerments, and although women play key roles as tantric partners in Abhayadatta's 'biographies', only four of the eighty-four siddhas are women. Given the difficulties associated with straightforwardly viewing Abhayadatta's text as a historical document, such roles that women have may be as much symbolic as actual. Also, despite the existence of some tantric texts written by women, the vast majority are written (or at least attributed) to men. Such qualifications notwithstanding, it does appear, however, that tantric Buddhism in this period did to some extent provide opportunities for women to function in a more egalitarian fashion than was possible in the broader (Buddhist) social and religious context.

Origins and influences

That tantric Buddhism did not evolve in isolation from the broader religious culture of its time has been noted. The devotional (*bhakti*) traditions focused on the gods Śiva, Viṣṇu, and Devī were a prominent part of Indian religion from at least the fourth century. Also significant, especially from the seventh century, were tantric forms of religion centred on these gods. In particular, tantric Śaivism had a following in areas, such as Kashmir, that were centres for tantric Buddhism. Indeed, by the seventh century, in the face of such competition, Buddhism seems to have been somewhat in decline. This, at least, is the picture conveyed by the journal of the famous seventh century Chinese Buddhist pilgrim Hsüan-tsang. In any case, it is clear that Buddhism was vying with other traditions for patronage and followers.

In response to the competing attractions and soteriologies of these non-Buddhist traditions, tantric Buddhism adopted a number of strategies. Essentially all of these can be seen as forms of inclusion, whereby non-Buddhist deities and rituals are incorporated as forms of Buddhism. One approach was to contend that the traditions concerned were never anything but Buddhist. Thus the *Mañjuśrīmūlakalpa* reveals that the rituals of the non-

Buddhist deities Tumberu and his sisters were originally taught many aeons ago by the Buddha. It is only recently that they have been taught by Śiva. A more general form of this strategy is found in the *Mahāvairocana Sūtra*. Here non-Buddhist traditions are presented as having been taught by Buddhas who, out of their compassionate skill in teaching according to individuals' differing needs, took the form of figures such as Maheśvara (Śiva) and Nārāyaṇa (Viṣṇu). From this perspective, all religion becomes Buddhist.

A second type of strategy is the (sometimes forcible) subjugation of non-Buddhist deities. Subjected deities go for refuge to the Buddha, after which their rituals may be incorporated though with new mantras substituted for the non-Buddhist ones. A highly vivid, as well as influential, example of this form of incorporation occurs in the *Tattvasaṃgraha*. This text contains a detailed narrative of the subjugation of Śiva by Vajrapāṇi. Śiva is particularly resistant to conversion, however. He has to be killed and revived, and finally trampled underfoot, along with his wife Umā, by Vajrapāṇi. After receiving tantric empowerments in this position from Vajrapāṇi's foot, Śiva achieves awakening and, renamed, becomes a Buddha in a distant world-system.[59] Davidson (1995a) has suggested that this story, which was to become one of Tibetan Buddhism's central myths, had its origins in the story-telling of itinerant Buddhist teachers who had to deal with competing religious traditions as they wandered from village to village. Only later, he believes, was it incorporated into the textual and monastic traditions.

With the Mahāyoga and Yoginī tantras, questions of origins arise in somewhat different form. Some scholars argue that these texts, and especially the Yoginī tantras as typified by the *Hevajra Tantra* with its adoption of cremation-ground practices, represent a radically new form of tantric Buddhism (see, for example, Snellgrove 1987a: 180–1). According to this view, such texts have their origin amongst groups of wandering non-celibate yogins that gathered, especially in cremation-grounds, to practise their rituals. Only later were they incorporated into the sphere of monastic Buddhism. It is further argued that this is the source not only for Buddhist Yoginī tantras, but also for Śaiva tantras that contain similar features, and that it represents a common yogic substratum that both traditions drew upon.[60] More recently Alexis Sanderson (1994) has questioned the validity of this sort of model. Sanderson, though agreeing that certain Śaiva and Buddhist tantric texts share a large number of features, argues that, in specific instances at least, this can be explained as the result of borrowing on the part of the Buddhists. He has been able to demonstrate convincingly that extensive passages in Cakrasaṃvara cycle tantras such as the *Laghusaṃvara*, the *Abhidhānottara*, and the *Saṃvarodaya*, were redacted from tantras in the Vidyāpītha section of the Śaiva canon. Sanderson also quotes a Śaiva text, the *Haracaritacintāmaṇi*, which makes it clear that the Śaiva tradition was quite aware that their texts had been used in this way (op. cit.: 93).

It appears, in conclusion, that the strategy of dealing with the threat of competing traditions by incorporating aspects of them continues into the period of the Yoginī tantras. The question of whether the Buddhist redactors of these texts were wandering yogins or monks remains to be settled, though whoever they were, they needed access to a range of Śaiva texts. Whatever the case – and paralleling earlier phases of Buddhism (tantric or otherwise) – the borrowed elements were assimilated into the Buddhist context, making tantric Buddhism, as Sanderson comments 'entirely Buddhist in terms of its function and self-perception' (op. cit.: 96).

Notes

1 The doctrinal position of the Buddha in context

1 Thus, the 'magic key' for understanding what is going on in Buddhism is the following: whenever you come across something new, or perhaps even strange, in your study of Buddhism ask yourself the following question: 'How might a Buddhist holding or practising that consider that doing so leads to the diminution or eradication of negative mental states, and the increasing or fulfilment of positive mental states?'

2 On what was, as far as we can tell, the Buddha's own view of the gods (*devas*) see Norman (1990–6; 1991 volume, papers 31 and 44).

3 See Gombrich (1988: 29). On Aśoka and Buddhism see Norman (1997: Ch. 7).

4 On purity and pollution in relationship to the caste system see Dumont (1988). Note, however, that when one speaks of 'impurity' or 'pollution' the polluting substance is not *as such* dirt. Caste is not a matter of hygiene. The pollution is metaphysical. One is born with it. One does not cease to be polluted by following a 'clean' occupation.

5 The Buddha was critical of the intrinsic supremacy of the brahmins, and with it the ideology of *varṇa*. But it would be misleading from this to infer, as some modern writers do, that the Buddha was 'anti-caste'. First, a criticism of the *varṇa* system is not in itself a comment on *jāti*, caste, although it could be transposed to the ideology that nevertheless underlies caste. For his part the Buddha spoke of the true brahmin as one who had spiritual insight and behaves accordingly (see the famous *Dhammapada* Ch. 26). In this sense the Buddha *affirmed* a hierarchy not of birth but of spiritual maturity. It is not obvious that the Buddha would have any comment to make about a brahmin who is *also* spiritually mature (understood in the Buddha's sense). The Buddha was not offering social reform. And

this is what one would expect. The Buddha was himself a renouncer of society.

6 Cf. Edgerton (1972: 165) on the *Bhagavad Gītā*:

> In fact, the Gītā, like the Upaniṣads, tends to promise complete emancipation to one who 'knows' any particularly profound religious or philosophic truth that it sets forth. This seems to have been characteristic of Hindu systems generally, at least in their early stages.

7 From the Pāli *Sāmaññaphala Sutta*, with the teachers' names in Pāli.
8 For further details see now the article by Cousins (1996a), reviewing Bechert (1991–2), and the Bechert volumes themselves.
9 This whole book is warmly recommended as an excellent, short, and easily accessible academic survey of the Buddha and his significance.
10 Norman (1997: 23) points out that *rāja* used for Gautama's father may at this time and in this context have simply meant someone from a *kṣatriya* class.
11 For a study of some Asian hagiographies see Granoff and Shinohara (1994).
12 See the account of the Buddha's last days in the Pāli *Mahāparinibbāna Sutta*.
13 On the nature and influence of oral transmission in Buddhism see Norman (1997: Ch. 3). On the process and influence of writing see op. cit.: Ch. 5.
14 Although Norman (1997: Ch. 8) expresses some caution about the whole concept of a 'canon', that he reminds us is a Western category. See also Collins (1990).
15 On the language or languages that the Buddha spoke, see Norman (1990–6: papers 38 and 42).
16 On the formation of the canon, with particular reference to the Pāli Canon, see Norman (1997: Ch. 8).
17 It has been found that preservation of texts orally can be just as accurate as literary preservation, if not more so. Where, for example, texts are chanted communally a mistake or interpolation is immediately noticeable and made public.
18 Usually taken as an epithet of the Buddha, but cf. Norman (1990–6; 1993 volume: 252, 258–60).
19 On whether *avidyā* would be best translated as 'misconception' or 'ignorance' see Matilal (1980). Perhaps, as Matilal argues, 'misconception' would be a better translation. But 'ignorance' has become fairly established in Buddhist Studies.
20 A common view of the later Buddhist tradition is that the Buddha did not answer these questions because he saw an incompatibility

between answering these questions and following the path. This is because the questions presuppose as some sort of absolutes categories like the world, the 'life-principle', and the *Tathāgata.* Actually these are simply conceptual constructs and do not exist from the point of view of a perception of how things really are. All these conceptual constructs presupposed as some sort of absolutes involve attachment, and are thus antithetical to liberation. Thus any answer to the questions would involve being enmeshed in attachment and grasping, or, as the Buddhist tradition has it, enmeshed in 'views' (*dṛṣṭi*; Pāli: *diṭṭhi*). It would thus be incompatible with not only the enlightenment of Māluṅkyāputta but also the enlightenment of the Buddha (see Gethin (1998: 67–8); see also Norman (1990–6; 1993 volume: 251–63)).

21 What he actually says is that 'if one practises the things the Buddha declared to be obstacles, they are no obstacles'. But I follow Richard Gombrich (1996: 22–3) in taking this as a euphemism for sexual intercourse.

22 This interpretation is supported in the sutta by the Buddha's subsequently relating the wrong approach here to the holding of 'views' (*dṛṣṭi*; Pāli: *diṭṭhi*). On the meaning of the expression 'view' here see the recent paper by Rupert Gethin (1997b). He comments that 'even so-called "right views" can be "views" (*diṭṭhi*) in so far as they can become fixed and the objects of attachment' (op. cit.: 217–18). Thus inasmuch as the content of a particular true statement becomes an object of attachment, it becomes a 'view' and should be abandoned. But it does not thereby become less than true. Moreover there is an implication here that rigid and unnecessary adherence to a particular formulation of a doctrinal position, again even if true, would also indicate a 'view'.

2 Mainstream Buddhism: the basic thought of the Buddha

1 Translated in Nārada (1980: 50), with *dukkha* substituted for 'suffering'. Cf. Vetter (1998).

2 On 'Death and the Tathāgata' see Norman (1990–6; 1993 volume: 251–63).

3 See e.g. Bhattacharya (1973), and Perez-Remon (1981). Cf. Collins (1982a) and Collins' combative review-article (1982b) of Perez-Remon.

4 'Intentional' here is being used in a technical philosophical sense that goes back at least as far as the philosopher Franz Brentano (1838–1917). In this context one speaks of 'intentional objects', meaning objects of intentional, i.e. mental, states. Mental states, like wishes, beliefs, or cognitions, are *about* something. That which they are about is their intentional object. It is their referent. Mental states are

distinguished from non-mental states by this 'intentionality'. This use of 'intention' is different from 'intention' when involving the will, as when we say 'I have the intention of going to London', or '*Karman* involves intention' or when we refer to the second link in the Noble Eightfold Path as 'right intention'.

5 And note that, as philosophers like Sartre have pointed out, it is arguably possible to have negative intentional objects, such as absences (see Sartre's comments on perceiving the *absence* of Pierre in the café in *Being and Nothingness* (1966: Ch. 1: 2)). Thus being a cognitive object need not in itself imply a 'positive reality' at all.

6 I have deliberately quoted here for all its faults from the famous translation by Woodward (quoted in Norman 1990–6; 1996 volume: 18). This translation is often cited in order to give an 'Advaita-like', or 'True Self' interpretation of Buddhism.

7 For a comprehensive and sophisticated study of nirvāṇa see now Collins (1998).

8 The translations are those of Gethin (1998: 81), who gives the interpretation of the eightfold path in a very handy table. I am more than usually indebted to his clear and readable explanation here.

9 This 'seeing' is not necessarily to be identified simply with holding a correct opinion or belief. On this complex issue see Gethin (1997b: esp. 223).

10 For an extremely useful and comprehensive book recently published in English on the monastic code see Thanissaro Bhikkhu (1994). 'Right speech' and 'right action' between them cover four of the five precepts which (it is hoped) will be observed by all Buddhists, including lay Buddhists. The other precept is refraining from intoxicants. On the precepts see Gethin (1998: 170 ff.).

11 There is some dispute among scholars about the translation of *kuśala* (Pāli: *kusala*) and their opposite by 'wholesome' and 'unwholesome' respectively, rather than, say, 'virtuous' and 'unvirtuous', or even 'good' and 'bad'. See Cousins (1996b).

12 See Gethin (1998: 184–6); cf. the slightly different account in Harvey (1990: 250–1). On 'applied thought and examination' see Cousins (1992).

13 See the similar comments in this connection by Gombrich (1996: 15–16).

14 Cf. here Hirakawa (1990: 6), who argues that rebirth is not essential to the Buddha's teachings since his concern was totally with liberation. The Buddha simply took over rebirth from the wider Indian religious environment. I do not agree. The Buddha's concern with liberation was precisely liberation from among other things continued rebirth. It was because the Buddha accepted rebirth that the search for liberation was so acute for him. Otherwise at least old age

and death (that thus comes but once) would not be so frightening (indeed old age could be avoided by an early death). Moreover since *ucchedavāda* would then be true, many wicked deeds would never bring about their unpleasant results for their perpetrators (*karman* would thus collapse). All would attain the final cessation of greed, hatred, and delusion, and all suffering, at death. It is difficult to see what would be left of Buddhism as it is traditionally understood with a denial of rebirth.

15 Note the translation here. The Pāli text does not say that form lacks a Self, or does not have a Self, or is Selfless, or whatever. Grammatically it quite straightforwardly says material form *is not Self*. See here Norman (1997: 26–8).

16 Note the very 'upaniṣadic' flavour to this. The Self that the Buddha's fellow renunciates were looking for is that which involves *complete control* (the Self as the 'inner controller' familiar from the Upaniṣads), and which is *beyond all suffering* (possibly, although not necessarily, the Self as bliss (*ānanda*)). It is also, as we shall see, *unchanging* (for it is that which lies behind all change). These are the characteristics of an *ātman*. The Buddha was not interested in abstract philosophising. He was interested in answering particular spiritual problems, and it should not be surprising to find his expression reflecting the context in which he was offering his advice. See here Gombrich (1996: 15–17).

17 On the aggregates see Gethin (1986 and 1998: 135–6).

18 See Norman (1990–6: paper 48) and (1997: 27); and Gombrich (1990b: 13 ff.) cf. Gombrich (1996: Ch. 2).

19 By far the best study on Not-Self, indeed the standard work, is Collins (1982a).

20 For an influential later source that makes this point very clear see the Pāli *Milindapañha* (the 'Questions of [King] Milinda') 2: 1: 1. Using the example of a chariot, it is pointed out that a chariot is not identifiable with any one part of the chariot (such as the wheels). There is no one constituent that is *the* chariot. And there certainly is not any *additional* thing called 'the chariot', behind all the constituents such as wheels, pole, axle, and so on. But we can still talk of a chariot for practical purposes, using a convenient label, in dependence upon the various constituents of the chariot.

21 Translated in Gethin (1998: 141). The word '*dharma*' (Pāli: *dhamma*) here is a specific technical usage of the term. It is sometimes used in this sense quite widely simply to mean something like 'thing'. More specifically, it refers to a 'phenomenon', something experienced or capable of being experienced (without any implication that there is some more fundamental reality, a 'noumenon', behind the phenomenon). In much of Buddhist philosophy (the Abhidharma;

Pāli: Abhidhamma) dharma comes to refer to what is actually there in all our experiences. It is a plurality, the plurality of 'actuals'. Thus it comes to mean (in e.g. Vaibhāṣika Abhidharma) the ultimate reals ('substances'; *dravyas*) that provide the experiential basis out of which the world as given to us and lived by us is constructed. It has become common among scholars to use the lower case 'd' (and depending on context the plural) when referring to dharmas in this sense, in order to distinguish this use of the term from the 'Dharma', that which was discovered and taught by the Buddha. Unfortunately the situation is further complicated by another overlapping use of '*dharmas*', again in plural and with a lower case 'd'. This is the term used to refer to objects of the sixth sense, the mind. In this sense '*dharmas*' refers broadly speaking to objects of thought, the objects when one e.g. anticipates or remembers.

22 See the *Visuddhimagga* and the *Abhidharmakośa*, in the excellent discussion in Gethin (1998: 149–59).

23 It might be suggested that if *karman* is to be thought of as moral or immoral, then it must be more than just the intention. Clearly if the immoral act were to be the *intention* to kill then nothing would be added morally or indeed in terms of following the Buddhist path by actually carrying out the killing. Buddhist tradition, recognising this, has added that for a full *karman* to have occurred various other factors are necessary. One must *recognise* the object for what it is (i.e. in the case of killing, recognise that *X* is a *living creature*), have the *intention* to do the deed, actually *perform* the deed, and the expected and hoped for result of the deed must really *occur* (i.e. the being dies). The Theravāda tradition on this topic, described in Gethin (1998: 120) precedes this list of four with one other, that the object must in some sense be present (i.e. there must be a living creature). A good Tibetan source, based on other Indian texts, is Pabongka Rinpoche (1991: 442 ff.). This text adds a further factor, the *delusion* involved. This in fact refers to the presence of greed, hatred, or delusion. The effect of this is to leave open the possibility of performing e.g. an act of killing without the presence of greed, hatred, or delusion. Thus such an act of killing would not be an unwholesome act (at least, not a fully unwholesome act). Perhaps this formulation reflects Mahāyāna views of 'skilful means' or 'skill-in-means' (*upāyakauśalya*), whereby it does indeed become possible for a bodhisattva to kill with compassion and thus not perform an unwholesome deed. See later.

24 The best study of all of this is Collins (1982a). For philosophical reflections, and a critique of the coherence of much of this, see Williams (1998a: Chs 2 and 5). See also the review articles by Pettit (1999) and Siderits (2000), with conjoined replies by Williams.

25 Note here that obviously the relationship between the arising of feelings and the arising of craving cannot be one of simple cause and effect (in accordance with the formula 'This being, that occurs' etc.). This is because it is possible for feelings to arise and craving *not* to follow. If that were not the case, the twelve-fold formula of dependent origination would be a completely closed deterministic system, and liberation would become impossible.

26 There appears prima facie to be a problem (or at least some tension) here. Acts are called 'wholesome' (*kuśala/kusala*) not just because they are virtuous, or good, but because in terms of the Buddhist soteriological project they are also conducive to furthering one's progress on the path to enlightenment. Yet wholesome acts do not themselves lead to enlightenment. They are acts (*karman*), and as such they lead to future pleasures including favourable rebirths in order to allow further pleasures to take place. As with all Indian gnostic systems, enlightenment is the result of gnosis, knowing. Yet it cannot be denied that wholesome acts do further the path to liberation.

27 There is a view that all twelve links are intended to apply not over three lifetimes, but to *each moment*. While some ingenuity may go into this application it seems doubtful that this was the original intention of the twelvefold formula. But then, was there an original intention at all? This view of the 'simultaneous' occurrence of the twelve factors, and some other views as well, is treated critically in the great Sarvāstivāda compendium, the *Mahāvibhāṣā*. See Potter (*et al.*) (1996: 114) and the textual references in that volume.

28 For more on whether this makes Buddhism an ethic of intention or, rather, a teleological ethics where good and bad (wholesome and unwholesome) are dependent upon the contribution of the relevant intention towards a soteriological goal, see Keown (1992).

29 There is often a lot of confusion about this in the West, particularly in the media. In saying that e.g. pains are the karmic results of unwholesome intentions in the past, including past lives, the Buddha considers that he is simply describing the 'is' of the factual situation. This explains why people have pains. The factual situation is indeed considered by the Buddha to entail an 'ought'. This 'ought' is the 'ought' of avoiding unwholesome intentions and the actions that commonly flow from them. Thus one will bring about a situation where one will not suffer pains in the future. The Buddhist tradition does *not* consider that the factual situation of pains, granted the truth of karmic causation, entails that one should treat the person in pain as e.g. not to be pitied, not to be helped, to be ignored 'because it is their own fault'.

30 Cf. Kṛṣṇa's criticisms in *Bhagavad Gītā* Ch. 3. This urge to bring to

an end all action may be related (if only subconsciously) to the Jain act of *sallekhanā*, holy death through self-directed starvation. See Jaini (1979: 227–3) and Tukol (1976).

31 Thus Gombrich wants to maintain that a close reading of the sources shows that the Buddha taught kindness and compassion as a means of attaining liberation. As Gombrich admits, this is not the traditional Buddhist way of understanding these texts. He has returned to this point in his 1998 paper.

32 For an outstanding description of Buddhist cosmology see Gethin (1998: Ch. 5), to which I am very indebted, and also Gethin (1997a).

33 Often characterised by rampant hunger, reflecting cultural ideas of the dead as hungry, needing to be fed, and therefore preying on their living descendants. Cf. my earlier reference to the late Vedic idea of feeding the dead through certain sacrificial rituals, keeping them alive in the afterlife through the appropriate actions, *karman*.

34 Interestingly, in the *Sangīti Sutta* ('Discourse that is a Recital') of the *Dīgha Nikāya* in the Pāli Canon we find lists of both five destinies (D: III: 234) and six destinies (D: III: 264), showing some instability among the early Buddhist sources.

35 Extensive accounts of the Buddhist cosmology cannot be found in the earliest sources, that presuppose a common heritage of realms of gods, hells, rebirth, and so on but do not give very much by way of elaborate discussion. For some material see e.g. the *Kevaddha Sutta* ('Discourse to Kevaddha') of the *Dīgha Nikāya*. The short account here is based largely on Gethin (1998) and Lamotte (1988: 31–3), that draw on later elaborations particularly from Abhidhamma/Abhidharma sources.

36 I shall not give the details. All of these realms can be found tabulated very nicely in Gethin (1998: 116–17). Of these six desire realm heavens, one particularly worth noting is the fourth, the Tuṣita realm, since that is said to be where a Buddha-to-be, a bodhisattva, resides in his life immediately before descending to earth to undergo his last life and become a Buddha. 'Tuṣita' in Sanskrit means 'contented' (Pāli: Tusita), and the lifespan there is said to be 16,000 'divine years' (a very long time, but nothing compared with the many aeons of the higher gods).

37 An example, the *Kevaddha Sutta* tells us, would be Great Brahmā (*Mahābrahmā*). Lower gods such as Sakka describe him as

> the Supreme One, the Mighty One, the All-seeing One, the Ruler, the Lord of all, the Controller, the Creator, the Chief of all, appointing to each his place, the Ancient of days, the Father of all that are and are to be.
>
> (*Kevaddha Sutta*, trans. Rhys-Davids 1889: 281)

But in what is partly intended as a (rather amusing) Buddhist joke Mahābrahmā is portrayed as really being pompous, a bit of a bully, and quite ignorant (although not wanting the other gods to know the fact). He pretends his own omniscience, dwelling on the plane of the form realm corresponding to the highest level of the first *dhyāna*. Thus by the standards of god realms he is actually quite low down in the system.

38 See also the *Brahmajāla Sutta*, the 'Discourse on the Net of Brahmā' Ch. 2.

39 The stage of 'never-returner' is the third of the four levels of the 'Noble One', the *Ārya*, one who has attained the 'fruit of the path' by following the teaching of a Buddha. The first of these is 'stream-enterer' (Sanskrit.: *srotāpanna*; Pāli: *sotāpanna*). One becomes a stream-enterer through abandoning the first three of the ten fetters (*saṃyojana*), the 'view of individuality', doubt, and clinging to precepts and vows. In finally and deeply abandoning these one will be reborn at the most a further seven times before becoming enlightened. On also permanently weakening the next two fetters, sensual desire and aversion, one becomes a 'once-returner' (Sanskrit: *sakṛdāgāmin*; Pāli: *sakadāgāmin*), who will be reborn as a human being no more than one further time. On completely abandoning all these five fetters one becomes a never-returner and is on death reborn in one of the highest planes of the form realm. One will never be reborn as a human again. One will attain enlightenment in that 'pure abode'. On completely and irrevocably eradicating all ten fetters (including now the five of desire for form, desire for the formless, pride, agitation, and ignorance) one becomes enlightened, an *arhat* (Sanskrit) or *arahat* (Pāli). See Gethin (1998: 72–3, 193–4).

40 It is said that if one is dominated by greed, other things being equal one becomes a ghost. If hatred, one plummets to hell. And if ignorance, one becomes an animal. This is all very neat, but as we have seen actually ignorance is the key to all states in saṃsāra.

41 Presumably the monk *also* engages in acts animated by non-greed, non-hatred, and non-delusion.

42 Note however that just as one born in the human realm *can* experience states of mind associated with other planes, so with some restrictions one born in other planes can too. Thus one born in a hell can experience a wholesome state of mind, and this can be one means to create the seeds of emergence from the hell. Another means may be the maturation of a previous wholesome *karman* for some reason. Likewise one in, say, one of the form reams corresponding to the third *dhyāna* can presumably experience an unwholesome state of mind or the maturation of an unwholesome *karman* and be reborn on a lower plane. But one born in the pure abodes corresponding

to the fourth *dhyāna* cannot fall further. Since throughout infinite saṃsāra we have all had infinite rebirths, Buddhists consider it follows that we have all been reborn many if not infinite times in all the planes of rebirth from which it is possible to rise or fall. Thus it follows that we have all been familiar many, many times with the states of mind associated with those planes.

43 For further information on Buddhist cosmology see Reynolds and Reynolds (1982), Kloetzli (1983), Kongtrul (1995), and Sadakata (1997). The Kongtrul text is Tibetan, but it is based on Indian sources.

44 On the *brahmavihāras* as means of attaining enlightenment, see Gombrich (1996: 60 ff. and 1998).

45 See here, for example, the *Sāmaññaphala Sutta*, where attaining these *iddhis* is specifically lauded as a 'fruit of being a drop-out'. It is sometimes said in works on Buddhism that these wondrous abilities were seen by the Buddha as a hindrance on the path, and were not to be developed or demonstrated. I am not so sure. The Buddha was well aware that they could become objects of attachment, and their cultivation was not what the path was all about. False claims to having such abilities are condemned in the *Vinaya*. But there are many cases where the Buddha and other monks of great attainment used such powers in order to teach, practise, or help others. One can be sure that the Buddha's possession of these and similar abilities would have been expected by his disciples and others. See Gethin (1998: 186).

46 On the translation of *prajñā/paññā* as 'wisdom' see Williams (1989: 42–5).

47 Compare this with the Mahāyāna 'Perfection of Wisdom' (*Prajñāpāramitā*) literature, and the Madhyamaka tradition of philosophy (see pp. 131–52). Cf. also Buddhaghosa's description of the next stage (21: 53 ff.), where the meditator is said to see all as 'empty' (Pāli: *suñña*; Sanskrit: *śūnya*).

48 This is enough to give the reader an idea of one widely held Buddhist structure for the path of meditation. Buddhaghosa was writing in Sri Lanka. For a summary of Vasubandhu's structure, that both reflects, and was very influential on, various north Indian traditions including Mahāyāna sources, see Gethin (1998: 194–8).

49 The expression 'Theravāda' means 'Doctrine of the Elders'. 'Sarvāstivāda' means 'Doctrine of those who hold that All Exist'. The alternative name 'Vaibhāṣika' for Sarvāstivāda, commonly used in e.g. Tibetan Buddhism, refers to their adherence to the great compendium of Abhidharma, the *Mahāvibhāṣā*.

50 To 'reify' something (such as a process like growth) is to make it into a fixed singular *thing*, existent as such in its own right. A 'conceptual reification' occurs when the reification is brought about or

associated with the application of the concept. Thus because we have a single concept 'growth', we may reify growth into a fixed singular *thing*, instead of seeing it as a process. Or we may treat a forest as a singular thing, again through application of the unitary concept 'forest'.

51 Handy discussions of dharmas can be found in Lamotte (1988: 593 ff.) and Hirakawa (1990: 139 ff.).

52 These two are the second and third of the five aggregates. Consciousness, in the Abhidhamma list, is the fifth aggregate. Physical, or material, form, the first aggregate, as we can see, divides into a number of dhammas. So also does the aggregate of formations, which as a class has by far the most dhammas.

53 There also remains texts of another Abhidharma system (although not a Piṭaka) connected with Yogācāra, a school usually thought of as associated with the Mahāyāna perspective. The Yogācāra Abhidharma has 100 dharmas.

54 One can see here that for Vaibhāṣika Abhidharma the sense in which a dharma has 'own-existence', a *svabhāva*, and is therefore not causally dependent is one of not being dependent upon conceptual reification in the way that, say, a forest is. In spite of Madhyamaka (as we shall see), this is certainly not the same as maintaining that a dharma with a *svabhāva* is not the result of causes and conditions at all. All conditioned dharmas, i.e. most dharmas, are the results of causes and conditions. They are radically impermanent. But likewise all dharmas have a *svabhāva*. That is, they are simples and not conceptually reified out of pluralities.

3 The nature and origins of Mahāyāna Buddhism

1 On how early we can date the earliest Mahāyāna, however, note the comments made by Paul Harrison (1995: 55–6). We are dealing with a floating body of ideas that issues in a floating body of literature. That literature eventually comes to take a form identifiable as the one that we have now. This could be due to a series of factors some of which may be historical accidents.

2 I am using the expression 'non-Mahāyāna' here instead of the pejorative 'Hīnayāna'. I have done the same in Williams (1989), and in the present context of discussing Mahāyāna historically I think this is possibly the safest neutral expression. 'Theravāda' is quite unsatisfactory, since while the Theravāda school is the only one remaining of the traditions of Buddhism that originated prior to the rise of Mahāyāna, historically as we have seen there were many more. In India in classical times the Theravāda was far from being the most important. It is indeed very difficult to show where

Mahāyāna sources knew of, or were reacting against, specifically Theravāda doctrines and practices. However clearly 'non-Mahāyāna' will not do for discussions of Buddhism as a whole. Nowadays I am inclined to favour the expression 'Mainstream Buddhism' for non-Mahāyāna, as used currently by Paul Harrison but possibly originating with Eric Cheetham (see the latter's series of booklets published by The Buddhist Society, London, 1985 onwards). 'Mainstream Buddhism' indicates rather nicely what appears to me to be the relationship between non-Mahāyāna and Mahāyāna, where Mahāyāna in India is a particular sort of occurrence within (and possibly very much a minority within) Buddhism, i.e. Mainstream Buddhism, non-Mahāyāna Buddhism.

3 The nearest case I know of is a discussion in the *Abhidharmadīpa* (Chs 4 and 6). This text dates from possibly the sixth century CE. The point made there is that there is indeed a bodhisattva vehicle to Buddhahood taught in the regular mainstream *Tripiṭaka*. This *Tripiṭaka* provides the only authentic Buddhist texts. Thus the so-called 'Mahāyāna sūtras' are inauthentic.

4 Perhaps what really needs explaining is why the Mahāyāna vision has become so dominant in certain parts of the Buddhist world *outside* India. The answer to that question may have something to do with the relative ease of transmission of Mahāyāna Buddhism to other and eventually non-Indic cultures.

5 Cf. however Sasaki (1994), who would want to argue that this non-doctrinal understanding of *saṃghabheda* emerged only during the time of Aśoka (third century BCE). I remain unconvinced, but anyway since Mahāyāna itself seems to have emerged first during or after the time of Aśoka, it would not affect the point as regards Mahāyāna and schism.

6 The First Council is traditionally held to have occurred immediately after the death of the Buddha, when those of his disciples who were enlightened recited and agreed the Buddha's teachings as they had heard them. They thus compiled the canon, the *Tripiṭaka*.

7 I am familiar with the problematic case of Saicho in eighth-ninth century Japan. He certainly *spoke* of establishing a Mahāyāna Vinaya in opposition to the non-Mahāyāna monastic Vinayas. Of course, as regards the issue of *saṃghabheda* and the Vinaya my concern here is with Indian Buddhism.

8 See Harrison (1995): 'Mahāyāna was a pan-Buddhist movement – or better, a loose set of movements – rather like Pentecostalism or Charismatic Christianity, running across sectarian boundaries' (1995: 56).

9 For Schopen's methodological reflections on what he sees as a 'Protestant' tendency among modern scholars to privilege tex-

tual resources rather than archaeological evidence see Schopen (1991b).

10 Note, incidentally, the extreme paucity of literary remains for Mahāyāna found on Indian soil. Very little indeed by way of ancient Mahāyāna texts have been found in 'India proper'.

11 For a short recent statement of the more traditional view, see Yuichi Kajiyama in Yoshinori Takeuchi (1993: 142–5). Kajiyama takes as his starting point the oft-stated association of the laity with stūpas and the relic cult, relying on the Buddha's purported statement in the *Mahāparinibbāna Sutta* that monks should have nothing to do with the cult of relics. This would be a concern of the laity. Schopen 1991c (see also 1992) has convincingly argued that this is based on a misreading of the sūtra (cf. here Schopen with Vetter (1994: esp. 1247 ff.)). The allied association of the rise of Mahāyāna with cults centred on stūpas and relics has been criticised in Schopen (1977). The originator of the widely accepted theory associating the stūpa cult, the laity, and the origins of the Mahāyāna is the Japanese scholar Akira Hirakawa (1963 and 1990, for example). Schopen (1985) shows that from the very earliest donative inscriptions, monks and nuns – often very learned monks and nuns – had been important donors at stūpas. The proportion of Sangha members increased as time passed until they were frequently in the overwhelming majority. Moreover it is also monks and nuns who are overwhelmingly associated with inscriptions identifiable as Mahāyāna, 'the Mahāyāna was a monk dominated movement' (1985: 26). Hirakawa's perspective is also criticised in an excellent paper by Paul Harrison (1995), and has recently begun to be criticised even within Japanese circles (see Sasaki 1994). Vetter (1994) suggests a sympathetic but, I think, unconvincing reappraisal of Hirakawa's argument.

12 Schopen (1992: 107) makes the same point about misunderstanding the rhetorical devices of the Mahāyāna sūtras. He contrasts the picture of the non-Mahāyāna monk as 'self-centered' and 'indolent' given in some (modern) works on Mahāyāna that rely uncritically on the picture obtained from the Mahāyāna sūtras, with the picture of altruism and social involvement provided by the inscriptional evidence.

13 See Williams (1989: 20–6). See also Harrison (1995: 57 ff. and especially 68).

14 But cf. Williams (1989: 26–8) for a suggestion that this sort of antagonism was not so prevalent in the very earliest Mahāyāna literature.

15 Perhaps this association of early Mahāyāna with forest-dwelling meditators could have something to do with a point I note in Williams

(1989: 10–11). The period that may have seen the origins of the Mahāyāna appears to have been characterised by

> an awareness of living in the 'last days', an era when things are on the decline, or are not what they were, 'life under siege', . . . it is possible that Mahāyānists saw their own practices and beliefs in this context as bulwarks against moral and spiritual decline.

Harrison (1995) suggests that the fact that many of the early Mahāyānists were forest dwelling ascetic meditators may be the reason why we find so little archaeological evidence for them.

16 Note also the reference in e.g. Schopen (1994: 47) to relics as 'infused with morality, infused with concentration, wisdom, release and knowledge and vision'. In other words, relics are infused with the very qualities that make a Buddha a Buddha. But these qualities are also the qualities (*dharmas*) often referred to as the 'collection of dharmas' (*dharmakāya*) in certain Buddhist philosophical texts (Williams 1989: 171). Thus texts that say that one should take refuge not in the physical body of the Buddha but in his *dharmakāya*, his Buddha-qualities, could be said to be indicating not just the need to become a Buddha through expressing in oneself those qualities constitutive of a Buddha (as previously thought). They could be indicating also the continuing presence of the Buddha, even though dead, his presence as the *dharmakāya* pervading his relics. Transcending death, the Buddha is present in the monastery still. Cf. however Harrison (1995: 62) on Mahāyāna as 'the work of a predominantly monastic order of meditators engaged in strenuous ascetic practices, people asserting, in short, that the Buddha is to be found in and through the realisation of the dharma, not the worship of relics'.

17 Perhaps we can also associate the occurrence of visions and its importance in the origins of at least some strands of Mahāyāna with the occurrence, or considered occurrence, also of magical power. Harrison (1995: 66) suggests that meditation and associated powers (not to mention the miraculous bodhisattvas) would have given Mahāyānists an edge in a crucial factor among the religious in ancient India, the competition for limited resources. Essentially this is competition for donations from supporting non-religious ('laity') eager for spiritual merit, and often also access to magical power and miraculous results.

18 Note the suggestion in Schopen (1987a: 212) that dying and being oneself buried in the presence of the Buddha (i.e. in the vicinity of a stūpa) was thought to lead to a rebirth in a heaven. The earliest Pure

Lands are modelled on heavens. It is not surprising that once the idea of Pure Lands had developed death associated with being in the presence of the Buddha (a stated result of *buddhānusmṛti*) would lead to rebirth in a Pure Land rather than a heaven.

4 Some schools of mainstream Buddhist thought

1 That is, from about the middle of the second century CE. The *Mahāvibhāṣā* is conceived as an elaborate commentary on the *Jñānaprasthāna*, one of the seven books of the Sarvāstivādin Abhidharma. It details extensive doctrinal debates both within Sarvāstivāda and with others, as well as formulating what became Sarvāstivādin orthodoxy.

2 What follows is a simplified summary of part of Williams (1981). See also Williams (1977), and Cox (1995) and, briefly, (1998).

3 And not, as books often have it, the three *times* (past, present, and future) exist. The issue of the ontological status of time is different.

4 For criticisms see in particular the *Abhidharmakośabhāṣya* 5: 25 ff. A summary can be found in Potter (1999: 554–7).

5 There is a problem with much of this. We have seen already that past dharmas exert causal efficacy as well. Thus 'doing what it does' cannot be definitive of a present dharma. In response to such criticisms, later Sarvāstivādins like Saṃghabhadra distinguish between the 'activity' that is definitive of a present dharma, and any other causal capacity of functioning that the dharma may exert. The present 'activity' consists in bringing about the next dharma of the same type in the causal sequence. Thus the present activity of a visual consciousness dharma consists in conditioning the visual consciousness dharma of the next moment. This type of activity always occurs when a dharma is present. Any other causal capacity (such as bringing about a karmic result, or serving as the object of a cognition) may or may not occur. It is not definitive of the *present* occurrence of a dharma.

6 There is another interpretation of this type of cause. Here it is said that they are 'simultaneous causes' because they co-operate simultaneously in producing the effect (Hirakawa 1990: 180). Since the standard Sarvāstivāda view is that the simultaneous cause occurs simultaneously with its effect (see Saṃghabhadra, in Potter 1999: 704), this explanation is much less satisfactory.

7 The other types of causes are known as the 'concomitant cause' (*saṃprayuktahetu*), the 'universal cause' (*sarvatrāgahetu*), and the 'cause of fruition' (*vipākahetu*). The *vipākahetu* is illustrated by a morally good cause producing a *pleasant* effect, and should be

contrasted with the *sabhāgahetu*. The four conditions are: (i) causal condition (*hetupratyaya*); (ii) the condition that is the (cessation of the) immediately preceding (*samantarapratyaya*); (iii) the condition that is the referential object (in the case of e.g. perception) (*ālambanapratyaya*); and (iv) the predominant condition (*adhipatipratyaya*).

8 Saṃghabhadra's commentary to the *Abhidharmakośa*, probably called the *Nyāyānusāra*, represents the orthodox Sarvāstivādin response to Vasubandhu.

9 Note that it follows from this that I am the one who possesses the *prāpti* series, that is, I possess the series of possessions. But what makes the possession itself *mine*? What is it for my series ('me') to possess the possession series? Later Sarvāstivādins spoke of a 'possession of possession' or 'secondary possession', in a relationship of mutual possession with the first possession, thus attempting to avoid an infinite regress. The first possession possesses (as well as the wicked intention) 'possession of possession', and 'possession of possession' possesses the first possession.

10 The non-enlightened person has 'non-possession' of enlightenment, from which he or she must be disconnected in order for enlightenment to occur. Note in all this that eliminating negative taints and attaining enlightenment is thought of in Sarvāstivāda as severing possessions, and giving rise to the possessions of non-possessions. This no doubt reflects a system where dharmas, such as negative taints, cannot be eliminated as such since they continue to exist in the three times. For a full discussion on all of this, and other unique teachings of Sarvāstivāda, see Cox (1995).

11 For the sake of simplicity I have omitted in this account the second moment of a perceptual act. That moment is the stage of 'mental perception' and is also said to be *nirvikalpa*. The *savikalpa* stages follow. For a more detailed summary of Diṅnāga's and Dharmakīrti's epistemology, see Williams (1996).

12 For a thorough study of the surviving materials, and their doctrines, see Bhikshu Thich Tien Chau (1997). See also Cousins (1994) and the references therein, especially note 6.

13 I have more to say on the philosophy of some of these issues in Williams (1998a: esp. Chs 3 and 5).

14 The *Kathāvatthu* (esp. Ch. 18) criticises a number of strange views that appear to have some similarity to the supramundane doctrine. These include the claim that even the excreta of a Buddha excel all other substances in perfume, and also the claim that Buddhas have never actually been present in the world of men. These views are not found in the *Mahāvastu*. It is not clear whether any group actually held them. Perhaps they were simply debating points.

5 Mahāyāna philosophy

1 Note that Perfection of Wisdom literature was composed throughout the period of Mahāyāna Buddhism in India. One should avoid the rather simplistic model that would see the earlier period alone of Mahāyāna as 'Prajñāpāramitā'.

2 See the definition of *prajñā* given in the *Abhidharmakośabhāṣya* as 'discernment of dharmas' (*dharmapravicayaḥ*). Incidentally, since *prajñā* is the result of understanding properly, it is debatable how helpful 'wisdom' is as a translation. Perhaps 'insight' would be better, but that is a term commonly used to translate the associated *vipaśyanā*.

3 Later Buddhist scholars will want to dissolve away the radical implications of saying that everything is like an illusion, arguing that this does not mean everything is illusory. Rather, things are *like* an illusion. This is because all things appear one way (as inherently existent, having primary existence) and exist in another (as conceptual constructs). But let us not dissolve away at this point the disturbing nature of a message that is described as frightening those who heard it for the first time.

4 The Perfection of Wisdom literature asserts that all things are secondary existents, conceptual constructs. This is the emptiness of dharmas as well as the emptiness of constructs. This idea of *dharmanairātmya*, absence of Self (here absence of own-existence) in dharmas, is also found in some schools of thought normally classed as 'non-Mahāyāna', or not showing in themselves Mahāyāna tendencies. Thus it would be wrong to use the teaching of emptiness of dharmas as in any way a *defining* characteristic of Mahāyāna. See Williams (1989: 46–7).

5 We also commonly find e.g. practices of recollection of the Buddha (*buddhānusmṛti*) said to serve as antidotes to fear. See, for example, Williams (1989: 218).

6 The level of the Disciple (*śrāvaka*) is that of one aiming for nirvāṇa, to become an arhat. The *pratyekabuddha* is another type of enlightenment classed by Mahāyāna writers with the arhat as both equalling the 'inferior vehicle' (*hīnayāna*).

7 The idea of giving away one's merit is not however unique to Mahāyāna, as it is often portrayed. See Schopen (1985).

8 Certainly this contradicts the oft-stated assertion that Madhyamaka holds no positions of its own. Even at this stage it can be seen that to assert literally that Madhyamaka has no position of its own would be to contradict the *Prajñāpāramitā* sūtras. Those sūtras clearly assert universal absence of *svabhāva*. It would also be to contradict Nāgārjuna's own avowal of *śūnyatāvāda*. Of course, if a person holds

that all is akin to illusions, and says that he or she holds no positions of his or her own, that person is on one level being manifestly consistent. This is because any position itself must be akin to an illusion. But on the level of illusion a Mādhyamika position of absence of *svabhāva* can still be put forward. This is even though the Mādhyamika (in a sense) has no position of his or her own. All this also corresponds with Nāgārjuna's own response in the *Vigrahavyāvartanī*.

9 See Ruegg (1981) and Lindtner (1982). Concerning the *Bodhicittavivaraṇa* see Williams (1984).

10 Note that although Tibetans often refer to Candrakīrti as the greatest Mādhyamika after Nāgārjuna, if references in other texts and extant Indian commentaries are anything to go by Candrakīrti had slight influence in India at all. We have to be very careful in reconstructing our picture of what was going on in India when using later non-Indian sources.

11 For further details on Mādhyamika texts and scholars see Williams (1989: 58–60) and Ruegg (1981).

12 I say this fully aware that Richard Hayes has recently raised questions, as yet undeveloped, about whether Madhyamaka reasoning really is aimed simply or primarily at the *svabhāvas* of its opponents. See Hayes (1994).

13 Remember that most of the dharmas (i.e. the conditioned (*saṃskṛta*) dharmas in Abhidharma) are very much the results of causes and conditions, succeeding each other in a rapid stream of conditionality.

14 For short summaries of some Madhyamaka critiques see Williams (1989: 65 ff.).

15 The arguments are taken from Buddhapālita's commentary. See Williams (1989: 65–6).

16 For a more detailed analysis of the two truths see Williams (1989: 69–72).

17 Note therefore that to maintain something is conventional, or merely conceptual, is to cut grasping after it and craving for it. This is not necessarily thought in Madhyamaka to devalue it. Buddhahood lacks inherent existence, as do all things. So does the welfare of sentient beings. But these have supreme (in one sense absolute) importance for the bodhisattva.

18 In other words Nāgārjuna's reply in *MMK* 24 while clever would not have been found convincing. The opponent would have felt there were insuperable problems in all as merely conceptual constructs, and avoided the problem of a block universe by simply denying the association of emptiness (as equalling *niḥsvabhāva*) with dependent origination.

19 This is not to say that Mādhyamikas could not construct a reply to their opponents here. They could argue that they are not playing this

primary existent versus secondary existent game at all. Theirs is a completely different project. It is to take any primary existent put forward by the opponent and analyse it. That is all. It is not the Mādhyamika's fault if there are problems for the opponent in the idea of all as *prajñaptimātra*. But on this level the debate between the two sides seems much more evenly balanced.

20 It is often thought that Madhyamaka is all to do with philosophy and has nothing much to do with meditation. This is, I think, wrong. Madhyamaka philosophy *is* the meditation. We are dealing here with insight meditation, not (as such) *dhyāna* states.

21 Even co-called 'unconditioned' dharmas are for Nāgārjuna dependently originated in some sense.

22 I am still doubtful that in the last analysis Nāgārjuna, with his reduction of *all* things to processes, can escape the accusations of having created a position where it is difficult to see how the existence of anything can be grounded at all (i.e. nihilism). But the situation is philosophically extremely subtle and complex. I plan to return to these issues in detail in a future book on Nāgārjuna's philosophy for the Routledge 'Arguments of the Philosophers' series. Another point: you may recall that for those who acquire the fifth purification there is said to be a danger that the meditator could become complacent and attached. One needs to tear oneself away from this in order to attain the sixth purification. I wonder if, for Nāgārjuna, a follower of Mahāyāna, the generation of compassion for others precisely created the moral imperative that served to lift him from a comfortable absorption in everything as processes.

23 See Powers (1995: 138–41). On the whole topic of Buddhist textual hermeneutics see Lopez (1988a). There is also a brief discussion in Williams (1989: 79–80).

24 Notice these alternatives of taking emptiness (*niḥsvabhāva*) literally. Both involve an interpretation that is nihilism. We have seen from the Abhidharma context why this would have seemed the obvious way to take these teachings.

25 There are some contemporary scholars who would want to argue that in the last analysis Yogācāra does not differ in ontology from Madhyamaka. They are just different, and perhaps complementary, ways of getting at the same thing. I completely disagree. Either Yogācāra is saying the same as Madhyamaka, i.e. all is a conceptual construct with nothing for it to be constructed out of, and therefore in this respect it actually *is* Madhyamaka (as is Yogācāra-Svātantrika Madhyamaka), or it is not. If it is not it differs from Madhyamaka in ontologically the strongest possible way. Notice that in the context of the *Saṃdhinirmocana Sūtra* the response to the 'nihilist' interpretation of emptiness is *not* to claim that emptiness does not mean

non-existence but rather it means dependent origination. The actual response is through the use of the three aspects, to limit the range of absence of *svabhāva*. This response strongly *contradicts* and *contrasts* with Madhyamaka. For some of those who in different ways would appear to disagree with me, however, see Rahula (1978), Willis (1979), Anacker (1984), Nagao (1991), and Harris (1991). For some further comments of my own see Williams (1989: Ch. 4), (1994a), (1998a: 243–8), and (1998b: 12–15).

26 Reference should also be made to the important later commentators and rivals Sthiramati and Dharmapāla. Dharmapāla's work was particularly well known and important in China. For more details on all this material see Williams (1989: 80–2).

27 There are those who would object to my calling it 'Mind', because this suggests a form of idealism. Also there are Yogācāra texts that state that consciousness has no more reality than anything else. But the denial of consciousness here is clearly in context a denial of the consciousness that is a subject opposed to an object. Denying consciousness is a corollary of denying duality. Yogācāra struggles to talk about a non-duality that it holds is beyond language. But the texts themselves state that if this denial entails denying consciousness as a primary existent serving as a substratum however we would then have nihilism. I have no objection to the use of 'idealism' for what is going on here. For more details see Williams (1989: Ch. 5).

28 Cf. the old argument that no matter whether I am hallucinating I cannot doubt that I am undergoing certain experiences. This means of course that in the Buddhist case *experience* must be a primary existent even if it is dependently-originated. So it is not enough to say that the dependent aspect in Yogācāra is not held to have real ontological existence (to have a *svabhāva*) because it is a dependent flow. The implication here would be denied in Yogācāra. If you grant that implication then of course you end up with Madhyamaka.

29 There is also an epistemological argument found in thinkers like Dharmakīrti and Śāntarakṣita. How does consciousness know 'external' physical objects, when consciousness itself is of a completely different order from matter? Consciousness has a reflexive quality of knowing (*svasaṃvedana*), while matter has no such reflexivity. Clearly only things of the same basic order of reality can contact each other. Thus either all must be matter, or all must be consciousness. But if all were matter then there would be no experience at all. Since there patently is experience, all must be consciousness.

30 Thus the substratum consciousness, sometimes referred to more literally as the 'storehouse consciousness', while beyond language and therefore direct individual appropriation, must still be individual

and personal to each sentient being. For a detailed study of the *ālayavijñāna* see Schmithausen (1987).

31 It is terribly easy to confuse the substratum consciousness in Yogācāra with the one reality, the non-dual dependent nature. They are *not*, however, the same. The substratum consciousness is only one of the eight (or for Paramārtha nine) consciousnesses. It thus follows that it cannot be identical with the one reality, the dependent nature. The issue of the substratum consciousness concerns individual psychology, not ontology.

32 Perhaps one should also mention in this Indian textual context the so-called 'Buddha Nature Treatise' (*Fo-hsing Lun*), that is attributed to Vasubandhu and known only in its Chinese version. It is quite likely however that this short text was actually composed in China during the sixth century by its purported translator Paramārtha (see King 1990 and 1991).

33 Ethical implications might also be drawn from the idea that all sentient beings have within them the Buddha-nature. It is related in *tathāgatagarbha* sūtras explicitly to the call for vegetarianism. See Ruegg (1980).

34 Although it was translated into Chinese, its influence in East Asia also seems to have been quite muted, possibly due to the enormous significance of the *Ta-cheng ch'i-hsin Lun* ('Awakening of Faith in the Mahāyāna') that was attributed, certainly falsely, to Aśvaghoṣa. It was probably a Chinese creation. In Tibet, on the other hand, the *Ratnagotravibhāga* has been extremely important.

35 Commonly in meditation systems (such as Mahāmudrā in Tibet, or Zen) where the idea of the Buddha-nature is extremely important this will be associated with allowing the conceptual mind connected with impurities to fade and the radiant pure enlightened and non-conceptual mind to shine forth. This is what it has always been doing, and it does so quite naturally of its own accord. Actually nothing has to be done, there is a letting-go of doing anything. Thus we can attempt to solve the apparent paradox of trying to bring about a state of unconditioned non-conceptuality.

6 The Buddha in Mahāyāna Buddhism

1 Thus Nāgārjuna points out in the *Madhyamakakārikā* Ch. 18 that the Buddha will even teach the Self to those who would benefit by it. This does not make the teaching of the Self *true*, of course.

2 Among others there is also a striking parable of a prodigal son.

3 Note that one way of putting this that is often encountered, that teachings have only a relative validity, is ambiguous and has, I think, led to a lot of misunderstanding of the notion of skill in means. It

could mean that the *teaching* is relative to context, or that *what is said in the teaching* is itself only relative to context. But take the case of 'All dharmas are empty' in a Madhyamaka context. *What* is said there is not skill in means in the sense that its truth is only relative to context, and not actually true. Emptiness for a Mādhyamika is indeed absolutely always true. Nevertheless whether or not to say it depends upon context, upon what is most helpful. Thus the teaching may be skill in means. Inasmuch as all the words of the Buddha are teachings, all such words are thus skill in means even where what they say is absolutely true.

4 The teaching of skill in means entails that if we look at actions alone we cannot be sure that an advanced bodhisattva will not infringe what is considered to be the normal moral code. But there is no suggestion here that somehow the normal moral code has ceased to apply. For more on bodhisattva ethics see Tatz (1986).

5 Chih-i dịd it through linking the *Lotus* with the *Mahāparinirvāṇa Sūtra*. That sūtra, as we have seen, teaches the *tathāgatagarbha*. Chih-i stressed that both were sūtras of the Buddha's last days.

6 Not three bodies as such. A Buddha can emanate many, many bodies (of 'magical transformation' (Griffiths)) in order to benefit sentient beings. Griffiths' 'classical doctrine' is in fact the position of the Indian Yogācāra treatises such as the *Mahāyānasūtrālaṃkāra* and the *Mahāyānasaṃgraha*. See also Eckel (1992).

7 The translations are from Griffiths. The *svabhāvakāya* (literally 'essence body') is sometimes referred to as the *svābhāvikakāya*, the *saṃbhogakāya* as the *sāṃbhogikakāya*, and the *nirmāṇakāya* as the *nairmāṇikakāya*. I do myself in Williams (1989). In retrospect this could cause some confusion.

8 On these factors in Vaibhāṣika Abhidharma, commonly various knowledges and attainments, and the five pure aggregates (*skandhas*) of a Buddha see Williams (1989: 171). Note that later systematists consider there is a problem in interpreting the true body of the Buddha as his teachings (*Dharma*). When we take refuge in the Buddha it cannot be his physical body we take refuge in. It thus must be his *dharmakāya*. But if *dharma* here = *Dharma* then there would be a confusion of the first of the three refuges (in the Buddha) with the second (in the *Dharma*).

9 Note therefore the contrast with the stūpa cult, that can be portrayed as concerning itself with that which is lower, the (remnants of) the physical body (*rūpakāya*) of the Buddha. Thus it becomes quite possible to claim that e.g. the Mahāyāna sūtras such as the *Prajñāpāramitā* sūtras are indeed the 'Teaching-body', the *dharmakāya*, of the Buddha. All admit that the *dharmakāya* is higher than the physical body. Therefore it makes sense to follow the sūtras

and even to establish shrines containing the sūtra, offering to it (as the Mahāyāna sūtras themselves advocate) incense, flowers, music, etc., the offerings traditionally made at stūpas. See here Kajiyama (1985).

10 Important is *Ratnāvalī* 3: 10, where Nāgārjuna points out that the *rūpakāya* of a Buddha arises due to his collection of merit and his *dharmakāya* due to his collection of gnosis (*jñāna*). The Buddha, as do we all, gains a physical body through his deeds in previous lives. He gains his qualities as a Buddha – what makes him a Buddha – or his teachings that genuinely lead to liberation, through his insight.

11 The conclusion that the true body of the Buddha is actually the same as the ultimate, emptiness, is implicit rather than explicit in these hymns. Nevertheless it seems to me it is from sources like this that the later 'cosmic' interpretation of the *dharmakāya* evolved. Note that if the true body of the Buddha is emptiness then since emptiness is the true nature of everything – and on the level of emptiness itself it is not possible to distinguish between different emptinesses – so the true body of the Buddha is the true nature of all things. The idea of referring to emptiness as a 'body' presumably was influenced by the idea of the Buddha-dharmas, the collection of ultimates that uniquely characterise a Buddha. Since some of these are cognitive, it may also be possible to find the Buddha's mind, his knowing of emptiness (i.e. *prajñā*), expressed as his *dharmakāya*.

12 Manifested through a 'revolution of the basis' that destroyed the tainted dependent aspect. See the discussion of Yogācāra on pp. 156–60.

13 Although note that on a basis of mind-only there is one way of looking at the *dharmakāya* (suggested by the classical sources) that would enable one to maintain that all the cosmos (the *dharmadhātu*) is actually the *dharmakāya*. There is only pure non-dual consciousness. Thus there is only the *dharmakāya*.

14 Not a doctrinally precise way of putting it, since the *dharmakāya* does not *do* anything. But I like the image. A *saṃbhogakāya* could still be called Śākyamuni. Cf. here the *Lotus Sūtra* and the Buddha's lifespan.

15 I have also relied particularly on Lopez (1988b), a very accessible and well-written account of the bodhisattva path based mainly on these Indian sources, the *Daśabhūmika Sūtra*, and the *Madhyamakāvatāra* ('Supplement to Madhyamaka') of Candrakīrti. See also Williams (1989: Ch. 9).

16 See Kamalaśīla's first *Bhāvanākrama* in e.g. Beyer (1974: 103). This point concerning the absolute necessity of integrating wisdom with means (the proper moral etc. bodhisattva activities) was crucial to the situation (actually Tibetan) that produced the *Bhāvanākramas*. For more details see Williams (1989: 193–7).

17 See Kamalaśīla in Beyer (1974: 111 ff.). Kamalaśīla's work is classed as Madhyamaka.

18 Thus *of course* it is proper for the bodhisattva to engage in e.g. removing poverty as well as unjust social systems and ideologies. On the bodhisattva stages see in particular the *Daśabhūmika Sūtra*, and Candrakīrti's *Madhyamakāvatāra*. On the perfections see especially also the *Bodhicaryāvatāra*. Note as well the phenomenon of 'transference of merit'. All Buddhist traditions hold that it is an appropriate religious act to pray that the merit that might otherwise accrue from a particular virtuous deed should be transferred to another party. In Mahāyāna it is held to be the appropriate response of a bodhisattva to gaining merit that the merit should be given away for the benefit of all sentient beings (i.e. all beings with consciousness, all beings that are alive and can therefore feel pleasure and pain). I doubt that the theory of *karman* in Buddhism was ever in ancient times and in practice (and probably even in theory) held to be so rigid (i.e. as a law) that the transference of merit was thought to be impossible. See Williams (1989: 207–8) and Schopen (1985).

19 This is a little strange, since it was necessary to have direct non-conceptual insight into emptiness in order to attain the first bodhisattva stage. It is possible that the scheme of five paths that has the first bodhisattva stage attained at the third path, that of seeing, was originally a different path-structure to Buddhahood from that of the ten stages.

20 Is it in completing the sixth or at the seventh stage that one finally goes irreversibly beyond the position of an arhat? In Williams (1989: 211) I suggested the sixth. Here, following Candrakīrti's *Madhyamakāvatāra*, I suggest the seventh. One might think that all forces leading to rebirth and suffering would be overcome in completing the perfection of wisdom. There appears to be different views on this topic.

21 Until that time, although the bodhisattva sees in meditation how it really is, in coming out of meditation he or she still sees things the way an unenlightened being sees things although, of course, he or she knows that is not really how it is. Now this is beginning to change.

22 Note also in this context the comment by the historian A. L. Basham (1981: 37) that inscriptional evidence points to a northern origin for the belief in 'celestial' bodhisattvas.

23 There is some evidence from other sources that this regret was acutely felt at times (see Williams 1989: 218–19). The common reference to going beyond fear possibly reflects the turbulent times associated with the centuries after the collapse of the Mauryan empire (from the late third century BCE onwards), the very period of the initial

growth of Mahāyāna. Pure Land cults can be traced back well into this period. In terms of a sociological connection between religious change and wider changes in society, one could also suggest a connection between the changing status of the Buddha and the gradual socialisation of the Buddhist Sangha. This socialisation is reflected in the growth of larger stable monastic units in a closer formal relationship with the local communities, creating a wider society embracing two alternative careers, lay and monastic. This contrasts with the original model of society and complete renunciation as its negation. Instead of the Buddha as someone who has gone beyond and is no longer available, paralleling the position of the renunciate in relationship to the society he or she has renounced, the Buddha now comes to be seen as the head of the alternative society. He is thus the equivalent in the spiritual society of the king in the lay society. Thus the Buddha becomes the king who can do what even secular kings cannot. He is thereby thought of as present, on the model of an emperor. And in turbulent times, what secular kings cannot do is perform the proper duty (*Dharma*) of kings according to the Brāhmanic social vision, the duty of protection, giving freedom from fear. Thus with the Buddha as the very-much-present spiritual king (if, like so many kings, unseen) we also find the advent of techniques whereby it is possible to make contact with the ever-present Buddha, techniques that are precisely said to grant protection, freedom from fear.

24 The full title of course being the *Pratyutpannabuddhasaṃmukhāvasthitasamādhi Sūtra*, 'The Samādhi of Direct Encounter with the Buddhas of the Present'.

25 Note that it is a *pure* Buddha Field that is the goal. This is superior to the heavens, and incidentally is superior therefore to the particular heavenly realm as a goal for rebirth (Tuṣita) in which non-Mahāyānists and Mahāyānists hold the next Buddha, Maitreya, is now residing. There is moreover not much point in striving to be reborn in an *impure* Buddha Field when a Pure Land is available.

26 Note that perhaps rather strangely, when compared with the Sukhāvatī cult, Akṣobhya is said by the sūtra eventually to die (enter *parinirvāṇa*), and the presence of his teaching in Abhirati will eventually come to an end.

27 According to Indian and East Asian sources 'Amitābha' (Infinite Light) and 'Amitāyus' (Infinite Life) both refer to the same Buddha. Tibetans, on the other hand, habitually distinguish them.

28 There is an unequivocal reference to Amitābha discovered in 1977 in a Kuṣāna inscription probably of the early second century CE. As Schopen (1987b) points out, the real significance is that this is the *only* such inscription from anywhere nearly so early a date. When

Amitābha next appears in inscriptions, in the seventh century, it is not as an independent cult figure but as part of an extended hymn of praise to the bodhisattva Avalokiteśvara. After that time Amitābha disappears from epigraphy. Schopen has also shown elsewhere (1977) how the goal of rebirth in Sukhāvatī takes on the role in Indian Mahāyāna Buddhism of a 'generalized religious goal' open to the Mahāyāna community as a whole quite divorced from any specific association with a cult of Amitābha.

29 Note that this differs from the way this crucial vow is interpreted by the Sanghavarman translation into Chinese, and understood in the East Asian Pure Land tradition. See *Sukhāvatīvyūha Sūtra*, trans. Cowell (15, 73).

30 Buddha Bhaiṣajyaguru (the 'Medicine Buddha') is also flanked by two attendant bodhisattvas.

31 On devotion to Amitābha/Amitāyus in India see also the so-called *Daśabhūmikavibhāṣā Śāstra*, attributed to Nāgārjuna, and the *Sukhāvatīvyūhopadeśa*, attributed to Vasubandhu. There is considerable doubt that these texts are by their attributed authors. The *Daśabhūmikavibhāṣā Śāstra* makes the point that reciting the name of the Buddha Amitāyus is a much easier way to practise than the traditional practices. See Williams (1989: 256–8). There is some evidence from the *Suhṛllekha*, more plausibly attributed to Nāgārjuna, that he was familiar with the Buddha Amitābha.

32 On Maitreya see now Sponberg and Hardacre (1988).

33 I hope my readers are too sophisticated to assume that all this has something to do with 'popular Buddhism', whatever that may mean. From a Mahāyāna point of view the bodhisattvas act from their immense compassion for the benefit of others in *whatever* way will be beneficial.

34 As can be seen in the rather interesting case of a statue of Avalokiteśvara found in Sri Lanka. See Mori (1997).

35 In spite of what is often said, if the mantra is written in correct Sanskrit it cannot mean grammatically 'Oh, the jewel in the lotus, *hūṃ*' or something like that (Thomas 1951: 187–8). Studholme (1999) argues in his unpublished doctoral thesis on this mantra in the *Kāraṇḍavyūha Sūtra* that the mantra perhaps originally meant 'In the jewel-lotus'. This refers to the common form of rebirth in Amitābha's Pure Land of Sukhāvatī. This rebirth was indeed associated with Avalokiteśvara from an early date. For more on Avalokiteśvara, and in particular his cult in Śrī Laṅka, see Holt (1991).

36 Perhaps this is a reference to the *Susthitamatiparipṛcchā Sūtra*. In that sūtra Mañjuśrī is said to have taken up a sword and lunged at the Buddha with the intention of killing him, the worst possible

misdeed, as a strategy to help those bodhisattvas whose spiritual progress had become delayed through guilt due to previous misdeeds. Misdeeds, while clearly wrong, are empty of inherent existence and do not condemn one as an inherently wicked person. Since misdeeds and their karmic effects are empty of *inherent* existence all can make progress and become enlightened.

7 Mantranaya/Vajrayāna – tantric Buddhism in India

1 For details of surviving Sanskrit manuscripts see Tsukamoto *et al.* (1989).
2 A number of useful (and generally) introductory discussions of tantric Buddhism in India can, however, be found in Eliade (1987) *The Encyclopedia of Religion.* See articles by Gomez, Hirakawa, Orzech, Ray, Snellgrove, and Wayman. Samuel (1993) and Snellgrove (1987a), especially the latter, are important sources for more detailed discussions.
3 See Urban (1999) for a perspective on the 'orientalist' dimension to early understandings of tantrism.
4 See, for example, Lopez (1995a and b).
5 As with early Mahāyāna Buddhism, dated Chinese translations supply some of the hardest evidence of the early textual history of tantric Buddhism. The third century date for the appearance of tantric Buddhist texts is based on the existence of a third century translation of the *Anantamukhasādhakadhāraṇī* by Chih-ch'ien. Hodge (1994) lists other Kriyā texts translated by Chih-ch'ien.
6 Precise numbers vary depending on the edition of the Kanjur and Tenjur consulted.
7 The existence of a non-Mahāyāna (Theravāda) form of tantric Buddhism in Southeast Asia should be noted (see Cousins 1997).
8 Though the term *mantrayāna* is often used in preference to *mantranaya* in (academic) discussions of tantric Buddhism, it does not appear in texts until well after the appearance of the term *Vajrayāna* (see de Jong 1984: 93), upon which it is probably modelled. As a result *mantranaya* is the more appropriate term to describe the self-perception of pre-Vajrayāna tantric Buddhism.
9 See Hodge (1994: 59), and Snellgrove (1988: 1359) for alternative lists of significant features.
10 Of the following features, probably only ritual use of maṇḍalas and analogical thinking are found in all historical phases of tantric Buddhism.
11 See Elder (1976), Wayman (1973: 128–35), Newman (1988), and Samuel (1993: 414–19) for discussion of the problems associated with the use of allusive language in tantric Buddhism.

12 On the body in tantric Buddhism (and Hinduism) see Samuel (1989).

13 For example, in the Puruṣasūkta (*Ṛg Veda* x: 90) where the body of the sacrificial cosmic man (*puruṣa*) is correlated with a series of categories.

14 See Skorupski (1998) for a summary of the contents of Kuladatta's ritual compendium the *Kriyāsaṃgraha*.

15 For example, in Vilāsavajra's *Nāmasaṃgīti* commentary, the *Nāmamantrārthāvalokinī*. Buddhaguhya, also eighth century, lists *Kriyā*, *Ubhaya* ('dual'), and *Yoga* as the three categories (Hodge 1994: 58).

16 A fourfold categorisation is found in the Indian texts, but into Kriyā, Caryā, Yoga, and Yogottara tantras (see Parahitarakṣita's commentary on Nāgārjuna's *Pañcakrama*, ed. de la Vallée Poussin: 39), surely the precursor of the fivefold list ending with the Yoganiruttara tantras.

17 The numbers of texts assigned here and below to the various Kanjur tantra categories is taken from the Tohoku catalogue of the Derge (sDe dge) edition. See Ui (1934).

18 See note 5.

19 See Lopez (1996: 165 ff.) for a discussion of the dhāraṇī at the end of the *Heart Sūtra* (*gate gate pāragate pārasaṃgate bodhi svāhā*), which is often taken by Indian commentators as a summary of the Mahāyāna path.

20 The *Nāmasaṃgīti* is significant in part because, unlike most of the Yoga tantras, it was not supplanted by later developments in India. It was interpreted not only as a Yoga Tantra but also both as a Mahāyoga and as more than one type of Yoginī tantra. For a discussion of this text see Tribe (1997a).

21 For Vilāsavajra's *Nāmasaṃgīti* commentary, which may be the earliest tantric commentary that survives in Sanskrit, see *Nāmamantrārthāvalokinī*.

22 For a detailed study of the evolution of the five Buddhas, the Buddha families and the system of correlations and correspondences see Yoritomi (1990). Unfortunately, this work is mainly in Japanese, although there is an English summary (1990: 693–716). See Snellgrove (1987a: 209–213) for discussion and diagrams of the Vajradhātu maṇḍala.

23 See Tsuda (1978) for a detailed discussion of the different perspectives of the *Mahāvairocana Sūtra* and *Tattvasaṃgraha Sūtra*.

24 Though Vilāsavajra, in his *Nāmasaṃgīti* commentary, written in the late eighth century, enumerates just three categories of tantras, Kriyā, Caryā, and Yoga, he cites a number of works, such as the *Guhyasamāja* and *Vajrabhairava Tantras*, subsequently classed as Mahāyoga tantras. The eleventh to twelfth century murals at Alchi

in Ladakh depict Yoga and Mahāyoga maṇḍalas side by side, also suggesting that these two classes of texts may have coexisted as a single phase in the development of tantric Buddhism (see Pal and Fournier 1988; Goepper and Poncar 1996).

25 There is no scholarly consensus on the date of the *Guhyasamāja Tantra*. Wayman has argued since 1968 (see 1973: 12–23) for an early fourth century origin and continues to do so (1995: 141). Matsunaga, in the introduction (1978: xxvii) to his edition of the *Guhyasamāja Tantra* argues convincingly for a mid to late eighth century origin.

26 The fierce deity Vajrabhairava, who has the head of a bull, is a form of Yamāntaka, related (as his destroyer) to Yama, the bull-headed god of death (see Siklós 1996).

27 For a detailed study of the *Guhyasamāja Tantra* and its exegetical traditions see Wayman (1977).

28 A composite text that does not fit this characterisation is the *Saṃpuṭa Tantra*. For an overview of its contents see the introduction to Skorupski's edition of the text of Chapter 1.

29 Vajravārāhī's importance is demonstrated by the existence of a collection of some forty-six sādhana texts devoted to her in a work with the title *Vajravārāhīsādhanasaṃgraha*. This also appears to be known as the *Guhyasamayasaṃgraha*, or *Guhyasamayasādhanamālā*. Doctoral research into some of these texts has been carried out by Elizabeth English at Oxford University.

30 For example, with Cakrasaṃvara cycle texts such as the *Laghusaṃvara Tantra*.

31 There is a growing literature on the *Kālacakra Tantra*. See Bahulkar (1995), Brauen (1998), Cicuzza and Sferra (1997), Newman (1995), Simon (1985), and Wallace (1995).

32 As the gathering contains both female and male practitioners, the term *ḍākinī* has to be understood to include ḍākinīs and their male counterparts, *ḍākas*. See Tsuda (*Saṃvarodaya Tantra*, 54–60) for a discussion of the meaning of *ḍākinījālasaṃvara* within the context of the *Saṃvarodaya Tantra*. At another level the 'assembly' occurs within the body of the practitioner, in which case the ḍākinīs are identified with the energy channels (*nāḍī*) of the subtle body.

33 This tradition of 'crazy wisdom' was transmitted to Tibet where it continued to sound as an underlying note in Tibetan Buddhism that was often critical of institutional monasticism. For a study of *sahaja* in India see Kvaerne (1975).

34 See Templeman (1994).

35 For information on Abhayākaragupta see the introduction to the facsimile edition of the *Niṣpannayogāvalī* by Gudrun Bühnemann.

36 *Nāmasaṃgīti* (trans. Davidson, in Lopez: 120).

37 The terms *Sahajayāna* and *Kālacakrayāna*, sometimes found in discussions of tantric Buddhism (e.g. Gomez 1987: 376), can be misleading. They denote separate *yānas* even less than the term *Vajrayāna* does. Rather, they can be seen as representing competing emphases (or even, competing soteriologies) within the phase of Vajrayāna Buddhism typified by the Yoginī tantras.

38 See Snellgrove (1987a: 240–2) for a translation of this important passage. See Lessing and Wayman (1968: 25 ff.) for a Tibetan account of how the awakening of the Buddha is understood to have occurred according to the different classes of tantras and their commentators.

39 For Buddhism, speech is always a form of action. Thus mantras have to be understood as a particular form of speech act. Discussion of the nature of mantras can quickly become philosophically complex. See Lopez (1996: 165 ff.) on some of the issues, within the context of his examination of the *Heart Sūtra*'s mantra.

40 See Wayman (1975) and Alper (1989) for discussions of mantras in the broader Indian context. For 'tantric' features of early and Theravāda Buddhism, see Skilling (1992), Jackson (1994). There are philosophical issues connected with the use of mantras in Buddhism, however. In particular, it is hard to see how they work (in the sense of having guaranteed efficacy). Mahāyāna Buddhism generally sees language as having a contingent relationship with phenomena ('the world'), whereas the use of mantras appears to be predicated on the existence of necessary connections (a view generally acceptable to non-Buddhists in India).

41 See *Nāmamantrārthāvalokinī* (trans. Tribe: 127) and Lessing and Wayman (1968: 270) for these two explanations. In fact, the two meanings – 'adornment' and 'essence' – are not unrelated and probably derive from a more basic meaning in which *maṇḍa* denotes the scum of rice broth. The scum is both regarded as the best part of the broth, the cream (hence 'essence'), as well as adorning it (hence 'adornment'). Commentaries are often termed 'ornaments' (*alaṃkāra*), i.e. works that elaborate or express the meaning of the root text.

42 Useful material on maṇḍalas, including some good reproductions, can be found in exhibition catalogues by Leidy and Thurman (1997) and Rhie and Thurman (1991). See also Brauen (1998), Cozort (1995), Lalou (1930), Macdonald (1962), Vira and Chandra (1995).

43 See Pal and Fournier (1988) and Goepper and Poncar (1996).

44 See *Sādhanamālā* and *Sādhanaśataka*/*Sādhanaśatapañcāśikā* for collections of sādhanas in Sanskrit. For a study a Buddhist tantric iconography based on the *Sādhanamālā*, see Bhattacharyya (1958, also 2nd edition).

45 Tantric ritual is said to engage all facets of the practitioner since body, speech, and mind (the standard tripartite analysis of the individual) are occupied with mudrās, mantras, and visualisation, respectively.

46 This series of divisions may well reflect the historical development of tantric meditation traditions, whereby stages previously seen as final are incorporated by revaluing them as preparatory.

47 On the two stages of tantric mediation see Beyer (1973: 108 ff.). On Nāropa's yogas see Guenther (1963).

48 Scholars differ on how to best translate the term *abhiṣeka*, literally meaning 'sprinkling', and which has associations with royal consecration. It is for this reason that Snellgrove, for example, prefers 'consecration' as a translation. I follow others (e.g. Sanderson 1994) in adopting 'empowerment', which gives some sense of the intended empowering function of tantric *abhiṣeka*. For a discussion of the role of notions of royalty in tantric Buddhism, see Snellgrove (1959).

49 For two examples of Yoga tantra initiation rituals, see *Sarvadurgatipariśodhana Tantra* (trans. Skorupski: 100–7), and Snellgrove (1987a: 217–20), from the *Tattvasaṃgraha*.

50 It is often assumed that the fourth empowerment is an invariable feature of Mahāyoga and Yoginī tantra initiations. However, Isaacson (1998) has pointed out that wider examination of the literature reveals a more complex picture. The *Guhyasamāja* contains no reference to a fourth empowerment. While 'mainstream' Yoginī tantras such as the *Hevajra* and those of the *Cakrasaṃvara* cycle do, others, for example the *Caṇḍamahāroṣaṇa*, do not. Isaacson observes, moreover, that there is no commentarial consensus as to the nature or status of the fourth empowerment.

51 Although the *Bodhipathapradīpa* was essentially composed for a Tibetan audience, Atiśa's solution to the problem of the secret and wisdom empowerments was not generally adopted in Tibet. Monks did (and do) take these empowerments, but symbolically rather than literally. See also Davidson (1995b).

52 For example, Munidatta's commentary on *Caryāgīti* 5: 2, which takes it as stating 'By abandoning, o yogins, the delusion of the woman of flesh-and-blood, obtain the perfection of the Great Seal!' (trans. Kvaerne 1975: 105).

53 This verse is also found in the *Guhyasamāja Tantra* (xvi: 60).

54 The same is true for the late Tibetan biographies of siddhas, for examples of which see Guenther (1963) and Templeman (1989).

55 See Beyer (1973) and Willson (1986) for material related to Tārā. On Chinnamuṇḍā, a form of Vajrayoginī, see Benard (1994).

56 This is vividly exemplified, in the context of (near) contemporary Indian society, in Satyajit Ray's powerful film *Devī*, in which a young

girl's freedom is lost as a result of her being recognised as an embodiment of Devī, 'the goddess'.

57 See also Ray (1980).

58 See, for example, the story of Saraha, author of the *Dohākośas* (*Caturaśītisiddhapravṛtti*, trans. Dowman: 68).

59 For English translations of this episode see Davidson (1995a) and Snellgrove (1987a: 136–41). Also see Davidson (1991) for further analysis and interpretation of the developing myth.

60 See Beyer (1973: 42), Gomez (1987: 375–6), and Ruegg (1989b: 173) for examples of this view.

Bibliography of works cited

Primary sources

In the case of Indian Buddhist works an edition of the Sanskrit or Pāli text is cited where available. The Tibetan and/or Chinese translations are given, using the Tohoku (T) for the Tibetan and the Taisho number for the Chinese, unless there is a standard or relatively accessible more recent edition familiar to us. An asterisk indicates a hypothetical Sanskrit reconstruction from a Chinese title. Where possible, the most easily available and reasonably reliable English translation of each primary source mentioned in the essay is given. Where no English translation is available but there is one in French or German we are familiar with that has been given instead.

Most of the philosophical texts mentioned here have been summarised in detail in three volumes (to date) of the *Encyclopedia of Indian Philosophies*. Consult individual volumes for details:

Potter, K. H., with Buswell, R. E., Jaini, P. S., and Reat, N. R. (eds) (1996) *Encyclopedia of Indian Philosophies: Volume VII: Abhidharma Buddhism to 150 A.D.*, Delhi: Motilal Banarsidass.

Potter, K. H. (ed.) (1999) *Encyclopedia of Indian Philosophies: Volume VIII: Buddhist Philosophy from 100 to 350 A.D.*, Delhi: Motilal Banarsidass.

Potter, K. H. and Williams, P. (eds) (forthcoming) *Encyclopedia of Indian Philosophies: Volume IX: Buddhist Philosophy from 350 A.D.*, Delhi: Motilal Banarsidass.

Abhidhānottara Tantra: Sanskrit at Nepal–German Manuscript Preservation Project reel E 695/3. T. 369. No Chinese. For translation see M. Kalff (1979) 'Selected chapters from the Abhidhānottaratantra: The union of female and male deities', unpublished Ph.D. thesis, Columbia University, New York.

Abhidharmadīpa (Vimalamitra? Īśvara?): P. S. Jaini (ed.) (1977) *Abhidharmadīpa with Vibhāṣāprabhāvṛtti*, critically edited with notes and introduction, Patna: Kashi Prasad Jayaswal Research Institute. No translation, but a summary available in Jaini's 'Introduction'.

Abhidharmakośa(bhāṣya) (Vasubandhu): Swami Dwarikadas Shastri (ed.) (1970–4) *Abhidharmakośa and Bhāṣya of Acharya Vasubandhu with Sphutārthā commentary of Acarya Yaśomitra*, Varanasi: Bauddha Bharati. Five volumes. T. 4090. Taisho 1558/1559. English in L. de La Vallée Poussin (trans.) (1998–90) *Abhidharmakośabhāṣyam*, English translation by Leo M. Pruden, Berkeley, Calif.: Asian Humanities Press. Four volumes.

Abhidharmasamuccaya (Asaṅga): V. V. Gokhale (ed.) (1947) 'Fragments from the Abhidharmasamuccaya of Asaṃga', *Journal of the Bombay Branch of the Royal Asiatic Society*, New Series 23: 13–38. T. 4049. Taisho 1605. French translation in W. Rahula (trans.) (1971) *Le Compendium de la Super-doctrine (Philosophie) (Abhidharmasamuccaya) d'Asaṅga*, Paris: École Française d'Extrême-Orient.

Abhisamayālaṃkāra (Maitreyanātha?): Sanskrit text contained within the *Abhisamayālaṃkārāloka* of Haribhadra in P. L. Vaidya (ed.) (1960) *Aṣṭasāhasrikā Prajñāpāramitā, with Haribhadra's Commentary called Āloka*, Darbhanga: The Mithila Instititute of Post-Graduate Studies and Research in Sanskrit Learning. T. 3786. No Chinese. English in E. Conze (trans.) (1954) *Abhisamayālaṃkāra*, introduction and translation from original text, with Sanskrit-Tibetan index, Rome: Instituto Italiano per il Medio ed Estremo Oriente.

Advayavajrasaṃgraha: A collection of some twenty short works ascribed to Advayavajra. Sanskrit in H. Shastri (ed.) (1927) *Advayavajrasaṃgraha*, Baroda: Oriental Institute. No Chinese. No Tibetan translation references. Some works may have been translated into Tibetan. English translation of one text, the *Pañcakāra*, by D. Snellgrove, in E. Conze, I. B. Horner, D. Snellgrove, and A. Waley (eds.) (1964) *Buddhist Texts Through the Ages*, New York: Harper & Row.

Aggañña Sutta: Pāli text in T. W. Rhys Davids and J. Estlin Carpenter (eds) (1966) *The Dīgha Nikāya*, London: published for the Pāli Text Society by Luzac. Three volumes. Originally published 1890–1911. English in M. Walshe (trans.) (1987) *Thus Have I Heard: The Long Discourses of the Buddha*, London: Wisdom. Another translation in T. W. Rhys Davids (trans.) (1899–21) *Dialogues of the Buddha*, London: Pāli Text Society. Three volumes.

Ajātaśatrukaukṛtyavinodana Sūtra: Sanskrit lost. Appears not to have been translated into English. T. 216. Taisho 629.

Akṣayamatinirdeśa Sūtra: No extant Sanskrit version. T. 175. Taisho 397 (12)/403. Translated in J. Braarvig (trans.) (1993)

'*Akṣayamatinirdeśa Sūtra: The Tradition of Imperishability' in Buddhist Thought*, Oslo: Solum Forlag.

Akṣobhyavyūha Sūtra: Indian original lost. T. 50. Taisho 310 (6)/313. Translated in Garma C. C. Chang (ed.) (1983) *A Treasury of Mahāyāna Sūtras: Selections from the Mahāratnakūṭa Sūtra*, translated from the Chinese by the Buddhist Association of the United States, University Park, Pa.: Pennsylvania State University Press.

Alagaddūpama Sutta: Pāli text in V. Trenckner (ed.) (1991–4) *The Majjhima-Nikāya*, London: Pāli Text Society. Reprint of a work originally published in 1888–1925. Four volumes. Translation in I. B. Horner (trans.) (1954–9) *Middle Length Sayings*, London: published for the Pāli Text Society by Luzac. Three volumes. Another translation in Bhikkhu Ñāṇamoli and Bhikkhu Bodhi (trans.) (1995) *The Middle Length Discourses of the Buddha: A New Translation of the Majjhima Nikāya*, original translation by Bhikkhu Ñāṇamoli; translation edited and revised by Bhikkhu Bodhi, Boston: Wisdom, in association with the Barre Center for Buddhist Studies.

Anantamukhasādhakadhāraṇī: Sanskrit appears to be lost. T. 140 (cf. 525). Taisho 1009–17. No translation.

Anattalakkhaṇa Sutta: Pāli text in M. Leon Feer (ed.) (1973–80) *The Saṃyutta-nikāya of the Sutta-piṭaka*, London: Pāli Text Society. Originally published London: Frowde, 1884–1904 and London: Luzac, 1960. Six volumes. Translation in C. Rhys Davids (Vols 1–2) and F. L. Woodward (Vols 3–5) (trans.) (1917–30) *The Book of the Kindred Sayings*, London: Pāli Text Society. Five volumes.

Aṅgulimālīya Sūtra: No complete Sanskrit version. T. 213. Taisho 99. Appears not yet to have been translated.

Aṅguttara Nikāya: Pāli text in R. Morris (vols 1–2) and E. Hardy (vols 3–5) (eds) (1961–81) *The Aṅguttara-nikāya*, 2nd edition revised by A. K. Warder, London: published for the Pāli Text Society by Luzac. Originally published London: Frowde, 1885–1910. Six volumes. Translation in F. L. Woodward (Vols 1, 2, and 5) and E. M. Hare (Vols 3, 4) (trans.) (1932–6) *The Book of the Gradual Sayings*, London: Pāli Text Society.

Aṣṭasāhasrikāprajñāpāramitā: Sanskrit text in P. L. Vaidya (ed.) (1960) *Aṣṭasāhasrikā Prajñāpāramitā, with Haribhadra's commentary called Āloka*, Darbhanga: The Mithila Instititute of Post-Graduate Studies and Research in Sanskrit Learning. T. 12. Taisho 220 (4)(5)/224–228. English translation by E. Conze (trans.) (1973) *The Perfection of Wisdom in Eight Thousand Lines and its Verse Summary*, Bolinas: Four Seasons Foundation.

Avataṃsakasūtra: Some Sanskrit portions surviving. See under *Daśabhūmika Sūtra* and *Gaṇḍavyūha Sūtra*. T. 44/104. Taisho 278–9. English translation from the Chinese in T. Cleary (trans.) (1984–7)

The Flower Ornament Scripture: A Translation of the Avataṃsaka Sūtra, Boulder, C.: Shambhala Publications. Three volumes. Vol. 3 published in Boston.

Bar do thos grol: Translated in R. A. F. Thurman (trans.) (1994) *The Tibetan Book of the Dead: Liberation Through Understanding in the Between*, New York, Toronto, London, Sydney, Auckland: Bantam Books.

Bhagavad Gītā: Translated in W. J. Johnson (trans.) (1994) *The Bhagavad Gītā*, Oxford and New York: Oxford University Press.

Bhāvanākrama (Kamalaśīla): Sanskrit and Tibetan of first *Bhāvanākrama*, together with an English summary, in G. Tucci (ed.) (1958) *Minor Buddhist Texts, Part II*, Rome: Instituto Italiano per il Medio ed Estremo Oriente. For English see also S. Beyer (trans.) (1974) *The Buddhist Experience: Sources and Interpretations*, Encino, Calif.: Dickenson. T. 3915. As far as we know, the Sanskrit of the second (T. 3916) and third (T. 3917) *Bhāvanākramas* is missing. Nor are we familiar with a translation of the second *Bhāvanākrama*. Third *Bhāvanākrama* translated into French by Étienne Lamotte in P. Demiéville (1952) *Le Concile de Lhasa*, Paris: Bibliothèque de l'Institut des Hautes Études Chinoises, Imprimerie Nationale de France. See also G. Tucci (ed.) (1971) *Minor Buddhist Texts: Part III*, Rome: Instituto Italiano per il Medio ed Estremo Oriente. Cf. the Taisho 1664.

Bodhicaryāvatāra (Śāntideva): For the Sanskrit see P. L. Vaidya (ed.) (1960) *Bodhicaryāvatāra of Śāntideva, with the commentary Pañjikā of Prajñākaramati*, Darbhanga: The Mithila Instititute of Post-Graduate Studies and Research in Sanskrit Learning. T. 3871. Taisho 1662. English in K. Crosby and A. Skilton (trans.) (1995) *Śāntideva: The Bodhicaryāvatāra*, Oxford: Oxford University Press.

Bodhicittavivaraṇa (Nāgārjuna?): Complete Sanskrit version lost. Tibetan text, with Sanskrit fragments, in Chr. Lindtner (ed. and trans.) (1982) *Nāgārjuniana: Studies in the Writings and Philosophy of Nāgārjuna*, Copenhagen: Akademisk Forlag. Cf. Taisho 1661.

Bodhipathapradīpa (Atiśa, with a commentary attributed to Atiśa): Sanskrit lost, no Chinese version. T. 3947. Cf. T. 4465. Translated in R. Sherburne (trans.) (1983) *A Lamp for the Path and Commentary*, London: Allen and Unwin.

Brahmajāla Sutta: Pāli text in T. W. Rhys Davids and J. Estlin Carpenter (eds) (1966) *The Dīgha Nikāya*, London: published for the Pāli Text Society by Luzac. Three volumes. Originally published 1890–1911. English in M. Walshe (trans.) (1987) *Thus Have I Heard: The Long Discourses of the Buddha*, London: Wisdom. Another translation in T. W. Rhys Davids (trans.) (1899–21) *Dialogues of the Buddha*, London: Pāli Text Society. Three volumes.

Buddhacarita (Aśvaghoṣa): Sanskrit text and English translation in E. H. Johnston (ed. and trans.) (1935–6) *The Buddhacarita; or Acts of the Buddha*, cantos i to xiv translated from the original Sanskrit supplemented by the Tibetan version, Calcutta: published for the University of the Panjab, Lahore, by Baptist Mission Press. Johnston has also translated Chapters 15 to 28 in E. H. Johnston (1937) 'The Buddha's mission and last journey: Buddhacarita, xv to xxviii', *Acta Orientalia* 15: 26–62, 85–111, 231–52, 253–86. Chs 1–17 translated by E. B. Cowell (ed.) (1969) in *Buddhist Mahāyāna Texts*, New York: Dover Publications. Originally Volume 49 of F. Max Müller (ed.) (1894) *The Sacred Books of the East*, Oxford: Clarendon Press. Taisho 192. T. 4156.

Caṇḍamahāroṣaṇa Tantra: Sanskrit part edited with an English translation by Christopher S. George (1974) *The Caṇḍamahāroṣaṇa Tantra: Chapters I–VIII: A Critical Edition and English Translation*, New Haven, Connecticut: American Oriental Society. T. 431. No Chinese.

Caryāgīti: Old Bengali text, Tibetan translation, and English translation in Per Kvaerne (1977) *An Anthology of Buddhist Tantric Songs: A Study of the Caryāgīti*, Oslo: Universitetsforlaget. Second edition, Bangkok: White Orchid Press, 1986. This also contains the Sanskrit text and Tibetan translation of Munidatta's commentary to the *Caryāgīti*. No Chinese.

Catuḥśatakakārikā (Āryadeva): Full Sanskrit text lost. Fragments, with Tibetan, and translation in K. Lang (trans.) (1986) *Āryadeva's Catuḥśataka: On the Bodhisattva's Cultivation of Merit and Knowledge*, Copenhagen: Akademisk Forlag. T. 3846. Taisho 1570–1 (Chs 9–16). Tibetan translated together with a commentary by rGyal tshab rje (1364–1432 CE), by R. Sonam (trans.) (1994) *The Yogic Deeds of Bodhisattvas: Gyel-tsap on Āryadeva's Four Hundred*, Ithaca, N. Y.: Snow Lion.

Catuḥstava (Nāgārjuna): Sanskrit, with an English translation, in F. Tola and C. Dragonetti (trans.) (1995) *On Voidness: A Study on Buddhist Nihilism*, Delhi: Motilal Banarsidass. Sanskrit, Tibetan, and English of *Lokātītastava* and *Acintyastava* in Chr. Lindtner (ed. and trans.) (1982) *Nāgārjuniana: Studies in the Writings and Philosophy of Nāgārjuna*, Copenhagen: Akademisk Forlag. T. 1119/1120/1122/1128. No Chinese.

Caturaśītisiddhapravṛtti (Abhayadatta): No Sanskrit. Facsimile of Tibetan blockprint edition in J. B. Robinson (trans.) (1979) *Buddha's Lions: The Lives of the Eighty-four Siddhas. Caturaśīti-siddha-pravṛtti by Abhayadatta*, Berkeley, Calif.: Dharma Publishing. No Chinese. English translation by (i) Robinson (above); (ii) Keith Dowman (trans.) (1985) *Masters of Mahāmudrā: Songs and Histories of the Eighty-Four Buddhist Siddhas*, Albany, N. Y.: State University of New York Press.

Cūlamāluṅkya Sutta: Pāli text in V. Trenckner (ed.) (1991–4) *The Majjhima-Nikāya*, London: Pāli Text Society. Reprint of a work originally published in 1888–1925. Four volumes. Translation in I. B. Horner (trans.) (1954–9) *Middle Length Sayings*, London: published for the Pāli Text Society by Luzac. Three volumes. Another translation in Bhikkhu Ñāṇamoli and Bhikkhu Bodhi (trans.) (1995) *The Middle Length Discourses of the Buddha: A New Translation of the Majjhima Nikāya*, original translation by Bhikkhu Ñāṇamoli; translation edited and revised by Bhikkhu Bodhi, Boston: Wisdom, in association with the Barre Center for Buddhist Studies.

Ḍākārṇava Tantra: Sanskrit in manuscripts only. No further details. T. 372. No Chinese. No translation.

Daśabhūmika Sūtra: Sanskrit in P. L. Vaidya (ed.) (1967) *Daśabhūmikasūtra*, Darbhanga: The Mithila Instititute of Post-Graduate Studies and Research in Sanskrit Learning. Tibetan in the appropriate portion of the *Avataṃsaka Sūtra*, T. 44. Taisho 278 (22)/279 (26)/285–7. Translated from the Sanskrit by M. Honda in Denis Sinor (ed.) (1968) *Studies in South, East and Central Asia*, Delhi: Śata-Piṭaka Series. Translated from the Chinese in Vol. 2 of T. Cleary (trans.) (1984–7) *The Flower Ornament Scripture: A Translation of the Avataṃsaka Sūtra*, Boulder, Co.: Shambhala Publications. Three volumes. Vol. 3 published in Boston.

Daśabhūmikavibhāṣā Śāstra (Nāgārjuna?): No Sanskrit or Tibetan. Taisho 1521. Appears not yet to have been translated in its entirety, although we have seen reference to J. Eracle (1981) *Le Chapitre de Nāgārjuna sur la Pratique Facile, suivi du Sūtra qui loue la Terre de Purité*, Bruxelles (Ch. 9, no further details available).

Dhammacakkappavattana Sutta: Pāli text in M. Leon Feer (ed.) (1973–80) *The Saṃyutta-nikāya of the Sutta-piṭaka*, London: Pāli Text Society. Originally published London: Frowde, 1884–1904 and London: Luzac, 1960. Six volumes. Translation in C. Rhys Davids (Vols 1–2) and F. L. Woodward (Vols 3–5) (trans.) (1917–30) *The Book of the Kindred Sayings*, London: Pāli Text Society. Five volumes.

Dhammapada: Pāli text with English translation in John Ross Carter and M. Palihawadana (trans.) (1992) *Sacred Writings, Buddhism: The Dhammapada*, New York: Quality Paperback Book Club. Originally published Oxford: Oxford University Press, 1987.

Dharmadharmatāvibhāga (Maitreyanātha?): Sanskrit lost. Tibetan in G. M. Nagao and J. Nozawa (eds) (1955) *Studies in Indology and Buddhology, Presented in Honour of Professor Susumu Yamaguchi on the Occasion of the Sixtieth Birthday*, Kyoto: Hozokan. There is, apparently, a Chinese version although we have not been able to trace its Taisho number. As far as we know to date no translation appears to have been published.

Dharmasūtras: Translation in P. Olivelle (trans.) (1999) *The Law Codes of Ancient India*, Oxford and New York: Oxford University Press.

Dīgha Nikāya: Pāli text in T. W. Rhys Davids and J. Estlin Carpenter (eds) (1966) *The Dīgha Nikāya*, London: published for the Pāli Text Society by Luzac. Three volumes. Originally published 1890–1911. English in M. Walshe (trans.) (1987) *Thus Have I Heard: The Long Discourses of the Buddha*, London: Wisdom. Another translation in T. W. Rhys Davids (trans.) (1899–21) *Dialogues of the Buddha*, London: Pāli Text Society. Three volumes.

Dohākośa (Saraha): Apabhrāṃśa text in P. C. Bagchi (ed.) (1938) *Dohākośa*, Calcutta: Calcutta Sanskrit Series. English translations (i) by David Snellgrove, in E. Conze, I. B. Horner, D. Snellgrove, and A. Waley (eds) (1964) *Buddhist Texts Through the Ages*, New York: Harper and Row; (ii) in Guenther (1973) and (1993). Tibetan text and French translation by M. Shahidullah (trans.) (1928) *Les Chants Mystiques de Kāṇha et de Saraha*, Paris: Adrien-Maisonneuve. No Chinese.

Fo-hsing Lun (Vasubandhu?): No Sanskrit or Tibetan version. See S. B. King (1991) *Buddha Nature*, Albany, N. Y.: State University of New York Press.

Gaṇḍavyūha Sūtra: Sanskrit text in P. L. Vaidya (ed.) (1960) *Gaṇḍavyūhasūtra*, Darbhanga: The Mithila Instititute of Post-Graduate Studies and Research in Sanskrit Learning. Tibetan included at the appropriate point of the translation of the *Avataṃsaka Sūtra*, T. 44. Taisho 278 (31)(34)/279 (36)(39)/293–5. Translated from the Chinese in Vol. 3 of T. Cleary (trans.) (1984–7) *The Flower Ornament Scripture: A Translation of the Avataṃsaka Sūtra*, Boulder, Co.: Shambhala Publications. Three volumes. Vol. 3 published in Boston.

Guhyasamāja Tantra: Sanskrit text in (i) Benoytosh Bhattacharyya (ed.) (1931) *Guhyasamāja Tantra or Tathāgataguhyaka*, Baroda: Oriental Institute (reprinted in 1967); (ii) S. Bagchi (ed.) (1965) *Guhyasamāja Tantra*, Darbhanga: The Mithila Instititute of Post-Graduate Studies and Research in Sanskrit Learning (in effect a reprint of Bhattacharyya's edition); (iii) Yukei Matsunaga (ed.) (1978) *The Guhyasamāja Tantra: A New Critical Edition*, Osaka: Toho Shuppan. T. 442–3. Taisho 885. English translation by Eiji Takahashi (1981) in *Some Studies in Indian History*, Chiba: Funsbashi. English of selected chapters by (i) Francesca Fremantle, 'Chapter seven of the Guhyasamāja Tantra', in T. Skorupski (ed.) (1990) *Indo-Tibetan Studies: Papers in Honour and Appreciation of Professor David L. Snellgrove's Contribution to Indo-Tibetan Studies*, Tring: The Institute of Buddhist Studies (includes an edition of the Sanskrit of Ch. 7); (ii) Alex Wayman (1977) *Yoga of the Guhyasamājatantra: The Arcane Lore of Forty Verses*, Delhi: Motilal Banarsidass (Chs 6 and 12); (iii) by David Snellgrove, in E. Conze, I. B. Horner, D. Snellgrove, and A. Waley (eds) (1964) *Buddhist Texts Through the Ages*, New York: Harper & Row (Ch. 7).

Haracaritacintāmaṇi (Jayadratha): Sanskrit edited by Paṇḍita Śivadatta and K. P. Parab (1897) Bombay. No further details available.

Heart (Prajñāpāramitāhṛdaya) Sūtra: Sanskrit text and English translation in E. Conze (trans.) (1958) *Buddhist Wisdom Books: Containing the Diamond Sūtra [Vajracchedikā] and the Heart Sūtra [Hṛdaya]*, London: Allen and Unwin. For Sanskrit of both the longer and shorter versions see also P. L. Vaidya (ed.) (1961) *Mahāyāna-sūtra-saṃgraha Part 1*, Darbhanga: The Mithila Instititute of Post-Graduate Studies and Research in Sanskrit Learning. T. 21. Taisho 250–7.

Hevajra Tantra (Śrīhevajraḍākinījālasaṃvara): Sanskrit and Tibetan text, with English translation, in David Snellgrove (ed.) (1959) *The Hevajra Tantra*, Oxford: Oxford University Press. Two volumes. T. 417–8. Taisho 892. Sanskrit text with English translation also in G. W. Farrow and I. Menon (1992) *The Concealed Essence of the Hevajra Tantra, with the Commentary Yogaratnamālā*, Delhi: Motilal Banarsidass (see *Yogaratnamālā*).

Hevajrasekaprakriyā (author unknown): Sanskrit in Louis Finot (1934) 'Manuscrits sanscrits de sādhana retrouvés en Chine', *Journal Asiatique* 1–85. No Tibetan or Chinese known.

Hundred-thousand Verse (Śatasāhasrikā) Prajñāpāramitā Sūtra: Lost in Sanskrit as a full and independent text. T. 8. Taisho 220 (1). Some parts translated in E. Conze in collaboration with I. B. Horner, D. L. Snellgrove, and A. Waley (trans.) (1964) *Buddhist Texts Through the Ages*, New York: Harper & Row; and also E. Conze (trans.) (1978) *Selected Sayings from the Perfection of Wisdom*, Boulder, Co.: Prajñā Press.

Jñānaprasthāna (Kātyāyanīputra): No Sanskrit or Tibetan version surviving. Taisho 1543/1544. No translation in a European language.

Kālacakra Tantra: Sanskrit in (i) Raghu Vira and Lokesh Candra (eds) (1966) *Kālacakra-tantra and Other Texts*, Part 1, New Delhi: International Academy of Indian Culture; (ii) Biswanath Banerjee (ed.) (1985) *A Critical Edition of Śrī Kālacakratantra-rāja (Collated with the Tibetan Version)*, Calcutta: Asiatic Society. T. 362. No Chinese translation. No translation into a European language.

Kāmasūtra: English translation in A. Daniélou (trans.) (1994) *The Complete Kāma Sūtra*, Rochester, Vermont: Park Street Press.

Kāraṇḍavyūha Sūtra: Sanskrit in P. L. Vaidya (ed.) (1961) *Mahāyāna-sūtra-saṃgraha Part 1*, Darbhanga: The Mithila Instititute of Post-Graduate Studies and Research in Sanskrit Learning. T. 116. Taisho 1050. Short selections in E. J. Thomas (trans.) (1952) *The Perfection of Wisdom: The Career of the Predestined Buddhas; a Selection of Mahāyāna Scriptures*, London: J. Murray. There is an unpublished

French translation by E. Burnouf, and a detailed summary in A. Studholme (1999), 'On the history of the oṃ maṇipadme hūṃ mantra', unpublished Ph.D. thesis, University of Bristol.

Karmasiddhiprakaraṇa (Vasubandhu): Sanskrit text lost. T. 113. Taisho number unavailable. Translated into French by É. Lamotte (trans.) (1935–6) in *Mélanges Chinois et Bouddhiques* 4: 151–288. English in S. Anacker (1984) *Seven Works of Vasubandhu, the Buddhist Psychological Doctor*, Delhi: Motilal Banarsidass.

Karuṇāpuṇḍarīka Sūtra: Not translated, but edited in Sanskrit with a long introduction, summary, and notes in I. Yamada (ed.) (1968) *Karuṇāpuṇḍarīka Sūtra*, London: School of Oriental and African Studies, University of London. Two volumes. T. 112. Taisho 157–8.

Kathāvatthu (Moggaliputtatissa): Pāli text in A. C. Taylor (ed.) (1979) *Kathāvatthu* London: Pāli Text Society. Two volumes in one. Originally published London: Frowde, in two vols. Vol. 1, 1894; Vol. 2, 1897. Translation in Shwe Zan Aung and C. Rhys Davids (trans.) (1969) *Points of Controversy, or, Subjects of Discourse: Being a Translation of the Kathā-Vatthu from the Abhidhamma-piṭaka*, London: published for the Pāli Text Society by Luzac. Reprint of 1915 edition. Commentary by Buddhaghosa translated in B. C. Law (trans.) (1989) *The Debates Commentary*, Oxford: Pāli Text Society. Originally published London: Oxford University Press, 1940.

Kevaddha Sutta: Pāli text in T. W. Rhys Davids and J. Estlin Carpenter (eds) (1966) *The Dīgha Nikāya*, London: published for the Pāli Text Society by Luzac. Three volumes. Originally published 1890–1911. English in M. Walshe (trans.) (1987) *Thus Have I Heard: The Long Discourses of the Buddha*, London: Wisdom. Another translation in T. W. Rhys Davids (trans.) (1899–21) *Dialogues of the Buddha*, London: Pāli Text Society. Three volumes.

Kriyāsaṃgraha (also called *Kriyāsaṃgrahapañjikā*) (Kuladatta): Sanskrit: (manuscript facsimile) in Lokesh Candra (1977) *Kriyāsaṃgraha: A Sanskrit Manuscript from Nepal Containing a Collection of Tantric Ritual by Kuladatta*, New Delhi: International Academy of Indian Culture; edition of Chapter 7 by Ryugen Tanemura (1997) *Kriyāsaṃgraha of Kuladatta*, Tokyo, The Sankibo Press. T. 2531. No Chinese. See Skorupski (1998) for a summary of contents.

Kriyāsamuccaya (Darpaṇācārya): Sanskrit (manuscript facsimile) in Lokesh Candra (ed.) (1977) *Kriyāsamuccaya*, New Delhi: International Academy of Indian Culture. No English translation. No Tibetan known. No Chinese.

Kuan-wu-liang-shou-fo Ching (**Amitāyurdhyāna Sūtra/Amitāyurbuddhānusmṛti Sūtra*): No Sanskrit or Tibetan version. Taisho 365. Ryukoku University Translation Center (1984) *The Sūtra of Contemplation on the Buddha of Immeasurable Life as Expounded by Śākyamuni*

Buddha, Kyoto: Ryukoku University. All three Sukhāvatī sūtras (from the Chinese) in Inagaki Hisao, in collaboration with Harold Stewart (trans.) (1995) *The Three Pure Land Sutras*, Berkeley, Calif.: Numata Centre for Buddhist Translation and Research, and in E. B. Cowell (ed.) (1969) *Buddhist Mahāyāna Texts*, New York: Dover Publications. Originally Volume 49 of F. Max Müller (ed.) (1894) *The Sacred Books of the East*, Oxford: Clarendon Press.

Laghusaṃvara Tantra (Cakrasaṃvara Tantra): Sanskrit manuscript 13290, Oriental Institute, Baroda. T. 368. No Chinese. No translation.

Laṅkāvatāra Sūtra: Sanskrit text in P. L. Vaidya (ed.) (1963) *Saddharmalaṅkāvatārasūtram*, Darbhanga: The Mithila Instititute of Post-Graduate Studies and Research in Sanskrit Learning. T. 107–8. Taisho 670–2. English in D. T. Suzuki (trans.) (1973) *The Laṅkāvatāra Sūtra: A Mahāyāna Text*, London: Routledge and Kegan Paul.

Lokānuvartana Sūtra: Not yet translated in its entirety. Some verses edited in Sanskrit and translated with a discussion by P. Harrison (1982) 'Sanskrit fragments of a Lokottaravādin tradition', in L. A. Hercus, F. B. J. Kuiper, T. Rajapatirana, and E. R. Skrzypczak (eds) (1982) *Indological and Buddhist Studies: Volume in Honour of Professor J. W. de Jong on his Sixtieth Birthday*, Canberra: Faculty of Asian Studies. T. 200. Taisho 807.

Madhyamakakārikā (Nāgārjuna): Translated from the Sanskrit, with a Sanskrit edition, in K. K. Inada (1970) *Nāgārjuna: A Translation of his Mūlamadhyamakakārikā, with an Introductory Essay*, Tokyo: Hokuseido Press. An important version of the Sanskrit text is J. W. de Jong (ed.) (1977) *Nāgārjuna: Mūlamadhyamakakārikā*, Adyar, Madras: The Adyar Library and Research Centre. See also the Sanskrit embedded in the *Prasannapadā* commentary of Candrakīrti in P. L. Vaidya (ed.) (1960) *Madhyamakaśāstra of Nāgārjuna, with the Commentary Prasannapadā by Candrakīrti*, Darbhanga: The Mithila Instititute of Post-Graduate Studies and Research in Sanskrit Learning. T. 3824. Taisho contained in 1564.

Madhyamakāvatāra (Candrakīrti): Not available in Sanskrit or Chinese. T. 3861, T. 3862 includes the autocommentary. First five chapters, together with the commentary by Tsong kha pa (1357–1419), in J. Hopkins (ed. and trans.) (1980) *Compassion in Tibetan Buddhism: Tsong-ka-pa, with Kensur Lekden's Meditations of a Tantric Abbot*, London: Rider. Complete text, with his own commentary based on Tsong kha pa, in Geshe Kelsang Gyatso (1995) *Ocean of Nectar: Wisdom and Compassion in Mahāyāna Buddhism*, London: Tharpa Publications. Translation of verses only in C. W. Huntington, Jr with Geshe Namgyal Wangchen (1989) *The Emptiness of Emptiness*, Honolulu: University of Hawaii Press. See the review article on this book in Williams (1991).

Madhyamakāvatārațīkā (Jayānanda): Lost in Sanskrit, no Chinese version available. Tibetan text at T. 3870. No English translation.

Madhyāntavibhāga (Maitreyanātha?): Sanskrit with Vasubandhu's commentary and a translation in S. Anacker (1984) *Seven Works of Vasubandhu, the Buddhist Psychological Doctor*, Delhi: Motilal Banarsidass. T. 4021. Taisho 1601.

Mahāhatthipadopama Sutta: Pāli text in V. Trenckner (ed.) (1991–4) *The Majjhima-Nikāya*, London: Pāli Text Society. Reprint of a work originally published in 1888–1925. Four volumes. Translation in I. B. Horner (trans.) (1954–9) *Middle Length Sayings*, London: published for the Pāli Text Society by Luzac. Three volumes. Another translation in Bhikkhu Ñāṇamoli and Bhikkhu Bodhi (trans.) (1995) *The Middle Length Discourses of the Buddha: A New Translation of the Majjhima Nikāya*, original translation by Bhikkhu Ñāṇamoli; translation edited and revised by Bhikkhu Bodhi, Boston: Wisdom, in association with the Barre Center for Buddhist Studies.

Mahāmegha Sūtra: Sanskrit lost. Taisho 387/388; cf. Taisho 992–3. T. 232; cf. T. 657. No translation known. But cf. C. Bendall (1880) 'The Mahāmegha Sūtra', *Journal of the Royal Asiatic Society*, 286–311 (unseen).

Mahānidāna Sutta: Pāli text in T. W. Rhys Davids and J. Estlin Carpenter (eds) (1966) *The Dīgha Nikāya*, London: published for the Pāli Text Society by Luzac. Three volumes. Originally published 1890–1911. English in M. Walshe (trans.) (1987) *Thus Have I Heard: The Long Discourses of the Buddha*, London: Wisdom. Another translation in T. W. Rhys Davids (trans.) (1899–21) *Dialogues of the Buddha*, London: Pāli Text Society. Three volumes.

Mahāparinibbāna Sutta: Pāli text in T. W. Rhys Davids and J. Estlin Carpenter (eds) (1966) *The Dīgha Nikāya*, London: published for the Pāli Text Society by Luzac. Three volumes. Originally published 1890–1911. English in M. Walshe (trans.) (1987) *Thus Have I Heard: The Long Discourses of the Buddha*, London: Wisdom. Another translation in T. W. Rhys Davids (trans.) (1899–21) *Dialogues of the Buddha*, London: Pāli Text Society. Three volumes.

Mahāparinirvāṇa Sūtra: Sanskrit lost. T. 119–21. Taisho 374–7/390. English in K. Yamamoto (trans.) (1973–5) *The Mahāyāna Mahāparinirvāṇa-sūtra: A Complete Translation from the Classical Chinese Language in 3 Volumes*, annotated and with full glossary, index, and concordance by Kosho Yamamoto, Ube City, Japan: The Karinbunko. Three volumes. The translation is unfortunately marred by poor English. A revised version by T. Page of this translation is in the process of being published privately in booklet form by Nirvana Publications, UKAVIS, PO Box 4746, London SE11 4XF, England.

Mahāsatipaṭṭhāna Sutta: Pāli text in T. W. Rhys Davids and J. Estlin Carpenter (eds) (1966) *The Dīgha Nikāya*, London: published for the Pāli Text Society by Luzac. Three volumes. Originally published 1890–1911. English in M. Walshe (trans.) (1987) *Thus Have I Heard: The Long Discourses of the Buddha*, London: Wisdom. Another translation in T. W. Rhys Davids (trans.) (1899–21) *Dialogues of the Buddha*, London: Pāli Text Society. Three volumes. *Mahāsatipaṭṭhāna Sutta* also contained in Nyanaponika Thera (1969) *The Heart of Buddhist Meditation: A Handbook of Mental Training Based on the Buddha's Way of Mindfulness*, London: Rider.

Mahāsīhanāda Sutta: Pāli text in V. Trenckner (ed.) (1991–4) *The Majjhima-Nikāya*, London: Pāli Text Society. Reprint of a work originally published in 1888–1925. Four volumes. Translation in I. B. Horner (trans.) (1954–9) *Middle Length Sayings*, London: published for the Pāli Text Society by Luzac. Three volumes. Another translation in Bhikkhu Ñāṇamoli and Bhikkhu Bodhi (trans.) (1995) *The Middle Length Discourses of the Buddha: A New Translation of the Majjhima Nikāya*, original translation by Bhikkhu Ñāṇamoli; translation edited and revised by Bhikkhu Bodhi, Boston: Wisdom, in association with the Barre Center for Buddhist Studies.

Mahātaṇhāsaṅkhaya Sutta: Pāli text in V. Trenckner (ed.) (1991–4) *The Majjhima-Nikāya*, London: Pāli Text Society. Reprint of a work originally published in 1888–1925. Four volumes. Translation in I. B. Horner (trans.) (1954–9) *Middle Length Sayings*, London: published for the Pāli Text Society by Luzac. Three volumes. Another translation in Bhikkhu Ñāṇamoli and Bhikkhu Bodhi (trans.) (1995) *The Middle Length Discourses of the Buddha: A New Translation of the Majjhima Nikāya*, original translation by Bhikkhu Ñāṇamoli; translation edited and revised by Bhikkhu Bodhi, Boston: Wisdom, in association with the Barre Center for Buddhist Studies.

Mahāvairocanābhisaṃbodhi Sūtra (Mahāvairocana Sūtra): Sanskrit text lost except for fragments. T. 494. Taisho 848. English translations: (i) (of the Tibetan) by Stephen Hodge (forthcoming 2000) *Mahāvairocana-Abhisambodhi Tantra, with Buddhaguhya's Commentary*, Richmond: Curzon Press; (ii) by Chikyo Yamamoto (1990) *Mahāvairocanasūtra, translated from the Chinese of Śubhākarasiṃha and I-hsing*, New Delhi: International Academy of Indian Culture; (iii) of Chapter 2 by Alex Wayman (from Tibetan), in A. Wayman and R. Tajima (1992) *The Enlightenment of Vairocana*, New Delhi: Motilal Banarsidass; of Chapter 1 by Ryūjun Tajima (from Chinese), also in A. Wayman and R. Tajima (this is an English translation of Tajima's earlier French translation of the first chapter in Ryūjun Tajima (1936) *Étude sur le Mahāvairocana-Sūtra (Dainichikyo), avec la traduction commentée du premier chapitre*, Paris: Adrien Maisonneuve).

Mahāvastu: Sanskrit text edited in three volumes by É. Senart (ed.) (1882–97) *Le Mahāvastu*, Paris: Société Asiatiques. English translation in three volumes in J. J. Jones (trans.) (1949–56) *The Mahāvastu*, London: Luzac. No Tibetan or Chinese.

Mahāvibhāṣā: Sanskrit lost. Taisho 1545–7. No Tibetan. Sections translated from the Chinese in Louis de La Vallée Poussin (1930) 'Documents d'Abhidharma: Textes relatifs au nirvāṇa et aux asaṃskṛtas en général I-II', *Bulletin de l'École Française d'Extrême-Orient* 30: 1–28, 343–76; Louis de La Vallée Poussin (1936–1937a) 'Documents d'Abhidharma: La controverse du temps', in *Mélanges Chinois et Bouddhiques* 5: 7–158; and Louis de La Vallée Poussin (1936–1937b) 'Documents d'Abhidharma: Les deux, les quatre, les trois vérités', *Mélanges Chinois et Bouddhiques* 5: 159–87.

Mahāyānasaṃgraha (Asaṅga): Sanskrit not available. Tibetan and Chinese, with a French translation in É. Lamotte (ed. and trans.) (1938) *La Somme du Grand Véhicule d'Asaṅga (Mahāyānasaṃgraha)*, Tome 1–2: Versions tibétaine et chinoise (Hiuan-tsang); traduction et commentaire, Louvain: Bureaux du Muséon. Text and translation of the *Mahāyānasaṃgraha* and its commentaries, the *Mahāyānasaṃgrahabhāṣya* of Vasubandhu and the *Mahāyānasaṃgrahopanibandhana*, edited by Lamotte. English translation from the Chinese of Paramārtha's version in John P. Keenan (trans.) (1992) *The Summary of the Great Vehicle, by Bodhisattva Asaṅga*, Berkeley, Calif.: Numata Center for Buddhist Translation and Research. For Chapter 10 see also J. P. Keenan, P. J. Griffiths, and N. Hakamaya (1989) *The Realm of Awakening: A Translation and Study of the Tenth Chapter of Asaṅga's Mahāyānasaṅgraha*, New York: Oxford University Press. Includes Vasubandhu's *Mahāyānasaṃgrahabhāṣya* and Asvabhāva's *Mahāyānasaṃgrahopanibandhana*.

Mahāyānasūtrālaṃkāra (Maitreyanātha?): Sanskrit text (with *Bhāṣya*) and French translation in S. Lévi (ed. and trans.) (1907–11) *Asaṅga, Mahāyānasūtrālaṃkāra*, Paris: Librairie Honoré Champion. Two volumes. T. 4020 (*Bhāṣya* T. 4026). Taisho 1604.

Maitreyamahāsiṃhanāda Sūtra: No Sanskrit available. Now part of the *Ratnakūṭa* collection. Taisho 310, no. 23. T. 67 (i.e. pt 23 of the *Mahāratnakūṭa Sūtra*). No translation.

Maitreyavyākaraṇa: Sanskrit edited and translated into French by S. Lévi (1932) 'Maitreya le consolateur', *Études d'Orientalisme publiées par le Musée Guimet á la mémoire de Raymonde Linossier*, Paris: Leroux. Volume 2. The Tibetan appears to be missing from the Derge, Cone, and Peking bKa' 'gyurs, but it is found at Narthang 329 and Lhasa 350. Taisho 454. For a partial translation into English see E. Conze (trans.) (1959) *Buddhist Scriptures*, Harmondsworth: Penguin.

Majjhima Nikāya: Pāli text in V. Trenckner (ed.) (1991–4) *The Majjhima-Nikāya*, London: Pāli Text Society. Reprint of a work originally published in 1888–1925. Four volumes. Translation in I. B. Horner (trans.) (1954–9) *Middle Length Sayings*, London: published for the Pāli Text Society by Luzac. Three volumes. Another translation in Bhikkhu Ñāṇamoli and Bhikkhu Bodhi (trans.) (1995) *The Middle Length Discourses of the Buddha: A New Translation of the Majjhima Nikāya*, original translation by Bhikkhu Ñāṇamoli; translation edited and revised by Bhikkhu Bodhi, Boston: Wisdom, in association with the Barre Center for Buddhist Studies.

Mañjuśrībuddhakṣetraguṇavyūha Sūtra: Sanskrit lost. T. 59. Taisho 310 (15)/318–9. Translated in Garma C. C. Chang (ed.) (1983) *A Treasury of Mahāyāna Sūtras: Selections from the Mahāratnakūṭa Sūtra*, translated from the Chinese by the Buddhist Association of the United States, University Park, Pa.: Pennsylvania State University Press.

Mañjuśrīmūlakalpa: Sanskrit in (i) Gaṇapati Śāstri (ed.) (1920, 1922, 1925) *Mañjuśrīmūlakalpa*, Trivandrum: Trivandrum Sanskrit Series (three volumes); (ii) in P. L. Vaidya (ed.) (1964) *Mahāyānasūtrasaṃgraha: Part II*, Darbhanga: The Mithila Instititute of Post-Graduate Studies and Research in Sanskrit Learning. T. 543. Taisho 1191. French translations: (i) of Chapters 4–7 by Marcelle Lalou (1930) *Iconographie des Etoffes Paintes dans le Mañjuśrīmūlakalpa*, Paris: Librairie Orientaliste Paul Geuthner; of Chapters 2–3 by Ariane Macdonald (1962), *Le Maṇḍala du Mañjuśrīmūlakalpa*, Paris: Adrien-Maisonneuve.

Māyājāla Tantra: Sanskrit lost. T. 466/833. Taisho 890. No translation.

Milindapañha: Pāli text, edited by V. Trenckner (1986) in *The Milindapañho: Being Dialogues between King Milinda and the Buddhist Sage Nāgasena*, London: Pāli Text Society. Originally published Williams and Norgate, 1880. This edition, with appended indices, originally reprinted by the Royal Asiatic Society, 1928. Now reprinted with *Milinda-ṭīkā*. Translation in I. B. Horner (trans.) (1963–4) *Milinda's Questions*, London: Luzac. Two volumes.

Nāmamantrārthāvalokinī (Vilāsavajra): Sanskrit. Five chapters in A. H. F. Tribe (ed. and trans.) (1994) 'The Names of Wisdom: a critical edition and annotated translation of Chapters 1–5 of Vilāsavajra's commentary on the Nāmasaṃgīti, with introduction and textual notes', unpublished D.Phil. thesis, University of Oxford. English translation of five chapters in Tribe (above). T. 2533. No Chinese.

Nāmasaṃgīti (Mañjuśrīnāmasaṃgīti): Sanskrit in (i) I. P. Minaev (1887) *Buddhizm: Izledovaniya i Materialui: Vol. II*, St Petersburg (publisher's details unavailable); (ii) Raghu Vira (ed.) (1962) *Mañjuśrī-Nāma-Saṅgīti, edited in Sanskrit, Tibetan, Mongolian, and Chinese*, New

Delhi: International Academy of Indian Culture (Sanskrit reprint in *Kālacakra Tantra and Other Texts: Part I*, New Delhi: International Academy of Indian Culture, 1966); (iii) Durga Das Mukherji (ed.) (1963) *Āryamañjuśrī-nāmasaṃgīti: Sanskrit and Tibetan Texts*, Calcutta: Calcutta University Press; (iv) Ronald M. Davidson, 'The Litany of Names of Mañjuśrī', in Michel Strickmann (ed.) (1981) *Tantric and Taoist Studies in Honour of Professor R. A. Stein*, Vol. 1 *(Mélanges Chinois et Bouddhiques 20)*, Brussels: Institut Belge des Hautes Études Chinoises; (iv) Alex Wayman (ed. and trans.) (1985) *Chanting the Names Of Mañjuśrī: the Mañjuśrī-nāma-saṃgīti, Sanskrit and Tibetan texts, Translated with Annotation and Introduction*, Boston and London: Shambhala. English in (i) R. M. Davidson (above), reprinted as 'The Litany of Names of Mañjuśrī', in D. S. Lopez, Jr (ed.) (1995) *Religions of India in Practice*, Princeton, N.J.: Princeton University Press; (ii) in Wayman (above).

Niraupamyastava (Nāgārjuna): Sanskrit, with an English translation, in F. Tola and C. Dragonetti (trans.) (1995) *On Voidness: A Study on Buddhist Nihilism*, Delhi: Motilal Banarsidass. T. 1119. No Chinese.

Niṣpannayogāvalī (Abhayākaragupta): Sanskrit in (i) Benoytosh Bhattacharyya (ed.) (1949) *Niṣpannayogāvalī of Mahāpaṇḍita Abhayākaragupta*, Baroda: Oriental Institute; (ii) (manuscript facsimiles) Gudrun Bühnemann and Musachi Tachikawa (1991) *Niṣpannayogāvalī: Two Sanskrit Manuscripts from Nepal*, Tokyo: The Centre for East Asian Cultural Studies (see xvii–xviii for a bibliography of scholarship on individual chapters of the *Niṣpannayogāvalī*). T. 3141. No Chinese or English translation.

Nyāyānusāra (Saṃghabhadra): Available only in Chinese (Taisho 1562). Sections translated in C. Cox (1995) *Disputed Dharmas: Early Buddhist Theories on Existence*, Tokyo: The International Institute for Buddhist Studies.

Pañcakrama (Nāgārjuna): Sanskrit in (i) Louis de La Vallée Poussin (ed.) (1896) *Études et Textes Tantriques: Pañcakrama*, Gand: H. Engelcke and Louvain: J. B. Istas, Muséon; (ii) in Katsumi Mimaki and Toru Tomabechi (eds) (1994) *Pañcakrama: Sanskrit and Tibetan Texts Critically Edited with Verse Index, Plus Facsimile of the Sanskrit MSS*, Tokyo: The Toyo Bunko (note that both of these editions include Nāgārjuna's *Piṇḍīkṛtasādhana*, a separate work, initially thought to be part of the *Pañcakrama*). No Chinese. English translation of excerpts in Robert A. F. Thurman (trans.) (1995) *Essential Tibetan Buddhism*, New York: HarperCollins.

Pañcaviṃśatisāhasrikā Prajñāpāramitā Sūtra: Sanskrit partially edited by N. Dutt (ed.) (1934) *Pañcaviṃśatisāhasrikā Prajñāpāramitā*, London: Luzac. T. 9/3790. Taisho 220 (2)/221–3. English translation in E. Conze (trans.) (1975) *The Large Sūtra on Perfect Wisdom: With the*

Divisions of the Abhisamayālaṅkāra, Berkeley, Calif.: University of California Press.

Paramārthastava (Nāgārjuna): Sanskrit, with an English translation, in F. Tola and C. Dragonetti (trans.) (1995) *On Voidness: A Study on Buddhist Nihilism*, Delhi: Motilal Banarsidass. T. 1122. No Chinese.

Pradīpoddyotana (Ṣaṭkoṭivyākhyā) (Candrakīrti): Sanskrit edited in C. Chakravarti (ed.) (1984) *Guhyasamājatantra-pradīpoddyotanaṭīkā-ṣaṭkoṭivyākhyā*, Patna: Kashi Prasad Jayaswal Research Institute. T. 1785. The *Pradīpoddyotana's* opening *Nidāna-kārikā*: edition of Sanskrit and Tibetan in S. S. Bahulkar (ed.) (1996) 'The Guhyasamāja-Nidāna-Kārikāḥ [A Revised Edition]', *Dhīḥ* 21: 101–16; English translation (plus Sanskrit and Tibetan texts) in Wayman (1977). No Chinese.

Prajñopāyaviniścayasiddhi (Anaṅgavajra): Sanskrit in Benoytosh Bhattacharyya (ed.) (1929) *Two Vajrayāna Works*, Baroda: Oriental Institute. English translation of (most of) Chapters 1–3 by David Snellgrove, in E. Conze, I. B. Horner, D. Snellgrove, and A. Waley (eds and trans.) (1964) *Buddhist Texts Through the Ages*, New York: Harper & Row. No Tibetan translation known. No Chinese.

Pramāṇasamuccaya (Diṅnāga): Sanskrit lost. T. 4203 ff. Tibetan of Chapter 1, together with the Sanskrit fragments, edited and translated into English in M. Hattori (1968) *Dignāga on Perception: Being the Pratyakṣapariccheda of Dignāga's Pramāṇasamuccaya from the Sanskrit Fragments and the Tibetan Versions*, Cambridge, Mass.: Harvard University Press.

Pratyutpannabuddhasaṃmukhāvasthitasamādhi Sūtra: Sanskrit text lost apart from a few fragments. Tibetan edited by Paul Harrison (ed.) (1978) *The Tibetan Text of the Pratyutpanna-Buddha-Saṃmukhāvasthita-Samādhi-Sūtra*, Tokyo: The International Institute for Buddhist Studies. Translated by Paul Harrison (trans.) (1990) *The Samādhi of Direct Encounter with the Buddhas of the Present: An Annotated English Translation of the Tibetan Version of the Pratyutpanna-Buddha-Saṃmukhāvasthita-Samādhi-Sūtra, with Several Appendices relating to the History of the Text*, Tokyo: The International Institute for Buddhist Studies. Taisho 416–19.

Ratnagotravibhāga (Uttaratantra) (Maitreya[nātha]? (Tibetan tradition) Sāramati? (Chinese tradition)): Sanskrit (with its commentary (*Vyākhyā*)) in E. H. Johnston and T. Chowdhury (eds) (1950) *The Ratnagotravibhāga Mahāyānottaratantra Śāstra*, Patna: The Bihar Research Society. T. 4025–5. Taisho 1611. English translation in J. Takasaki (trans.) (1966) *A Study on the Ratnagotravibhāga (Uttaratantra): Being a Treatise on the Tathāgatagarbha Theory of Mahāyāna Buddhism, including a translation from the original Sansrit text*, Rome: Instituto Italiano per il Medio ed Estremo Oriente.

Ratnaguṇasaṃcayagāthā: Sanskrit text critically edited in A. Yuyama (ed.) (1976) *Prajñā-pāramitā-ratna-guṇa-saṃcaya-gāthā (Sanskrit recension A): Edited with an Introduction, Bibliographical notes, and a Tibetan Version from Tunhuang*, Cambridge: Cambridge University Press. T. 13. Taisho 229. Translated in E. Conze (trans.) (1973) *The Perfection of Wisdom in Eight Thousand Lines and its Verse Summary*, Bolinas: Four Seasons Foundation.

Ratnāvalī (Nāgārjuna): Sanskrit fragments edited by G. Tucci (ed.) (1934, 1936) 'The Ratnāvalī of Nāgārjuna', *Journal of the Royal Asiatic Society* 307–25; 1936: 237–52, 423–35. Tibetan edited in M. Hahn (ed.) (1982) *Nāgārjuna's Ratnāvalī: Volume 1: The Basic Texts (Sanskrit, Tibetan, Chinese)*, Bonn: Indica et Tibetica Verlag. Translated in J. Hopkins and Lati Rinpoche (trans.) (1975) *The Precious Garland; and The Song of the Four Mindfulnesses*, by Nāgārjuna and the Seventh Dalai Lama, London: George Allen and Unwin.

Ṛg Veda: Selections translated in Wendy Doniger O'Flaherty (trans.) (1981) *The Rig Veda*, Harmondsworth: Penguin Books.

Saddharmapuṇḍarīka Sūtra: Sanskrit text in P. L. Vaidya (ed.) (1960) *Saddharmapuṇḍarīkasūtra*, Darbhanga: The Mithila Instititute of Post-Graduate Studies and Research in Sanskrit Learning. T. 113. Taisho 262–5. English in L. Hurvitz (trans.) (1976) *Scripture of the Lotus Blossom of the Fine Dharma*, translated from the Chinese of Kumārajīva by Leon Hurvitz, New York: Columbia University Press. See also T. Kubo and A. Yuyama (trans.) (1993) *The Lotus Sūtra*, translated from the Chinese of Kumārajīva (Taisho, Volume 9, number 262) by Kubo Tsugunari and Yuyama Akira, Berkeley, Calif.: Numata Center for Buddhist Translation and Research.

Sādhanamālā: A collection of some two hundred and forty *sādhanas* by various authors. Sanskrit in Benoytosh Bhattacharyya (ed.) (1925, 1928) *Sādhanamālā*, Baroda: Oriental Institute. Two volumes. T. 3400–3644. No Chinese. English translation of two sādhanas in L. O. Gomez 'Two Tantric meditations: Visualizing the deity', in D. S. Lopez, Jr (ed.) (1995) *Buddhism in Practice*, Princeton, N. J.: Princeton University Press.

Sādhanaśataka and *Sādhanaśatapañcāśikā*: Two collections of *sādhanas* by various authors. Sanskrit (facsimile edition) in Gudrun Bühnemann (1994) *Two Buddhist Sādhana Collections in Sanskrit Manuscript*, Wien: Wiener Studien zur Tibetologie und Buddhismus-Kunde. T. 3306–99; T. 3143–3304. No Chinese.

Sāmaññaphala Sutta: Pāli text in T. W. Rhys Davids and J. Estlin Carpenter (eds) (1966) *The Dīgha Nikāya*, London: published for the Pāli Text Society by Luzac. Three volumes. Originally published 1890–1911. English in M. Walshe (trans.) (1987) *Thus Have I Heard: The Long Discourses of the Buddha*, London: Wisdom. Another translation in T. W. Rhys Davids (trans.) (1899–21) *Dialogues of the Buddha*, London: Pāli Text Society. Three volumes.

Saṃdhinirmocana Sūtra: No complete Sanskrit version surviving. Tibetan text and English translation, in J. Powers (trans.) (1995) *Wisdom of Buddha: The Saṃdhinirmocana Sūtra*, Berkeley, Calif.: Dharma Publishing. Taisho 675–9. Tibetan text and French translation in É. Lamotte (ed. and trans.) (1935) *Saṃdhinirmocana Sūtra*, Louvain: Bureaux du Recueil; Paris: Adrien-Maisonneuve.

**Sammitīyanikāya Śāstra*: No Sanskrit or Tibetan. Taisho 1649. English translation by K. Venkataramanan (trans.) (1953) 'Sammitīyanikāya Śāstra', *Viśva-Bharati Annals* 5: 155–242. T. 4021.

Saṃpuṭa Tantra (also known as *Saṃpuṭodbhava Tantra*): Sanskrit: (i) Edition of Chapter 1 by T. Skorupski, 'The Saṃpuṭa-tantra: Sanskrit and Tibetan versions of chapter one', in T. Skorupski (ed.) (1996) *The Buddhist Forum IV*, London: School of Oriental and African Studies, University of London; (ii) Edition and English translation of Chapters 1–4 in George Robert Elder (1978) 'The Saṃpuṭa Tantra: edition and translation, chapters I-IV', unpublished Ph.D. thesis, Columbia University, New York. T. 381. No Chinese.

Saṃvara Tantra (*Sarvabuddhasamāyogaḍākinījālasaṃvara Tantra*): Sanskrit lost. T. 366–7. No Chinese.

Saṃvarodaya Tantra: Sanskrit part edited in Shinichi Tsuda (ed. and trans.) (1974) *The Saṃvarodaya-Tantra: Selected Chapters*, Tokyo: Hokuseido Press. T. 373. No Chinese. English of these chapters also in Tsuda (above).

Saṃyutta Nikāya: Pāli text in M. Leon Feer (ed.) (1973–80) *The Saṃyutta-nikāya of the Sutta-piṭaka*, London: Pāli Text Society. Originally published London: Frowde, 1884–1904 and London: Luzac, 1960. Six volumes. Translation in C. Rhys Davids (Vols 1–2), and F. L. Woodward (Vols 3–5) (trans.) (1917–30) *The Book of the Kindred Sayings*, London: Pāli Text Society. Five volumes.

Saṅgīti Sutta: Pāli text in T. W. Rhys Davids and J. Estlin Carpenter (eds) (1966) *The Dīgha Nikāya*, London: published for the Pāli Text Society by Luzac. Three volumes. Originally published 1890–1911. English in M. Walshe (trans.) (1987) *Thus Have I Heard: The Long Discourses of the Buddha*, London: Wisdom. Another translation in T. W. Rhys Davids (trans.) (1899–21) *Dialogues of the Buddha*, London: Pāli Text Society. Three volumes.

Saptaśatikā (Seven Hundred Verse) Prajñāpāramitā: Sanskrit in P. L. Vaidya (ed.) (1961) *Mahāyāna-sūtra-saṃgraha Part 1*, Darbhanga: The Mithila Instititute of Post-Graduate Studies and Research in Sanskrit Learning. Taisho 220 (7)/232/233/310 (46). T. 24. English in E. Conze (trans.) (1973) *The Short Prajñāpāramitā Texts*, London: Luzac.

Sarvadurgatipariśodhana Tantra: Sanskrit and Tibetan texts and English translation in Tadeusz Skorupski (ed. and trans.) (1983) *The Sarvadurgatipariṣodhana Tantra, Elimination of all Evil Destinies*, Delhi: Motilal Banarsidass. No Chinese.

Sarvarahasya Tantra: Sanskrit lost. T. 481. Tibetan text and English translation in Alex Wayman (1984) 'The Sarvarahasya-tantra', *Acta Indologica* 6: 521–69. No Chinese.

Sekoddeśaṭīkā (Nāropa): Sanskrit in M. E. Carelli (ed.) (1941) *Sekoddeśaṭīkā of Nāḍapāda (Nāropa): Being a commentary Sekkodeśa section of the Kālacakra Tantra*, Baroda: Oriental Institute. T. 1353. No Chinese. No English translation.

Śrīmālādevīsiṃhanāda Sūtra: Complete Sanskrit version lost. T. 92. Taisho 310 (48)/353. English translation in A. Wayman and H. Wayman (trans.) (1974) *The Lion's Roar of Queen Śrīmālā: A Buddhist Scripture on the Tathāgatagarbha Theory*, New York: Columbia University Press. Translated also in Garma C. C. Chang (ed.) (1983) *A Treasury of Mahāyāna Sūtras: Selections from the Mahāratnakūṭa Sūtra*, translated from the Chinese by the Buddhist Association of the United States, University Park, Pa.: Pennsylvania State University Press.

Suhṛllekha (Nāgārjuna): Sanskrit text lost. T. 4182/4496. Taisho 1672–4. Translated from the Tibetan in L. Kawamura (trans.) (1975) *Golden Zephyr: Instructions from a Spiritual Friend; Nāgārjuna and Lama Mipham*, Emeryville, Calif.: Dharma Publishing. Another translation by Ven. Lozang Jamspal, Ven. Ngawang Samten Chophel, and P. Della Santina (trans.) (1978) *Nāgārjuna's Letter to King Gautamīputra*, Delhi, Varanasi, and Patna: Motilal Banarsidass.

Sukhāvatīvyūha Sūtras (Longer and *Shorter)*: Sanskrit text in P. L. Vaidya (ed.) (1961) *Mahāyāna-Sūtra-Saṃgraha*, Darbhanga: The Mithila Instititute of Post-Graduate Studies and Research in Sanskrit Learning. T. 49/115. Taisho 310 (5)/360–4 (*Longer*), 366–7 (*Shorter*). For the longer sūtra the best translation (from Sanskrit and Chinese) is that of L. O. Gomez (trans.) (1996) *Land of Bliss: The Paradise of the Buddha of Measureless Light*, Honolulu: University of Hawaii Press. All three Sukhāvatī sūtras are in E. B. Cowell (ed.) (1969) *Buddhist Mahāyāna Texts*, New York: Dover Publications. Originally Volume 49 of F. Max Müller (ed.) (1894) *The Sacred Books of the East*, Oxford: Clarendon Press, and (from the Chinese) Inagaki Hisao, in collaboration with Harold Stewart (trans.) (1995) *The Three Pure Land Sutras*, Berkeley, Calif.: Numata Center for Buddhist Translation and Research. See also Garma C. C. Chang (ed.) (1983) *A Treasury of Mahāyāna Sūtras: Selections from the Mahāratnakūṭa Sūtra*, translated from the Chinese by the Buddhist Association of the United States, University Park, Pa.: Pennsylvania State University Press.

Sukhāvatīvyūhopadeśa (Vasubandhu?): No Sanskrit or Tibetan version. Taisho 1524. For English see Minoru Kiyota, 'Buddhist devotional meditation: A study of the Sukhāvatīvyūhopadeśa', in M. Kiyota (ed.) (1978) *Mahāyāna Buddhist Meditation: Theory and Practice*, Honolulu: University Press of Hawaii.

Śūnyatāsaptati (Nāgārjuna): Sanskrit lost. Tibetan text edited with a translation Chr. Lindtner (ed. and trans.) (1982) *Nāgārjuniana: Studies in the Writings and Philosophy of Nāgārjuna*, Copenhagen: Akademisk Forlag. For another version of the text, and translation see F. Tola and C. Dragonetti (trans.) (1995) *On Voidness: A Study on Buddhist Nihilism*, Delhi: Motilal Banarsidass.

Susthitamatiparipṛcchā Sūtra: Sanskrit lost. T. 80. Taisho 310 (36). See Garma C. C. Chang (ed.) (1983) *A Treasury of Mahāyāna Sūtras: Selections from the Mahāratnakūṭa Sūtra*, translated from the Chinese by the Buddhist Association of the United States, University Park, Pa.: Pennsylvania State University Press.

Sutta Nipāta: Pāli text in D. Andersen and H. Smith (eds) (1990) *Sutta-Nipāta*, Oxford: Pāli Text Society. First published 1913. English in H. Saddhatissa (trans.) (1985) *Sutta-Nipāta*, London: Curzon. Also K. R. Norman (trans.) (1982) *The Group of Discourses (Sutta-nipāta)*, Vol. 2, revised translation with introduction and notes by K. R. Norman, Oxford: Pāli Text Society.

Ta-cheng ch'i-hsin Lun (**Mahāyānaśraddhotpāda* Śāstra, Aśvaghoṣa?): No Sanskrit or Tibetan. Taisho 1666–7. See Y. S. Hakeda (trans.) (1967) *The Awakening of Faith, Attributed to Aśvaghosha*, New York: Columbia University Press.

Ta-chih-tu Lun (**Mahāprajñāpāramitā Śāstra*, Nāgārjuna?): No Sanskrit or Tibetan. Taisho 1509. Partially translated in É. Lamotte (trans.) (1944–80), *Le Traité de la Grande Vertu de Sagesse de Nāgārjuna (Mahāprajñāpāramitāśāstra)*, Louvain: Université de Louvain, Institut Orientaliste. Five volumes. For selections see K. Venkata Ramanan (1966) *Nāgārjuna's Philosophy: As Presented in the Mahā-Prajñāpāramitā-Śāstra*, Rutland, Vermont, and Tokyo: Charles Tuttle. Delhi reprint by Motilal Banarsidass, 1976.

Tantrāvatāra (also titled *Tantrārthāvatāra*; Buddhaguhya): Sanskrit lost. T. 2501. No Chinese. No European translation.

Tārāviśvakarmabhava Tantra: Sanskrit lost. T. 726. English translation from Tibetan in Martin Willson (1986) *In Praise of Tārā: Songs to the Saviouress*, London: Wisdom. No Chinese.

Tathāgatagarbha Sūtra: Sanskrit lost. T. 258. Taisho 666–7. Translated from the Chinese by William H. Grosnick, 'The Tathāgatagarbha Sūtra', in D. S. Lopez (ed.) (1995) *Buddhism in Practice*, Princeton, N. J.: Princeton University Press.

Tattvasaṃgraha Sūtra (also known as *Sarvatathāgatatattvasaṃgraha*

Sūtra): Sanskrit text in Isshi Yamada (1981) *Sarvatathāgatatattvasaṃgrahanāmamahāyānasūtra: A Critical Edition Based on a Sanskrit Manuscript and Chinese and Tibetan Translations*, New Delhi: International Academy of Indian Culture. See also Lokesh Chandra and David Snellgrove (1981) *Sarvatathāgatatattvasaṃgraha, a Facsimile Reproduction of a Tenth Century Sanskrit Manuscript from Nepal*, New Delhi: International Academy of Indian Culture; Lokesh Chandra (1987) *Sarva-Tathāgata-Tattva-Saṅgraha: Sanskrit Text with Introduction and Illustrations of Maṇḍalas*, Delhi: Motilal Banarsidass. T. 479. Taisho 882/865–6. No translation into English. Excerpts in Snellgrove (1987a).

Tevijja Sutta: Pāli text in T. W. Rhys Davids and J. Estlin Carpenter (eds) (1966) *The Dīgha Nikāya*, London: published for the Pāli Text Society by Luzac. Three volumes. Originally published 1890–1911. English in M. Walshe (trans.) (1987) *Thus Have I Heard: The Long Discourses of the Buddha*, London: Wisdom. Another translation in T. W. Rhys Davids (trans.) (1899–21) *Dialogues of the Buddha*, London: Pāli Text Society. Three volumes.

**Tridharmaka Śāstra* (*San-fa-tu Lun*) (Giribhadra?): No Sanskrit or Tibetan. Taisho 1506. See the summary in Bhikshu Thich Thien Chau (1997) *The Literature of the Personalists of Early Buddhism*, English translation by Sara Boin-Webb, Ho Chi Minh City: Vietnam Buddhist Research Institute.

Triṃśikā (Vasubandhu): Sanskrit text and English translation in S. Anacker (1984) *Seven Works of Vasubandhu, the Buddhist Psychological Doctor*, Delhi: Motilal Banarsidass. T. 4055. Taisho 1586–7.

Trisvabhāvanirdeśa (Vasubandhu): Sanskrit text and English translation in S. Anacker (1984) *Seven Works of Vasubandhu, the Buddhist Psychological Doctor*, Delhi: Motilal Banarsidass. T. 4058 (cf. T. 3843). See also F. Tola and C. Dragonetti (1983) 'The Trisvabhāvakārikā of Vasubandhu', *Journal of Indian Philosophy* 9, 3: 225–66.

Upāyakauśalya Sūtra: Sanskrit text lost. T. 82/261. Taisho 310 (38)/345–6. See Garma C. C. Chang (ed.) (1983) *A Treasury of Mahāyāna Sūtras: Selections from the Mahāratnakūṭa Sūtra*, translated from the Chinese by the Buddhist Association of the United States, University Park, Pa.: Pennsylvania State University Press. Also M. Tatz (trans.) (1994) *The Skill in Means Upāyakauśalya Sūtra*, Delhi: Motilal Banarsidass. Tatz relies on the Tibetan version.

Vaidalyaprakaraṇa (Nāgārjuna): Sanskrit lost. No Chinese. Tibetan, together with an English translation, in F. Tola and C. Dragonetti (eds and trans.) *Nāgārjuna's Refutation of Logic (Nyāya): Vaidalyaprakaraṇa*, Delhi: Motilal Banarsidass.

Vajrabhairava Tantra: Sanskrit: partial manuscripts only. No further details. T. 468. Taisho 1242. Tibetan and Mongolian texts, and English translation in Bulcsu Siklós (ed. and trans.) (1996) *The Vajrabhairava Tantras: Tibetan and Mongolian Versions, English Translation and Annotations*, Tring: Institute of Buddhist Studies.

Vajracchedikā (Diamond) Sūtra: Sanskrit text edited with an English translation in E. Conze (ed. and trans.) (1974) *Vajracchedikā Prajñāpāramitā*, 2nd edition, with corrections and additions, Rome: Instituto Italiano per il Medio ed Estremo Oriente. Taisho 220 (9)/235–9. Also translated in E. Conze (trans.) (1958) *Buddhist Wisdom Books: Containing the Diamond Sūtra [Vajracchedikā] and the Heart Sūtra [Hṛdaya]*, London: Allen and Unwin.

Vajraḍāka Tantra: Sanskrit in manuscripts only. No further details. T. 370/371. No Chinese. No translation.

Vajrapāṇyabhiṣeka Tantra: Sanskrit lost. T. 496. No Chinese. No translation.

Vajraśekhara Tantra: Sanskrit lost. T. 480. Chinese untraced. No translation.

Vajrāvalī (Abhyayākaragupta): Facsimile edition of a Sanskrit manuscript in Lokesh Chandra (1977) *Vajrāvalī*, Delhi: International Academy of Indian Culture. T. 3140. No Chinese. No translation.

Vajravārāhīsādhanasaṃgraha (= *Guhyasamayasaṃgraha* or *Guhyasamayasādhanamālā*): For a translation and edition of one Sanskrit text (= *Vajravārāhīsādhana* of Umāpatideva), with reference to the Tibetan (T. 1581), see Elizabeth English (1999) 'Vajrayoginī: Her visualistation, rituals, and forms', unpublished D.Phil. thesis, University of Oxford. Another *sādhana*, the *Abhisamayamañjarī* of Śubhākaragupta, was published (Sanskrit) in *Dhīḥ*, Rare Buddhist Text Series 13: 123–54 (1992). For details of the other *sādhanas* see English (above).

Vigrahavyāvartanī (Nāgārjuna): Sanskrit text, with an English translation, in K. Bhattacharya (ed. and trans.) (1978) *The Dialectical Method of Nāgārjuna (Vigrahavyāvartanī)*, translated from the original Sanskrit with introduction and notes by Kamaleswar Bhattacharya; text critically edited by E. H. Johnston and Arnold Kunst, Delhi: Motilal Banarsidass. T. 3828 (verses)/3832 (autocommentary). Taisho 1631.

Vijñānakāya (Devaśarman): No Sanskrit or Tibetan version. Taisho 1539. No translation.

Vimalakīrtinirdeśa Sūtra: Full Sanskrit text lost. 'Restored' into Sanskrit, with the Tibetan text and a Hindi translation in Bhikṣu Prāsādika and Lal Mani Joshi (1981) *Vimalakīrtinirdeśasūtra*, Sarnath: Central Institute of Higher Tibetan Studies. Taisho 474–6. For English see É. Lamotte (trans.) (1976) *The Teaching of Vimalakīrti (Vimalakīrtinirdeśa)*, from the French translation with introduction and notes (*L'Enseignement de Vimalakīrti*) by Étienne Lamotte, rendered into English by Sara Boin, London: Pāli Text Society.

Vimalaprabhā (commentary to the *Kālacakra Tantra*): Sanskrit published by the Central Institute of Higher Tibetan Studies, Sarnath, Varanasi, in three vols: Vol. 1, J. Upadhyaya (ed.) (1986); Vol. 2, V. Dwivedi and S. S. Bahulkar (ed.) (1994); Vol. 3, V. Dwivedi and S. S. Bahulkar (ed.) (1994); T. 845. No Chinese. No translation.

Viṃśatikā (Vasubandhu): Sanskrit text and English translation in S. Anacker (1984) *Seven Works of Vasubandhu, the Buddhist Psychological Doctor*, Delhi: Motilal Banarsidass. T. 4056. Taisho 1588–91.

Visuddhimagga (Buddhaghosa): Pāli text in Swami Dwarikadas Śāstrī (ed.) (1977) *Visuddhimagga of Siri Buddhaghosācariya*, Varanasi: Bauddha Bharati. English in Ñāṇamoli Bhikkhu (trans.) (1975) *The Path of Purification (Visuddhimagga) by Bhadantācariya Buddhaghosa*, Kandy: Buddhist Publication Society. Third edition.

Yogācārabhūmi (Asaṅga?): Parts of the Sanskrit text have been edited (although not always very adequately). See V. Bhattacharya (ed.) (1957) *The Yogācārabhūmi of Acārya Asaṅga*, Calcutta: University of Calcutta; A. Wayman (ed.) (1960) 'The Sacittikā and Acittikā Bhūmi and the Pratyekabuddhabhūmi (Sanskrit texts)', *Indogaku Bukkyogaku Kenkyū* 8: 375–9; K. Shukla (ed.) (1973) *Śrāvakabhūmi of Ācārya Asaṅga*, Patna: K. P. Jayaswal Research Institute; U. Wogihara (ed.) (1971) *Bodhisattvabhūmi: A Statement of the Whole Course of the Bodhisattva*, two vols, Tokyo: Sankibo Buddhist Bookstore. (1st edition 1930–6.) T. 4035–22. Taisho 1579. Some of the most interesting ontological material has been translated in Janice Dean Willis (trans.) (1979) *On Knowing Reality: The Tattvārtha Chapter of Asaṅga's Bodhisattvabhūmi*, New York: Columbia University Press. See also M. Tatz (trans.) (1986) *Asaṅga's Chapter on Ethics; With the Commentary of Tsong-Kha-Pa, The Basic Path to Awakening, The Complete Bodhisattva*, Lewiston: Edwin Mellen Press.

Yogaratnamālā (commentary to the *Hevajra Tantra* by Kāṇha): Sanskrit in David Snellgrove (ed.) (1959) *The Hevajra Tantra*, Oxford: Oxford University Press. Two volumes. T. 1183. No Chinese. English translation also in G. W. Farrow and I. Menon (1992) *The Concealed Essence of the Hevajra Tantra, with the Commentary Yogaratnamālā*, Delhi: Motilal Banarsidass.

Yoginīsaṃcāra Tantra: Sanskrit in Nepal-German Manuscript Preservation Project A 48/5; A 43/11. T. 375. No Chinese. No translation.

Yuktiṣaṣṭikā (Nāgārjuna): Most verses lost in Sanskrit. Tibetan text edited and translated in Chr. Lindtner (ed. and trans.) (1982) *Nāgārjuniana: Studies in the Writings and Philosophy of Nāgārjuna*, Copenhagen: Akademisk Forlag; and also F. Tola and C. Dragonetti (trans.) (1995) *On Voidness: A Study on Buddhist Nihilism*, Delhi: Motilal Banarsidass. Taisho 1575.

Secondary sources

Alper, H. P. (ed.) (1989) *Understanding Mantras*, New York: State University of New York Press.

Anacker, S. (1984) *Seven Works of Vasubandhu, the Buddhist Psychological Doctor*, Delhi: Motilal Banarsidass.

Bahulkar, S. S. (1995) 'The Lokadhātupaṭala (chapter 1) of the Kālacakra Tantra', *Dhīḥ* 19: 163–82.

Bareau, A. (1963–71) *Recherches sur la Biographie du Bouddha dans les Sūtrapiṭaka et les Vinayapiṭaka Anciens*, Paris: École Française d'Extrême-Orient.

Basham, A. L. (1951) *History and Doctrines of the Ājīvikas: A Vanished Indian Religion*, London: Luzac.

—— (1981) 'The evolution of the concept of the bodhisattva', in Leslie S. Kawamura (ed.) *The Bodhisattva Doctrine in Buddhism*, Waterloo, Ont.: Wilfrid Laurier University Press.

Bechert, H. (1982) 'The importance of Aśoka's so-called schism edict', in L. A. Hercus, F. B. J. Kuiper, T. Rajapatirana, and E. R. Skrzypczak (eds) (1982) *Indological and Buddhist Studies: Volume in Honour of Professor J. W. de Jong on his Sixtieth Birthday*, Canberra: Faculty of Asian Studies.

—— (ed.) (1991–2) *The Dating of the Historical Buddha/Die Datierung des Historischen Buddha*, Göttingen: Vandenhoek und Ruprecht. Two volumes.

Benard, E. A. (1994) *Chinnamastā: The Aweful Buddhist and Hindu Tantric Goddess*, Delhi: Motilal Banarsidas.

Beyer, S. (1973) *The Cult of Tārā: Magic and Ritual in Tibet*, Berkeley, Calif.: University of California Press.

—— (1974) *The Buddhist Experience: Sources and Interpretations*, Encino, Calif.: Dickenson.

—— (1977) 'Notes on the vision quest in early Mahāyāna', in L. Lancaster (ed.) *Prajñāpāramitā and Related Systems: Studies in Honor of Edward Conze*, Berkeley, Calif.: University of California Press.

Bhattacharyya, B. (1958) *The Indian Buddhist Iconography*, Calcutta: K. L. Mukhopadhyay (2nd edition, 1963).

Bhattacharya, K. (1973) *L'Ātman-Brahman dans le Bouddhisme Ancien*, Paris: École Française d'Extrême-Orient.

Birnbaum, R. (1980) *The Healing Buddha*, London: Rider.

Brauen, M. (1998) *The Maṇḍala: Sacred Circle in Tibetan Buddhism*, trans. M. Willson, Boston: Shambhala. Originally published in 1992 as *Das Maṇḍala: Der Heilige Kreis im tantrischen Buddhismus*, Köln: Dumont.

Broido, M. M. (1988) 'Killing, lying, stealing, and adultery: a problem of interpretation in the Tantras', in D. S. Lopez, Jr (ed.) (1988) *Buddhist Hermeneutics*, Honolulu: University of Hawaii Press.
Carrithers, M. (1983) *The Buddha*, Oxford: Oxford University Press.
Chang, Garma C. C. (ed.) (1983) *A Treasury of Mahāyāna Sūtras: Selections from the Mahāratnakūṭa Sūtra*, translated from the Chinese by the Buddhist Association of the United States, Garma C. C. Chang, General Editor, University Park, Pa.: Pennsylvania State University Press.
Chau, Bhikshu Thich Thien (1997) *The Literature of the Personalists of Early Buddhism*, English translation by Sara Boin-Webb, Ho Chi Minh City: Vietnam Buddhist Research Institute.
Cheetham, E. (1985 onwards) *Fundamentals of Mainstream Buddhism*, London: The Buddhist Society. At least seven volumes.
Cicuzza, C. and Sferra, F. (1997) 'Brief notes on the beginning of the Kālacakra literature', *Dhīḥ* 23: 113–26.
Collins, S. (1982a) *Selfless Persons: Imagery and Thought in Theravāda Buddhism*, Cambridge, London, New York, New Rochelle, Melbourne, and Sidney: Cambridge University Press.
—— (1982b) 'Self and non-Self in early Buddhism', *Numen* XXIX, 2: 250–71.
—— (1990) 'On the very idea of the Pāli Canon', *Journal of the Pāli Text Society* XV: 89–126.
—— (1998) *Nirvāṇa and Other Buddhist Felicities: Utopias of the Pali imaginaire*, Cambridge: Cambridge University Press.
Conze, E. (1960) *The Prajñāpāramitā Literature*, 's Gravenhage: Mouton.
Cousins, L. (1992) 'Vitakka/vitarka and vicāra: Stages of samādhi in Buddhism and Yoga', *Indo-Iranian Journal* 35: 137–57.
—— (1994) 'Person and Self', in *Buddhism into the Year 2000: International Conference Proceedings*, Bangkok and Los Angeles: Dhammakaya Foundation.
—— (1995) 'Abhidhamma', in J. R. Hinnells (ed.) *A New Dictionary of Religions*, Oxford and Cambridge, Mass.: Blackwell.
—— (1996a) 'The dating of the historical Buddha: A review article', *Journal of the Royal Asiatic Society*, Third Series, 6, 1: 57–63.
—— (1996b) 'Good or skilful? Kusala in canon and commentary', *Journal of Buddhist Ethics*, Vol. 3. Online. Available HTTP: *http://jbe.la.psu.edu/3/cousins1.html* (1 October 1999).
—— (1997) 'Aspects of Esoteric Southern Buddhism', in P. Connolly and S. Hamilton (eds) *Indian Insights: Buddhism, Brahmanism and Bhakti: Papers from the Annual Spalding Symposium on Indian Religions*, London: Luzac.
—— (1998) 'Buddhism', in J. R. Hinnells (ed.) *A New Handbook of Living Religions*, London, New York, Ringwood, Ontario, and Auckland: Penguin Books.

Couture, A. (1994) 'A survey of French literature of ancient Indian Buddhist hagiography', in P. Granoff and K. Shinohara (eds) *Monks and Magicians: Religious Biographies in Asia*, Delhi: Motilal Banarsidass.

Cox, C. (1995) *Disputed Dharmas: Early Buddhist Theories on Existence*, Tokyo: The International Institute for Buddhist Studies.

—— (1998) 'Buddhism, Ābhidharmika schools of', in E. Craig (ed.) *Routledge Encyclopedia of Philosophy*, London: Routledge.

Cozort, D. (1995) *The Sand Maṇḍala of Vajrabhairava*, New York: Snow Lion.

Davidson, R. M. (1991) 'Reflections on the Maheśvara subjugation myth: Indic materials, Sa-skya-pa apologetics, and the birth of Heruka', *Journal for the International Association of Buddhist Studies* 14, 2: 197–235.

—— (1995a) 'The bodhisattva Vajrapāṇi's subjugation of Śiva', in D. S. Lopez, Jr (ed.) *Religions of India in Practice*, Princeton, N. J.: Princeton University Press.

—— (1995b) 'Atiśa's A Lamp for the Path to Awakening', in D. S. Lopez, Jr (ed.) *Buddhism in Practice*, Princeton, N. J.: Princeton University Press.

Demiéville, P. (1954) 'La Yogācārabhumi de Sangharakṣa', *Bulletin de l'École Française d'Extrême-Orient* XLIV, 2: 339–436.

Dumont, L. (1988) *Homo Hierarchicus: The Caste System and its Implications*, trans. Mark Sainsbury, Louis Dumont, and Basia Gulati, complete revised English edition, Delhi: Oxford University Press.

Eckel, M. D. (1992) *To See the Buddha: A Philosopher's Quest for the Meaning of Emptiness*, Princeton, N. J.: Princeton University Press.

Edgerton, F. (trans.) (1972) *The Bhagavad Gītā*, Cambridge, Mass.: Harvard University Press.

Elder, G. R. (1976) 'Problems of language in Buddhist Tantra', *History of Religions* 15, 3: 231–50.

Eliade, M. (1969) *Yoga Immortality and Freedom*, trans. W. R. Trask, 2nd edition, Princeton, N.J.: Princeton University Press.

—— (ed.) (1987) *The Encyclopedia of Religion*, New York: Macmillan. Sixteen volumes.

Frauwallner, E. (1973) *History of Indian Philosophy*, trans. V. M. Bedekar, Delhi: Motilal Banarsidass. Two volumes.

Gellner, D. (1992) *Monk, Householder and Tantric Priest: Newar Buddhism and its Hierarchy of Ritual*, Cambridge: Cambridge University Press.

Gethin, R. (1986) 'The five khandhas: Their treatment in the Nikāyas and early Buddhism', *Journal of Indian Philosophy* 14: 35–53.

—— (1997a) 'Cosmology and meditation: From the Agañña-sutta to the Mahāyāna, *History of Religions* 36, 3: 183–217.

—— (1997b) 'Wrong view (micchā-diṭṭhi) and right view (sammā-diṭṭhi) in the Theravāda Abhidhamma', in Kuala Lumpur Dhammajoti,

Asanga Tilakaratne, and Kapila Abhayawansa (eds) *Recent Researches in Buddhist Studies: Essays in Honour of Professor Y. Karunadasa*, Colombo: Y. Karunadasa Felicitation Committee, in collaboration with Chi Ying Foundation, Hong Kong.

—— (1998) *The Foundations of Buddhism*, Oxford and New York: Oxford University Press.

Goepper, R. and Poncar, J. (1996) *Alchi, Ladakh's Hidden Buddhist Sanctuary: The Sumtsek*, Boston: Shambhala Limited Editions.

Gombrich, R. (1971) *Precept and Practice: Traditional Buddhism in the Rural Highlands of Ceylon*, Oxford: Clarendon Press.

—— (1988) *Theravāda Buddhism: A Social History from Ancient Benares to Modern Colombo*, London: Routledge and Kegan Paul.

—— (1990a) 'How the Mahāyāna began', in Tadeusz Skorupski (ed.) *The Buddhist Forum: Volume 1: Seminar Papers 1987–1988*, London: School of Oriental and African Studies, University of London.

—— (1990b) 'Recovering the Buddha's message', in D. S. Ruegg and L. Schmithausen (eds) *Earliest Buddhism and Madhyamaka*, Leiden: E. J. Brill.

—— (1996) *How Buddhism Began: The Conditioned Genesis of the Early Teachings*, London and Atlantic Highlands, N. J.: Athlone Press.

—— (1998) *Kindness and Compassion as a Means to Nirvāṇa*, 1997 Gonda Lecture, Amsterdam: Royal Netherlands Academy of Arts and Sciences.

Gomez, L. O. (1987) 'Buddhism: Buddhism in India', in M. Eliade (ed.) *The Encyclopedia of Religion*, New York: Macmillan.

—— (1995) 'The whole universe as a sūtra', in Donald S. Lopez (ed.) *Buddhism in Practice*, Princeton, N. J.: Princeton University Press.

Granoff, P. and Shinohara, K. (eds) *Monks and Magicians: Religions Biographies in Asia*, Delhi: Motilal Banarsidass.

Grayling, A. (ed.) (1998) *Philosophy 2: Further Through the Subject*, Oxford: Oxford University Press.

Griffiths, P. J. (1990) 'Painting space with colors: Tathāgatagarbha in the Mahāyānasūtrālaṃkāra-corpus IX.22–37', in P. J. Griffiths and J. P. Keenan (eds) *Buddha Nature: A Festschrift in Honor of Minoru Kiyota*, Reno, Nev.: Buddhist Books International.

—— (1994) *On Being Buddha: The Classical Doctrine of Buddhahood*, Albany, N. Y.: State University of New York Press.

Griffiths, P. J. and Keenan, J. P. (eds) (1990) *Buddha Nature: A Festschrift in Honor of Minoru Kiyota*, Reno, Nev.: Buddhist Books International.

Grosnick, W. H. (1995) 'The Tathāgatagarbha sūtra', in Donald S. Lopez (ed.) *Buddhism in Practice*, Princeton, N. J.: Princeton University Press.

Guenther, H. V. (1963) *The Life and Teachings of Naropa*, London, Oxford, and New York: Oxford University Press.

—— (1973) *The Royal Song of Saraha: A Study in the History of Buddhist Thought*, Berkeley, Calif.: Shambhala. Originally published, Seattle: University of Washington Press, 1968.

—— (1993) *Ecstatic Spontaneity: Saraha's Three Cycles of Dohā*, Berkeley, Calif.: Asian Humanities Press.

Harris, I. (1991) *The Continuity of Madhyamaka and Yogācāra in Indian Mahāyāna Buddhism*, Leiden: E. J. Brill.

Harrison, P. (1978) 'Buddhānusmṛti in the Pratyutpanna-buddha-saṃmukhāvasthita-samādhi-sūtra', *Journal of Indian Philosophy* 6: 35–57.

—— (1982) 'Sanskrit fragments of a Lokottaravādin tradition', in L. A. Hercus, F. B. J. Kuiper, T. Rajapatirana, and E. R. Skrzypczak (eds) (1982) *Indological and Buddhist Studies: Volume in Honour of Professor J. W. de Jong on his Sixtieth Birthday*, Canberra: Faculty of Asian Studies.

—— (1987) 'Who gets to ride in the Great Vehicle? Self-image and identity among the followers of the early Mahāyāna', *The Journal of the International Association of Buddhist Studies* 10, 1: 66–89.

—— (1990) *The Samādhi of Direct Encounter with the Buddhas of the Present: An Annotated English Translation of the Tibetan Version of the Pratyutpanna-Buddha-Saṃmukhāvasthita-Samādhi-Sūtra, with Several Appendices relating to the History of the Text*, Tokyo: The International Institute for Buddhist Studies.

—— (1992) 'Is the Dharma-kāya the real "phantom body" of the Buddha?', *The Journal of the International Association of Buddhist Studies*15, 1: 44–94.

—— (1995) 'Searching for the origins of the Mahāyāna: What are we looking for?', *Eastern Buddhist* 28, 1: 48–69.

Harvey, P. (1990) *An Introduction to Buddhism: Teachings, History and Practices*, Cambridge: Cambridge University Press.

—— (1995) *The Selfless Mind: Personality, Consciousness and Nirvāṇa in Early Buddhism*, Richmond: Curzon Press.

Hayes, R. (1994) 'Nāgārjuna's appeal', *Journal of Indian Philosophy* 22: 299–378.

Hirakawa, A. (1963) 'The rise of Mahāyāna Buddhism and its relationship to the worship of stūpas', in *Memoirs of the Research Department of the Toyo Bunko*, Tokyo: Toyo Bunko.

—— (1987) 'Buddhist literature: Survey of texts', in M. Eliade (ed.) *The Encyclopedia of Religion*, New York: Macmillan.

—— (1990) *A History of Indian Buddhism: From Śākyamuni to Early Mahāyāna*, translated and edited by Paul Groner, Honolulu: University of Hawaii Press.

Hodge, S. (1994) 'Considerations on the dating and geographical origins of the Mahāvairocanābhisaṃbodhi-sūtra', in T. Skorupski and

U. Pagel (eds) *The Buddhist Forum III*, London: School of Oriental and African Studies, University of London.

Holt, J. C. (1991) *Buddha in the Crown: Avalokiteśvara in the Buddhist Traditions of Sri Lanka*, New York: Oxford University Press.

Hume, D. (1969) *A Treatise of Human Nature*, edited with an introduction by Ernest G. Mossner, Harmondsworth: Penguin Books.

Isaacson, H. (1994) 'Some problems in the Hevajratantra and its commentaries', unpublished, revised version of a paper given at the IXth World Sanskrit Conference in Melbourne, Australia in January 1994.

—— (1998) 'Tantric Buddhism in India (from c. A.D. 800 to c. A.D. 1200)', *Buddhismus in Geschichte und Gegenwart: Band II*, Universität Hamburg: 24–49.

Jackson, R. R. (1992) 'Ambiguous sexuality: Imagery and interpretation in Tantric Buddhism', *Religion* 22: 85–100.

—— 1994) 'A Tantric echo in Sinhalese Theravāda? Pirit ritual, the book of paritta and the Jinapañjaraya', *Dhīḥ* 18: 121–40.

Jaini, P. S. (1979) *The Jaina Path of Purification*, Berkeley, Calif.: University of California Press. Indian reprint, Delhi, Varanasi, and Patna: Motilal Banarsidass, 1979.

Jong, J. W. de (1984) 'A new history of Tantric literature in India' (English précis of the Japanese work, *Mikkyo kyoten seiritsushi-ron*, by Yukei Matsunaga, Kyoto, 1980), *Acta Indologica* VI: 91–113.

—— (1998) 'Notes on the text of Indrabhūti's Jñānasiddhi', in P. Harrison and G. Schopen (eds) *Sūryacandrāya: Essays in Honour of Akira Yuyama on the Occasion of his 65th Birthday*, Swisttal-Odendorf.

Kajiyama, Y. (1985) 'Stūpas, the mother of Buddhas, and dharma-body', in A. K. Warder (ed.) *New Paths in Buddhist Research*, Durham, N. C.: Acorn Press.

Keenan, J. (1990) 'The doctrine of Buddha nature in Chinese Buddhism – Hui-K'ai on Paramārtha', in P. J. Griffiths and J. P. Keenan (eds) (1990) *Buddha Nature: A Festschrift in Honor of Minoru Kiyota*, Reno, Nev.: Buddhist Books International.

Keown, D. (1992) *The Nature of Buddhist Ethics*, Basingstoke: Macmillan.

King, S. B. (1990) 'Buddha nature thought and mysticism', in P. J. Griffiths and J. P. Keenan (eds) (1990) *Buddha Nature: A Festschrift in Honor of Minoru Kiyota*, Reno, Nev.: Buddhist Books International.

—— (1991) *Buddha Nature*, Albany: State University of New York Press.

King, W. (1980) *Theravāda Meditation: The Buddhist Transformation of Yoga*, University Park, Pa.: Pennsylvania State University Press.

Kloetzli, R. (1983) *Buddhist Cosmology: From Single World System to Pure Land: Science and Theology in the Images of Motion and Light*, Delhi: Motilal Banarsidass.

Kongtrul, Jamgon Kongtrul Lodro Taye (1995) *Myriad Worlds: Buddhist Cosmology in Abhidharma, Kālacakra, and Dzog-chen*, translated and edited by the International Translation Committee, Ithaca, N. Y.: Snow Lion.

Kvaerne, P. (1975) 'On the concept of sahaja in Indian Buddhist Tantric literature', *Temenos* XI: 88–135.

—— (1977) *An Anthology of Buddhist Tantric Songs: A Study of the Caryāgīti*, Oslo: Universitetsforlaget. Second edition, Bangkok: White Orchid Press, 1986.

Lalou, M. (1930) *Iconographie des Etoffes Paintes dans le Mañjuśrīmūlakalpa*, Paris: Librairie Orientaliste Paul Geuthner.

Lamotte, É. (1960) 'Mañjuśrī', *T'oung Pao* 48: 1–96.

—— (1988) *History of Indian Buddhism: From the Origins to the Śaka Era*, translated from the French by Sara Boin-Webb, Louvain and Paris: Peeters Press.

Lati Rinbochay and Hopkins, J. (1979) *Death, Intermediate State and Rebirth in Tibetan Buddhism*, London: Rider.

La Vallée Poussin, L. de (1922) 'Tāntrism (Buddhist)', in J. Hastings (ed.) *Encyclopaedia of Religion and Ethics*, Vol. 12, New York: Charles Scribner's Sons.

Leidy, D. P. (1997) 'Place and process: Maṇḍala imagery in the Buddhist art of Asia', in D. P. Leidy and R. A. F. Thurman *Mandala, the Architecture of Enlightenment*, New York and Boston: Asia Society Galleries, Tibet House, and Shambhala.

Leidy, D. P. and Thurman, R. A. F. (1997) *Maṇḍala, the Architecture of Enlightenment*, New York and Boston: Asia Society Galleries, Tibet House, and Shambhala.

Lessing, F. D. and Wayman, A. (1968) *mKhas grub rje's Fundamentals of the Buddhist Tantras*, The Hague and Paris: Mouton. Second edition (1978) published as *Introduction to the Buddhist Tantric Systems, translated from mKhas grub rje's Rgyud sde spyiḥi rnam par gzag pa rgyas par brjod, with Original Text and Annotation*, New Delhi: Motilal Banarsidass.

Lewis, T. T. (1995) 'The power of mantra: A story of the five protectors', in D. S. Lopez, Jr (ed.) *Religions of India in Practice*, Princeton, N. J.: Princeton University Press.

Lindtner, Chr. (1982) *Nāgārjuniana: Studies in the Writings and Philosophy of Nāgārjuna*, Copenhagen: Akademisk Forlag.

Lopez, D. S., Jr (ed.) (1988a) *Buddhist Hermeneutics*, Honolulu: University of Hawaii Press.

—— (1988b) 'Sanctification on the bodhisattva path', in Richard Kieckhefer and George D. Bond (eds) *Sainthood: Its Manifestations in World Religions*, Berkeley, Calif.: University of California Press.

—— (ed.) (1995a) *Religions of India in Practice*, Princeton, N. J.: Princeton University Press.

—— (ed.) (1995b) *Buddhism in Practice*, Princeton, N. J.: Princeton University Press.

—— (1996) *Elaborations on Emptiness: Uses of the Heart Sūtra*, Princeton, N. J.: Princeton University Press.

Macdonald, A. (1962) *Le Maṇḍala du Mañjuśrīmūlakalpa*, Paris: Adrien-Maisonneuve.

Matilal, B. K. (1980) 'Ignorance or misconception? A note on avidyā in Buddhism', in Somaratna Balasooriya, André Bareau, Richard Gombrich, Siri Gunasingha, Udaya Mallawarachchi, and Edmund Perry (eds) *Buddhist Studies in Honour of Walpola Rahula*, London and Vimamsa, Sri Lanka: Gordon Fraser.

Matsunaga, Y. (1977) 'A history of Tantric Buddhism in India with reference to Chinese translations', in L. Kawamura and K. Scott (eds) *Buddhist Thought and Indian Civilization: Essays in Honour of Herbert V. Guenther on his 60th Birthday*, Emeryville, Calif.: Dharma Publishing.

Mori, S. (1997) 'The Avalokiteśvara bodhisattva statue at Dambegoda and its restoration – A study of Mahāyānism in Sri Lanka', in Kuala Lumpur Dhammajoti, Asanga Tilakaratne, and Kapila Abhayawansa (eds) *Recent Researches in Buddhist Studies: Essays in Honour of Professor Y. Karunadasa*, Colombo: Y. Karunadasa Felicitation Committee, in collaboration with Chi Ying Foundation, Hong Kong.

Nagao, G. M. (1991) *Mādhyamika and Yogācāra: A Study of Mahāyāna Philosophies*, translated by L. S. Kawamura in collaboration with G. M. Nagao, Albany, N. Y.: State University of New York Press.

Nakamura, H. (1980) *Indian Buddhism: A Survey with Bibliographical Notes*, Hirakata City: Kansai University of Foreign Studies.

Ñāṇamoli Bhikkhu (1992) *The Life of the Buddha: According to the Pāli Canon*, Kandy: Buddhist Publication Society. Third edition.

Nārada Mahā Thera (1980) *The Buddha and His Teachings*, Singapore: Stamford Press charitable reprint. No further publication details given.

Nattier, J. (1992) 'The Heart Sūtra: A Chinese apocryphal text?', *The Journal of the International Association of Buddhist Studies* 15, 2: 153–223.

Newman, J. (1988) 'Buddhist Sanskrit in the Kālacakra Tantra', *Journal of the International Association of Buddhist Studies* 11: 123–40.

—— (1995) 'Eschatology in the Wheel of Time Tantra', in D. S. Lopez, Jr (ed.) *Buddhism in Practice*, Princeton, N. J.: Princeton University Press.

Nihom, M. (1994) *Studies in Indian and Indo-Indonesian Tantrism: The Kuñjarakarṇadharmakathana and the Yogatantra*, Wien: Sammlung De Nobili Institut für Indologie der Universität Wien.

Norman, K. R. (1990–6) *Collected Papers*, Oxford: Pāli Text Society. Six volumes.

—— (1997) *A Philological Approach to Buddhism: The Bukkyo Dendo Kyokai Lectures 1994*, London: School of Oriental and African Studies, University of London.

Olivelle, P. (trans.) (1996) *Upaniṣads*, Oxford: Oxford University Press.

Orzech, C. D. (1987) 'Mahāvairocana', in M. Eliade (ed.) *The Encyclopedia of Religion*, New York: Macmillan.

Pabongka Rinpoche (1991) *Liberation in the Palm of Your Hand: A Concise Discourse on the Stages of the Path to Enlightenment*, trans. Michael Richards, edited in the Tibetan by Trijang Rinpoche, Boston: Wisdom.

Padoux, A. (1987) 'Tantrism', in M. Eliade (ed.) *The Encyclopedia of Religion*, New York: Macmillan.

Pagel, U. (1995) *The Bodhisattvapiṭaka: Its Doctrines, Practices and their Position in Mahāyāna Literature*, Tring: Institute of Buddhist Studies.

Pal, P. and Fournier, L. (1988) *Marvels of Buddhist Art: Alchi-Ladakh*, New York and Paris: Ravi Kumar.

Pas, J. F. (1977) 'The Kuan-wu-liang shou-Fo-ching: Its origin and literary criticism', in Leslie S. Kawamura and Keith Scott (eds) *Buddhist Thought and Asian Civilization: Essays in Honor of Herbert V. Guenther on his Sixtieth Birthday*, Emeryville, Calif: Dharma Publishing.

Perez-Remon, J. (1981) *Self and Non-Self in Early Buddhism*, The Hague, Paris, and New York: Mouton.

Pettit, J. W. (1999) Review article of Williams (1998a), in *Journal of Buddhist Ethics*, Vol. 6. Online. Available HTTP: http://jbe.la.psu.edu/6/pettit991.htm (1 October 1999). Reply by Williams. Online. Available HTTP: http://jbe.la.psu.edu/6/williams991.htm (1 October 1999).

Potter, K. H., with Buswell, Robert E., Jaini, Padmanabh S., and Reat, Noble Ross (eds) (1996) *Encyclopedia of Indian Philosophies: Volume VII: Abhidharma Buddhism to 150 A.D.*, Delhi: Motilal Banarsidass.

Potter, K. H. (ed.) (1999) *Encyclopedia of Indian Philosophies: Volume VIII: Buddhist Philosophy from 100 to 350 A.D.*, Delhi: Motilal Banarsidass.

Potter, K. H. and Williams, P. (eds) (forthcoming) *Encyclopedia of Indian Philosophies: Volume IX: Buddhist Philosophy from 350 A.D.*, Delhi: Motilal Banarsidass.

Rahula, W. (1978) *Zen and the Taming of the Bull: Towards the Definition of Buddhist Thought*, London: Gordon Fraser Gallery.

Ray, R. A. (1980) 'Accomplished women in Tantric Buddhism of medieval India and Tibet', in N. A. Falk and R. M. Gross (eds) *Unspoken Worlds: Women's Religious Lives in Non-Western Cultures*, San Francisco: Harper & Row.

—— (1987) 'Mahāsiddhas', in M. Eliade (ed.) *The Encyclopedia of Religion*, New York: Macmillan.

Reynolds, F. E., and Reynolds, M. B. (trans.) (1982) *Three Worlds According to King Ruang: A Thai Buddhist Cosmology*, Berkeley, Calif.: University of California.

Rhie, M. M. and Thurman, R. A. F. (1991) *Wisdom and Compassion: The Sacred Art of Tibet*, London: Thames and Hudson.

Rowell, T. (1935) 'The background and early use of the Buddha-kṣetra concept, chs 2–3', *Eastern Buddhist* o.s. 6, 4: 379–431.

—— (1937) 'The background and early use of the Buddha-kṣetra concept, ch. 4, plus appendices and bibliography', *Eastern Buddhist* o.s. 7, 2: 132–76.

Ruegg, D. S. (1980) 'Ahiṃsā and vegetarianism in the history of Buddhism', in Somaratna Balasooriya, André Bareau, Richard Gombrich, Siri Gunasingha, Udaya Mallawarachchi, and Edmund Perry (eds) *Buddhist Studies in Honour of Walpola Rahula*, London and Vimamsa, Sri Lanka: Gordon Fraser.

—— (1981) *The Literature of the Madhyamaka School of Philosophy in India*, Wiesbaden: O. Harrassowitz.

—— (1989a) *Buddha-nature, Mind and the Problem of Gradualism in a Comparative Perspective: On the Transmission and Reception of Buddhism in India and Tibet*, London: School of Oriental and African Studies, University of London.

—— (1989b) 'Review of Snellgrove, D. L. (1987) "Indo-Tibetan Buddhism: Indian Buddhists and their Tibetan Successors"', *Journal of the Royal Asiatic Society*, 1989, 1: 172–8.

Ruegg, D. S. and Schmithausen, L. (eds) (1990) *Earliest Buddhism and Madhyamaka*, Leiden: E. J. Brill.

Sadakata, A. (1997) *Buddhist Cosmology: Philosophy and Origins*, trans. Gaynor Sekimori, with a foreword by Hajime Nakamura, Tokyo: Kosei.

Samuel, G. (1989) 'The body in Buddhist and Hindu Tantra', *Religion* 19: 197–210.

—— (1993) *Civilized Shamans: Buddhism in Tibetan Societies*, Washington and London: Smithsonian Institution Press.

Sanderson, A. (1994) 'Vajrayāna: origin and function', in *Buddhism Into the Year 2000 (International Conference Proceedings)*, Bangkok and Los Angeles: Dhammakaya Foundation.

Sartre, J.-P. (1966) *Being and Nothingness*, trans. Hazel E. Barnes, New York: Washington Square.

Sasaki, S. (1994) 'A study of the origin of Mahāyāna Buddhism – on the Hirakawa theory'. A paper delivered at the conference of the International Association of Buddhist Studies in Mexico City. No publication details available.

Schmithausen, L. (1987) *Ālayavijñāna: On the Origin and the Early Development of a Central Concept of Yogācāra Philosophy*, Tokyo: International Institute for Buddhist Studies. Two volumes.

Schopen, G. (1975) 'The phrase "sa pṛthivīpradeśaś caityabhūto bhavet" in the Vajracchedikā: notes on the cult of the book in Mahāyāna', *Indo-Iranian Journal* 17: 147–81.

—— (1977) 'Sukhāvatī as a generalized religious goal in Sanskrit Mahāyāna sūtra literature', *Indo-Iranian Journal* 19: 177–210.

—— (1979) 'Mahāyāna in Indian inscriptions', *Indo-Iranian Journal* 21: 1–19.

—— (1985) 'Two problems in the history of Indian Buddhism: the layman/monk distinction and the doctrines of the transference of merit', *Studien zur Indologie und Iranistik* 10: 9–47. Reprinted in Schopen (1997).

—— (1987a) 'Burial "ad sanctos" and the physical presence of the Buddha in early Indian Buddhism', *Religion* 17: 193–225. Reprinted in Schopen (1997).

—— (1987b) 'The inscription on the Kuṣān image of Amitābha and the character of the early Mahāyāna in India', *The Journal of the International Association of Buddhist Studies* 10, 2: 99–137.

—— (1990) 'The Buddha as an owner of property and permanent resident in medieval Indian monasteries', *Journal of Indian Philosophy* 18, 3: 181–217. Reprinted in Schopen (1997).

—— (1991a) 'An old inscription from Amarāvatī and the cult of the local monastic dead in Indian Buddhist monasteries', *The Journal of the International Association of Buddhist Studies* 14, 2: 281–329. Reprinted in Schopen (1997).

—— (1991b) 'Archaeology and protestant presuppositions in the study of Indian Buddhism', *History of Religions* 31, 1: 1–23. Reprinted in Schopen (1997).

—— (1991c) 'Monks and the relic cult in the Mahāparinibbānasutta: an old misunderstanding in regard to monastic Buddhism', in Koichi Shinohara and Gregory Schopen (ed.) *From Benares to Beijing: Essays on Buddhism and Chinese Religion in Honour of Professor Jan Yün-hua*, Oakville, Ont.: Mosaic Press. Reprinted in Schopen (1997).

—— (1992) 'On avoiding ghosts and social censure: monastic funerals in the Mūlasarvāstivāda-Vinaya', *Journal of Indian Philosophy* 20: 1–39. Reprinted in Schopen (1997).

—— (1994) 'Ritual rights and bones of contention: more on monastic funerals and relics in the Mūlasarvāstivāda-Vinaya', *Journal of Indian Philosophy* 22: 31–80.

—— (1997) *Bones, Stones, and Buddhist Monks: Collected Papers on the Archaeology, Epigraphy, and Texts of Monastic Buddhism in India*, Honolulu: University of Hawaii Press.

—— (1999) 'The bones of a Buddha and the business of a monk: Conservative monastic values in an early Mahāyāna polemical tract', *Journal of Indian Philosophy* 27: 279–324.

Shaw, M. (1994) *Passionate Enlightenment: Women in Tantric Buddhism*, Princeton, N. J.: Princeton University Press.

Sherburne, R. (trans.) (1983) *A Lamp for the Path and Commentary by Atīśa*, London: George Allen and Unwin.

Siderits, M. (2000) 'The reality of altruism', review article of Williams (1998a) with reply in *Philosophy East and West* 50: 3.

Siklós, B. (1996) 'The evolution of the Buddhist Yama', in T. Skorupski (ed.) *The Buddhist Forum IV*, London: School of Oriental and African Studies, University of London.

Simon, B. (ed.) (1985) *The Wheel of Time: The Kalachakra in Context*, Madison, Wis.: Deer Park Books.

Skilling, P. (1992) 'The Rākṣā literature of the Śrāvakayāna', *Journal of the Pāli Text Society* 16: 109–82.

Skorupski, T. (1998) 'An analysis of the Kriyāsaṃgraha', in P. Harrison and G. Schopen (eds) *Sūryacandrāya: Essays in Honour of Akira Yuyama on the Occasion of his 65th Birthday*, Swisttal-Odendorf.

Snellgrove, D. L. (1959) 'The notion of divine kingship in Tantric Buddhism', in *Studies in the History of Religions* (supplements to *Numen*) 4: 204–18.

—— (1987a) *Indo-Tibetan Buddhism: Indian Buddhists and their Tibetan Successors*, London and Boston: Serindia and Shambhala.

—— (1987b) 'Celestial Buddhas and Bodhisattvas', in M. Eliade (ed.) *The Encyclopedia of Religion*, New York: Macmillan.

—— (1988) 'Categories of Buddhist Tantras', in G. Gnoli and L. Lanciotti (eds) *Orientalia Iosephi Tucci Memoriae Dicata, Serie Orientale Roma*, Rome: Instituto Italiano per il Medio ed Estremo Oriente, LVI, 3: 1353–84.

Snellgrove, D. L. and Skorupski, T. (1977 and 1980) *The Cultural Heritage of Ladakh*, Warminster: Aris and Phillips. Two volumes.

Sponberg, A., and Hardacre, H. (eds) (1988) *Maitreya, the Future Buddha*, Cambridge: Cambridge University Press.

Strawson, P. F. (1959) *Individuals: An Essay in Descriptive Metaphysics*, London: Methuen.

Studholme, A. (1999) 'On the history of the *oṃ maṇipadme hūṃ* mantra', unpublished Ph.D. thesis, University of Bristol.

Takeuchi, Y. (ed.) (1993) *Buddhist Spirituality: Indian, Southeast Asian, Tibetan, Early Chinese*, New York: Crossroad.

Tatz, M. (trans.) (1986) *Asaṅga's Chapter on Ethics; With the Commentary of Tsong-Kha-Pa; The Basic Path to Awakening, the Complete Bodhisattva*, Lewiston: Edwin Mellen Press.

Templeman, D. (1989) *Tāranātha's Life of Kṛṣṇācārya/Kāṇha*, Dharamsala: Library of Tibetan Works and Archives.

—— (1994) 'Dohā, Vajragīti and Caryā songs', in G. Samuel (ed.) *Tantra and Popular Religion in Tibet*, New Delhi: Aditya Prakashan.

Thanissaro Bhikkhu (1994) *The Buddhist Monastic Code*, Valley Centre, Calif.: Metta Forest Monastery.

Thomas, E. J. (1951) *The History of Buddhist Thought*, London: Routledge and Kegan Paul. Second edition.

Tola, F. and Dragonetti, C. (1995) *On Voidness: A Study on Buddhist Nihilism*, Delhi: Motilal Banarsidass.

Tribe, A. H. F. (1997a) 'Mañjuśrī and "The Chanting of Names" (Nāmasaṃgīti): Wisdom and its embodiment in an Indian Mahāyāna Buddhist text', in P. Connolly and S. Hamilton (eds) *Indian Insights: Buddhism, Brahmanism and Bhakti. Papers from the Annual Spalding Symposium on Indian Religions*, London: Luzac.

—— (1997b) 'Mañjuśrī: Origins, role and significance: Parts I and II', *The Western Buddhist Review*, 2: 49–123.

Tsuda, S. (1978) 'A critical Tantrism', *Memoirs of the Research Department of the Toyo Bunko* 36: 167–231.

Tsukamoto, K., Matsunaga, Y. and Isoda, H. (eds) (1989) *Bongo Butten no Kenkyū IV, Mikkyo Kyoten Hen* [A Descriptive Bibliography of the Sanskrit Buddhist Literature: Volume IV: The Buddhist Tantra], Kyoto: Heirakuji Shoten.

Tukol, T. K. (1976) *Sallekhanā is not Suicide*, Ahmedabad: L. D. Institute of Indology.

Ui, Hakuju *et al.* (1934) *A Complete Catalogue of the Tibetan Buddhist Canons*, Sendai: Tohoku Imperial University.

Urban, H. B. (1999) 'The Extreme Orient: The construction of "Tantrism" as a category in the orientalist imagination', *Religion* 29: 123–46.

Vetter, T. (1994) 'On the origin of Mahāyāna Buddhism and the subsequent introduction of Prajñāpāramitā', *Asiatische Studien/Études Asiatiques* 48, 4: 1241–81.

—— (1998) 'Explanations of dukkha', *Journal of the International Association of Buddhist Studies* 21, 2: 383–7.

Vira, R. and Chandra, L. (1995) *Tibetan Maṇḍalas (Vajrāvalī and Tantrasamuccaya)*, New Delhi: Aditya Prakashan.

Wallace, V. A. (1995) 'Buddhist Tantric medicine in the Kālacakratantra', *Pacific World, Journal of the Institute of Buddhist Studies, New Series* 11: 155–74.

Warder, A. K. (1970) *Indian Buddhism*, Delhi, Patna, and Varanasi: Motilal Banarsidass.

Wayman, A. (1973) *The Buddhist Tantras: Light on Indo-Tibetan Esotericism*, New York: Samuel Weiser.

—— (1975) 'The significance of mantras, from the Veda down to Buddhist Tantric practice', *Indologica Taurinensia* 3–4: 483–97.

—— (1977) *Yoga of the Guhyasamājatantra: The Arcane Lore of Forty Verses*, Delhi: Motilal Banarsidass.

—— (1981) 'Reflections on the theory of Barabuḍur as a maṇḍala', in L. O. Gomez and H. W. Woodward, Jr (eds) *Barabudur: History and Significance of a Buddhist Monument*, Berkeley, Calif. Asian Humanities Press.

—— (1984) *Buddhist Insight – Essays, Edited with an Introduction by George Elder*, Delhi: Motilal Banarsidass.

—— (1987) 'Buddhism, schools of: Esoteric Buddhism', in M. Eliade (ed.) *The Encyclopedia of Religion*, New York: Macmillan.

—— (1995) 'An historical review of Buddhist Tantras', *Dhīḥ* 20: 137–53.

Williams, P. (1977) 'Buddhadeva and temporality', *Journal of Indian Philosophy* 4: 279–94.

—— (1978) Review article of Karl H. Potter (ed.) (1977) *Indian Metaphysics and Epistemology: The Tradition of Nyāya-Vaiśeṣika up to Gaṅgeśa*, Princeton, N. J.: Princeton University Press, in the *Journal of Indian Philosophy* 6: 277–97.

—— (1981) 'On the Abhidharma ontology', *Journal of Indian Philosophy* 9: 227–57.

—— (1984) Review article of Chr. Lindtner (1982) *Nāgārjuniana: Studies in the Writings and Philosophy of Nāgārjuna*, Copenhagen: Akademisk Forlag, in *Journal of Indian Philosophy* 12: 73–104.

—— (1989) *Mahāyāna Buddhism: The Doctrinal Foundations*, London and New York: Routledge.

—— (1991) 'On the Interpretation of Madhyamaka Thought', *Journal of Indian Philosophy* 19: 191–218.

—— (1994a) 'An argument for cittamātra – reflections on Bodhicaryāvatāra 9: 28 (Tib. 27) cd', in Per Kvaerne (ed.) *Tibetan Studies: Proceedings of the 6th Seminar of the International Association for Tibetan Studies, Fagernes 1992*, Oslo: The Institute for Comparative Research in Human Culture. Reprinted in Williams (1998a).

—— (1994b) 'On altruism and rebirth: Philosophical comments on Bodhicaryāvatāra 8: 97–8', in Tadeusz Skorupski and Ulrich Pagel (eds) *The Buddhist Forum: Volume 3 1991–1993: Papers in Honour and Appreciation of Professor David Seyfort Ruegg's Contribution to Indological, Buddhist and Tibetan Studies*, London: School of Oriental and African Studies, University of London. Reprinted in Williams (1998a).

—— (1996) *Indian Philosophy: A Study Guide*, London: Birkbeck College Department of Philosophy, University of London. A slightly adapted version of this is printed in A. Grayling (ed.) (1998), *Philosophy 2: Further Through the Subject*, Oxford: Oxford University Press.

—— (1998a) *Altruism and Reality: Studies in the Philosophy of the Bodhicaryāvatāra*, Richmond: Curzon.

—— (1998b) *The Reflexive Nature of Awareness: A Tibetan Madhyamaka Defence*, Richmond: Curzon.

Willis, Janice Dean (trans.) (1979) *On Knowing Reality: The Tattvārtha Chapter of Asaṅga's Bodhisattvabhūmi*, New York: Columbia University Press.

Willson, M. (1986) *In Praise of Tārā: Songs to the Saviouress: Source Texts from India and Tibet on Buddhism's Great Goddess*, London: Wisdom.

Yoritomi, M. (1990) *Mikkyo butsu no kenkyū* [Studies on Esoteric Buddhas], Kyoto.

Index